Shojo Beat

Tail of the Moon

2

Story & Art by
Rinko Ueda

Volume 2

Chapter 8 3

Chapter 9 29

Chapter 10 55

Chapter 11 81

Chapter 12 109

Chapter 13 136

Chapter 14 165

Glossary 190

C O N T E N T S

Story Thus Far...

It is the Warring States Era. Usagi, who lives in the ninja village of Hojiro in southern Iga, is a failure as a kunoichi, or female ninja. At the age of 15, she is still unable to qualify as a ninja, so she is suddenly ordered to get married!

The man who has been selected for her is Hattori Hanzo, the most handsome man in all Iga. But after rushing over to meet Hanzo, she is told by Hanzo himself that he has no intention of getting married. Usagi begins to train hard so that Hanzo will accept her. But another prospective bride—Yuri—appears, making things much more difficult...

Then Usagi meets Hanzou, a relative of Hanzo's, and his girlfriend Sara. Usagi learns that her Hanzo and Sara were married before... Shocked by the news, Usagi cannot concentrate on her training, and Hanzo tells her to leave his place. A dejected Usagi returns to her village and meets up with Goemon, a childhood friend and...?!

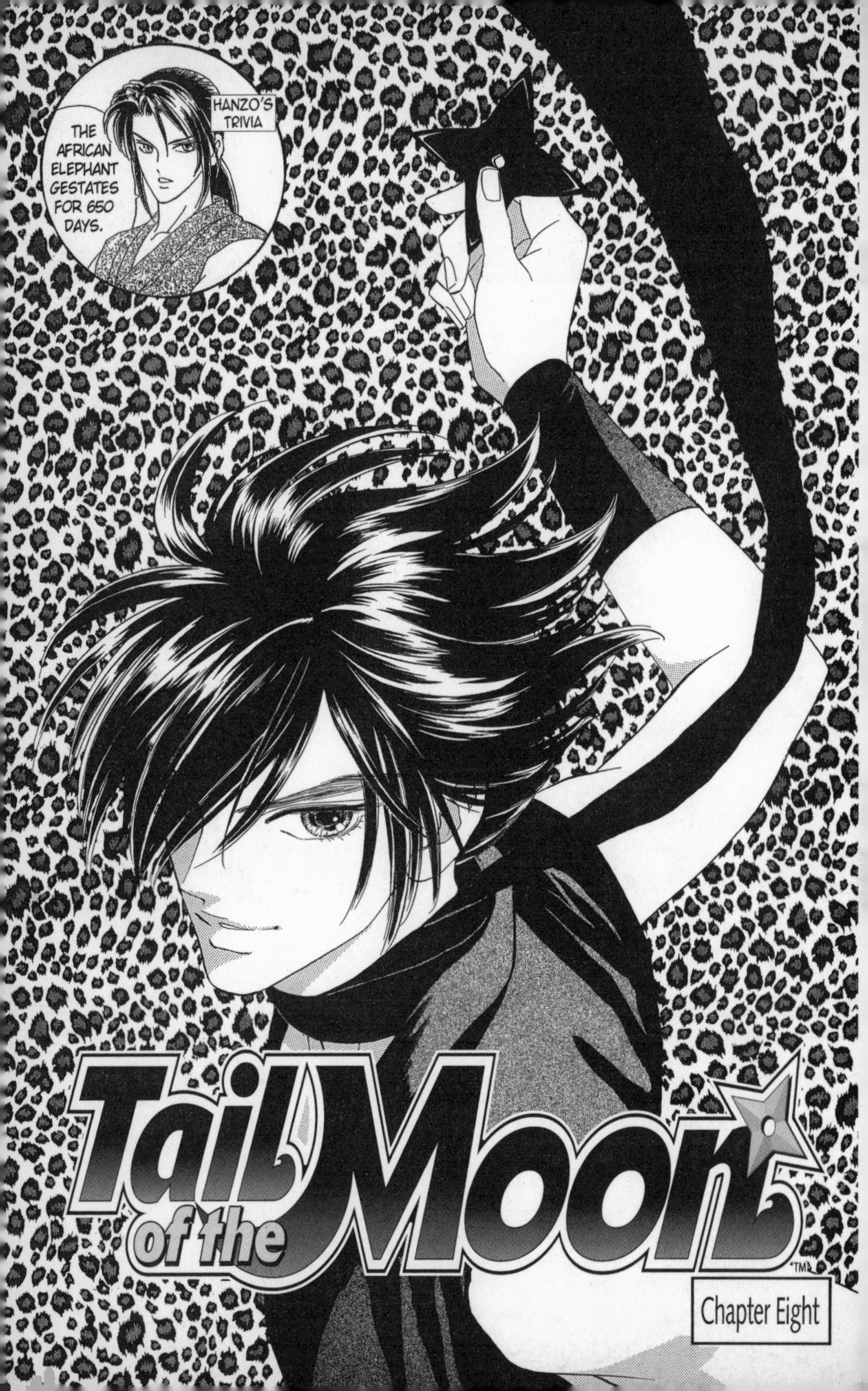
HANZO'S TRIVIA
THE AFRICAN ELEPHANT GESTATES FOR 650 DAYS.
Tail of the Moon™
Chapter Eight

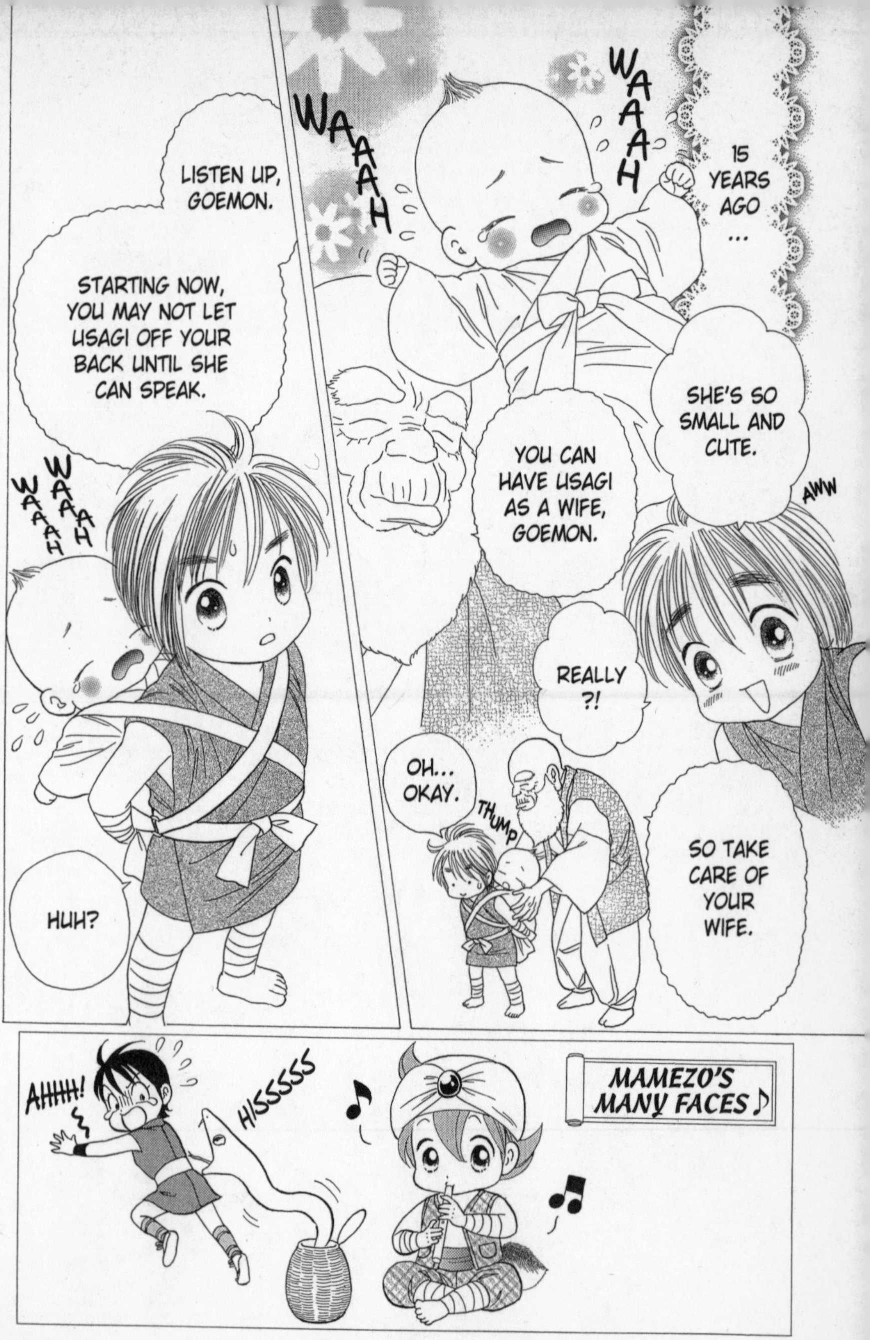
15 YEARS AGO ...
WAAAH
WAAAH
SHE'S SO SMALL AND CUTE.
AWW
YOU CAN HAVE USAGI AS A WIFE, GOEMON.
REALLY ?!
SO TAKE CARE OF YOUR WIFE.
OH... OKAY.
THUMP
LISTEN UP, GOEMON.
STARTING NOW, YOU MAY NOT LET USAGI OFF YOUR BACK UNTIL SHE CAN SPEAK.
WAAAAH
WAAAAH
HUH?
MAMEZO'S MANY FACES♪
HISSSSS
AHHHH!

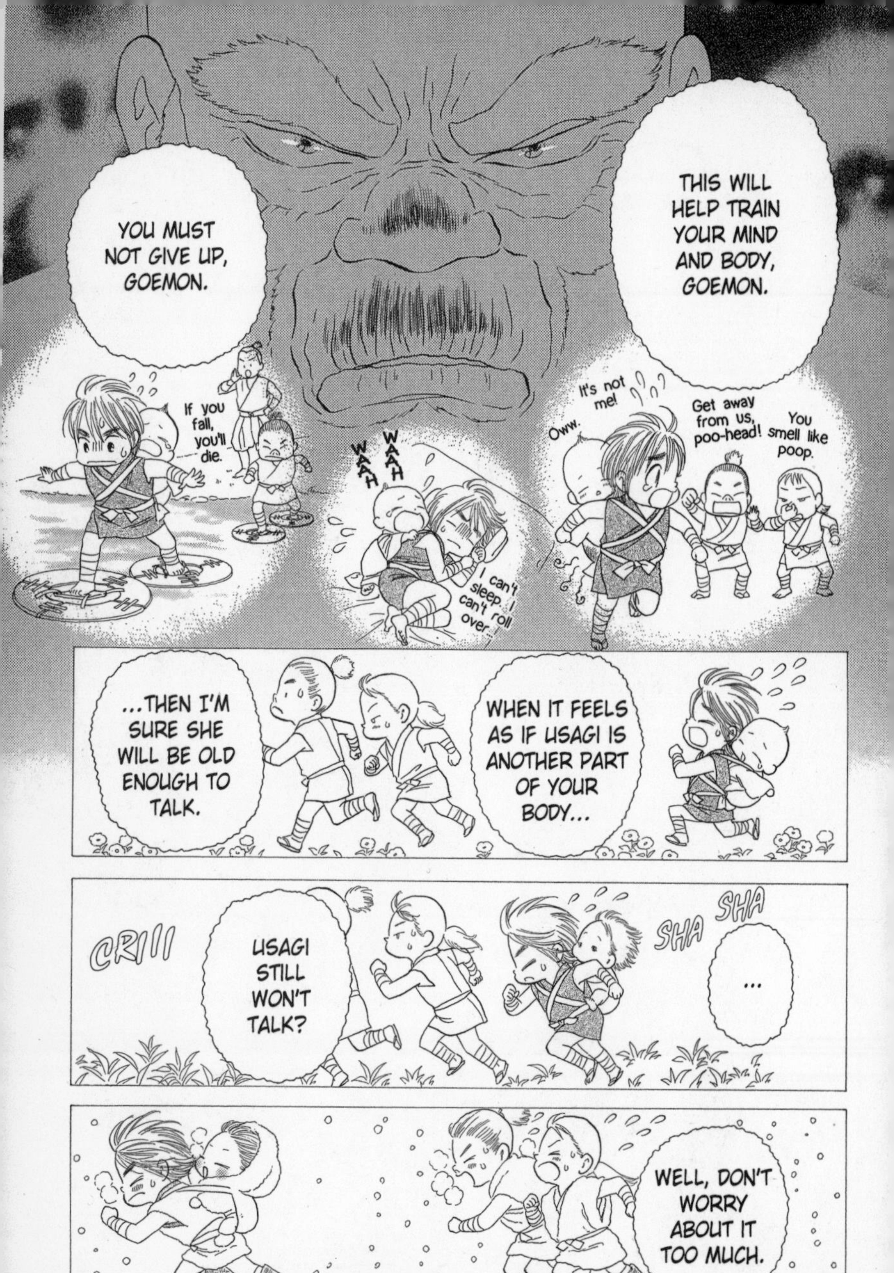
THIS WILL HELP TRAIN YOUR MIND AND BODY, GOEMON.
YOU MUST NOT GIVE UP, GOEMON.
You smell like poop.
Get away from us, poo-head!
It's not me!
Oww.
WAAH WAAH
I can't sleep. I can't roll over...
If you fall, you'll die.
WHEN IT FEELS AS IF USAGI IS ANOTHER PART OF YOUR BODY...
...THEN I'M SURE SHE WILL BE OLD ENOUGH TO TALK.
SHA SHA
...
USAGI STILL WON'T TALK?
CRIII
WELL, DON'T WORRY ABOUT IT TOO MUCH.

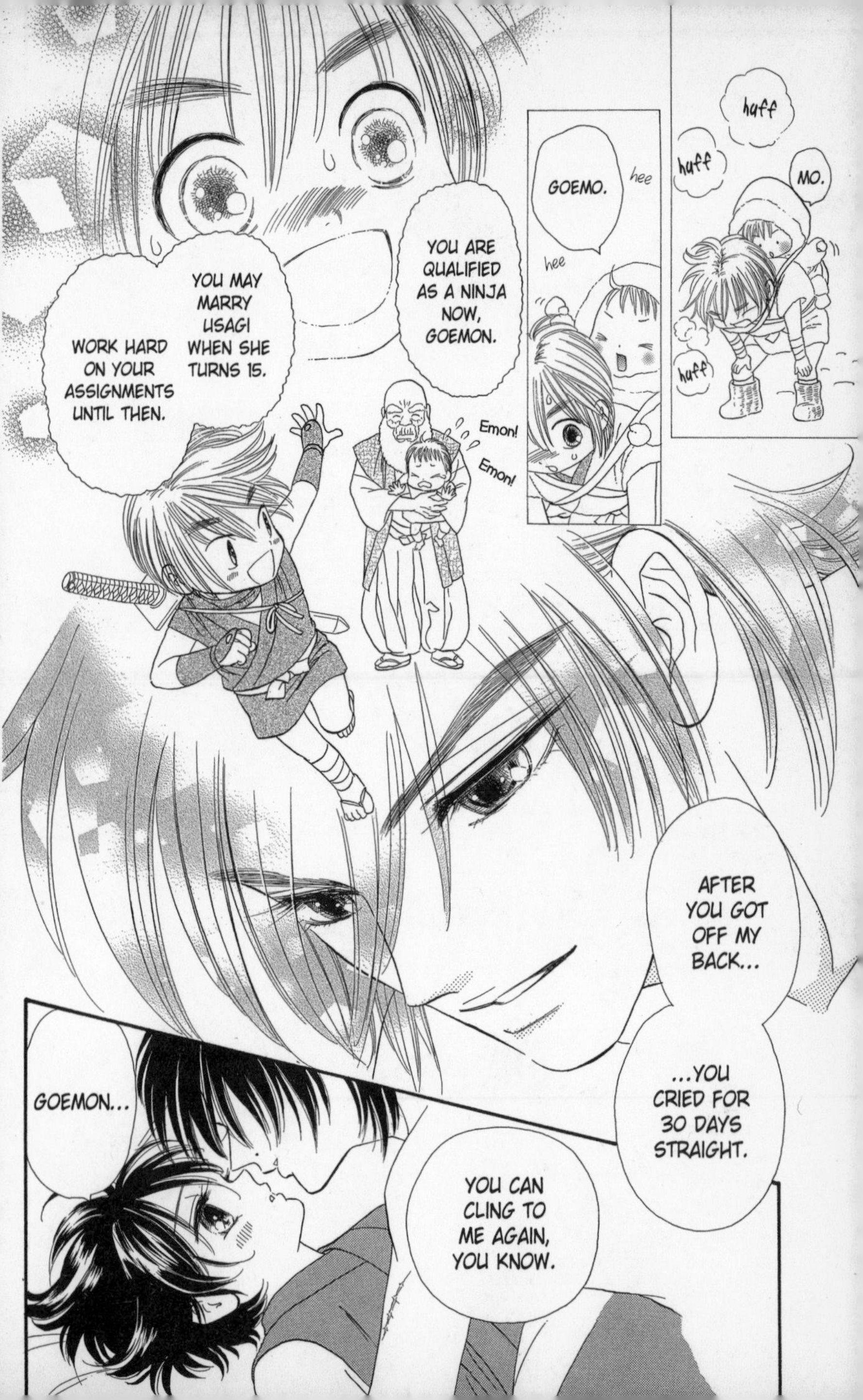
huff
huff
MO.
huff
GOEMO.
hee
hee
YOU ARE QUALIFIED AS A NINJA NOW, GOEMON.
YOU MAY MARRY USAGI WHEN SHE TURNS 15.
WORK HARD ON YOUR ASSIGNMENTS UNTIL THEN.
Emon!
Emon!
AFTER YOU GOT OFF MY BACK...
...YOU CRIED FOR 30 DAYS STRAIGHT.
YOU CAN CLING TO ME AGAIN, YOU KNOW.
GOEMON...

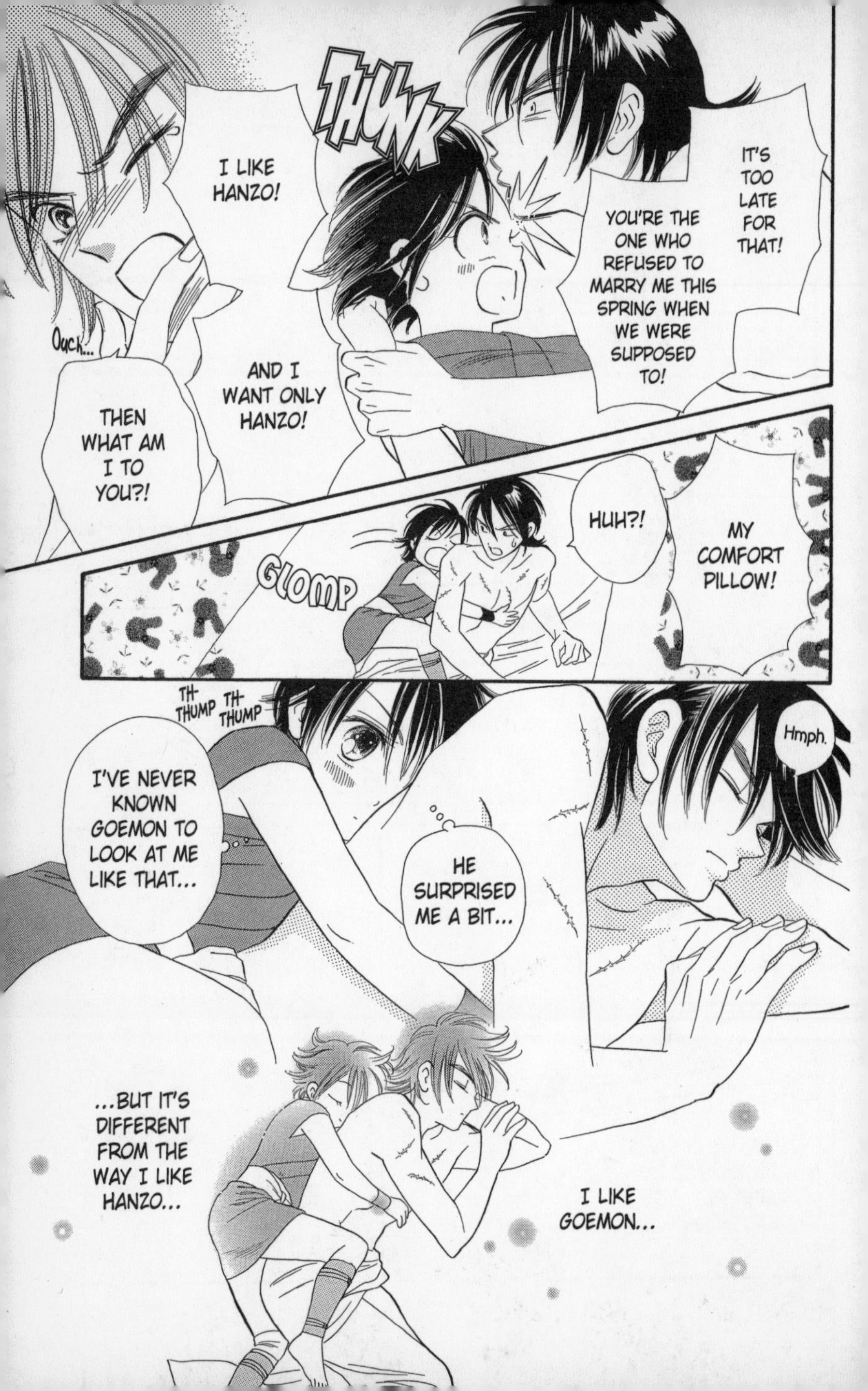
IT'S TOO LATE FOR THAT!
YOU'RE THE ONE WHO REFUSED TO MARRY ME THIS SPRING WHEN WE WERE SUPPOSED TO!
THUNK
I LIKE HANZO!
AND I WANT ONLY HANZO!
Ouch...
THEN WHAT AM I TO YOU?!
MY COMFORT PILLOW!
HUH?!
GLOMP
Hmph.
TH-THUMP TH-THUMP
HE SURPRISED ME A BIT...
I'VE NEVER KNOWN GOEMON TO LOOK AT ME LIKE THAT...
I LIKE GOEMON...
...BUT IT'S DIFFERENT FROM THE WAY I LIKE HANZO...

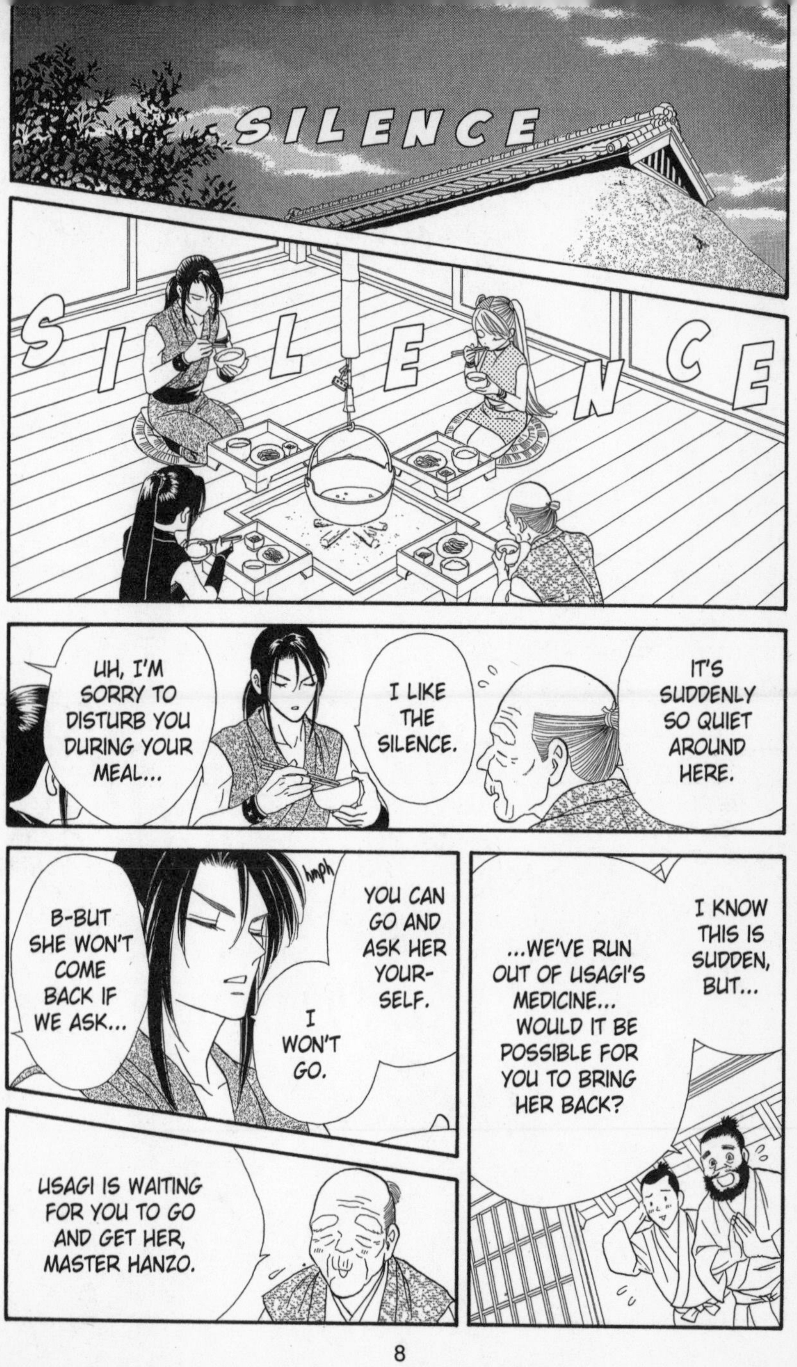
SILENCE
SILENCE
IT'S SUDDENLY SO QUIET AROUND HERE.
I LIKE THE SILENCE.
UH, I'M SORRY TO DISTURB YOU DURING YOUR MEAL...
I KNOW THIS IS SUDDEN, BUT...
...WE'VE RUN OUT OF USAGI'S MEDICINE... WOULD IT BE POSSIBLE FOR YOU TO BRING HER BACK?
hmph
YOU CAN GO AND ASK HER YOURSELF.
I WON'T GO.
B-BUT SHE WON'T COME BACK IF WE ASK...
USAGI IS WAITING FOR YOU TO GO AND GET HER, MASTER HANZO.

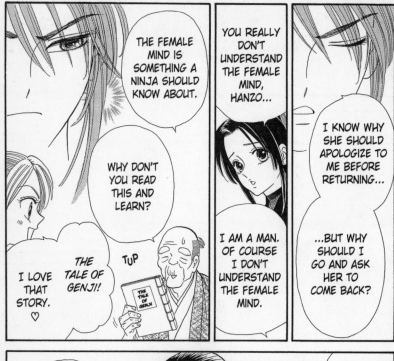

I KNOW WHY SHE SHOULD APOLOGIZE TO ME BEFORE RETURNING...
...BUT WHY SHOULD I GO AND ASK HER TO COME BACK?
YOU REALLY DON'T UNDERSTAND THE FEMALE MIND, HANZO...
I AM A MAN. OF COURSE I DON'T UNDERSTAND THE FEMALE MIND.
THE FEMALE MIND IS SOMETHING A NINJA SHOULD KNOW ABOUT.
WHY DON'T YOU READ THIS AND LEARN?
TUP
THE TALE OF GENJI
THE TALE OF GENJI!
I LOVE THAT STORY. ♡
I'VE READ IT MANY TIMES AS WELL.
LADY MURASAKI IS SUCH A WONDERFUL WOMAN AND...
IT SOUNDS LIKE A SOPHISTICATED NOVEL.
HEY, LADY MURASAKI IS *MY* FAVORITE!
I'LL READ IT LATER.

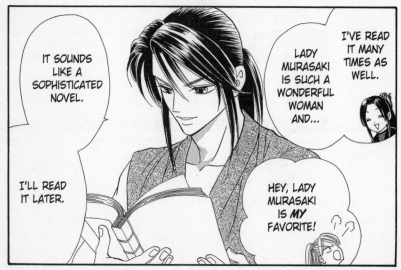

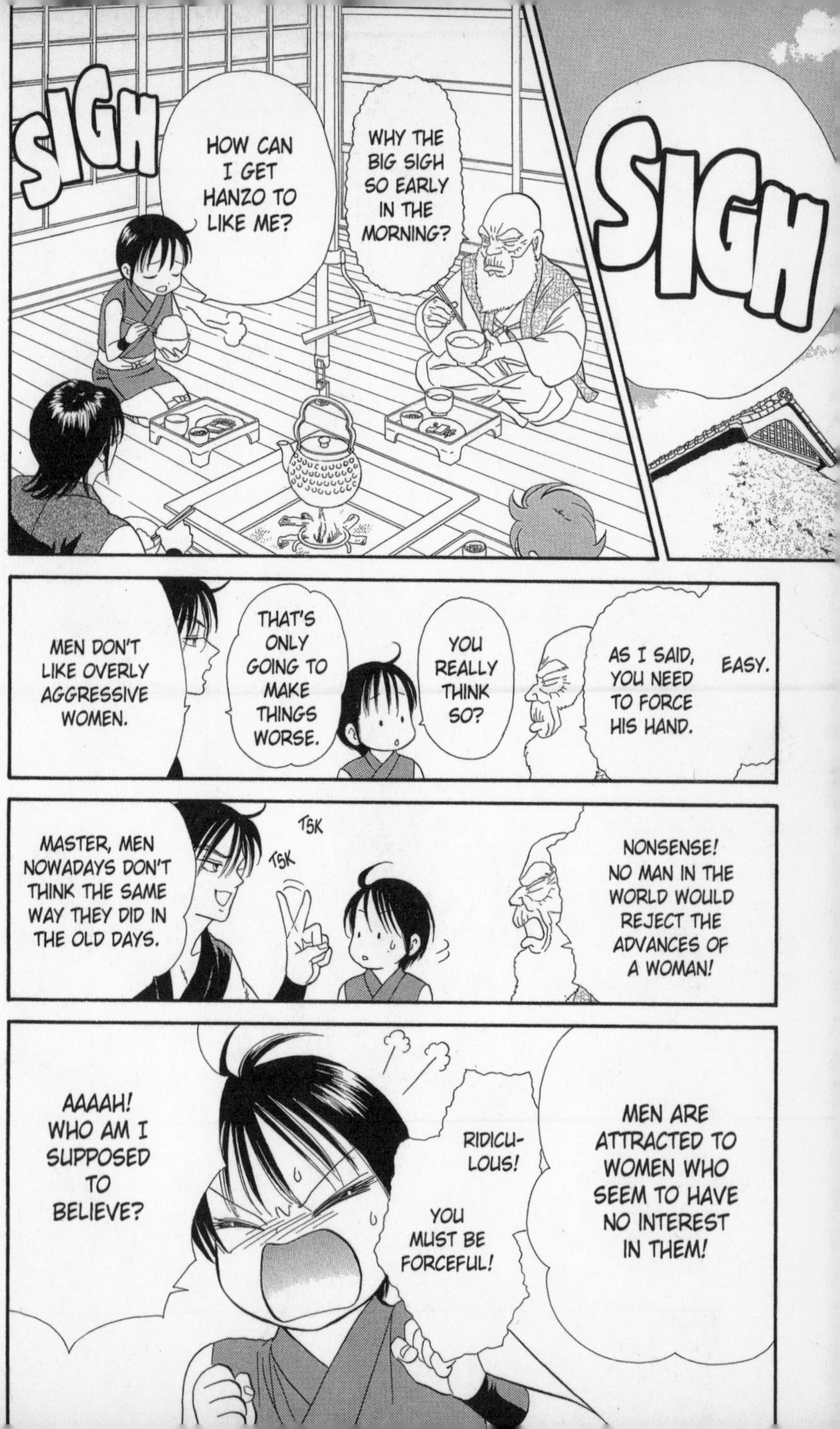
SIGH
WHY THE BIG SIGH SO EARLY IN THE MORNING?
HOW CAN I GET HANZO TO LIKE ME?
SIGH
EASY.
AS I SAID, YOU NEED TO FORCE HIS HAND.
YOU REALLY THINK SO?
THAT'S ONLY GOING TO MAKE THINGS WORSE.
MEN DON'T LIKE OVERLY AGGRESSIVE WOMEN.
NONSENSE! NO MAN IN THE WORLD WOULD REJECT THE ADVANCES OF A WOMAN!
TSK
TSK
MASTER, MEN NOWADAYS DON'T THINK THE SAME WAY THEY DID IN THE OLD DAYS.
MEN ARE ATTRACTED TO WOMEN WHO SEEM TO HAVE NO INTEREST IN THEM!
RIDICULOUS!
YOU MUST BE FORCEFUL!
AAAAH! WHO AM I SUPPOSED TO BELIEVE?

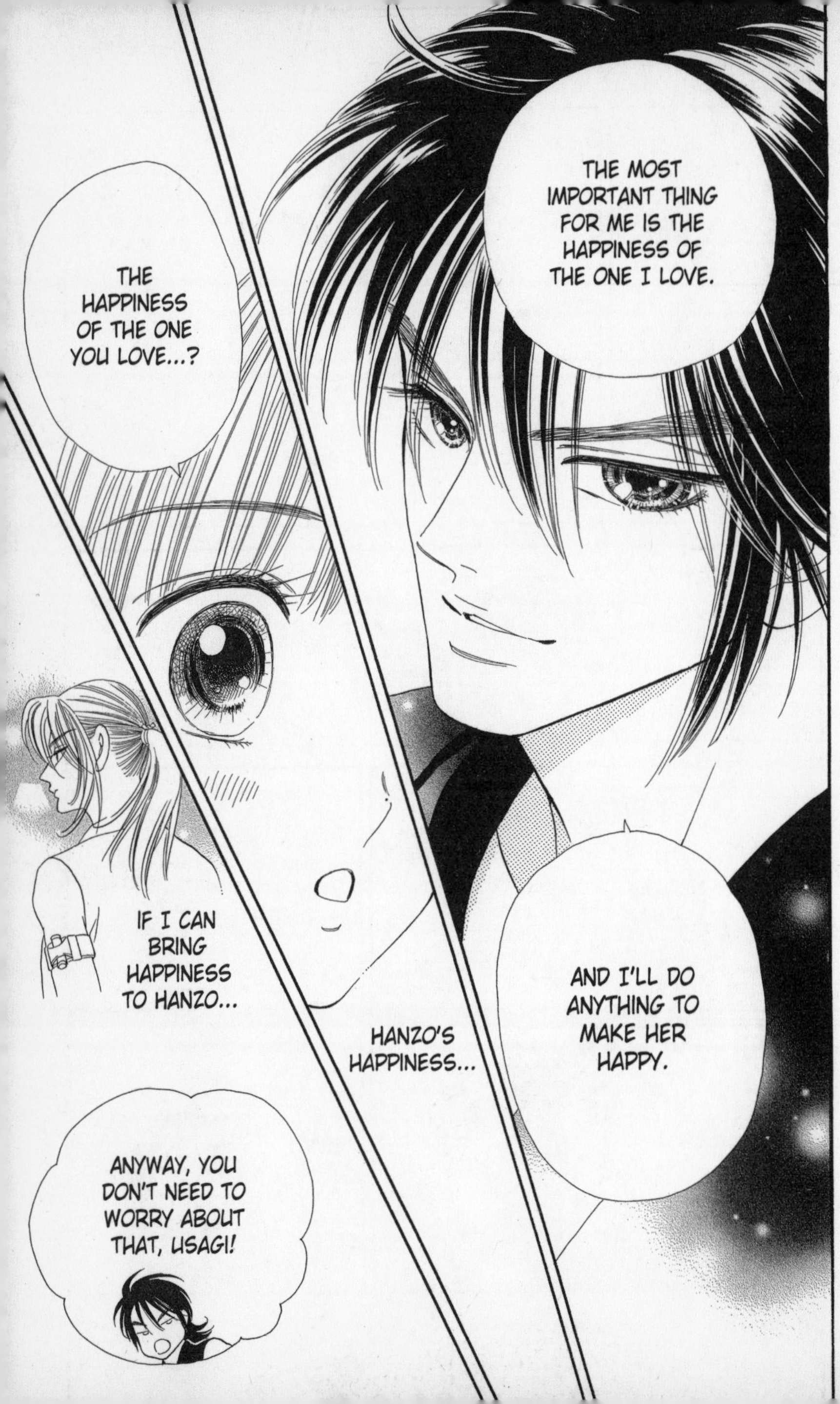
THE MOST IMPORTANT THING FOR ME IS THE HAPPINESS OF THE ONE I LOVE.
AND I'LL DO ANYTHING TO MAKE HER HAPPY.
THE HAPPINESS OF THE ONE YOU LOVE...?
HANZO'S HAPPINESS...
IF I CAN BRING HAPPINESS TO HANZO...
ANYWAY, YOU DON'T NEED TO WORRY ABOUT THAT, USAGI!

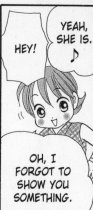

ALL YOU NEED TO DO IS BECOME MY WIFE. ♪
Are you joking again ?!
TUG
USA, ARE YOU GOING TO MARRY GOEMON?
YEAH, SHE IS. ♪
HEY!
OH, I FORGOT TO SHOW YOU SOMETHING.
THE COOL SWORD HANZO GAVE ME...
AAAAAAAH!
I FORGOT IT BACK IN THE VILLAGE!
I'M GOING BACK TO GET IT!
DASH
H-HOW CAN YOU JUST GO BACK TO HANZO'S VILLAGE...
I'm jealous.
HURRY HOME, MAMEZO.
WE HAVE THE ANNUAL NINJA SKILL CONTEST TODAY.
OH, THE CONTEST IS TODAY?
USAGI, WHY DON'T YOU ENTER IT?
SNARF SNARF
NO WAY.
I'VE NEVER BEEN IN IT BEFORE.
OH, WELL ...
THAT'S A SHAME. THE PRIZE THIS YEAR IS A LOVE POTION...

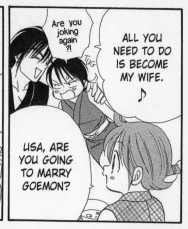

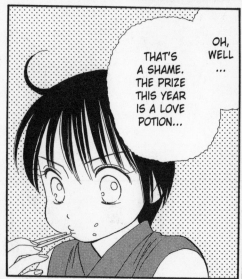

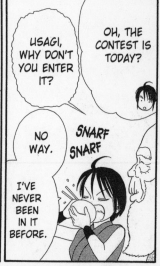

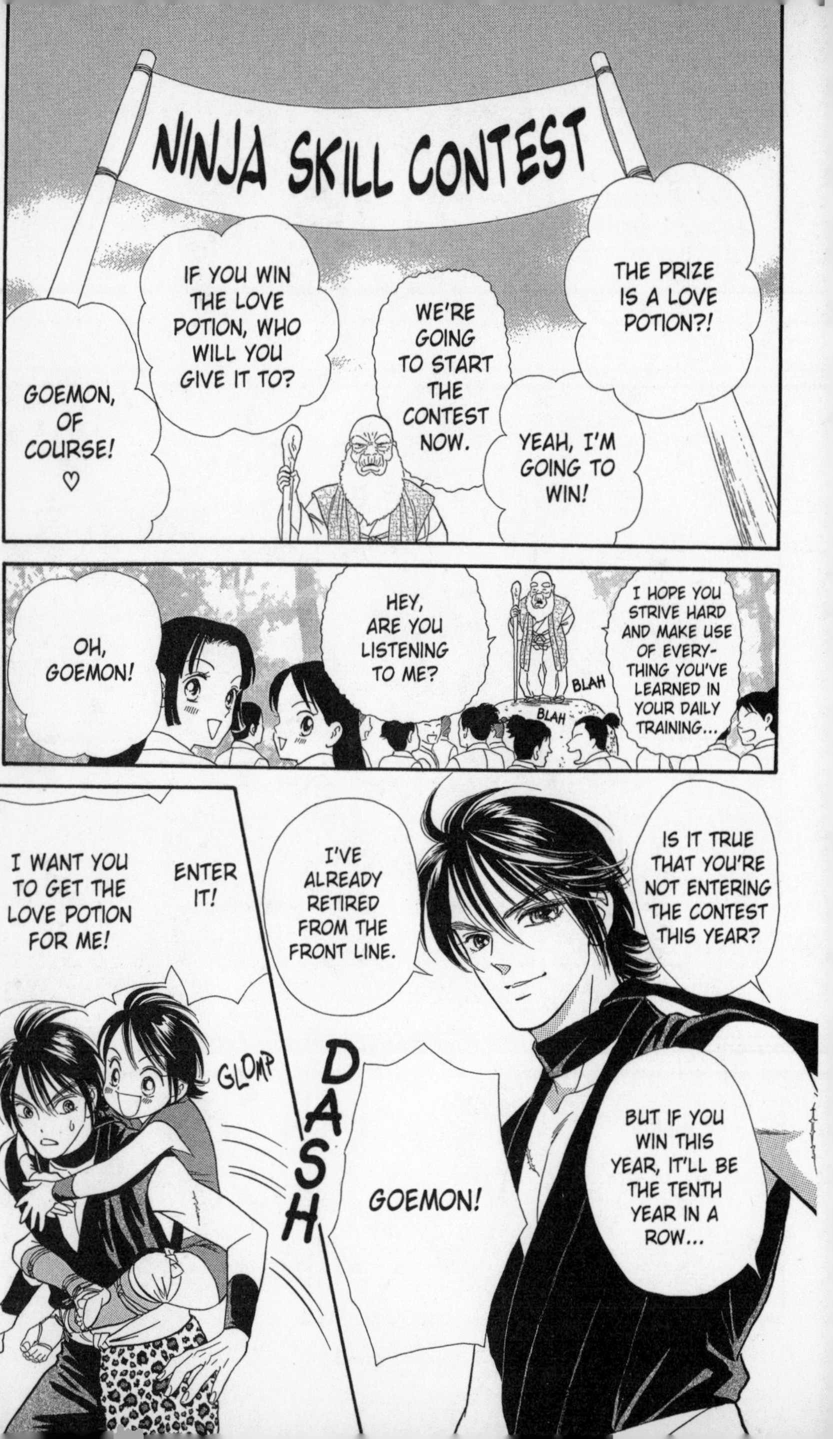
NINJA SKILL CONTEST
THE PRIZE IS A LOVE POTION?!
YEAH, I'M GOING TO WIN!
WE'RE GOING TO START THE CONTEST NOW.
IF YOU WIN THE LOVE POTION, WHO WILL YOU GIVE IT TO?
GOEMON, OF COURSE! ♡
I HOPE YOU STRIVE HARD AND MAKE USE OF EVERY-THING YOU'VE LEARNED IN YOUR DAILY TRAINING...
BLAH
BLAH
HEY, ARE YOU LISTENING TO ME?
OH, GOEMON!
IS IT TRUE THAT YOU'RE NOT ENTERING THE CONTEST THIS YEAR?
I'VE ALREADY RETIRED FROM THE FRONT LINE.
BUT IF YOU WIN THIS YEAR, IT'LL BE THE TENTH YEAR IN A ROW...
GOEMON!
DASH
ENTER IT!
I WANT YOU TO GET THE LOVE POTION FOR ME!
GLOMP

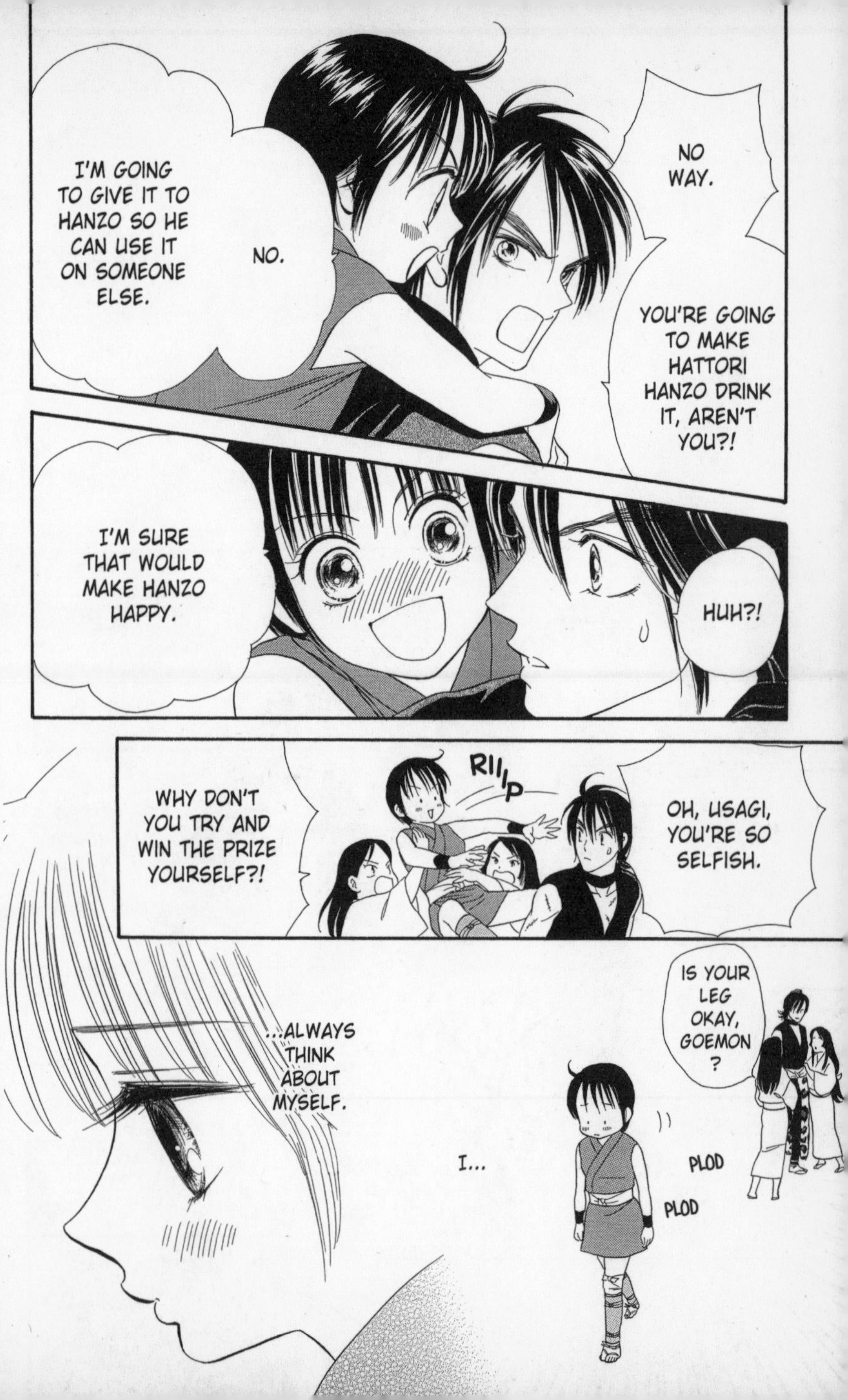
NO WAY.
YOU'RE GOING TO MAKE HATTORI HANZO DRINK IT, AREN'T YOU?!
NO.
I'M GOING TO GIVE IT TO HANZO SO HE CAN USE IT ON SOMEONE ELSE.
HUH?!
I'M SURE THAT WOULD MAKE HANZO HAPPY.
OH, USAGI, YOU'RE SO SELFISH.
RIIIP
WHY DON'T YOU TRY AND WIN THE PRIZE YOURSELF?!
IS YOUR LEG OKAY, GOEMON?
PLOD
PLOD
I...
...ALWAYS THINK ABOUT MYSELF.

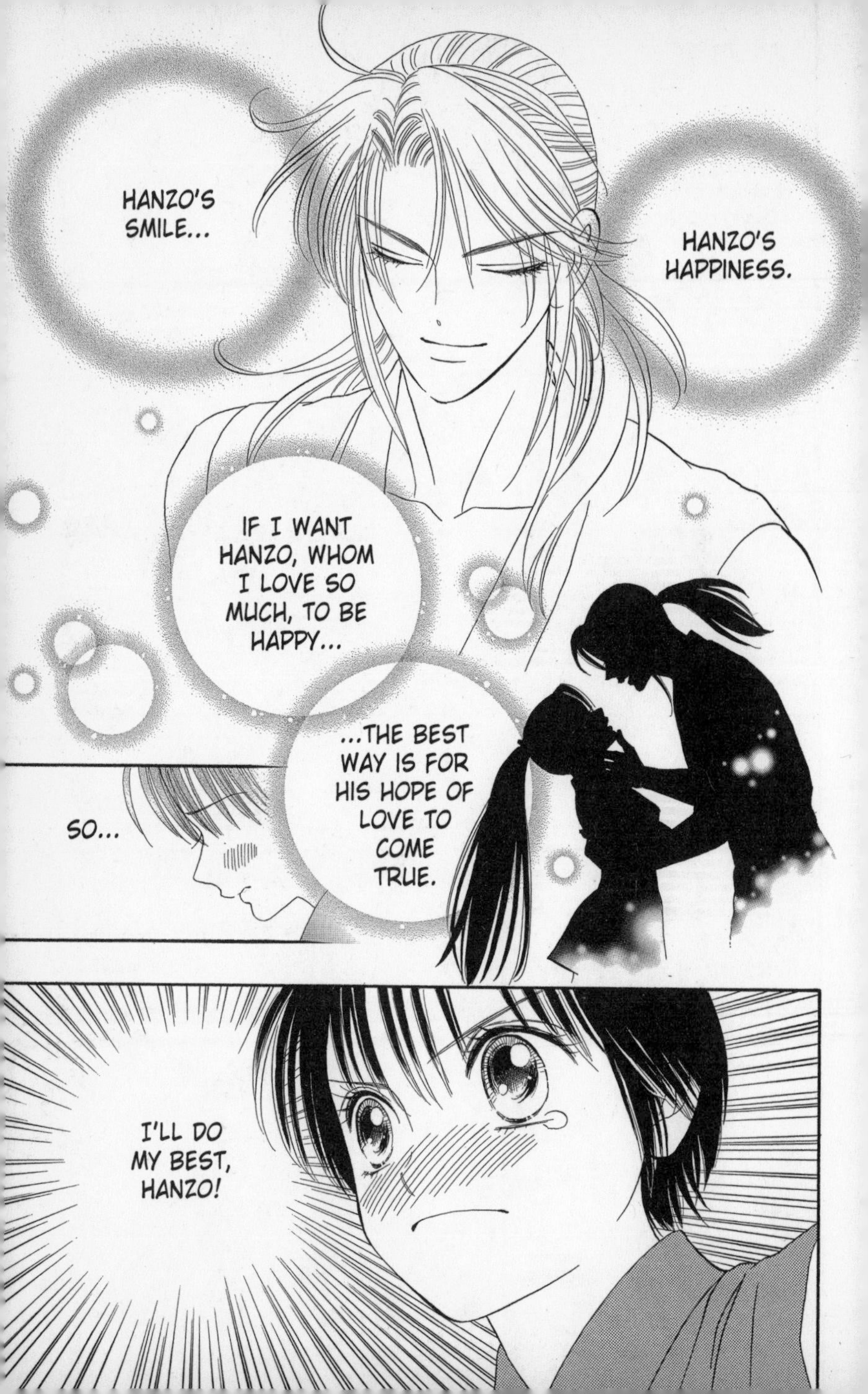
HANZO'S HAPPINESS.
HANZO'S SMILE...
IF I WANT HANZO, WHOM I LOVE SO MUCH, TO BE HAPPY...
...THE BEST WAY IS FOR HIS HOPE OF LOVE TO COME TRUE.
SO...
I'LL DO MY BEST, HANZO!

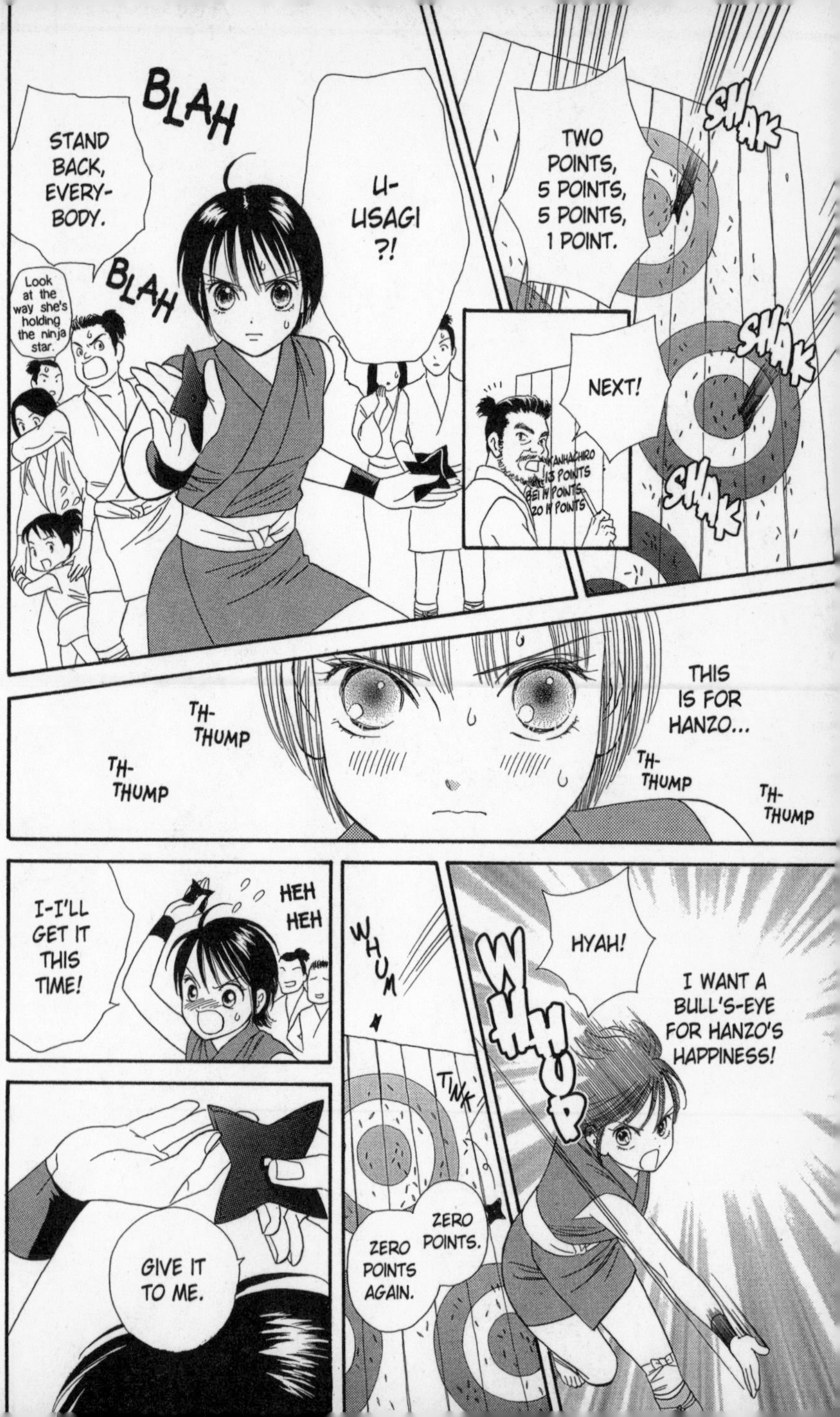
SHAK
TWO POINTS, 5 POINTS, 5 POINTS, 1 POINT.
SHAK
SHAK
NEXT!
ANHACHIRO
13 POINTS
BEI 14 POINTS
ZO 14 POINTS
U-USAGI ?!
BLAH
STAND BACK, EVERY-BODY.
BLAH
Look at the way she's holding the ninja star.
THIS IS FOR HANZO...
TH-THUMP
TH-THUMP
TH-THUMP
TH-THUMP
HYAH!
I WANT A BULL'S-EYE FOR HANZO'S HAPPINESS!
WHHUP
WHUM
TINK
ZERO POINTS.
ZERO POINTS AGAIN.
HEH HEH
I-I'LL GET IT THIS TIME!
GIVE IT TO ME.

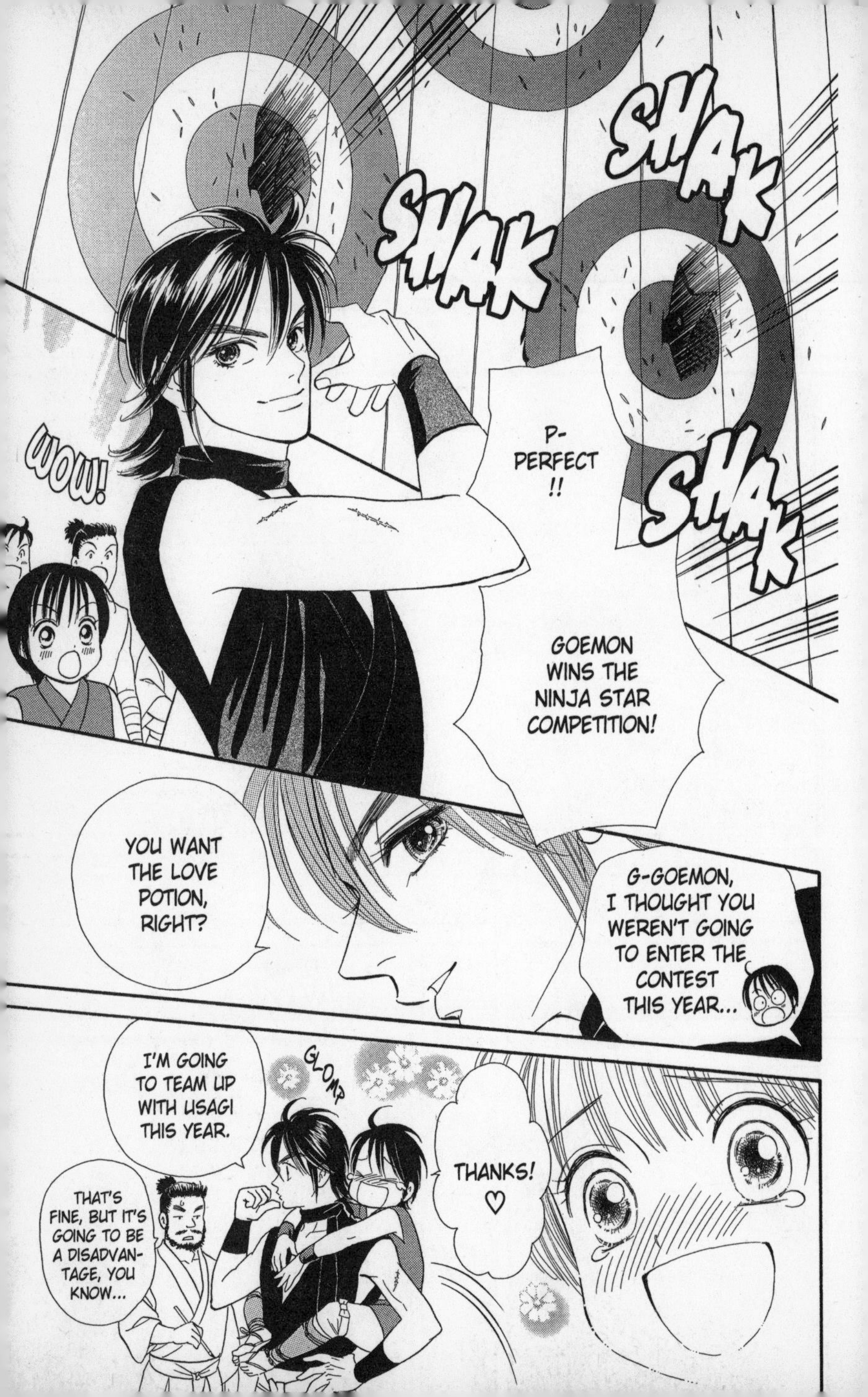
SHAK
SHAK
P-PERFECT!!
SHAK
GOEMON WINS THE NINJA STAR COMPETITION!
WOW!
G-GOEMON, I THOUGHT YOU WEREN'T GOING TO ENTER THE CONTEST THIS YEAR...
YOU WANT THE LOVE POTION, RIGHT?
THANKS! ♡
GLOMP
I'M GOING TO TEAM UP WITH USAGI THIS YEAR.
THAT'S FINE, BUT IT'S GOING TO BE A DISADVANTAGE, YOU KNOW...

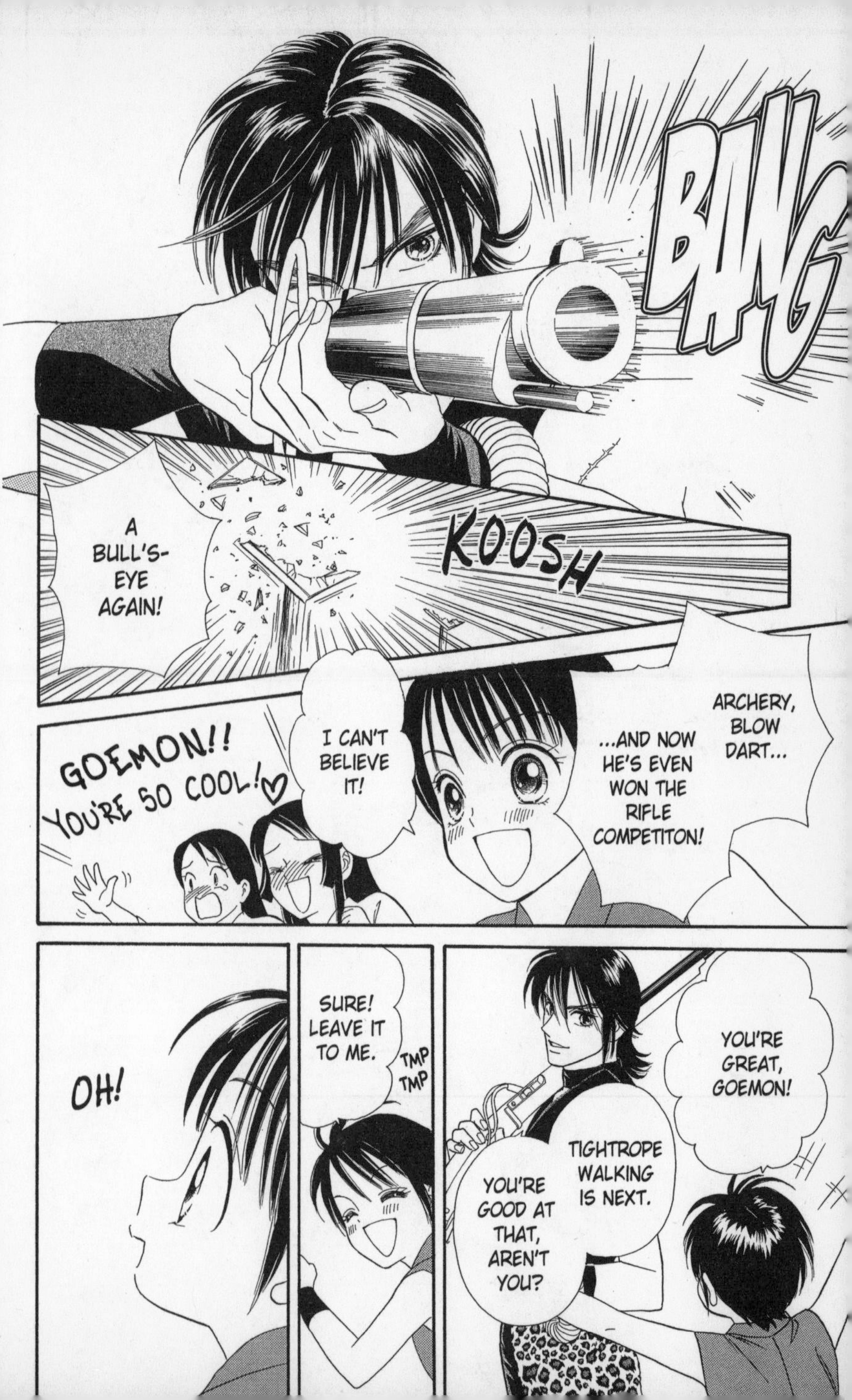
BANG
KOOSH
A BULL'S-EYE AGAIN!
ARCHERY, BLOW DART...
...AND NOW HE'S EVEN WON THE RIFLE COMPETITON!
I CAN'T BELIEVE IT!
GOEMON!! YOU'RE SO COOL!♥
YOU'RE GREAT, GOEMON!
TIGHTROPE WALKING IS NEXT.
YOU'RE GOOD AT THAT, AREN'T YOU?
SURE! LEAVE IT TO ME.
TMP TMP
OH!

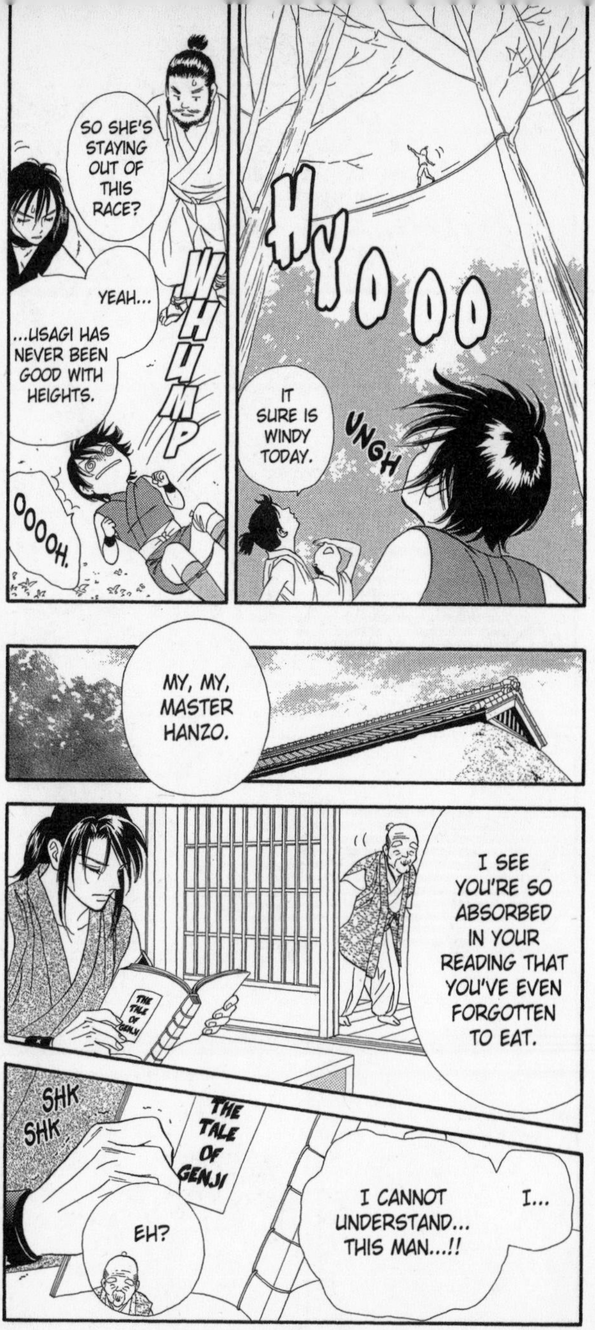
HYOOO
IT SURE IS WINDY TODAY.
UNGH
SO SHE'S STAYING OUT OF THIS RACE?
YEAH...
...USAGI HAS NEVER BEEN GOOD WITH HEIGHTS.
WHUMP
OOOOH.
MY, MY, MASTER HANZO.
I SEE YOU'RE SO ABSORBED IN YOUR READING THAT YOU'VE EVEN FORGOTTEN TO EAT.
THE TALE OF GENJI
I...
I CANNOT UNDERSTAND... THIS MAN...!!
THE TALE OF GENJI
EH?
SHK SHK

✿ GREETINGS! ✿

Hello for the second time! It's Ue-Rin here.

This time I'd like to share with you the profiles of the various characters.

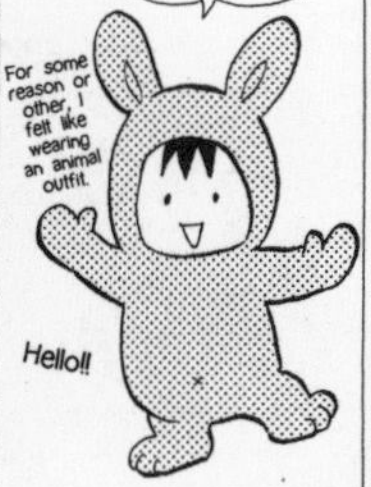
For some reason or other, I felt like wearing an animal outfit.
Hello!!

By the way, my birthday is September 30th. My blood type is B, and my zodiac sign is Libra.

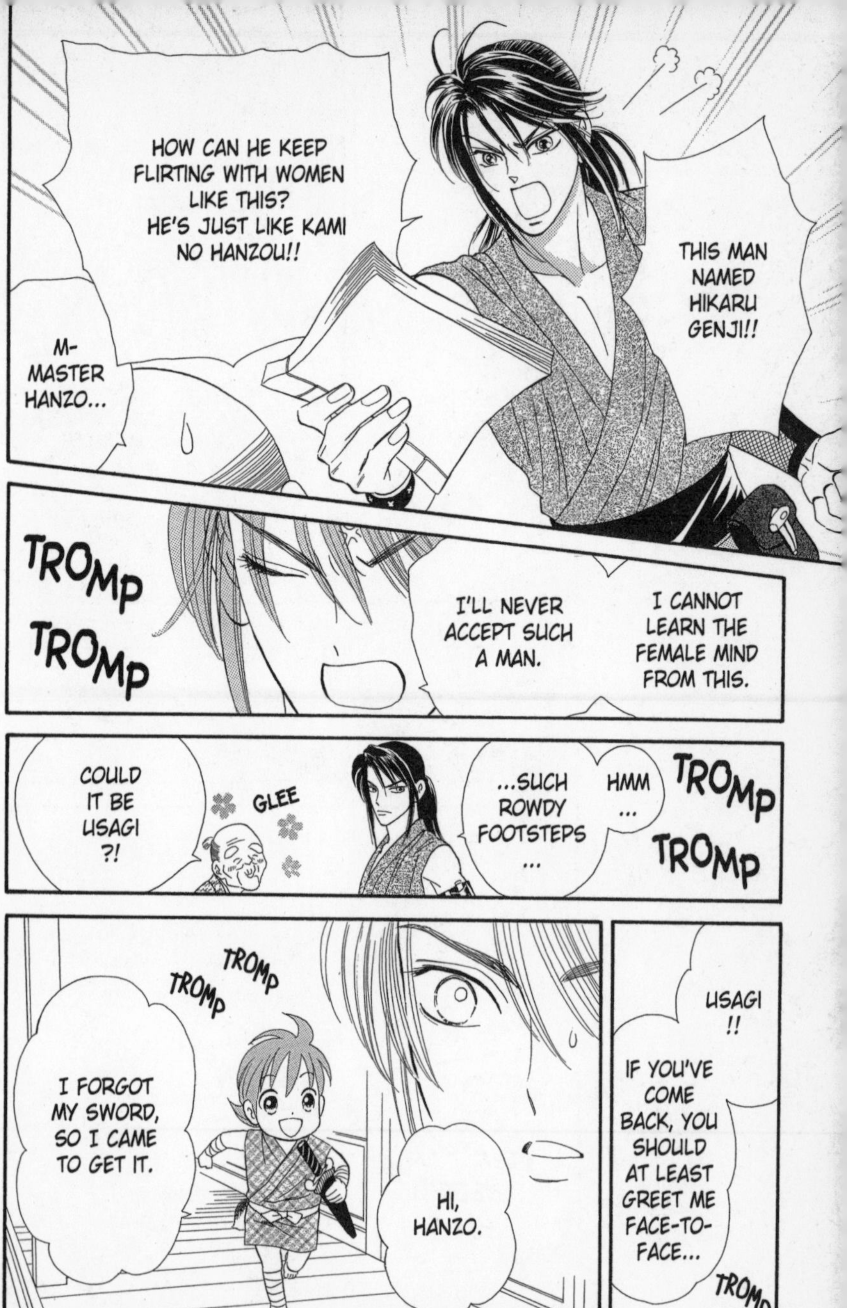
HOW CAN HE KEEP FLIRTING WITH WOMEN LIKE THIS? HE'S JUST LIKE KAMI NO HANZOU!!
THIS MAN NAMED HIKARU GENJI!!
M-MASTER HANZO...
I CANNOT LEARN THE FEMALE MIND FROM THIS.
I'LL NEVER ACCEPT SUCH A MAN.
TROMP
TROMP
TROMP
TROMP
HMM...
...SUCH ROWDY FOOTSTEPS...
GLEE
COULD IT BE USAGI?!
USAGI!!
IF YOU'VE COME BACK, YOU SHOULD AT LEAST GREET ME FACE-TO-FACE...
TROMP
HI, HANZO.
TROMP
TROMP
I FORGOT MY SWORD, SO I CAME TO GET IT.

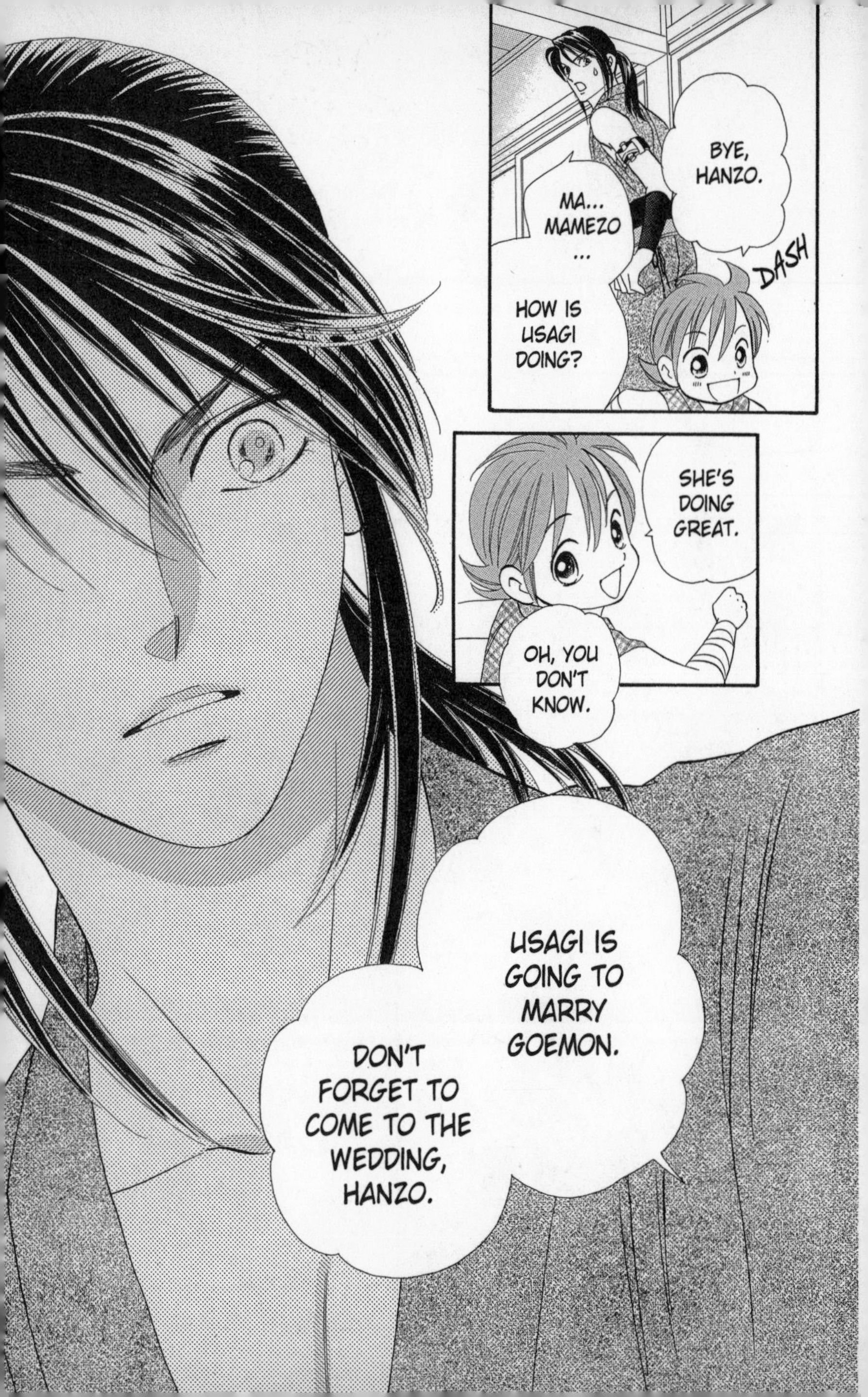
BYE, HANZO.
MA... MAMEZO ...
DASH
HOW IS USAGI DOING?
SHE'S DOING GREAT.
OH, YOU DON'T KNOW.
USAGI IS GOING TO MARRY GOEMON.
DON'T FORGET TO COME TO THE WEDDING, HANZO.

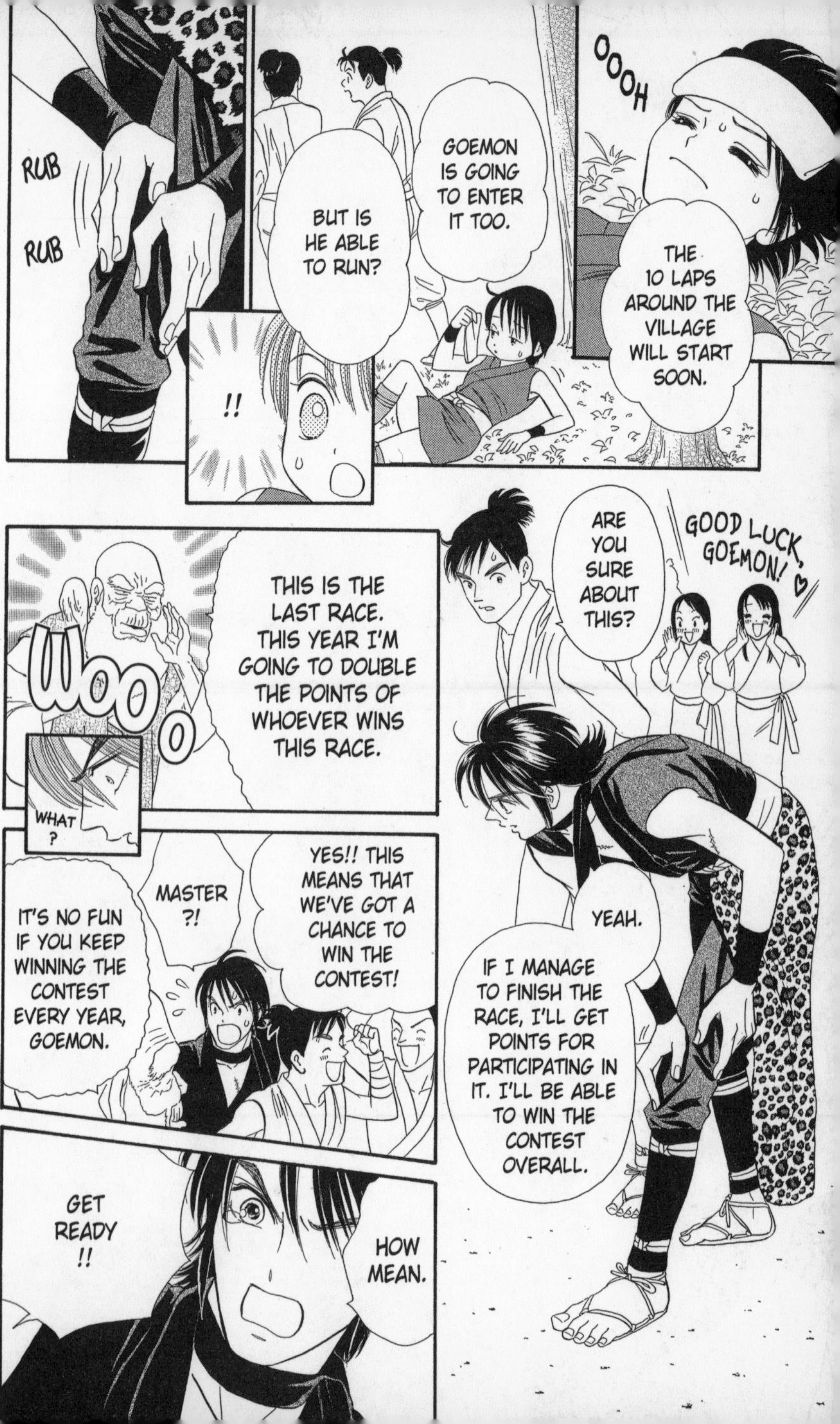
OOOH
THE 10 LAPS AROUND THE VILLAGE WILL START SOON.
GOEMON IS GOING TO ENTER IT TOO.
BUT IS HE ABLE TO RUN?
!!
RUB
RUB
GOOD LUCK, GOEMON! ♥
ARE YOU SURE ABOUT THIS?
YEAH.
IF I MANAGE TO FINISH THE RACE, I'LL GET POINTS FOR PARTICIPATING IN IT. I'LL BE ABLE TO WIN THE CONTEST OVERALL.
THIS IS THE LAST RACE. THIS YEAR I'M GOING TO DOUBLE THE POINTS OF WHOEVER WINS THIS RACE.
WOOO
WHAT?
YES!! THIS MEANS THAT WE'VE GOT A CHANCE TO WIN THE CONTEST!
MASTER ?!
IT'S NO FUN IF YOU KEEP WINNING THE CONTEST EVERY YEAR, GOEMON.
HOW MEAN.
GET READY !!

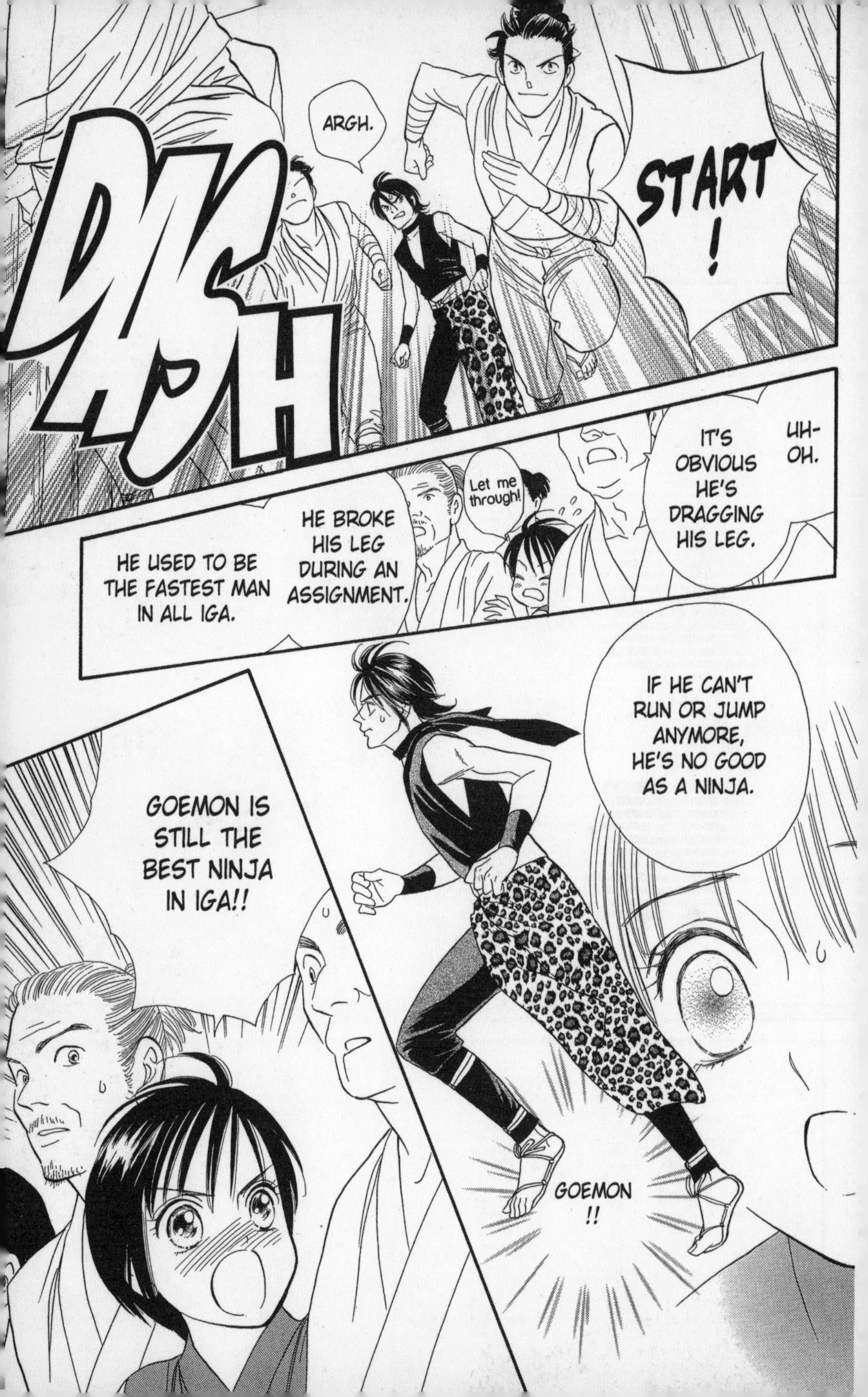
START!
ARGH.
DASH
UH-OH.
IT'S OBVIOUS HE'S DRAGGING HIS LEG.
Let me through!
HE BROKE HIS LEG DURING AN ASSIGNMENT.
HE USED TO BE THE FASTEST MAN IN ALL IGA.
IF HE CAN'T RUN OR JUMP ANYMORE, HE'S NO GOOD AS A NINJA.
GOEMON!!
GOEMON IS STILL THE BEST NINJA IN IGA!!

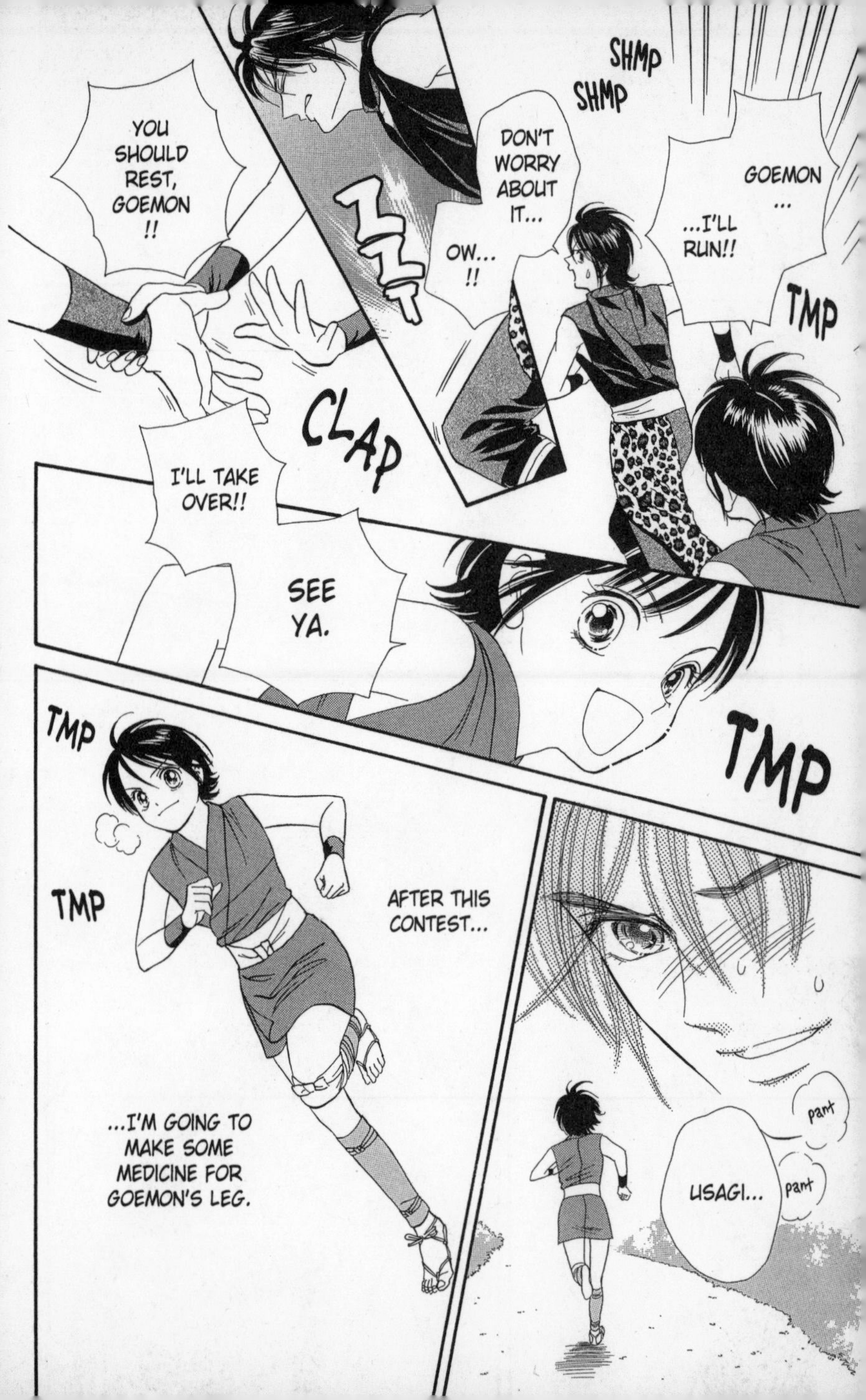
SHMP
SHMP
GOEMON ...
...I'LL RUN!!
TMP
DON'T WORRY ABOUT IT...
OW... !!
YOU SHOULD REST, GOEMON !!
CLAP
I'LL TAKE OVER!!
SEE YA.
TMP
USAGI...
pant
pant
TMP
TMP
AFTER THIS CONTEST...
...I'M GOING TO MAKE SOME MEDICINE FOR GOEMON'S LEG.

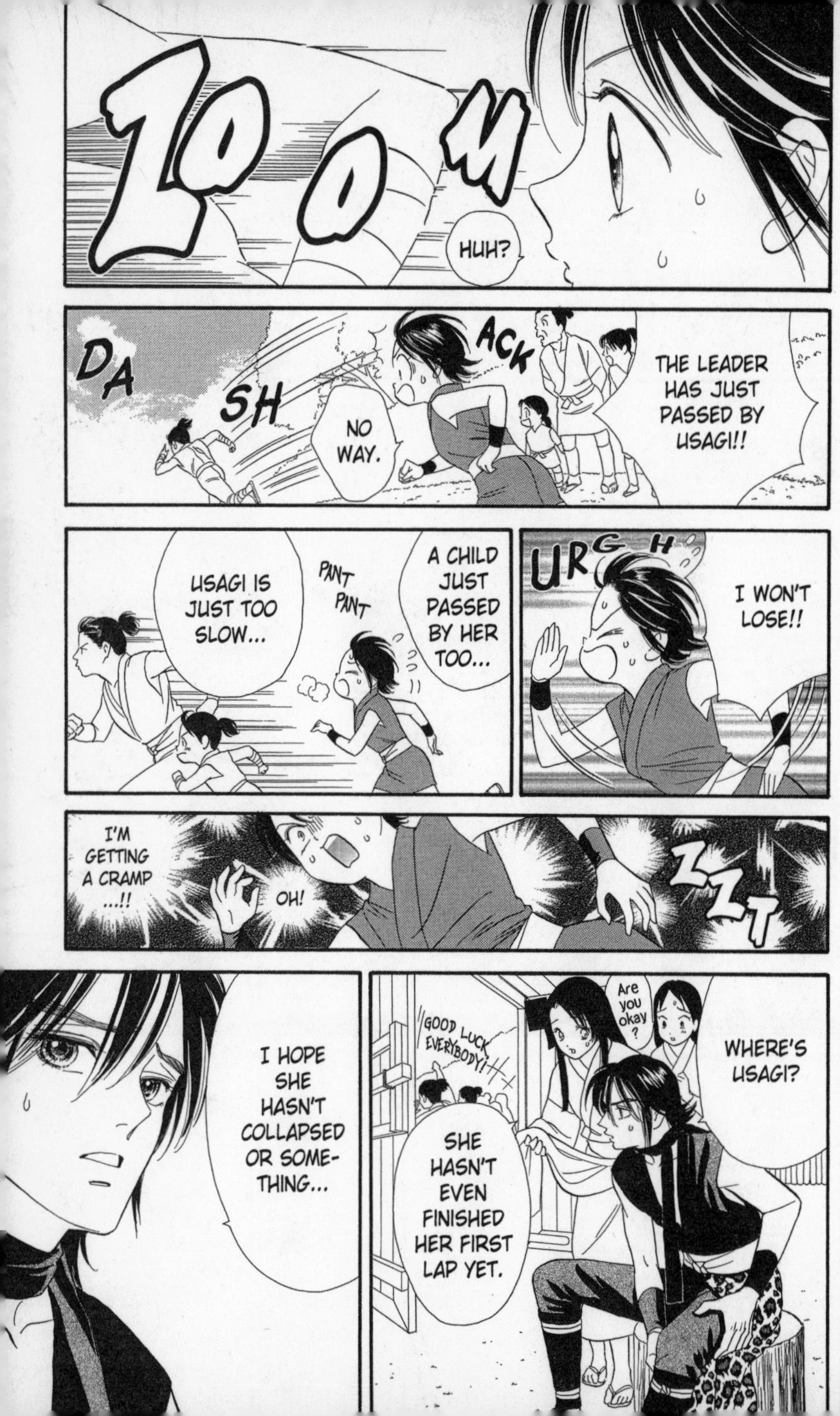
ZOOOM
HUH?
THE LEADER HAS JUST PASSED BY USAGI!!
ACK
NO WAY.
DASH
URGH
I WON'T LOSE!!
A CHILD JUST PASSED BY HER TOO...
PANT PANT
USAGI IS JUST TOO SLOW...
ZZZT
OH!
I'M GETTING A CRAMP ...!!
WHERE'S USAGI?
Are you okay?
GOOD LUCK EVERYBODY!!
SHE HASN'T EVEN FINISHED HER FIRST LAP YET.
I HOPE SHE HASN'T COLLAPSED OR SOMETHING...

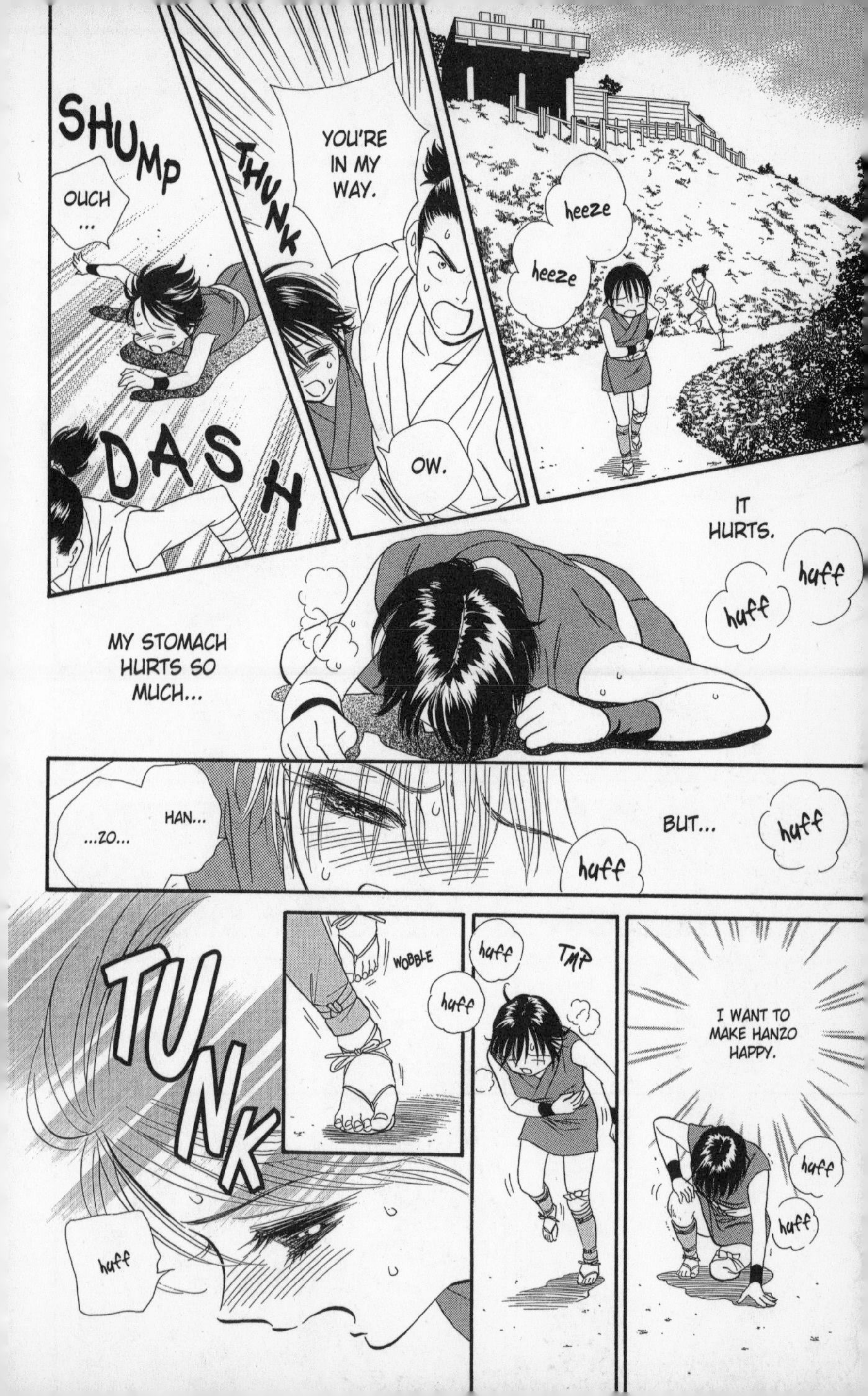
heeze
heeze
YOU'RE IN MY WAY.
THUNK
OW.
SHUMP
OUCH ...
DASH
IT HURTS.
huff
huff
MY STOMACH HURTS SO MUCH...
huff
BUT...
huff
HAN...
...ZO...
I WANT TO MAKE HANZO HAPPY.
huff
huff
TMP
huff
huff
WOBBLE
TUNK
huff

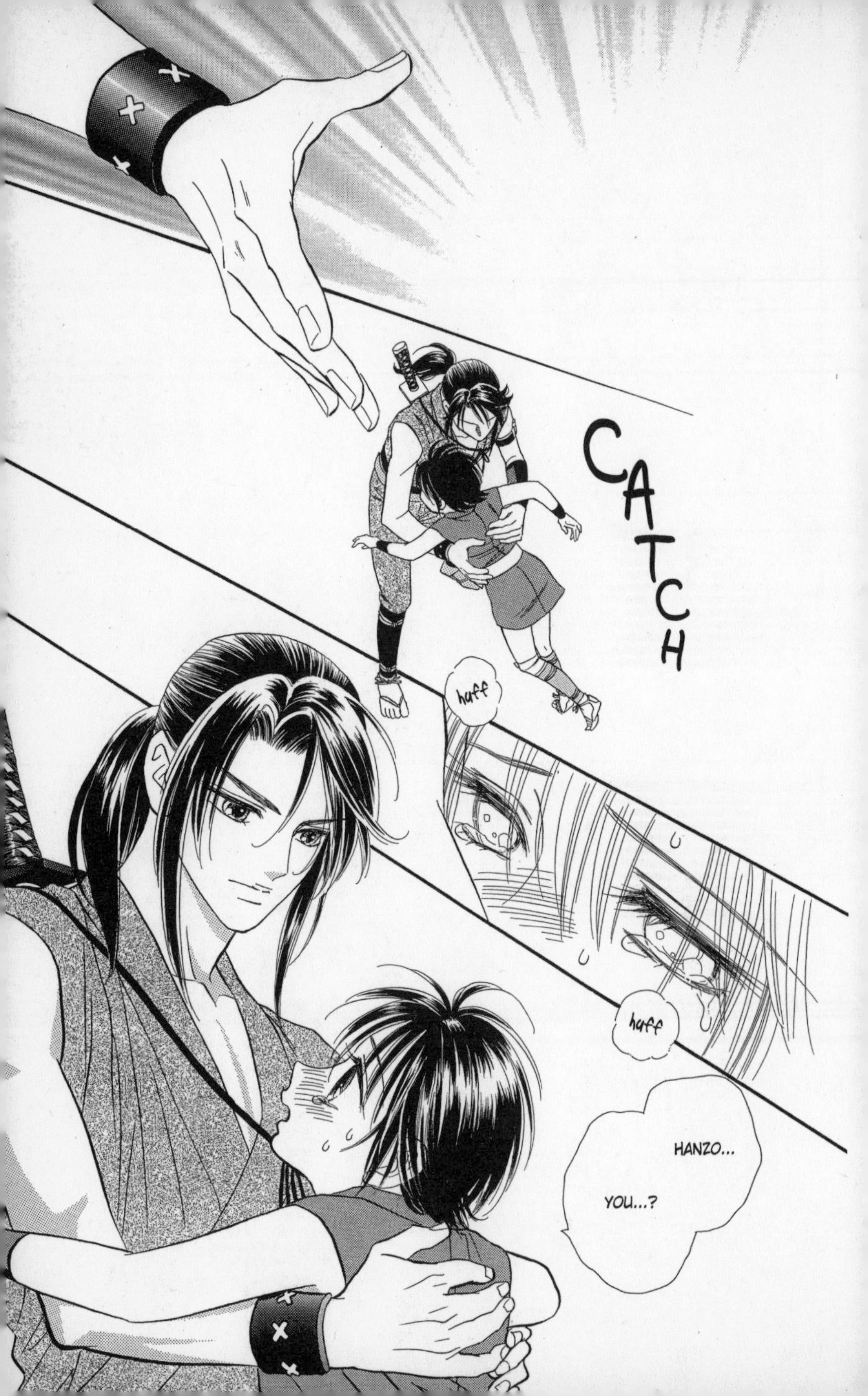
CATCH
huff
huff
HANZO...
YOU...?

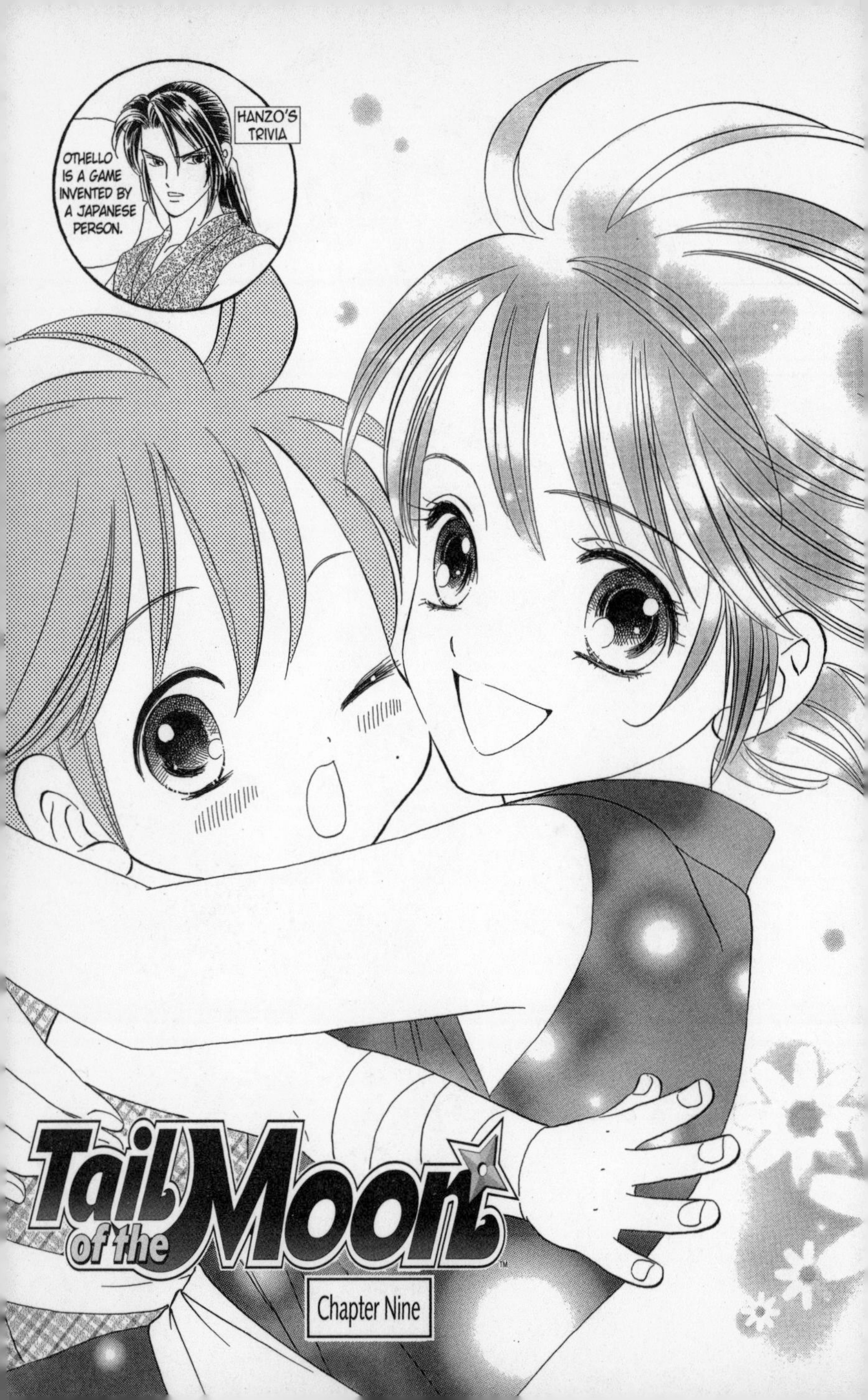
HANZO'S TRIVIA
OTHELLO IS A GAME INVENTED BY A JAPANESE PERSON.
Tail of the Moon™
Chapter Nine

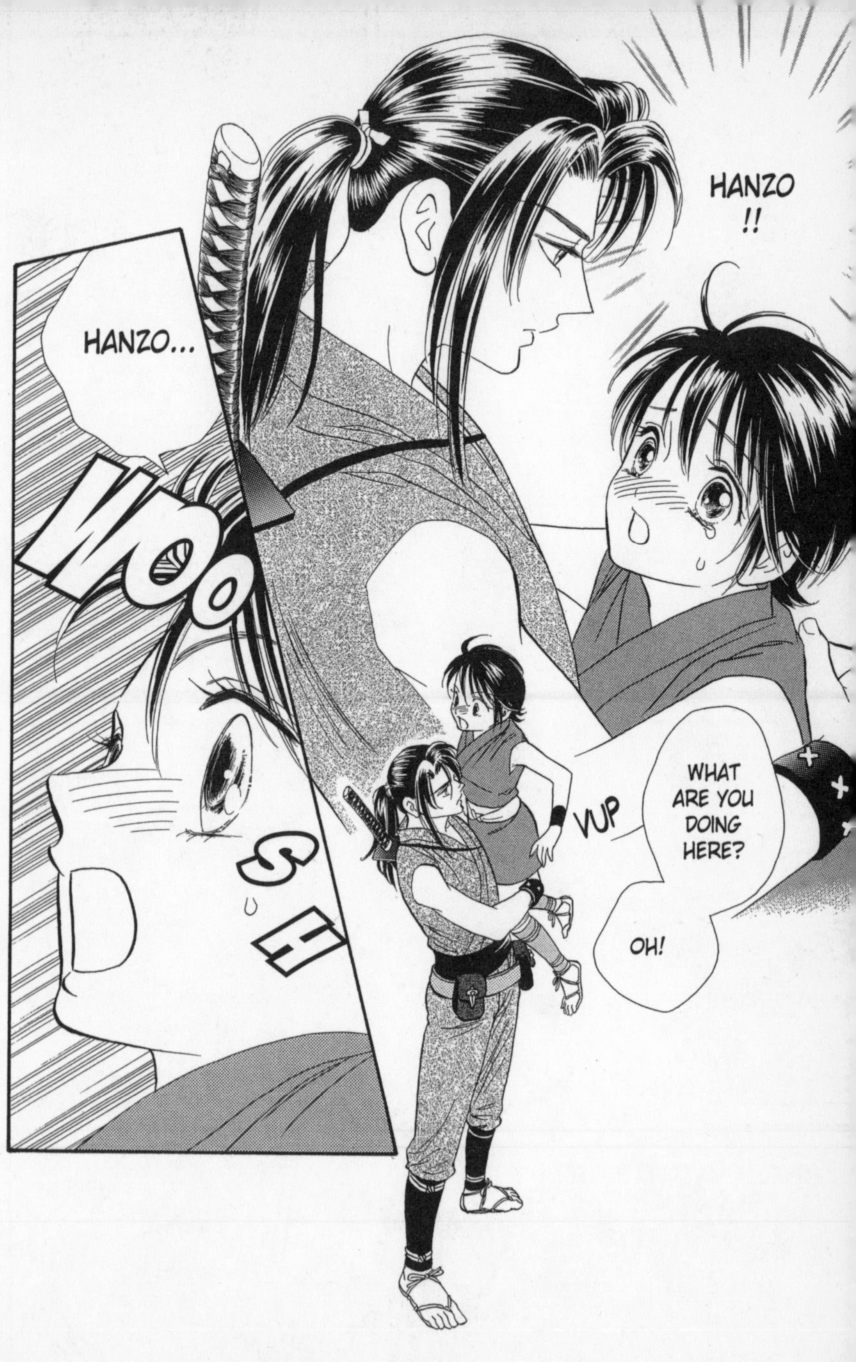
HANZO !!
WHAT ARE YOU DOING HERE?
OH!
VUP
HANZO...
WOOSH

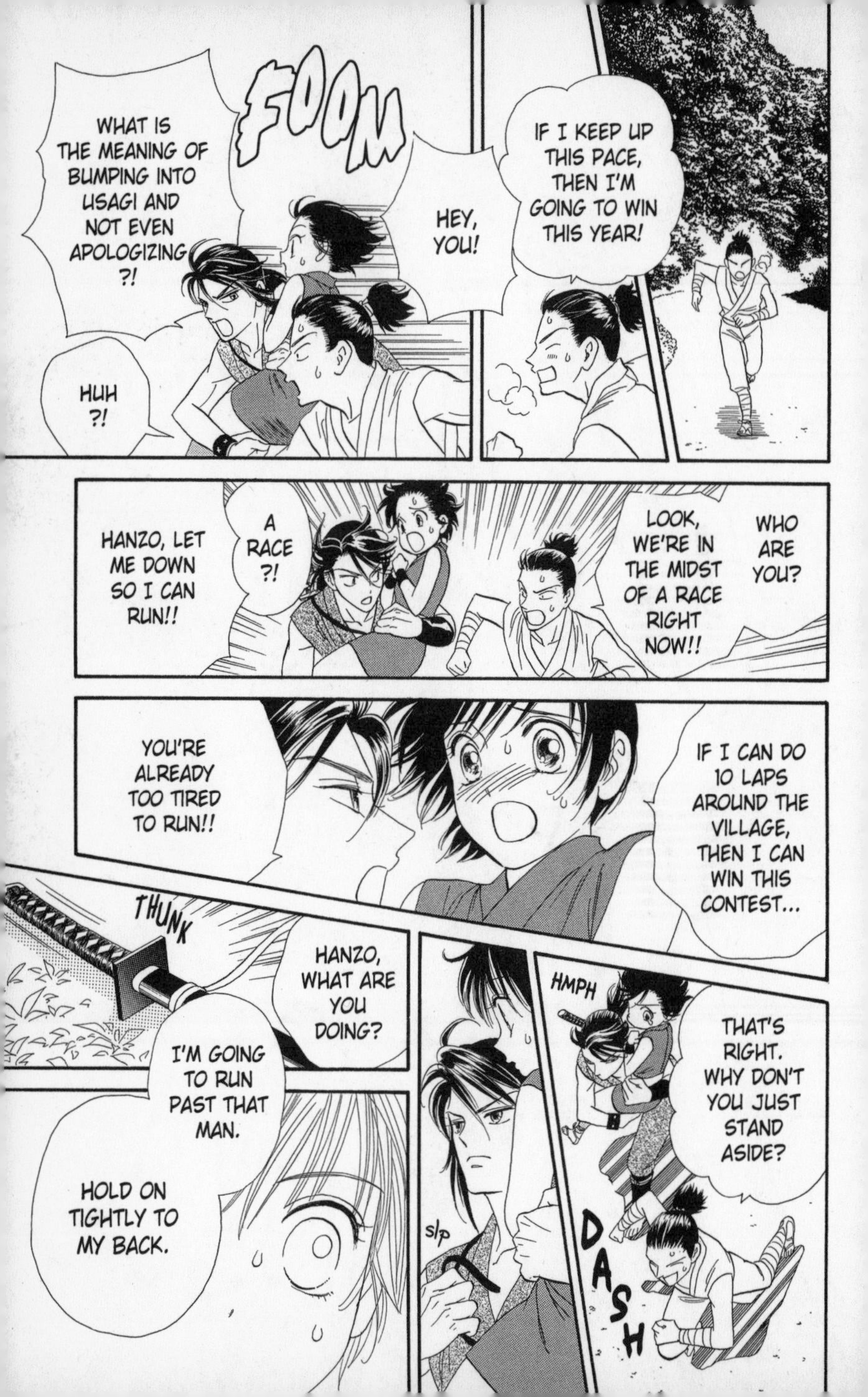
IF I KEEP UP THIS PACE, THEN I'M GOING TO WIN THIS YEAR!
FOOM
HEY, YOU!
WHAT IS THE MEANING OF BUMPING INTO USAGI AND NOT EVEN APOLOGIZING?!
HUH?!
WHO ARE YOU?
LOOK, WE'RE IN THE MIDST OF A RACE RIGHT NOW!!
A RACE?!
HANZO, LET ME DOWN SO I CAN RUN!!
IF I CAN DO 10 LAPS AROUND THE VILLAGE, THEN I CAN WIN THIS CONTEST...
YOU'RE ALREADY TOO TIRED TO RUN!!
THAT'S RIGHT. WHY DON'T YOU JUST STAND ASIDE?
HMPH
DASH
slp
THUNK
HANZO, WHAT ARE YOU DOING?
I'M GOING TO RUN PAST THAT MAN.
HOLD ON TIGHTLY TO MY BACK.

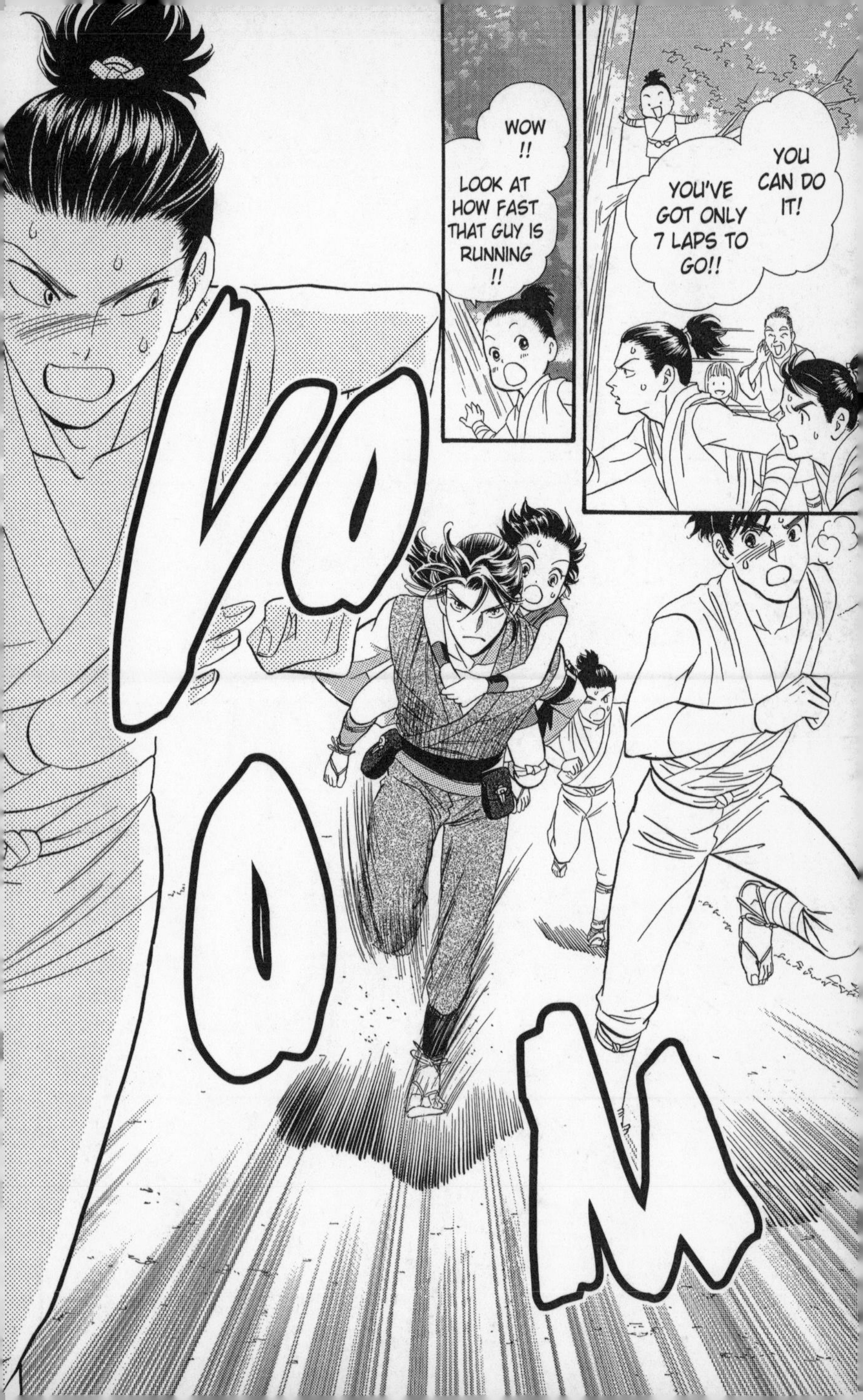
YOU CAN DO IT!
YOU'VE GOT ONLY 7 LAPS TO GO!!
WOW!!
LOOK AT HOW FAST THAT GUY IS RUNNING!!
VOOM

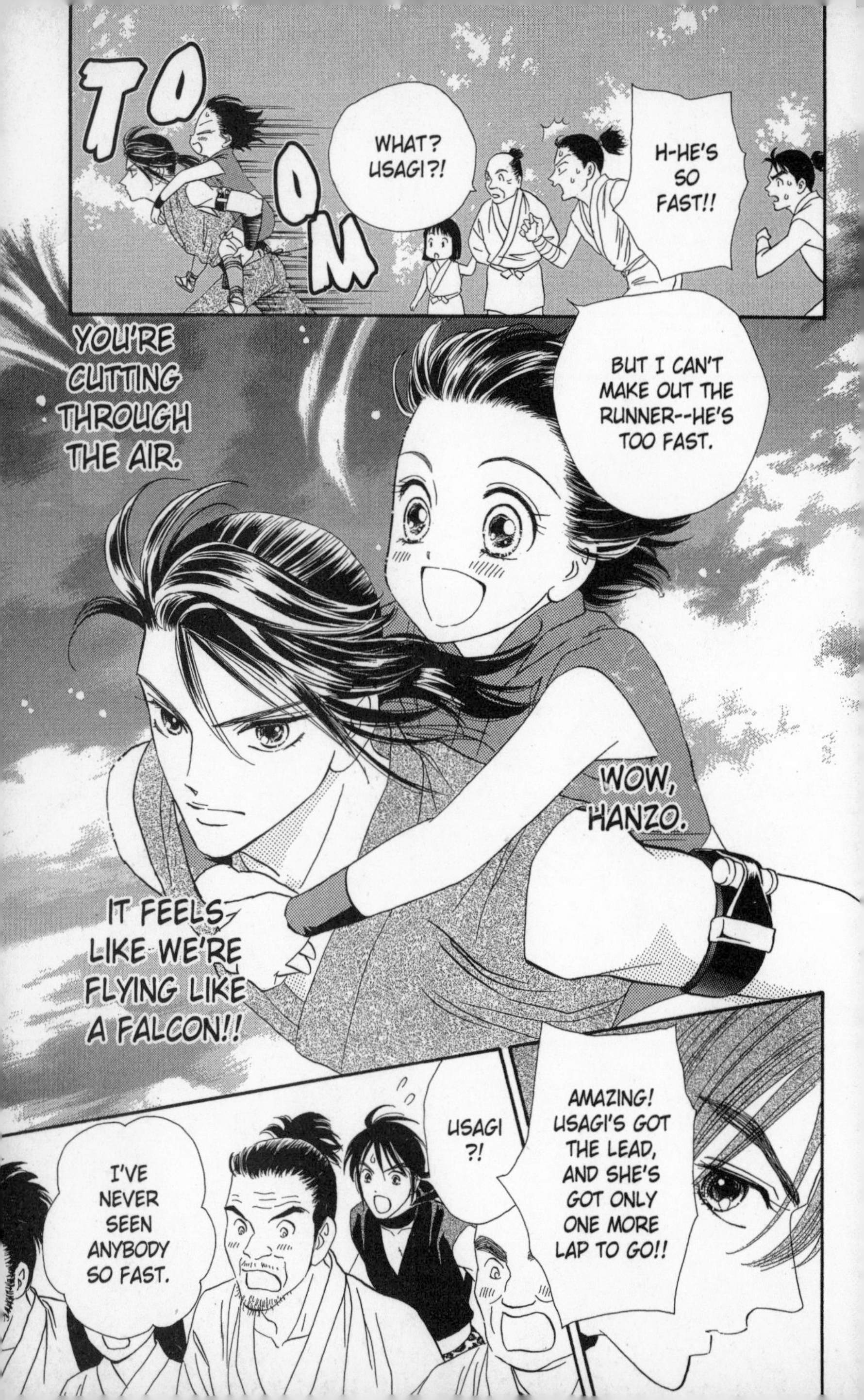
H-HE'S SO FAST!!
WHAT? USAGI?!
TOOM
BUT I CAN'T MAKE OUT THE RUNNER--HE'S TOO FAST.
YOU'RE CUTTING THROUGH THE AIR.
WOW, HANZO.
IT FEELS LIKE WE'RE FLYING LIKE A FALCON!!
AMAZING! USAGI'S GOT THE LEAD, AND SHE'S GOT ONLY ONE MORE LAP TO GO!!
USAGI ?!
I'VE NEVER SEEN ANYBODY SO FAST.

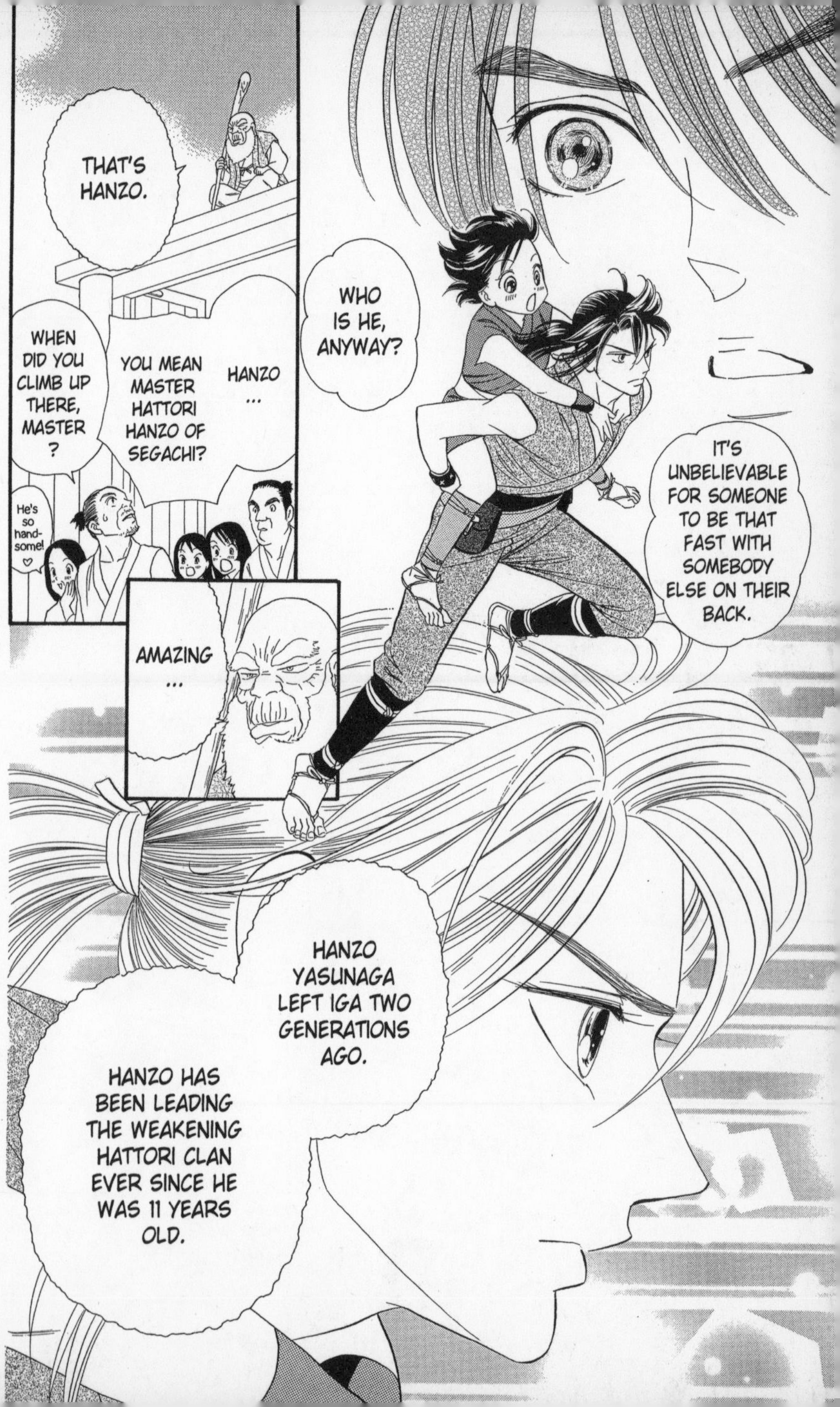
WHO IS HE, ANYWAY?
IT'S UNBELIEVABLE FOR SOMEONE TO BE THAT FAST WITH SOMEBODY ELSE ON THEIR BACK.
THAT'S HANZO.
HANZO ...
YOU MEAN MASTER HATTORI HANZO OF SEGACHI?
WHEN DID YOU CLIMB UP THERE, MASTER ?
He's so hand-some! ♡
AMAZING ...
HANZO YASUNAGA LEFT IGA TWO GENERATIONS AGO.
HANZO HAS BEEN LEADING THE WEAKENING HATTORI CLAN EVER SINCE HE WAS 11 YEARS OLD.

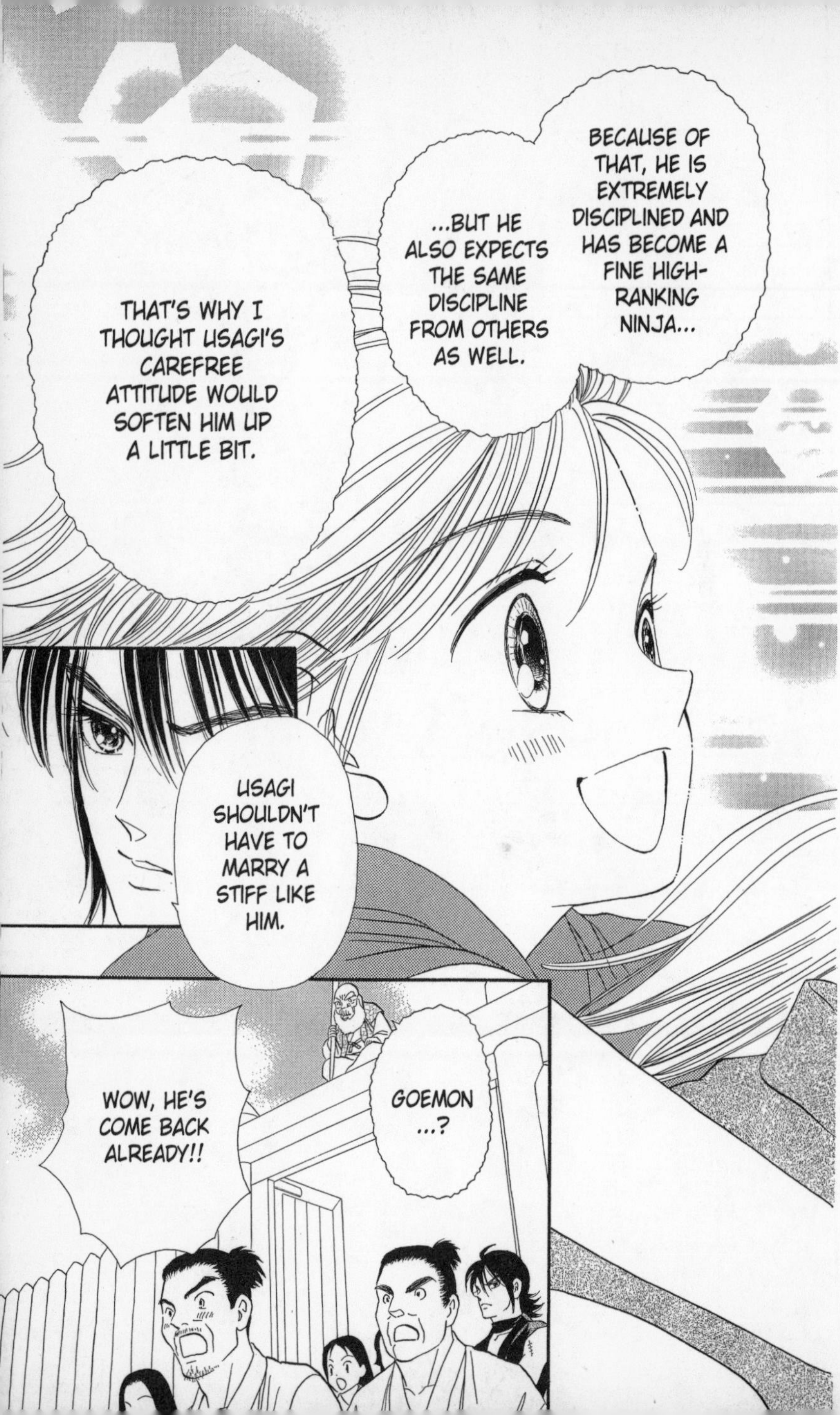
BECAUSE OF THAT, HE IS EXTREMELY DISCIPLINED AND HAS BECOME A FINE HIGH-RANKING NINJA...
...BUT HE ALSO EXPECTS THE SAME DISCIPLINE FROM OTHERS AS WELL.
THAT'S WHY I THOUGHT USAGI'S CAREFREE ATTITUDE WOULD SOFTEN HIM UP A LITTLE BIT.
USAGI SHOULDN'T HAVE TO MARRY A STIFF LIKE HIM.
GOEMON ...?
WOW, HE'S COME BACK ALREADY!!

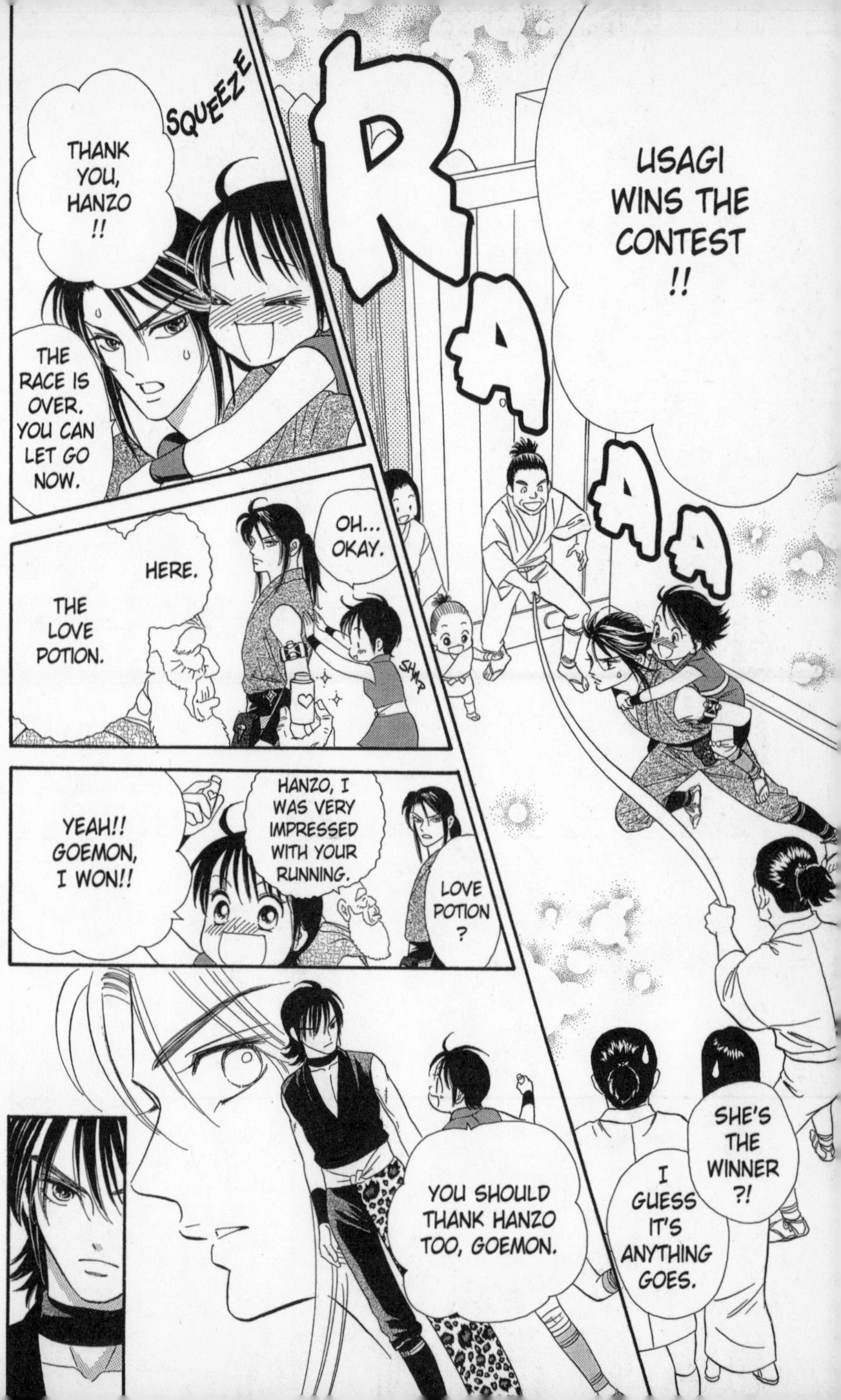
RAAAA
USAGI WINS THE CONTEST!!
SHE'S THE WINNER?!
I GUESS IT'S ANYTHING GOES.
SQUEEZE
THANK YOU, HANZO!!
THE RACE IS OVER. YOU CAN LET GO NOW.
OH... OKAY.
SHMP
HERE.
THE LOVE POTION.
LOVE POTION?
HANZO, I WAS VERY IMPRESSED WITH YOUR RUNNING.
YEAH!! GOEMON, I WON!!
YOU SHOULD THANK HANZO TOO, GOEMON.

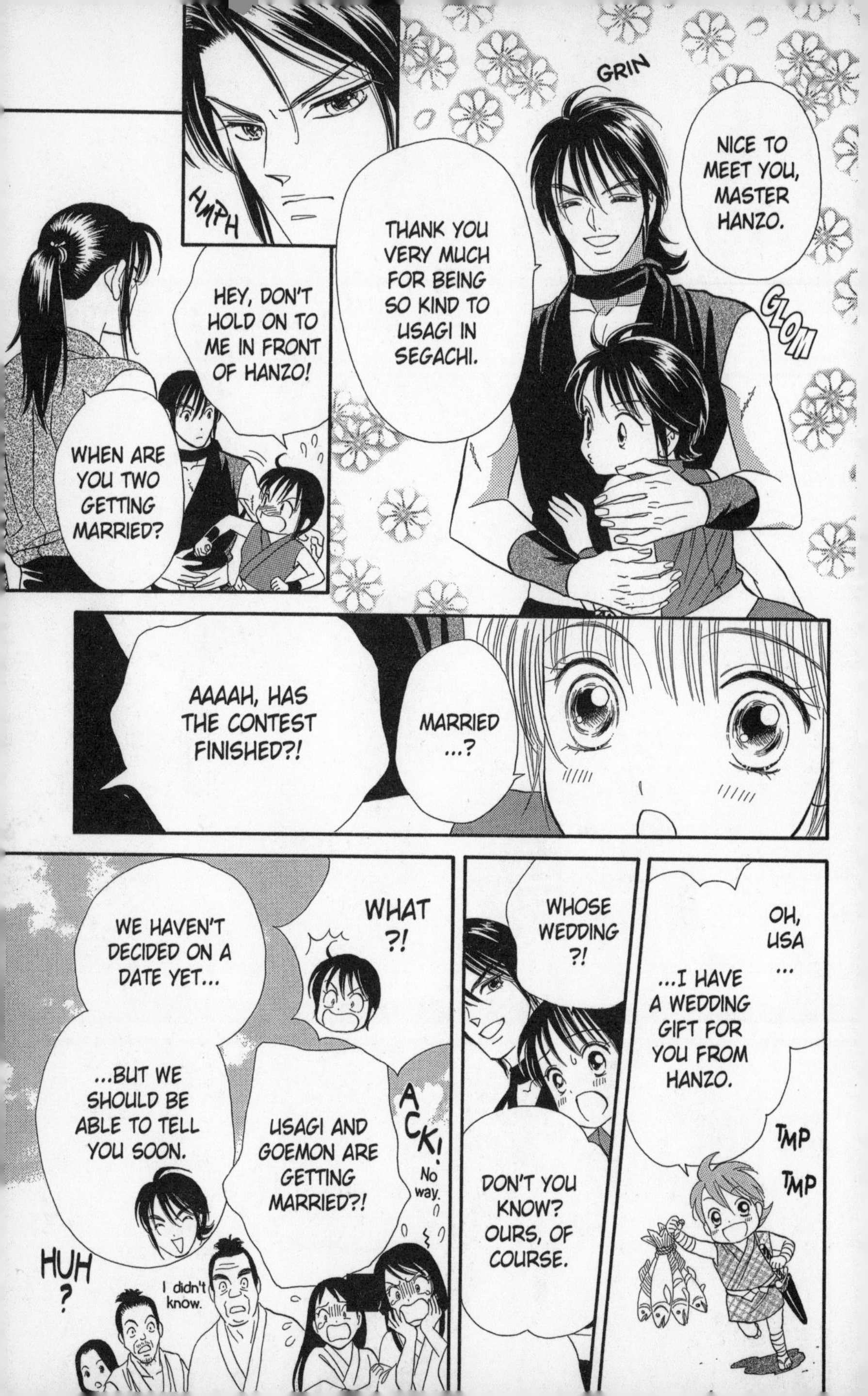
GRIN
NICE TO MEET YOU, MASTER HANZO.
GLOM
THANK YOU VERY MUCH FOR BEING SO KIND TO USAGI IN SEGACHI.
HMPH
HEY, DON'T HOLD ON TO ME IN FRONT OF HANZO!
WHEN ARE YOU TWO GETTING MARRIED?
MARRIED ...?
AAAAH, HAS THE CONTEST FINISHED?!
OH, USA ...
...I HAVE A WEDDING GIFT FOR YOU FROM HANZO.
TMP
TMP
WHOSE WEDDING ?!
DON'T YOU KNOW? OURS, OF COURSE.
WHAT ?!
WE HAVEN'T DECIDED ON A DATE YET...
...BUT WE SHOULD BE ABLE TO TELL YOU SOON.
USAGI AND GOEMON ARE GETTING MARRIED?!
ACK!
No way.
HUH ?
I didn't know.

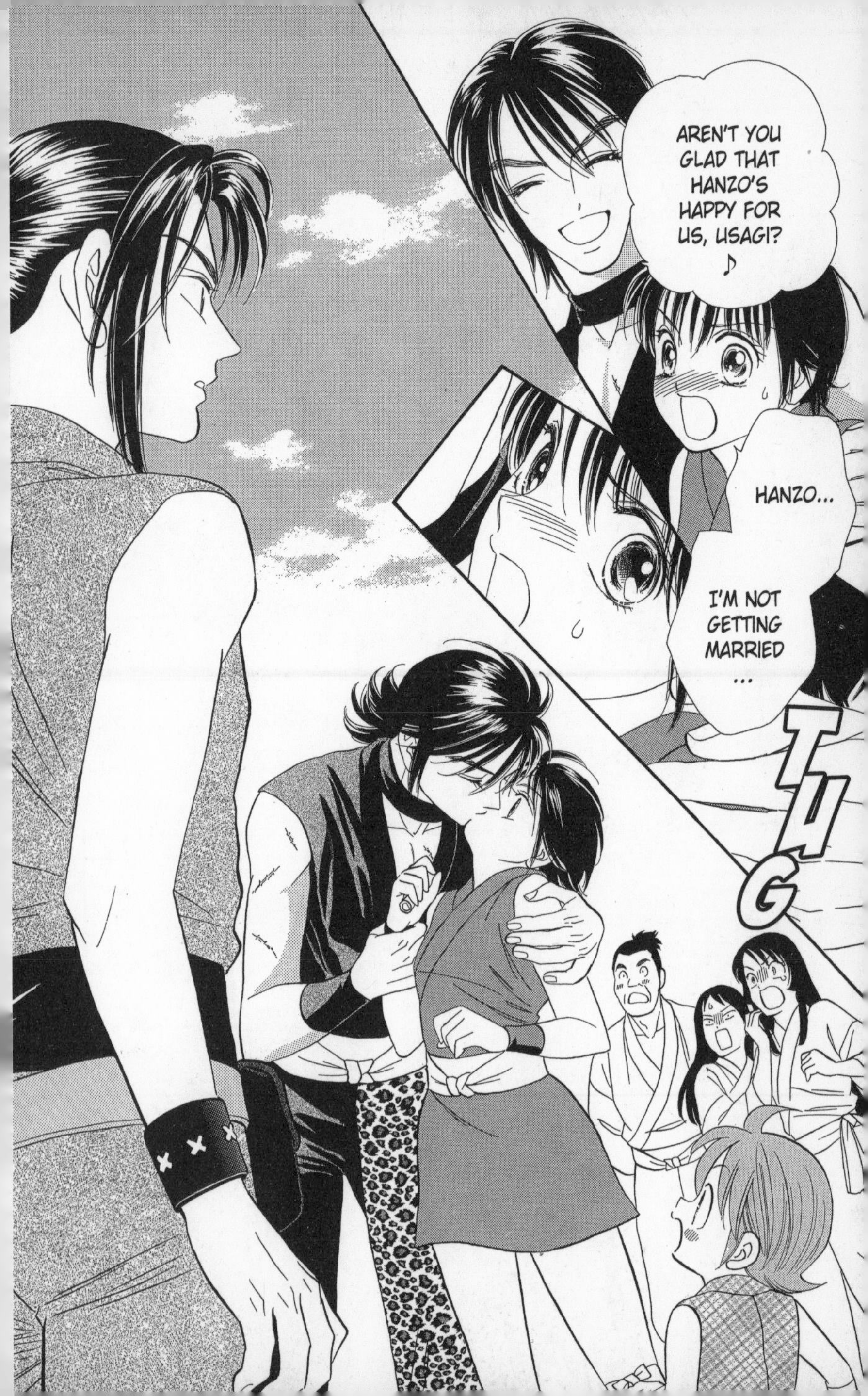
AREN'T YOU GLAD THAT HANZO'S HAPPY FOR US, USAGI? ♪
HANZO...
I'M NOT GETTING MARRIED ...
TUG

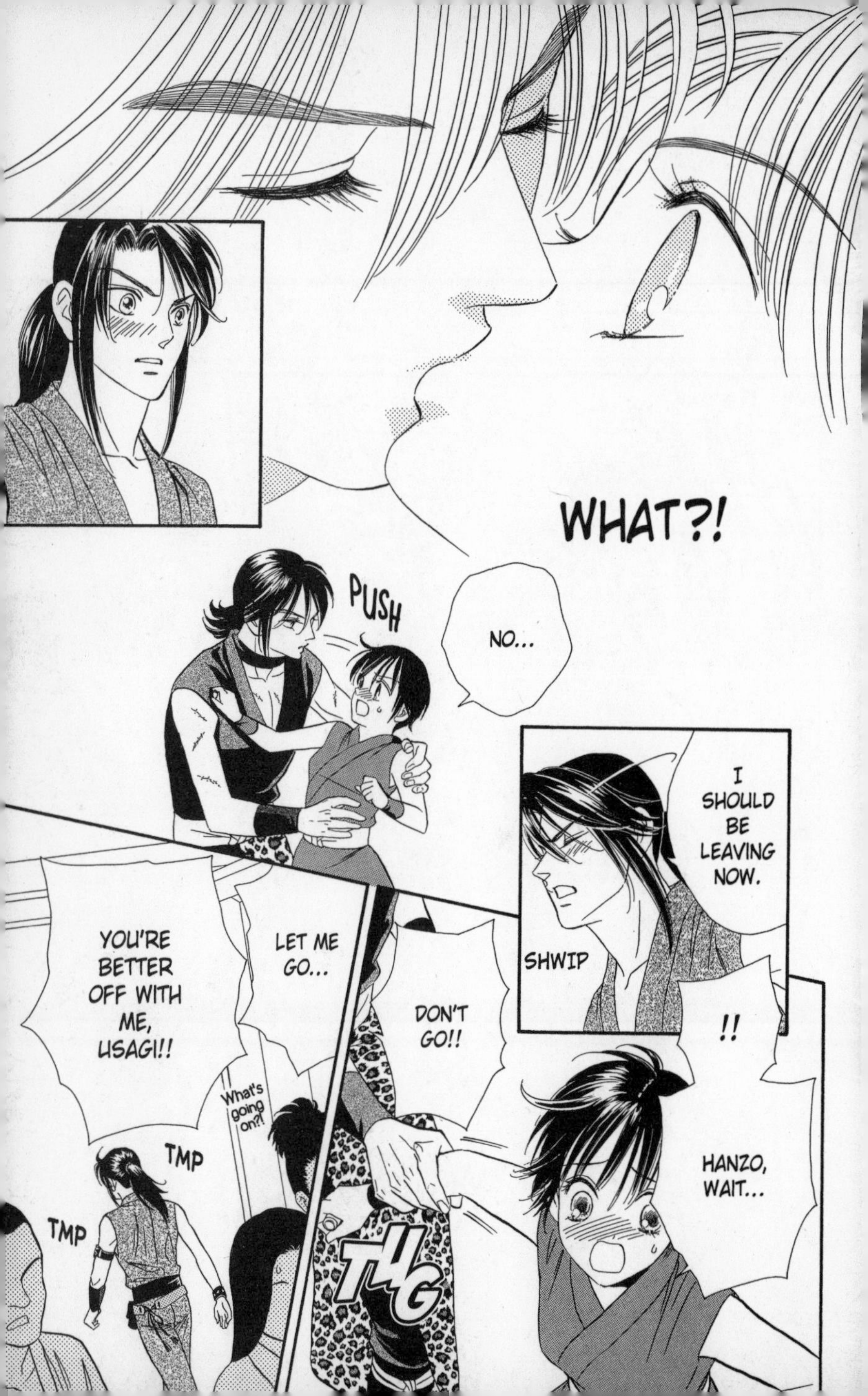
WHAT?!
NO...
PUSH
I SHOULD BE LEAVING NOW.
SHWIP
!!
HANZO, WAIT...
DON'T GO!!
THG
LET ME GO...
What's going on?!
YOU'RE BETTER OFF WITH ME, USAGI!!
TMP
TMP

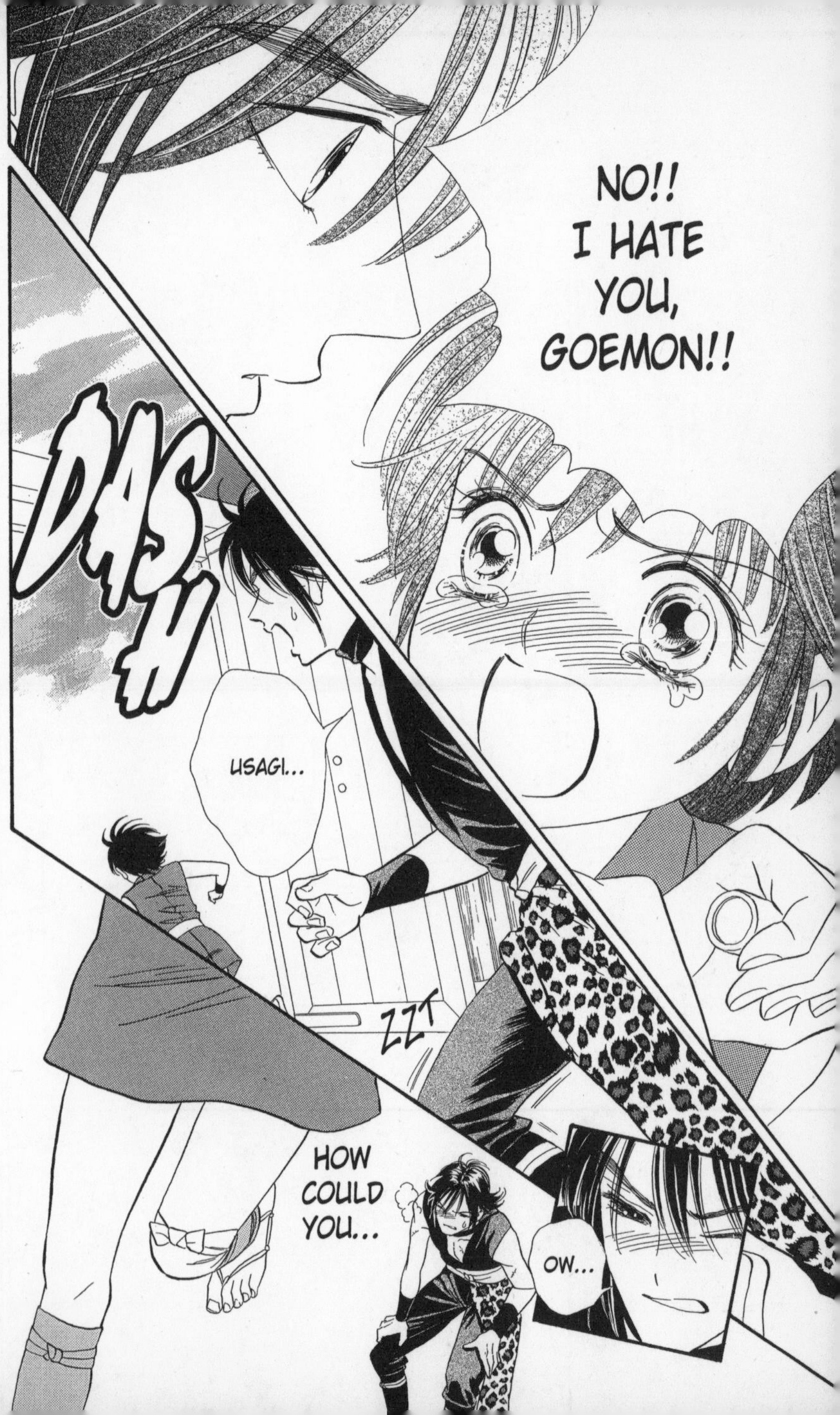
NO!! I HATE YOU, GOEMON!!
DASH
USAGI...
ZZT
OW...
HOW COULD YOU...

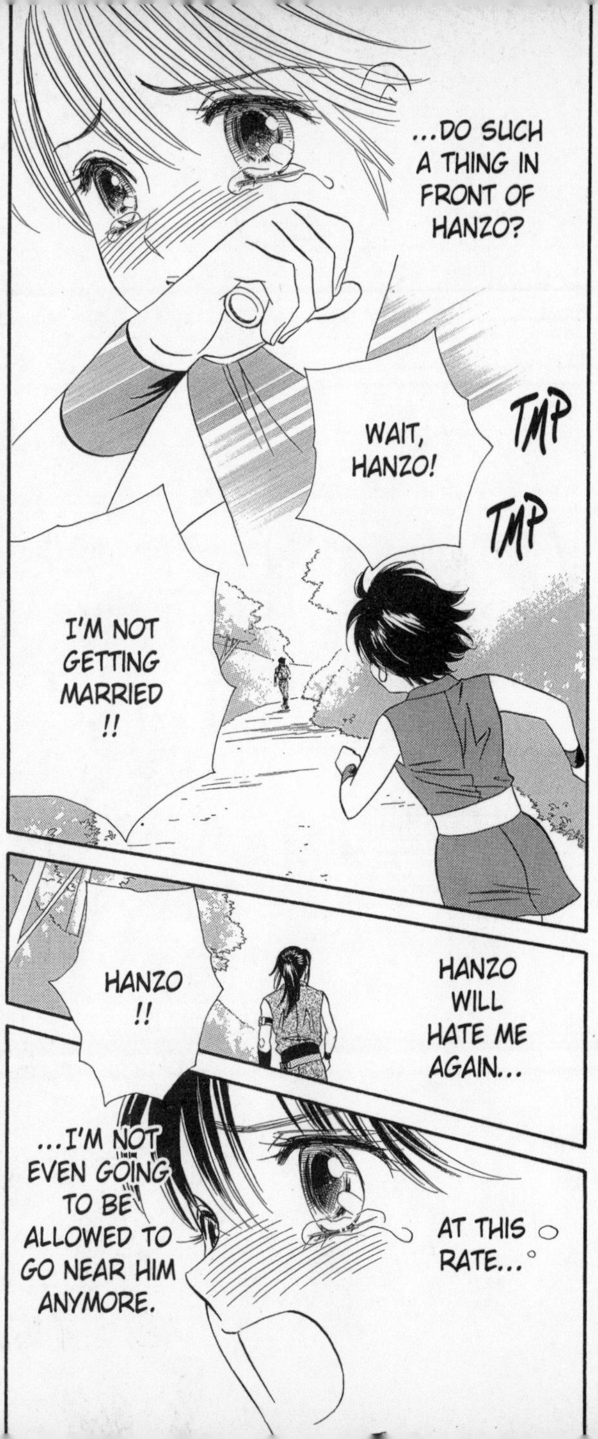
...DO SUCH A THING IN FRONT OF HANZO?
WAIT, HANZO!
TMP
TMP
I'M NOT GETTING MARRIED !!
HANZO WILL HATE ME AGAIN...
HANZO !!
AT THIS RATE...
...I'M NOT EVEN GOING TO BE ALLOWED TO GO NEAR HIM ANYMORE.

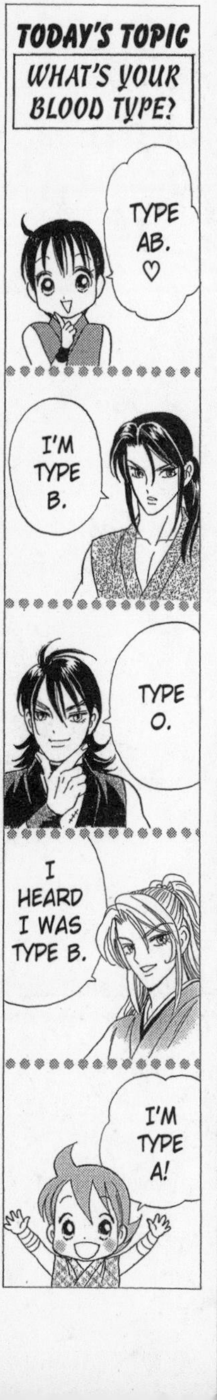
TODAY'S TOPIC
WHAT'S YOUR BLOOD TYPE?
TYPE AB. ♡
I'M TYPE B.
TYPE O.
I HEARD I WAS TYPE B.
I'M TYPE A!

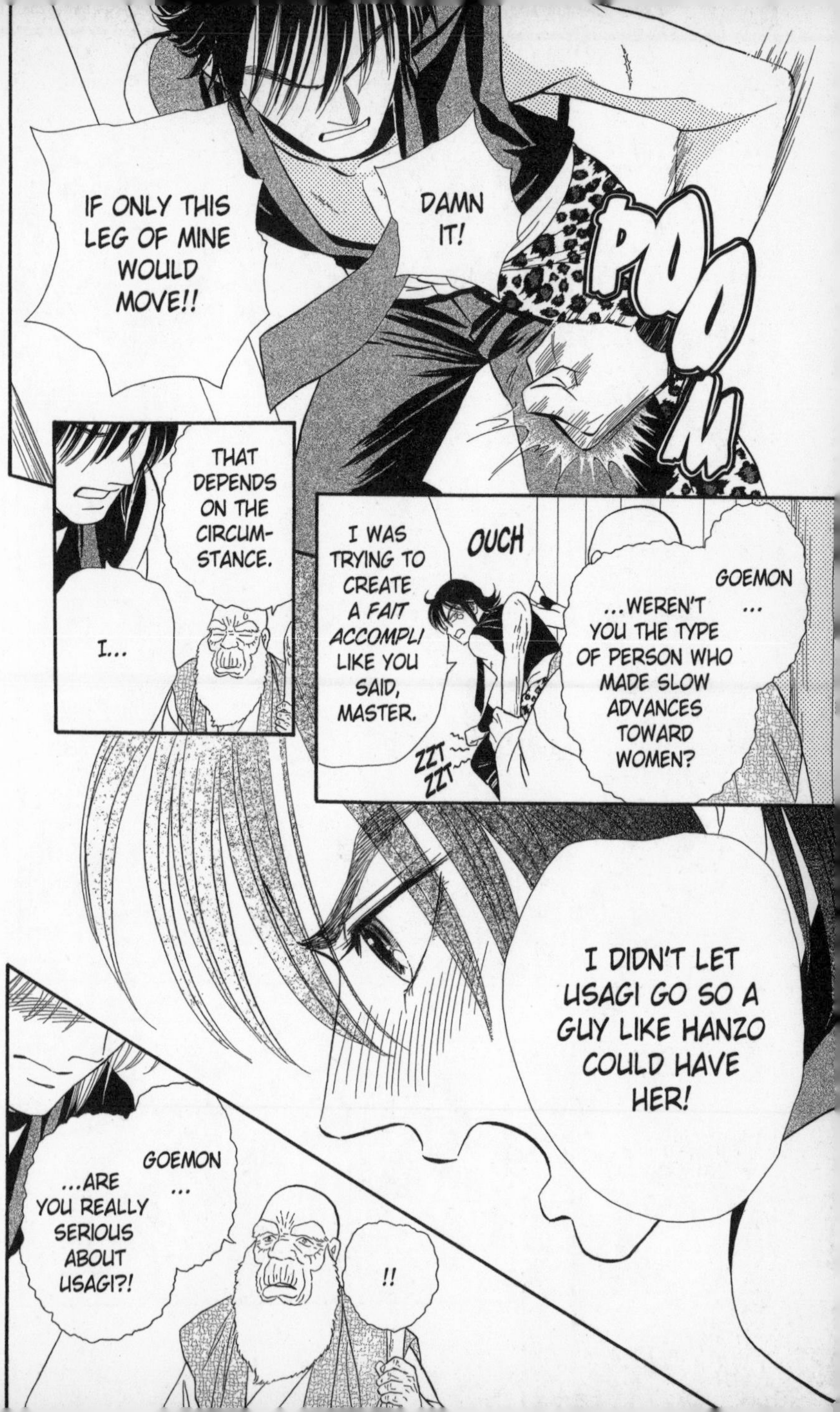
POOM
DAMN IT!
IF ONLY THIS LEG OF MINE WOULD MOVE!!
GOEMON ...WEREN'T YOU THE TYPE OF PERSON WHO MADE SLOW ADVANCES TOWARD WOMEN?
OUCH
I WAS TRYING TO CREATE A *FAIT ACCOMPLI* LIKE YOU SAID, MASTER.
ZZT ZZT
THAT DEPENDS ON THE CIRCUM-STANCE.
I...
I DIDN'T LET USAGI GO SO A GUY LIKE HANZO COULD HAVE HER!
!!
GOEMON ...ARE YOU REALLY SERIOUS ABOUT USAGI?!

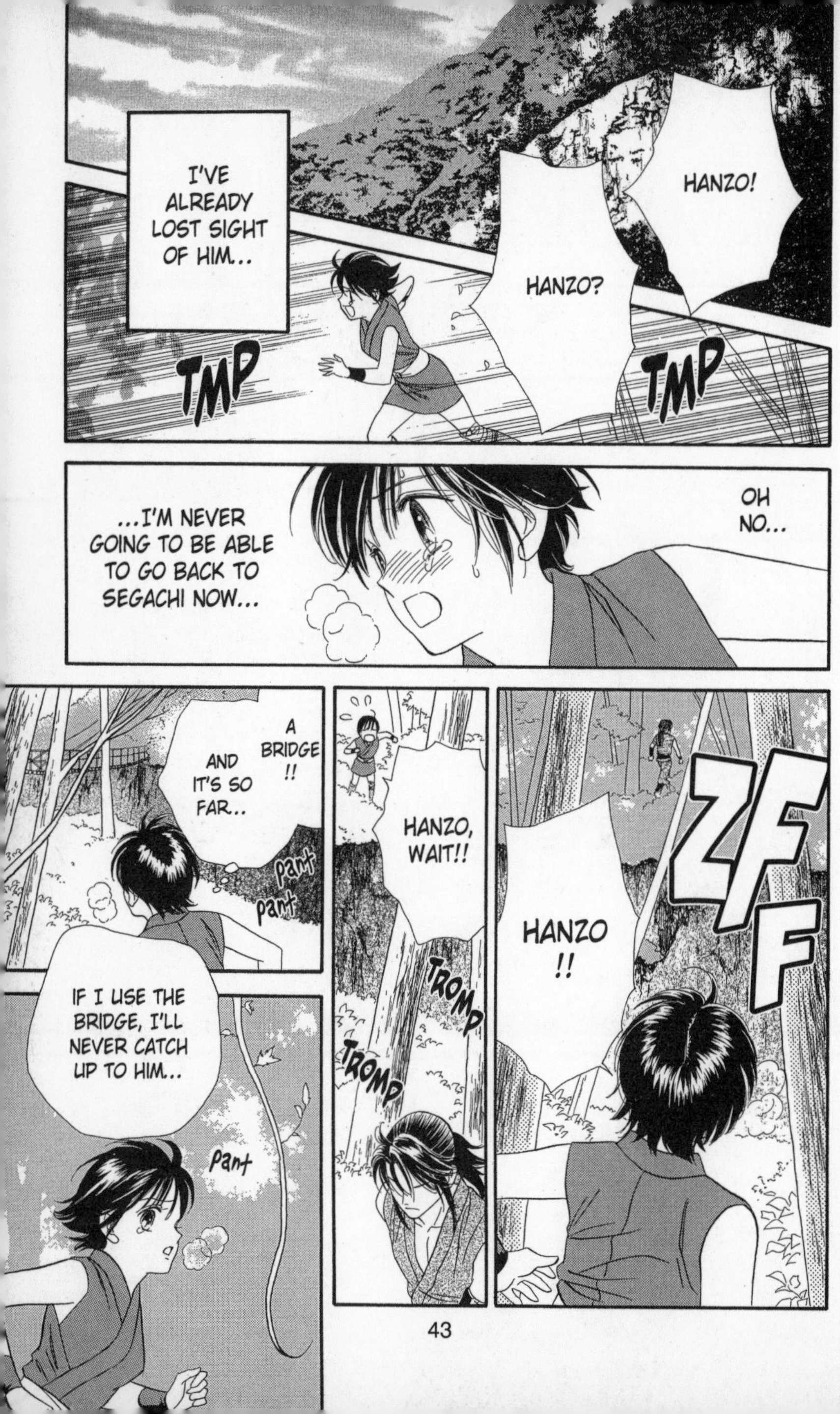
HANZO!
TMP
HANZO?
I'VE ALREADY LOST SIGHT OF HIM...
TMP
OH NO...
...I'M NEVER GOING TO BE ABLE TO GO BACK TO SEGACHI NOW...
ZFF
HANZO !!
HANZO, WAIT!!
TROMP
TROMP
A BRIDGE !!
AND IT'S SO FAR...
pant
pant
IF I USE THE BRIDGE, I'LL NEVER CATCH UP TO HIM...
pant

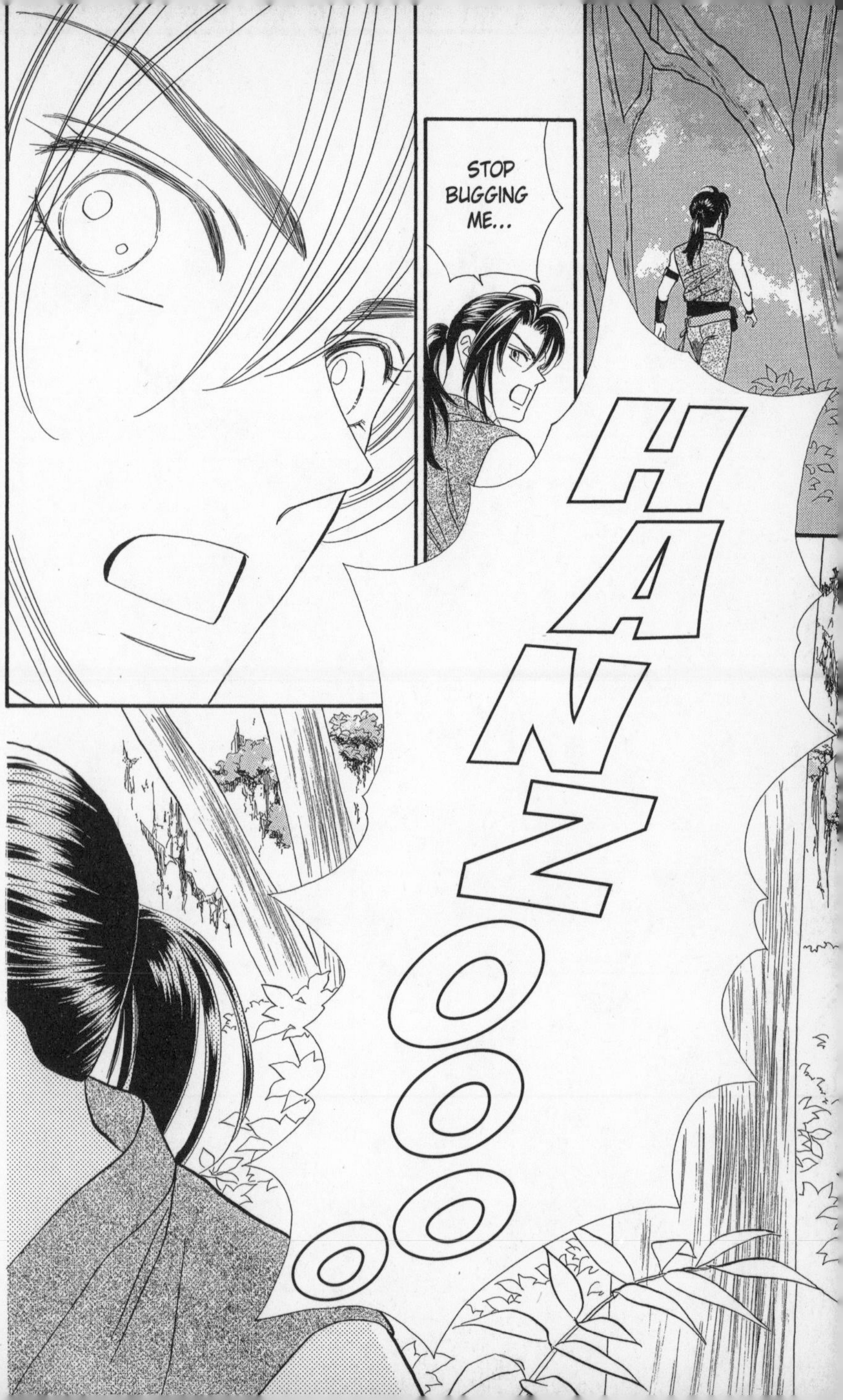
STOP BUGGING ME...
HANZOOOOO

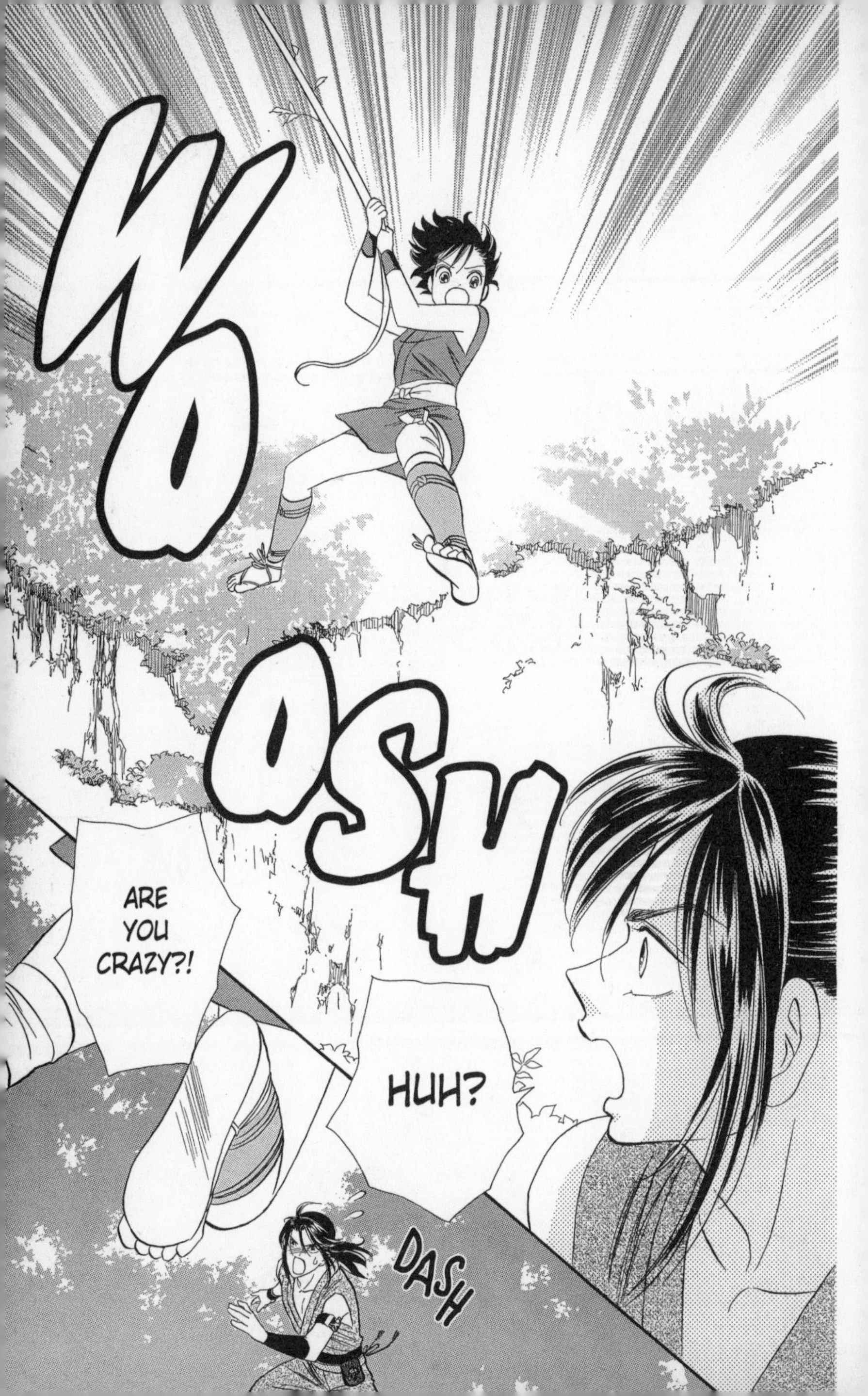
WHOOSH
HUH?
ARE YOU CRAZY?!
DASH

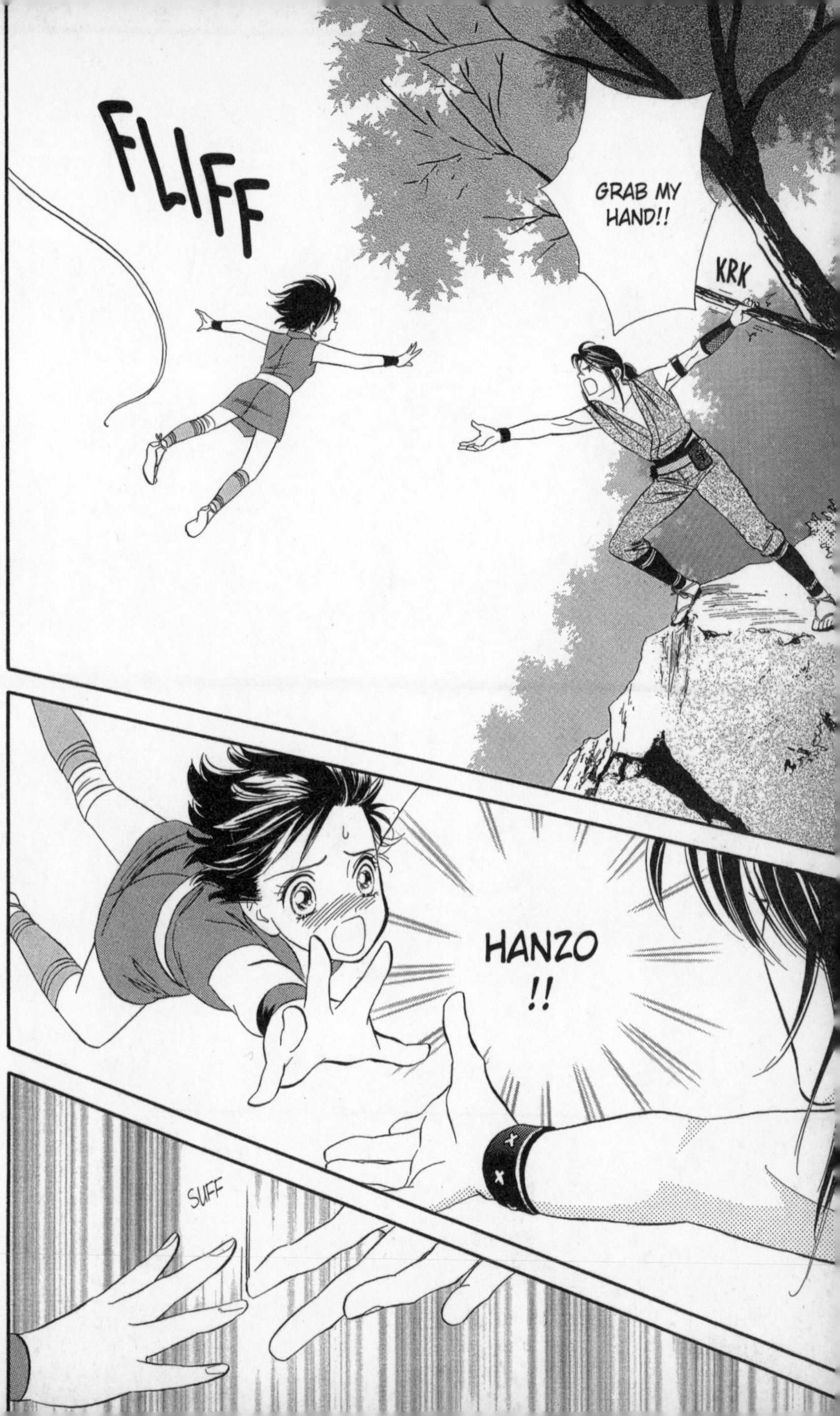
GRAB MY HAND!!
KRK
FLIFF
HANZO !!
SUFF

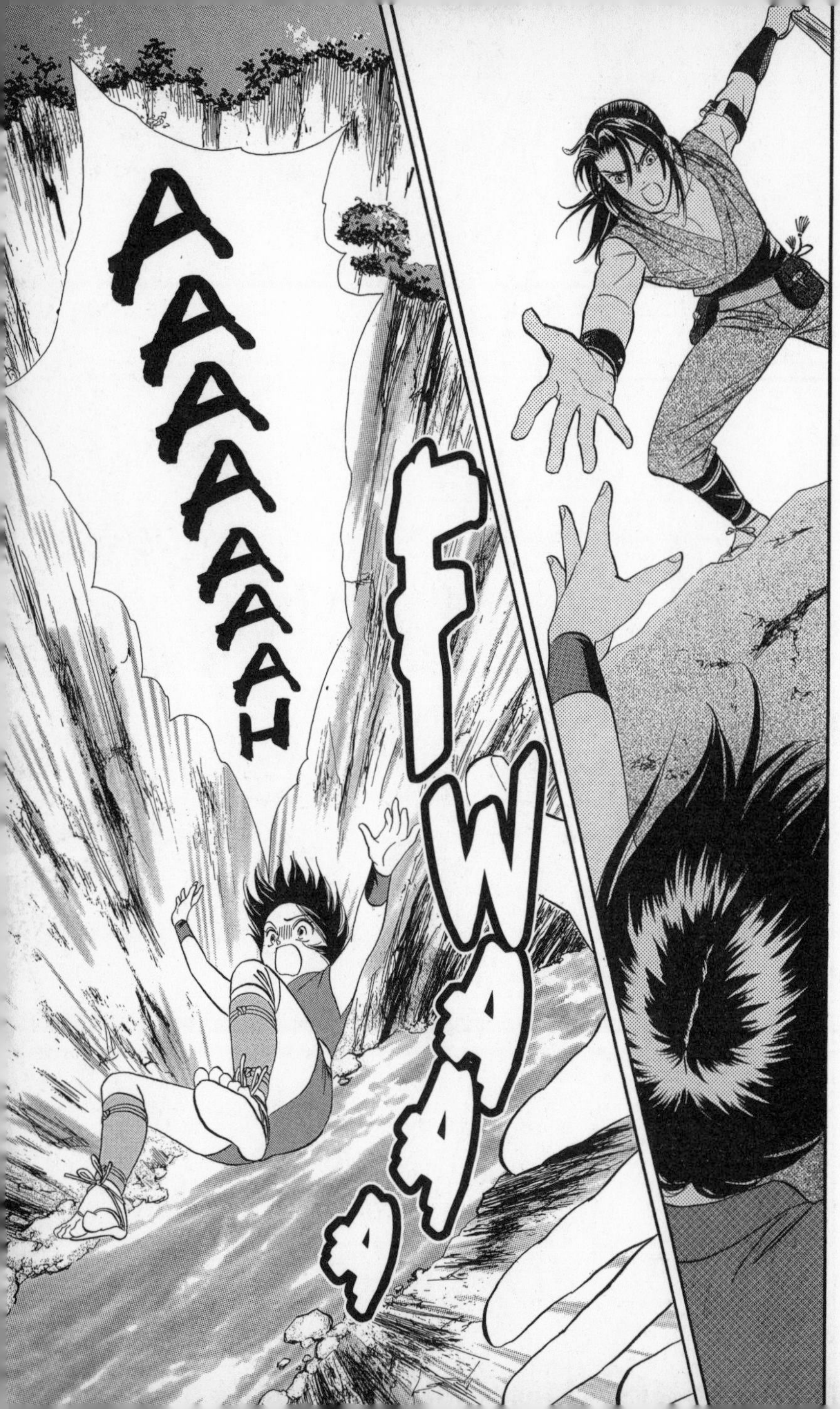
AAAAAAAH
fwaaaa

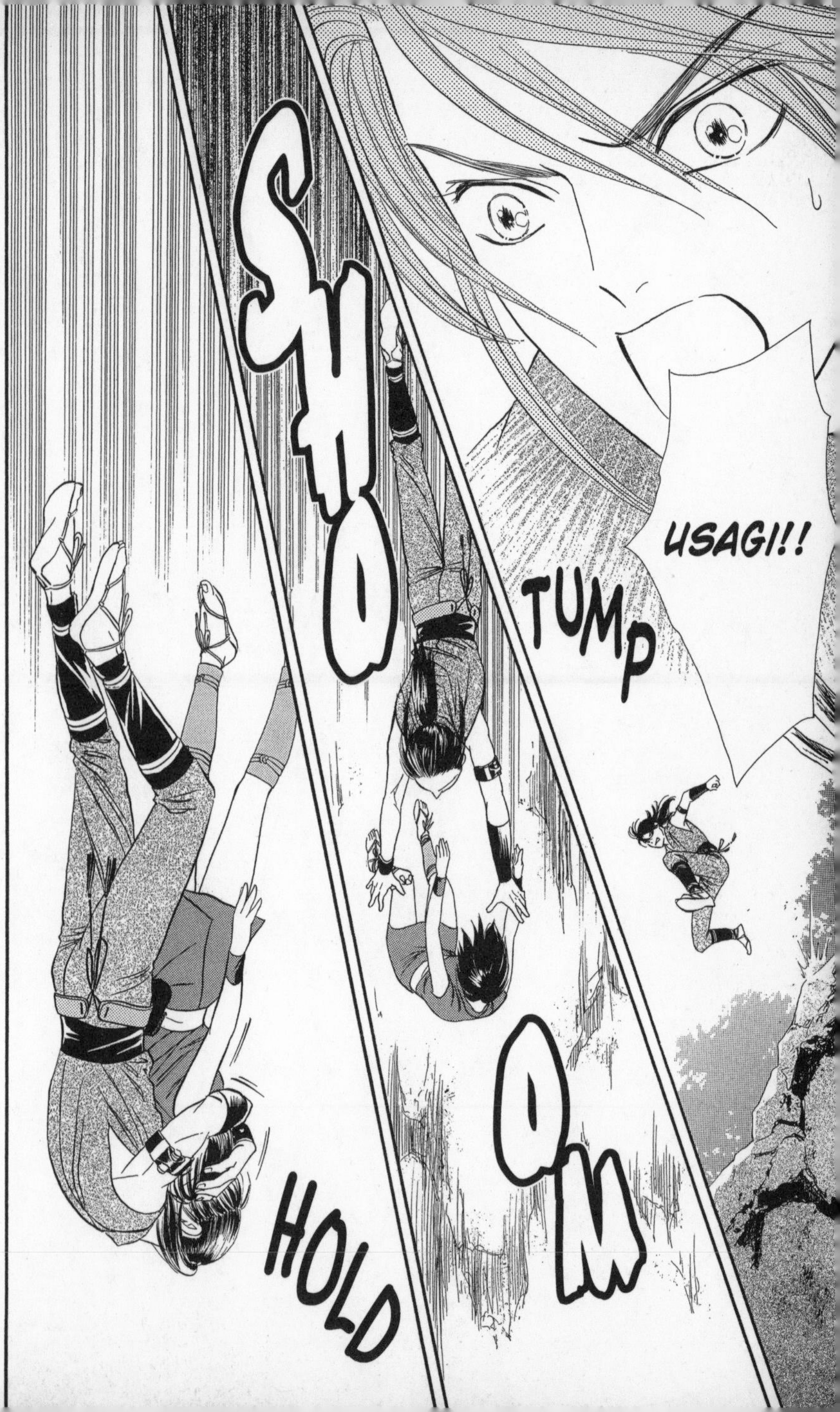
USAGI!!
TUMP
SHOO
OM
HOLD

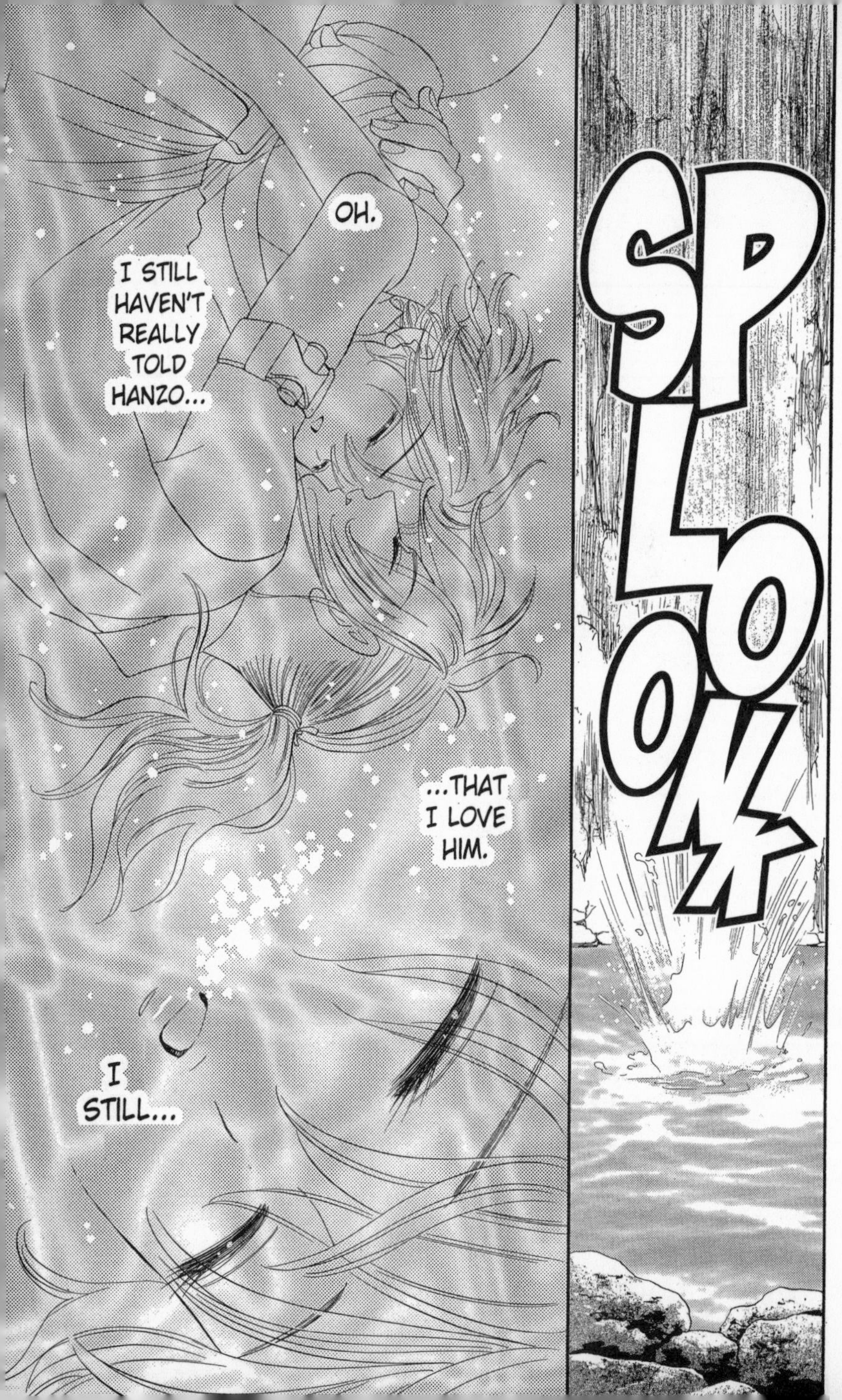
SPLOOK
OH.
I STILL HAVEN'T REALLY TOLD HANZO...
...THAT I LOVE HIM.
I STILL...

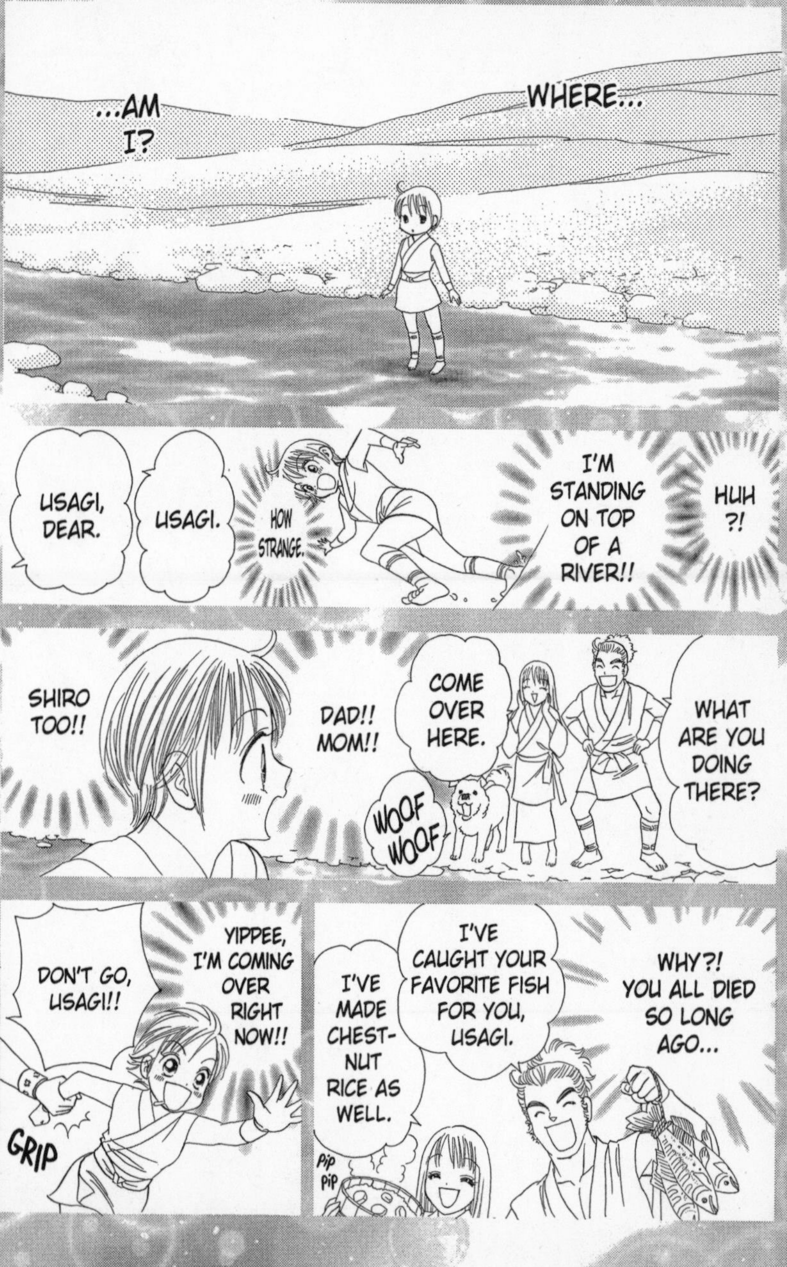
WHERE...
...AM I?
HUH?!
I'M STANDING ON TOP OF A RIVER!!
HOW STRANGE.
USAGI.
USAGI, DEAR.
WHAT ARE YOU DOING THERE?
COME OVER HERE.
WOOF WOOF
DAD!! MOM!!
SHIRO TOO!!
WHY?! YOU ALL DIED SO LONG AGO...
I'VE CAUGHT YOUR FAVORITE FISH FOR YOU, USAGI.
I'VE MADE CHEST-NUT RICE AS WELL.
Pip pip
YIPPEE, I'M COMING OVER RIGHT NOW!!
DON'T GO, USAGI!!
GRIP

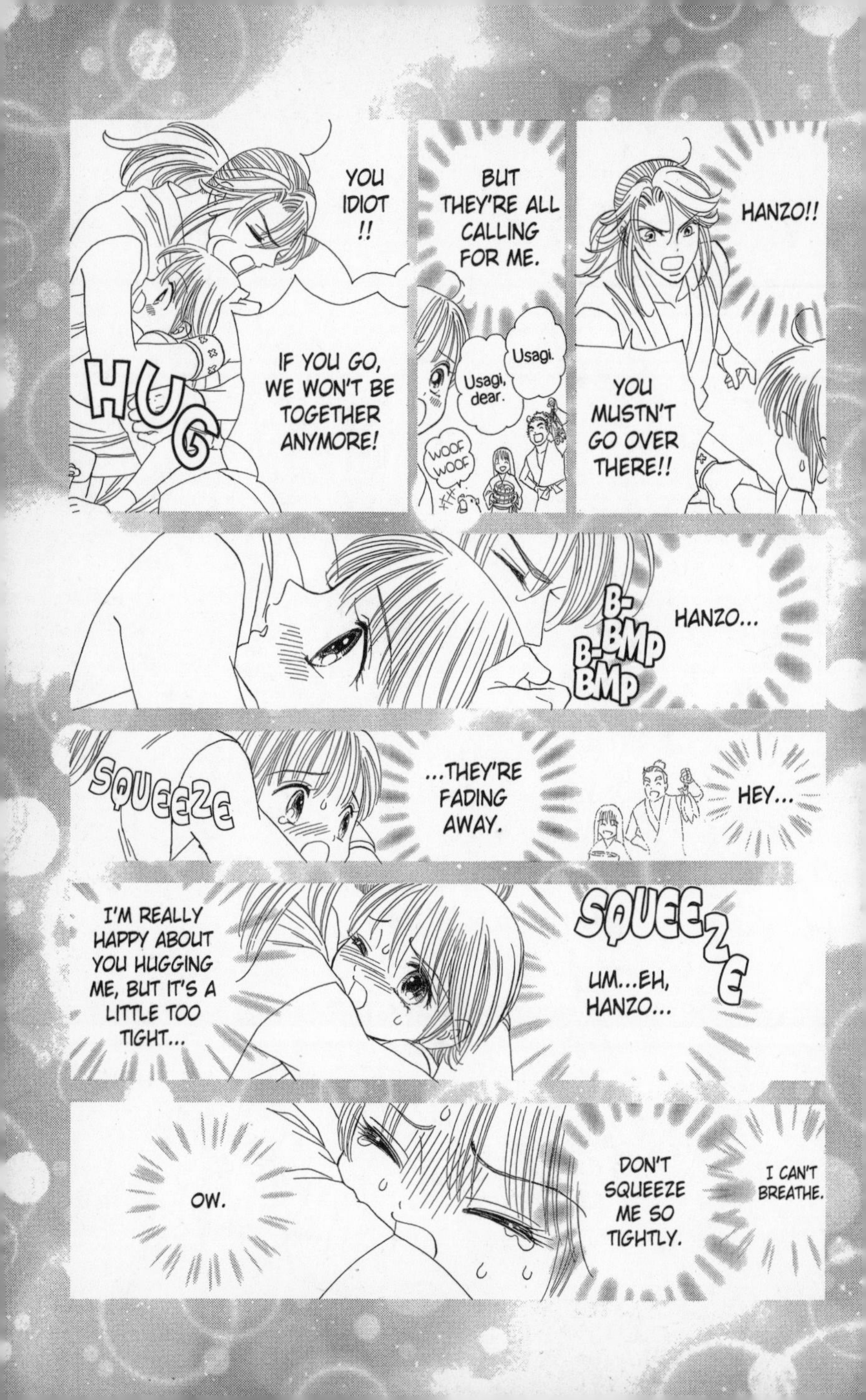
HANZO!!
YOU MUSTN'T GO OVER THERE!!
BUT THEY'RE ALL CALLING FOR ME.
Usagi.
Usagi, dear.
WOOF WOOF
YOU IDIOT !!
HUG
IF YOU GO, WE WON'T BE TOGETHER ANYMORE!
HANZO...
B-BMP B-BMP
HEY...
...THEY'RE FADING AWAY.
SQUEEZE
UM...EH, HANZO...
SQUEEZE
I'M REALLY HAPPY ABOUT YOU HUGGING ME, BUT IT'S A LITTLE TOO TIGHT...
I CAN'T BREATHE.
DON'T SQUEEZE ME SO TIGHTLY.
OW.

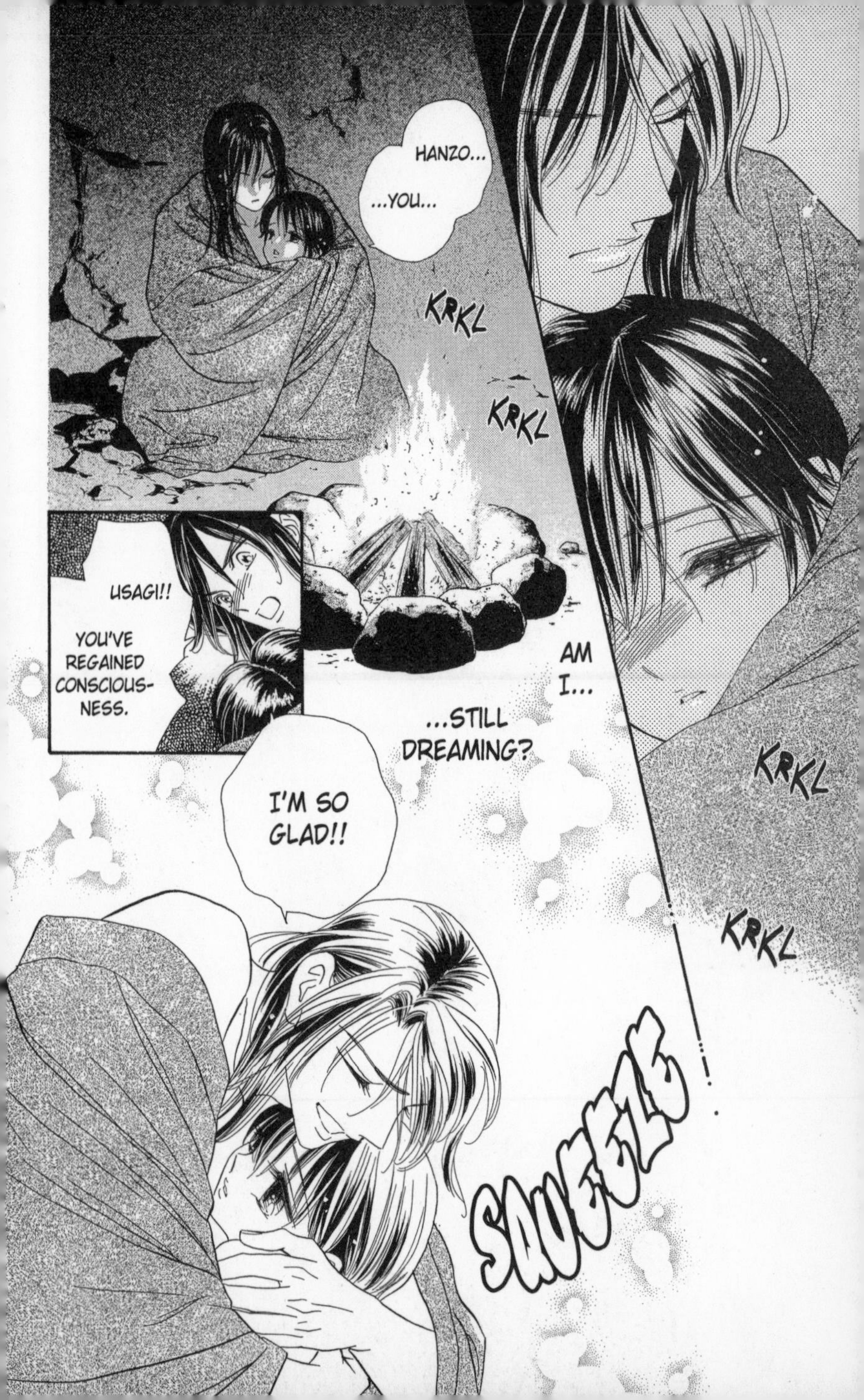
KRKL
KRKL
AM I...
...STILL DREAMING?
HANZO...
...YOU...
KRKL
KRKL
USAGI!!
YOU'VE REGAINED CONSCIOUS-NESS.
I'M SO GLAD!!
SQUEEZE

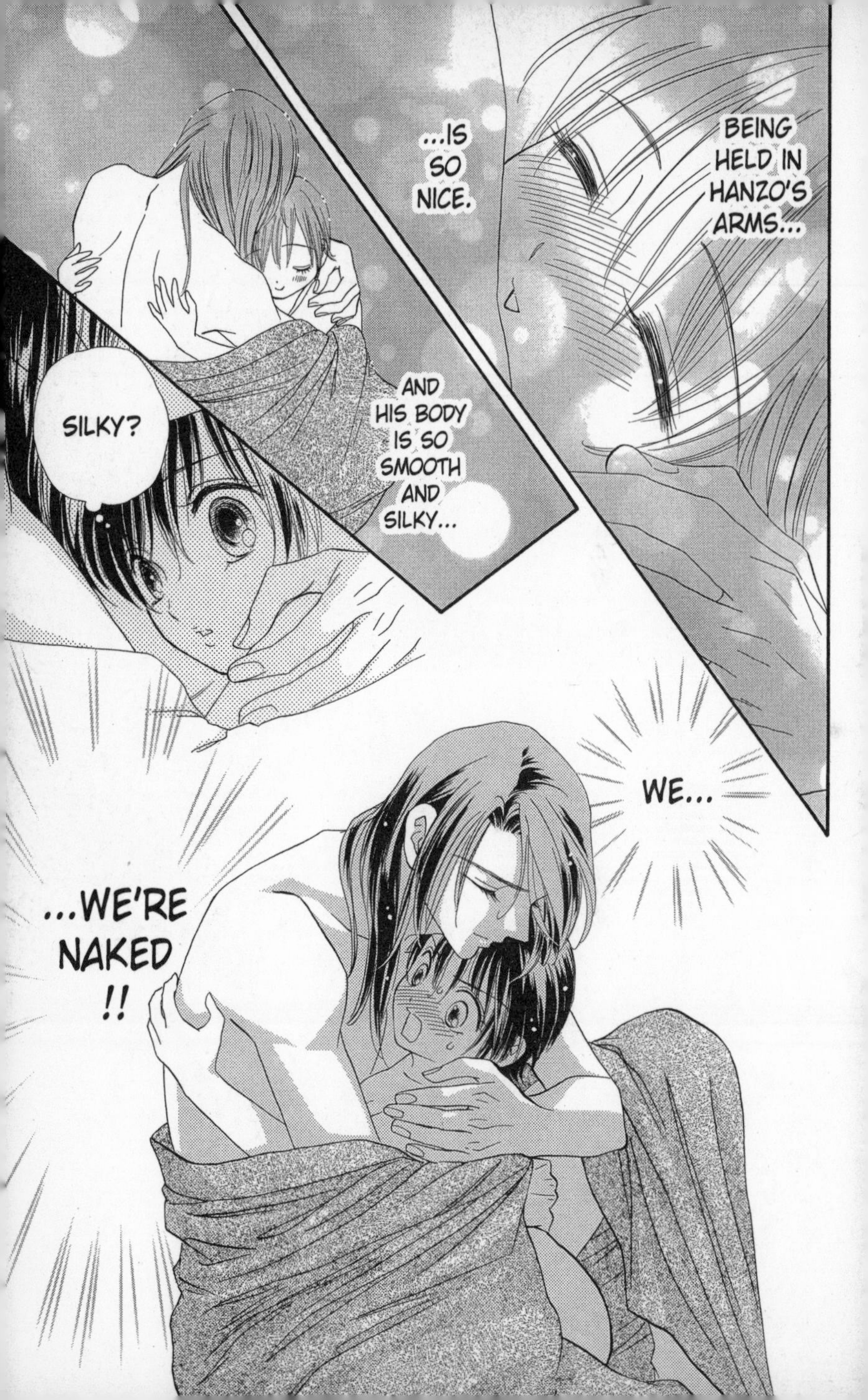
BEING HELD IN HANZO'S ARMS...
...IS SO NICE.
AND HIS BODY IS SO SMOOTH AND SILKY...
SILKY?
WE...
...WE'RE NAKED !!

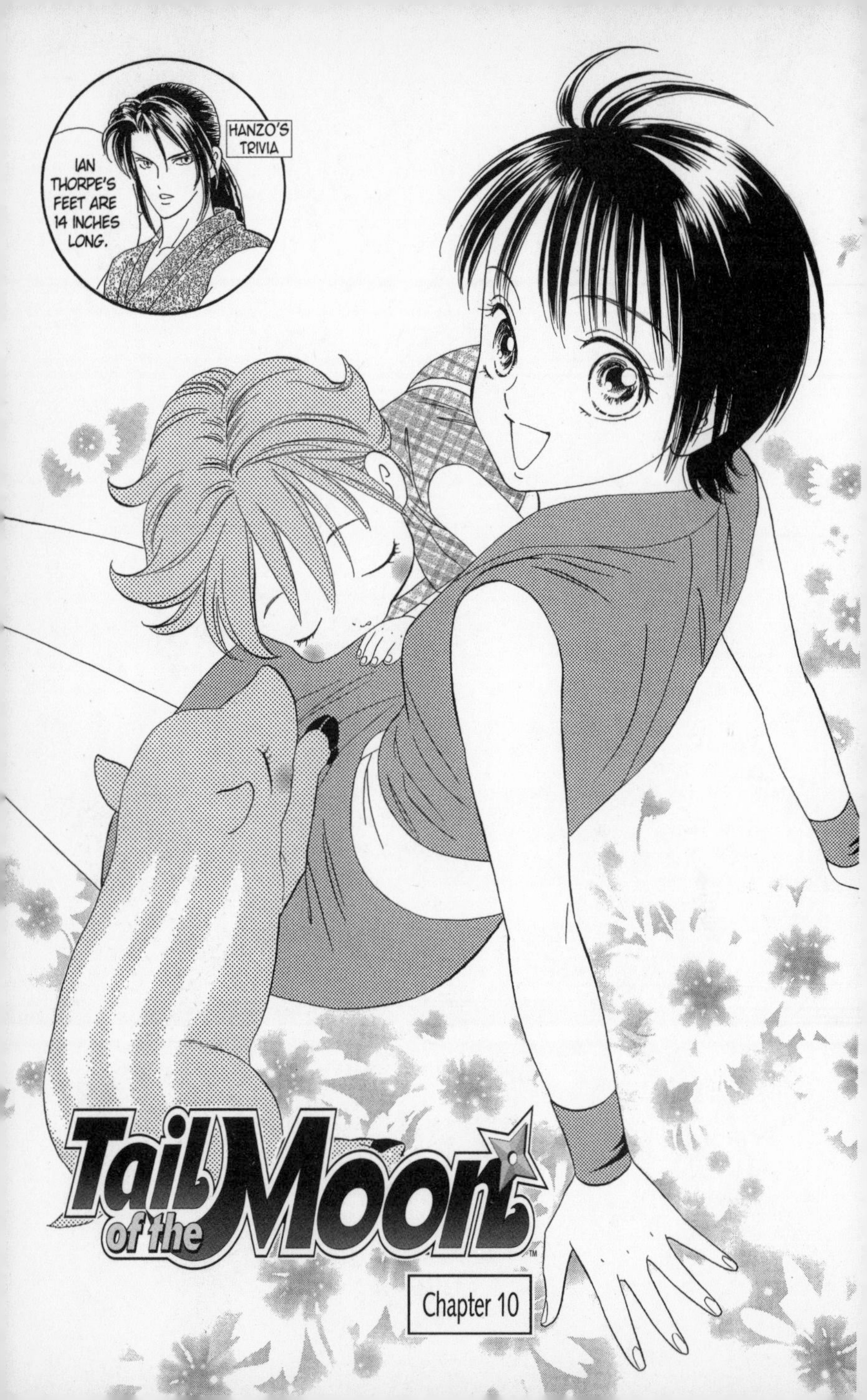
HANZO'S TRIVIA
IAN THORPE'S FEET ARE 14 INCHES LONG.
Tail of the Moon™
Chapter 10

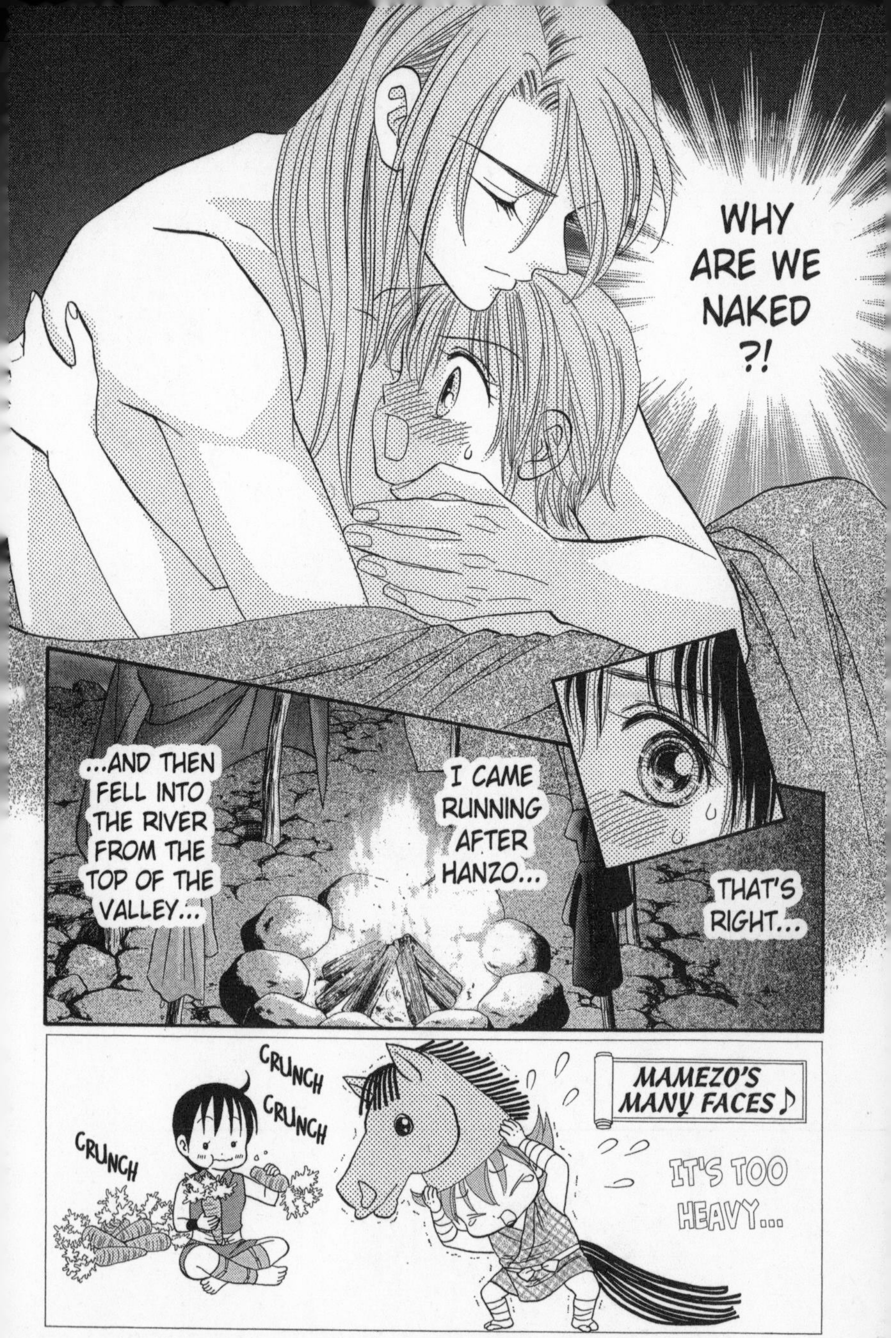
WHY ARE WE NAKED ?!
THAT'S RIGHT...
I CAME RUNNING AFTER HANZO...
...AND THEN FELL INTO THE RIVER FROM THE TOP OF THE VALLEY...
MAMEZO'S MANY FACES♪
IT'S TOO HEAVY...
CRUNCH
CRUNCH
CRUNCH

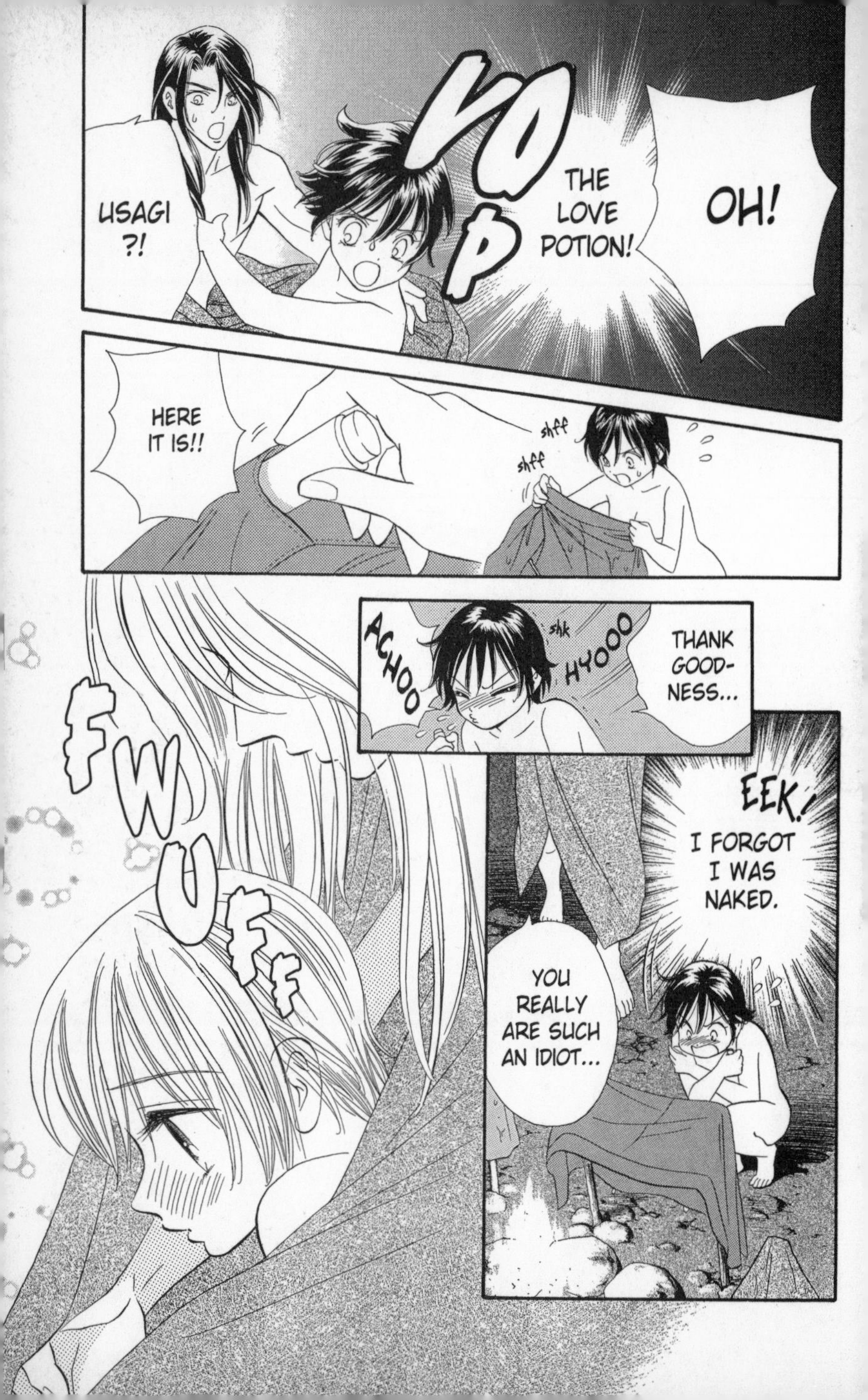
OH!
THE LOVE POTION!
VOOP
USAGI ?!
shff
shff
HERE IT IS!!
THANK GOOD-NESS...
HYOOO
shk
ACHOO
EEK!
I FORGOT I WAS NAKED.
YOU REALLY ARE SUCH AN IDIOT...
FWUFF

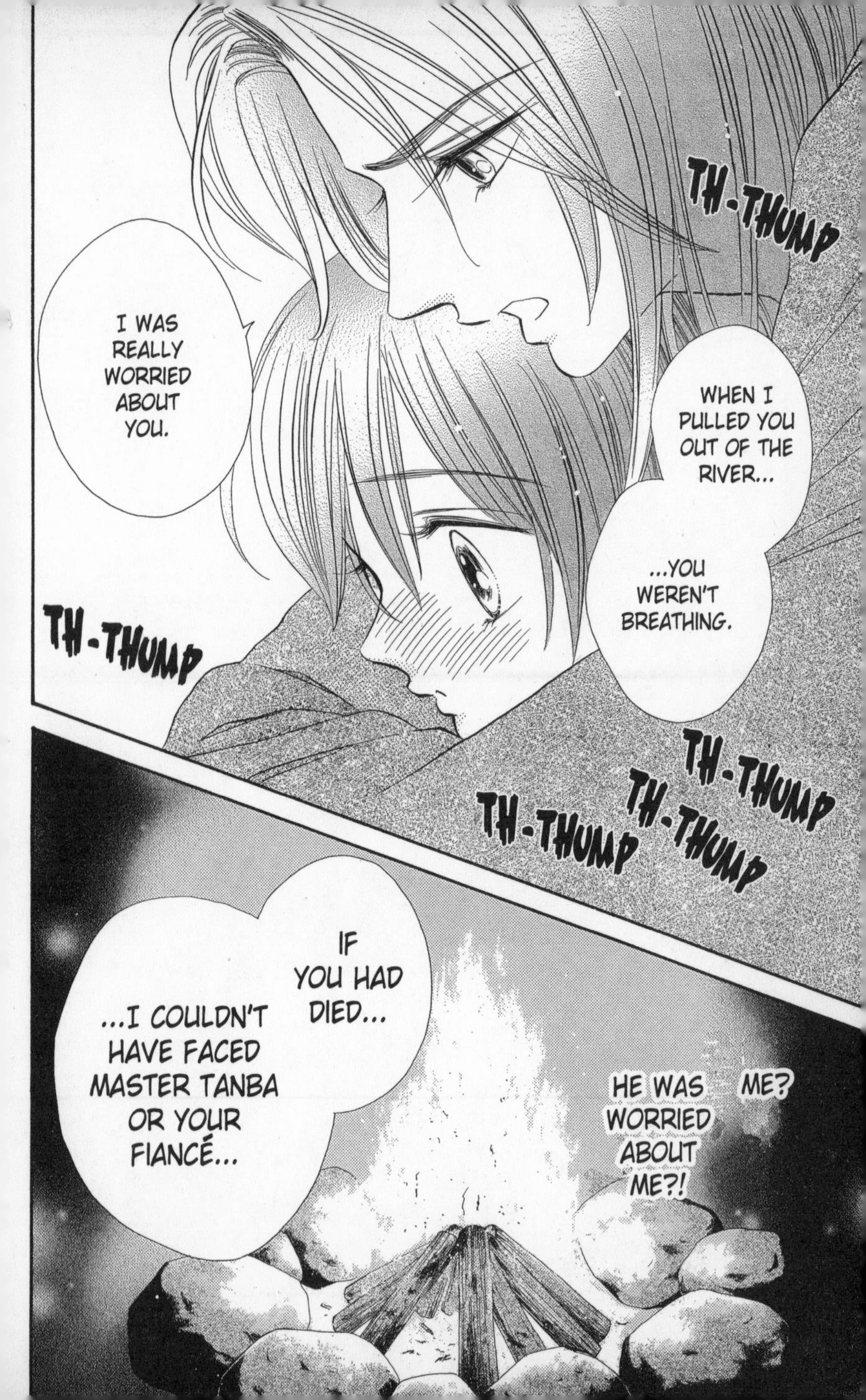
TH-THUMP
WHEN I PULLED YOU OUT OF THE RIVER...
...YOU WEREN'T BREATHING.
I WAS REALLY WORRIED ABOUT YOU.
TH-THUMP
TH-THUMP
TH-THUMP
TH-THUMP
ME?
HE WAS WORRIED ABOUT ME?!
IF YOU HAD DIED...
...I COULDN'T HAVE FACED MASTER TANBA OR YOUR FIANCÉ...

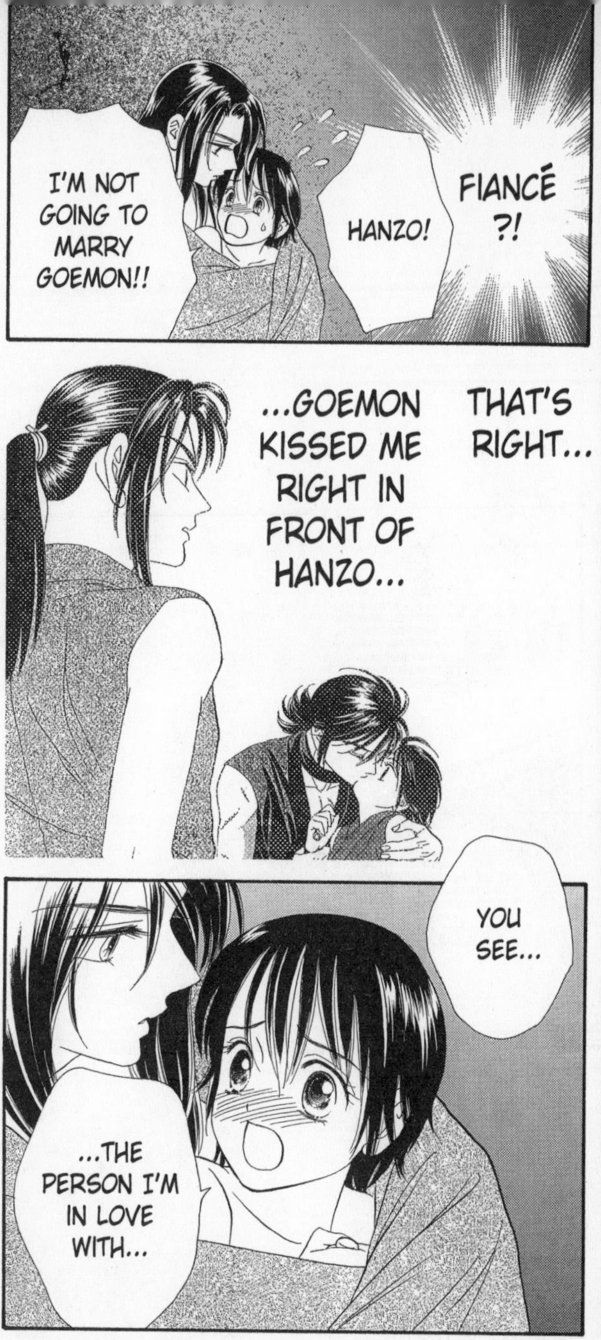
FIANCÉ ?!
HANZO!
I'M NOT GOING TO MARRY GOEMON!!
THAT'S RIGHT...
...GOEMON KISSED ME RIGHT IN FRONT OF HANZO...
YOU SEE...
...THE PERSON I'M IN LOVE WITH...

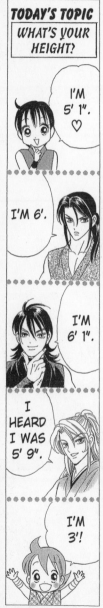

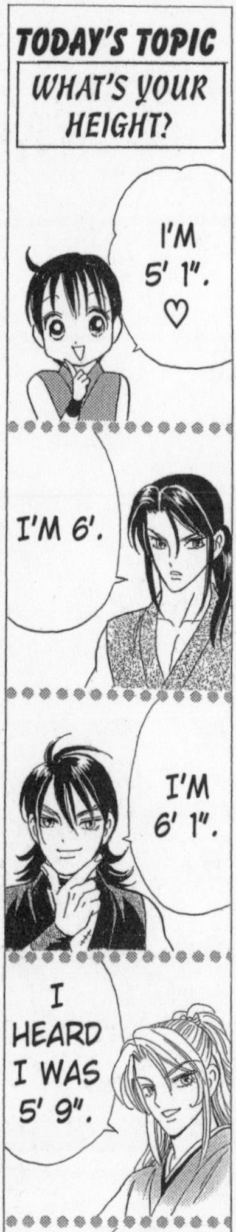
TODAY'S TOPIC
WHAT'S YOUR HEIGHT?
I'M 5' 1". ♡
I'M 6'.
I'M 6' 1".
I HEARD I WAS 5' 9".
I'M 3'!

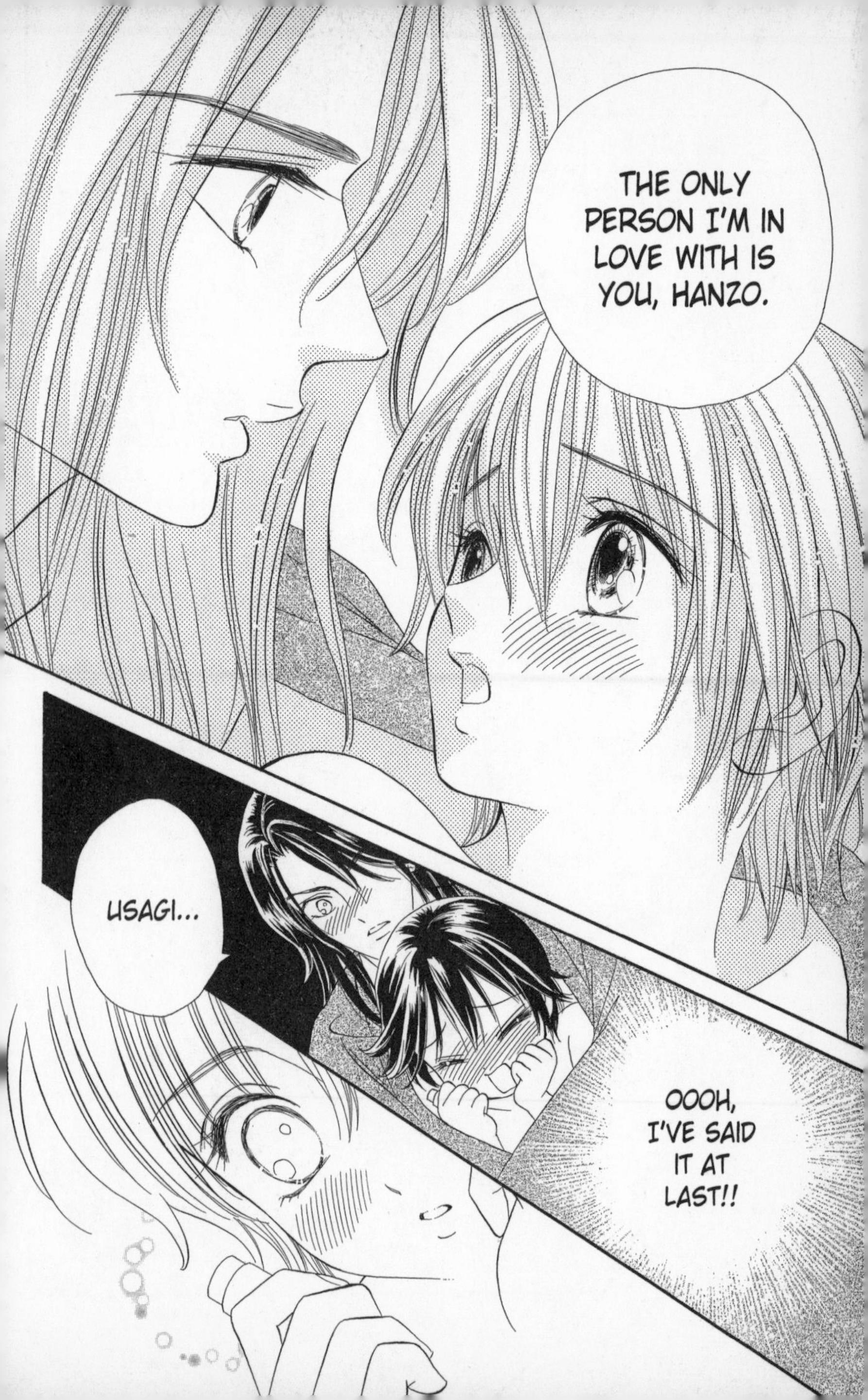
THE ONLY PERSON I'M IN LOVE WITH IS YOU, HANZO.
OOOH, I'VE SAID IT AT LAST!!
USAGI...

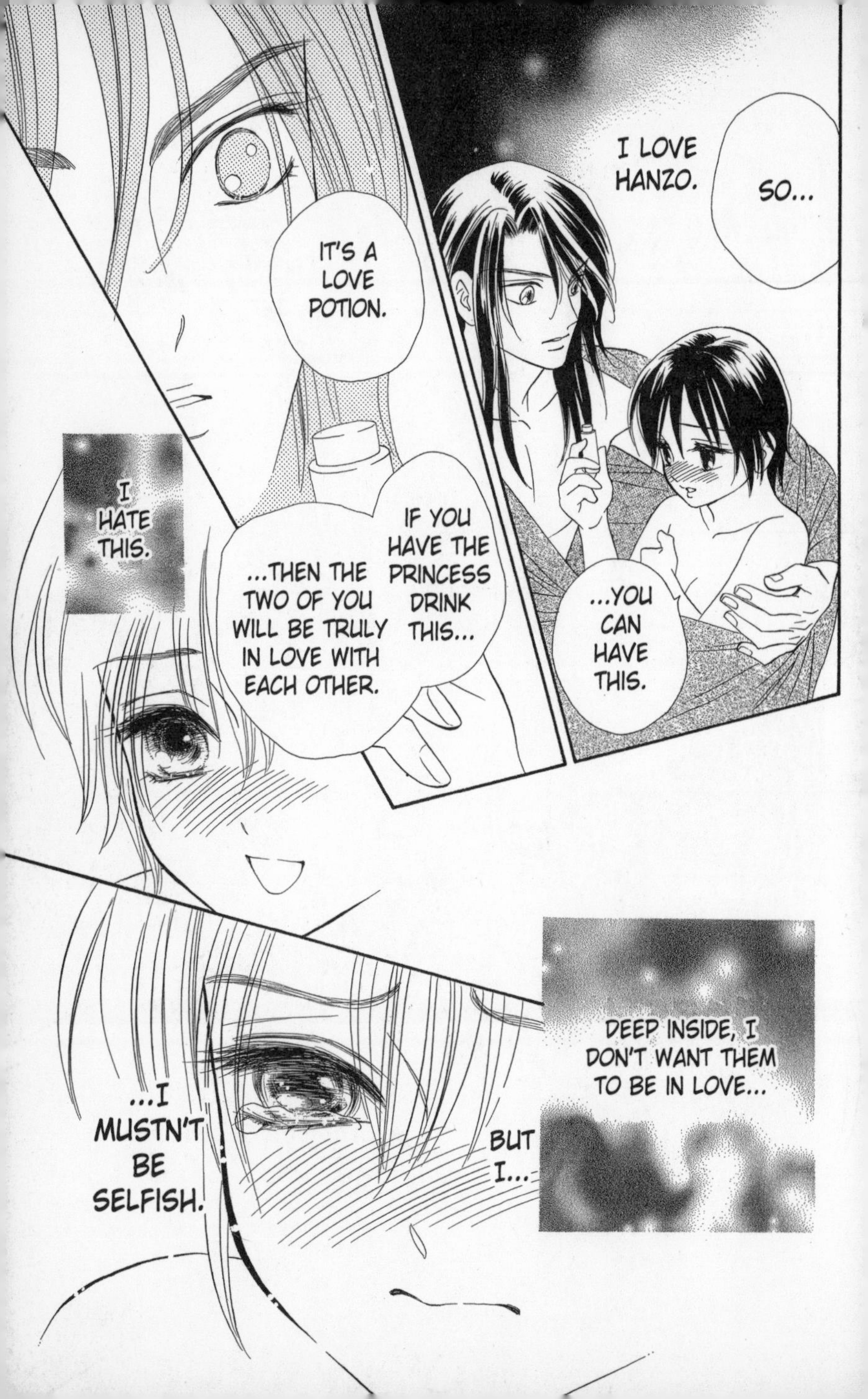
I LOVE HANZO.
SO...
...YOU CAN HAVE THIS.
IT'S A LOVE POTION.
IF YOU HAVE THE PRINCESS DRINK THIS...
...THEN THE TWO OF YOU WILL BE TRULY IN LOVE WITH EACH OTHER.
I HATE THIS.
DEEP INSIDE, I DON'T WANT THEM TO BE IN LOVE...
BUT I...
...I MUSTN'T BE SELFISH.

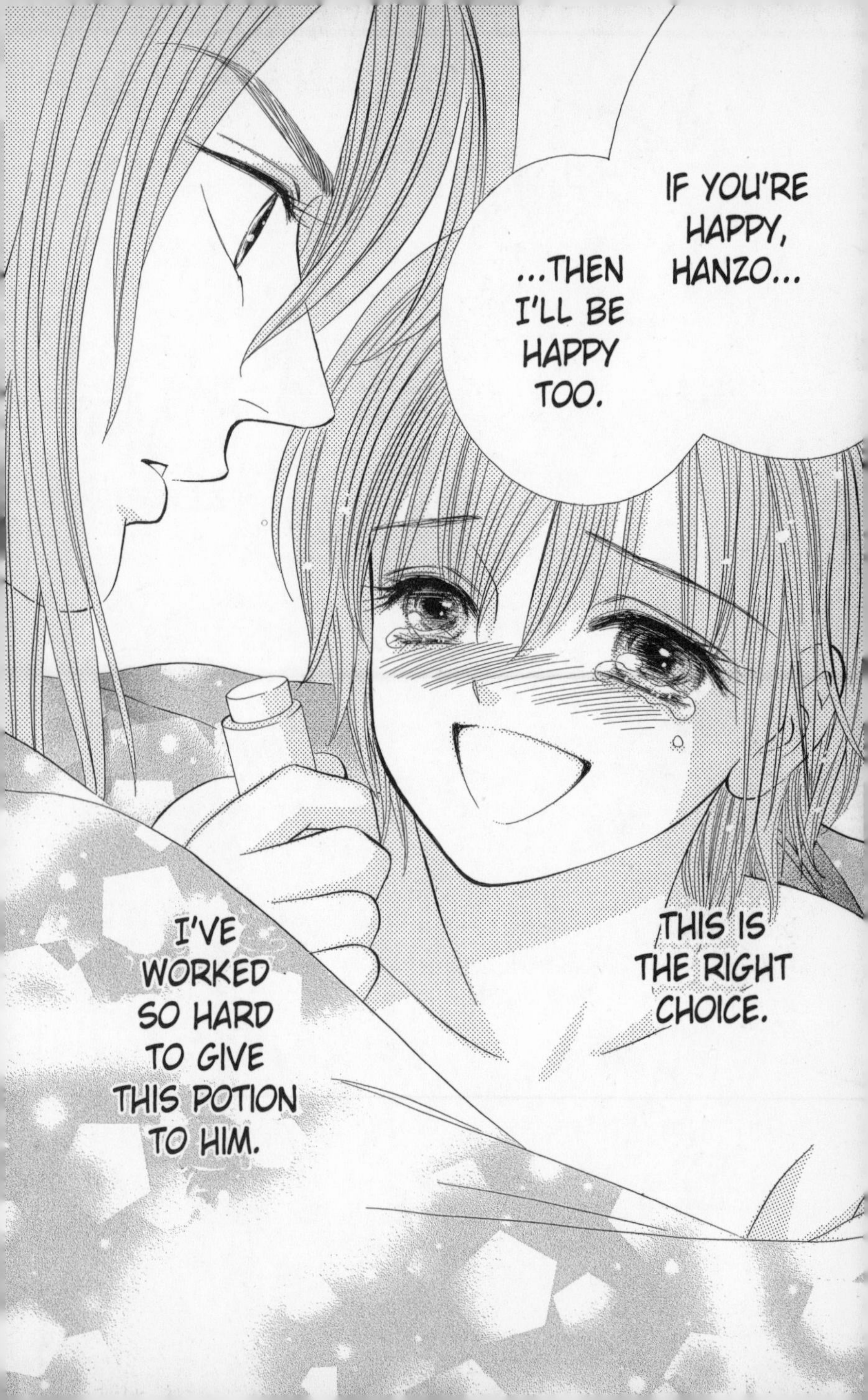
IF YOU'RE HAPPY, HANZO...
...THEN I'LL BE HAPPY TOO.
THIS IS THE RIGHT CHOICE.
I'VE WORKED SO HARD TO GIVE THIS POTION TO HIM.

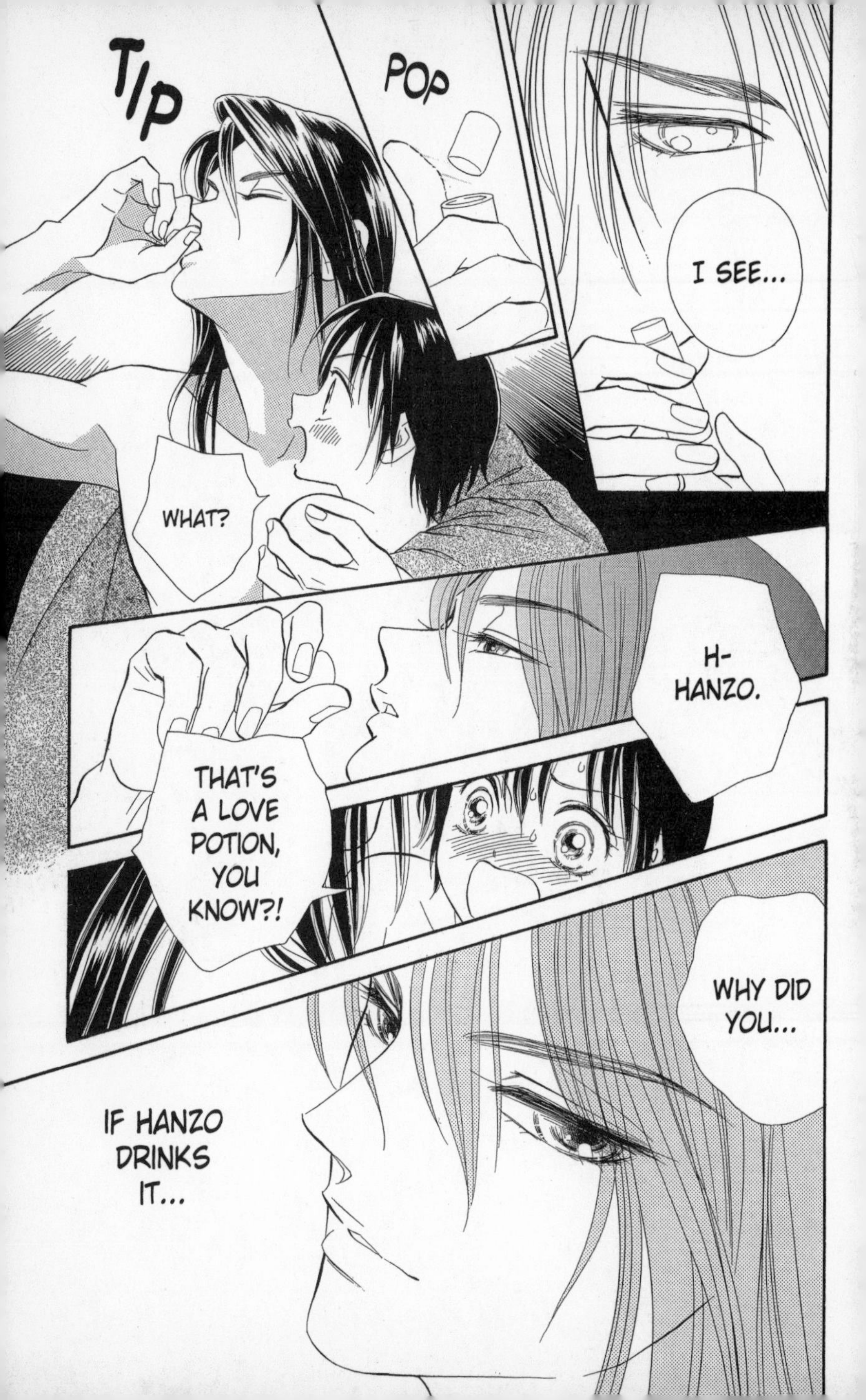
I SEE...
POP
TIP
WHAT?
H- HANZO.
THAT'S A LOVE POTION, YOU KNOW?!
WHY DID YOU...
IF HANZO DRINKS IT...

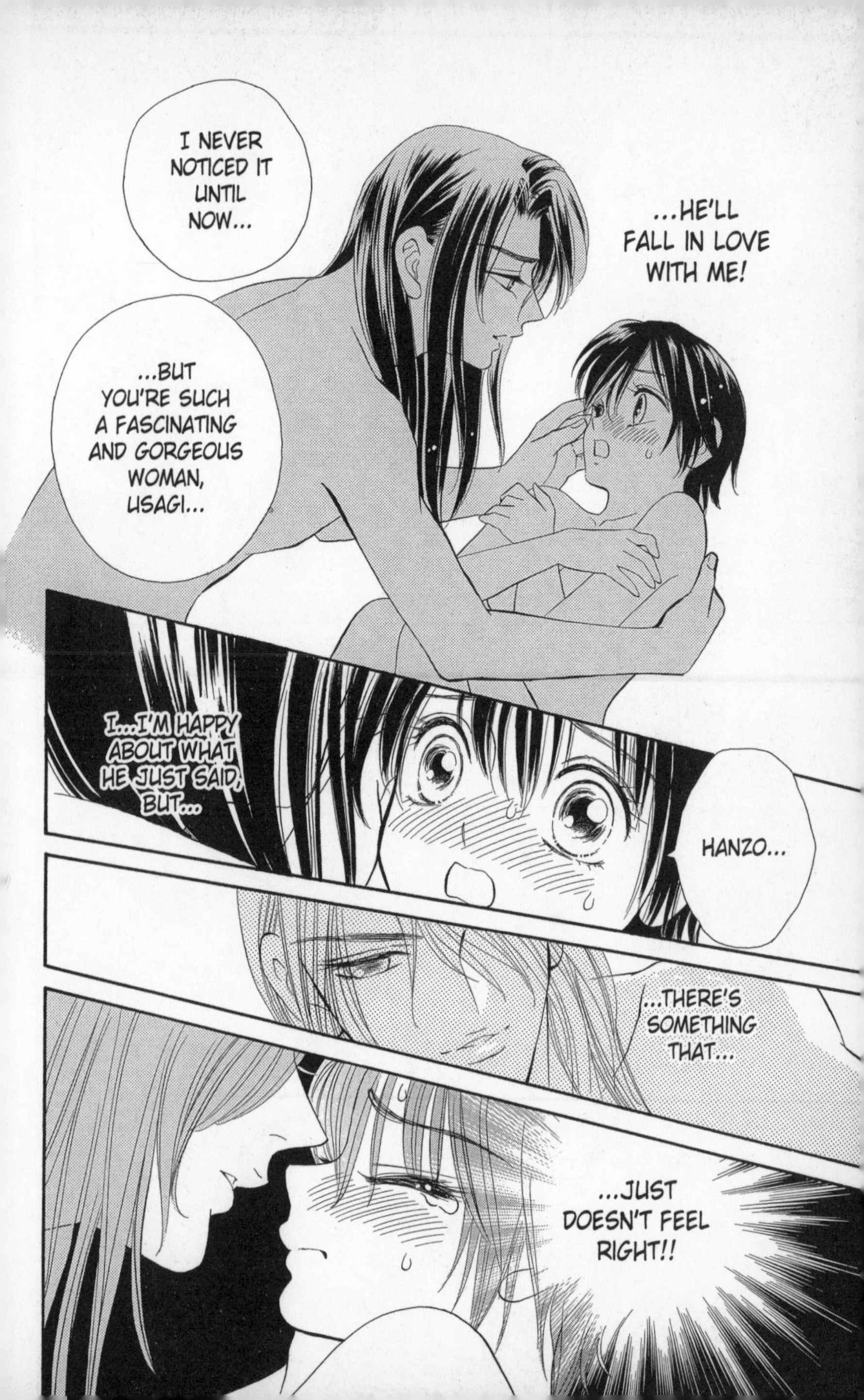
...HE'LL FALL IN LOVE WITH ME!
I NEVER NOTICED IT UNTIL NOW...
...BUT YOU'RE SUCH A FASCINATING AND GORGEOUS WOMAN, USAGI...
HANZO...
I...I'M HAPPY ABOUT WHAT HE JUST SAID, BUT...
...THERE'S SOMETHING THAT...
...JUST DOESN'T FEEL RIGHT!!

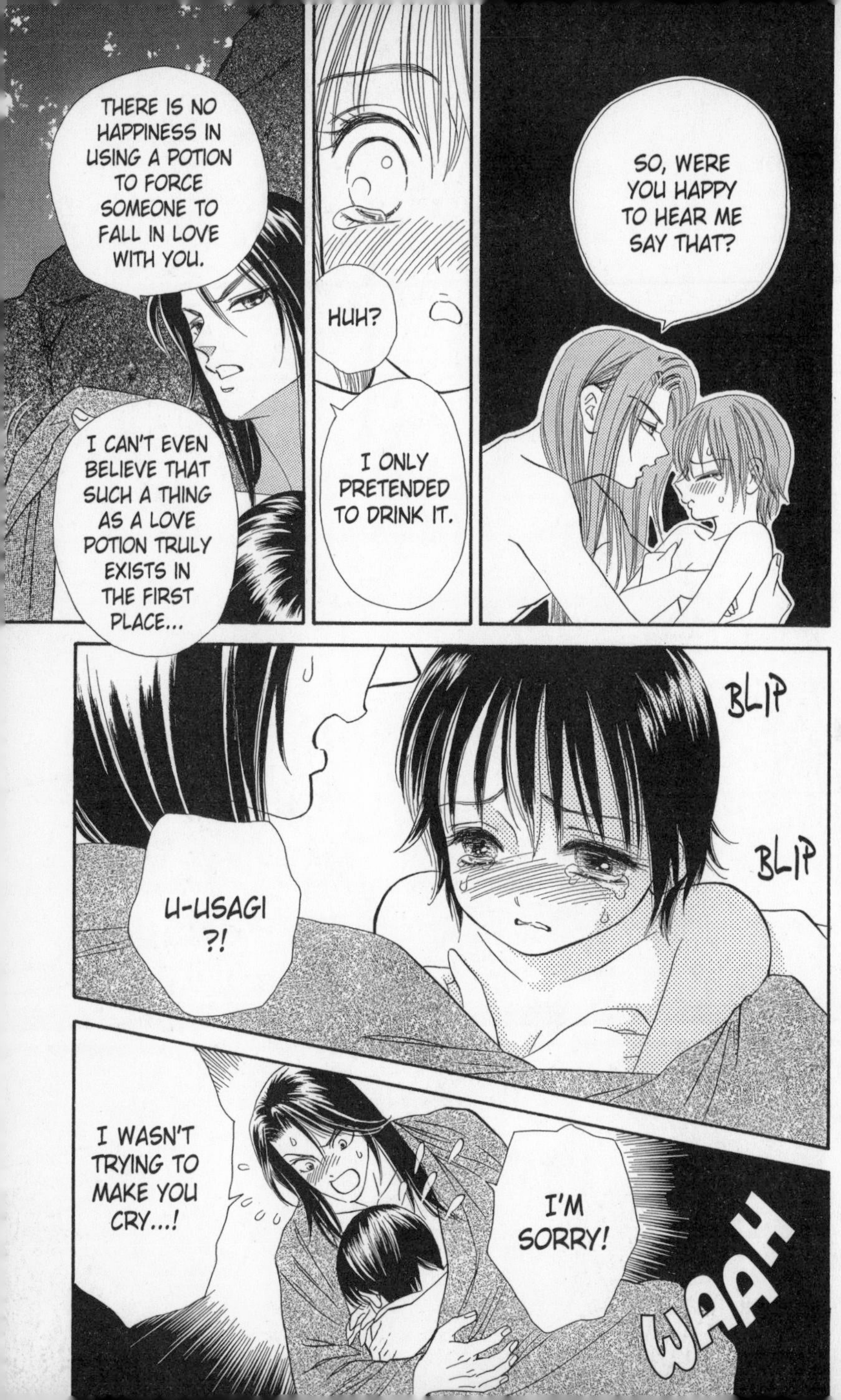
SO, WERE YOU HAPPY TO HEAR ME SAY THAT?
HUH?
I ONLY PRETENDED TO DRINK IT.
THERE IS NO HAPPINESS IN USING A POTION TO FORCE SOMEONE TO FALL IN LOVE WITH YOU.
I CAN'T EVEN BELIEVE THAT SUCH A THING AS A LOVE POTION TRULY EXISTS IN THE FIRST PLACE...
BLIP
BLIP
U-USAGI ?!
I'M SORRY!
WAAH
I WASN'T TRYING TO MAKE YOU CRY...!

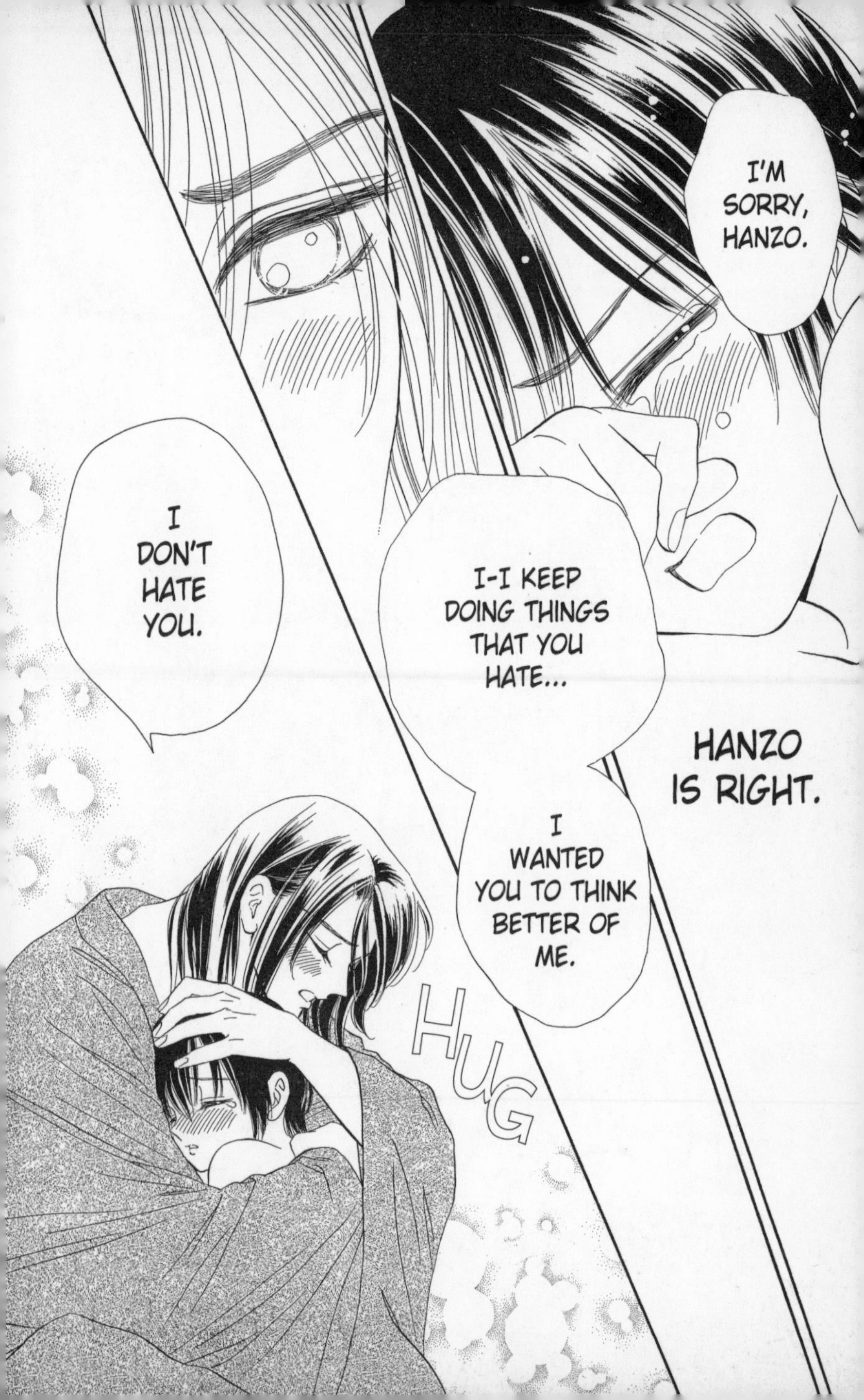
I'M SORRY, HANZO.
I-I KEEP DOING THINGS THAT YOU HATE...
I WANTED YOU TO THINK BETTER OF ME.
HANZO IS RIGHT.
I DON'T HATE YOU.
HUG

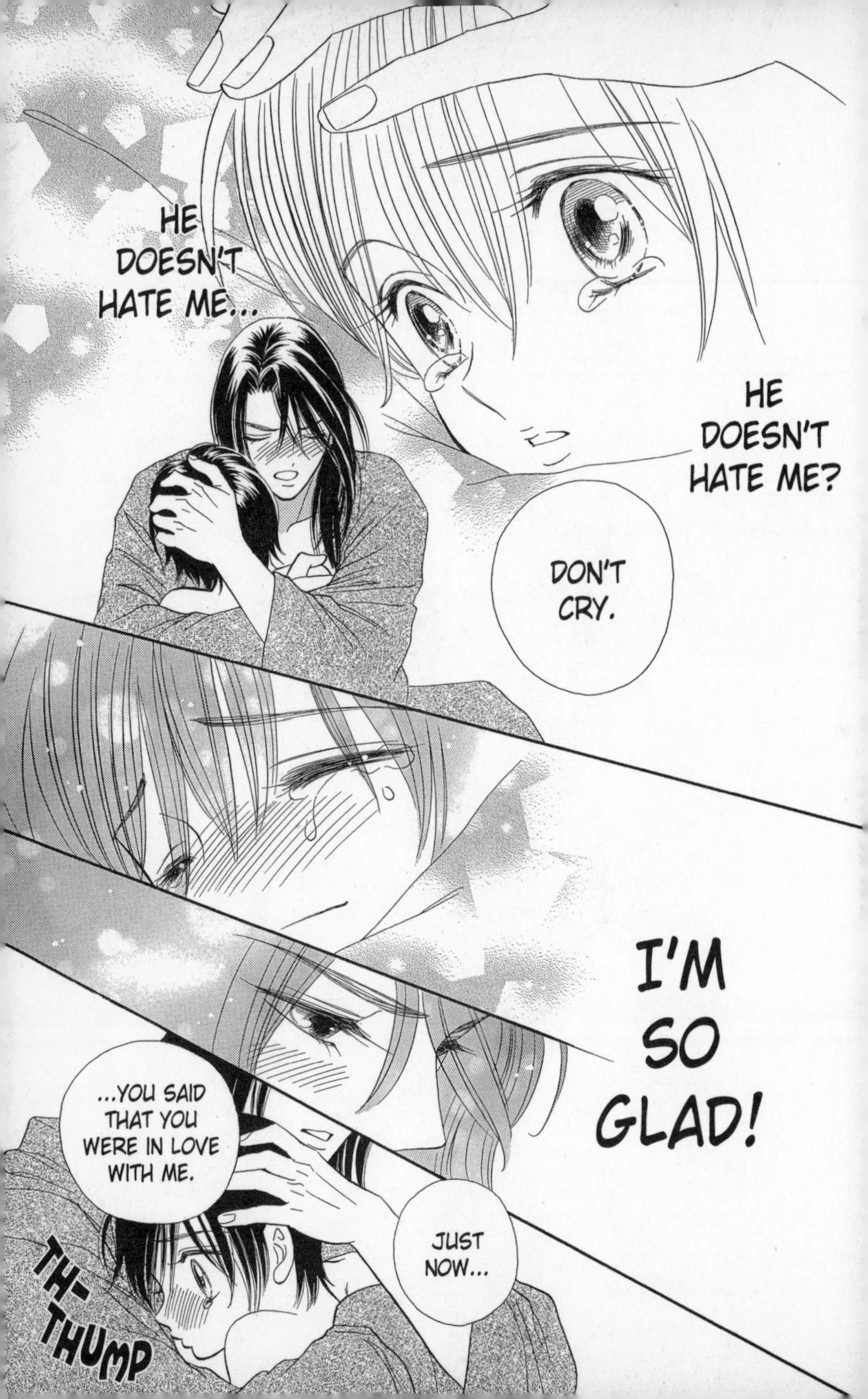
HE DOESN'T HATE ME...
HE DOESN'T HATE ME?
DON'T CRY.
I'M SO GLAD!
...YOU SAID THAT YOU WERE IN LOVE WITH ME.
JUST NOW...
TH-THUMP

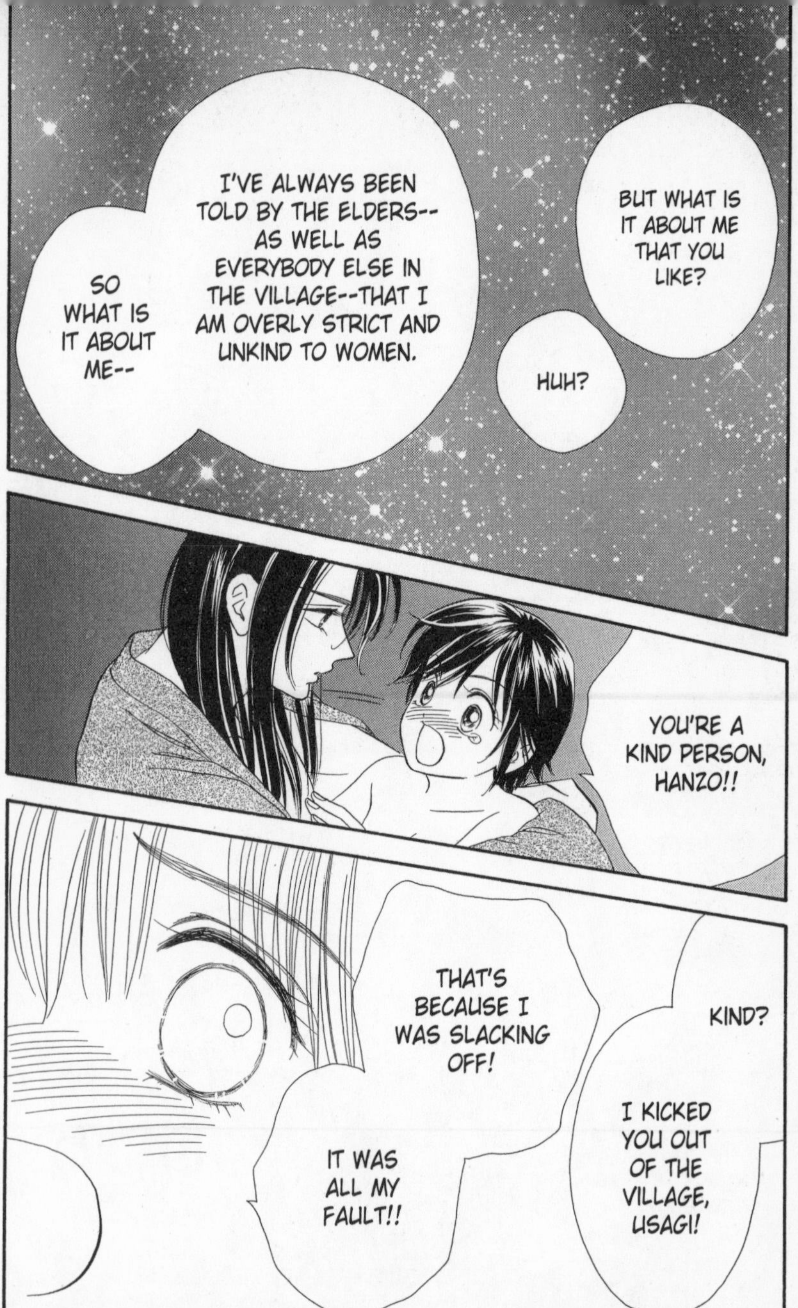
BUT WHAT IS IT ABOUT ME THAT YOU LIKE?
HUH?
I'VE ALWAYS BEEN TOLD BY THE ELDERS-- AS WELL AS EVERYBODY ELSE IN THE VILLAGE--THAT I AM OVERLY STRICT AND UNKIND TO WOMEN.
SO WHAT IS IT ABOUT ME--
YOU'RE A KIND PERSON, HANZO!!
KIND?
I KICKED YOU OUT OF THE VILLAGE, USAGI!
THAT'S BECAUSE I WAS SLACKING OFF!
IT WAS ALL MY FAULT!!

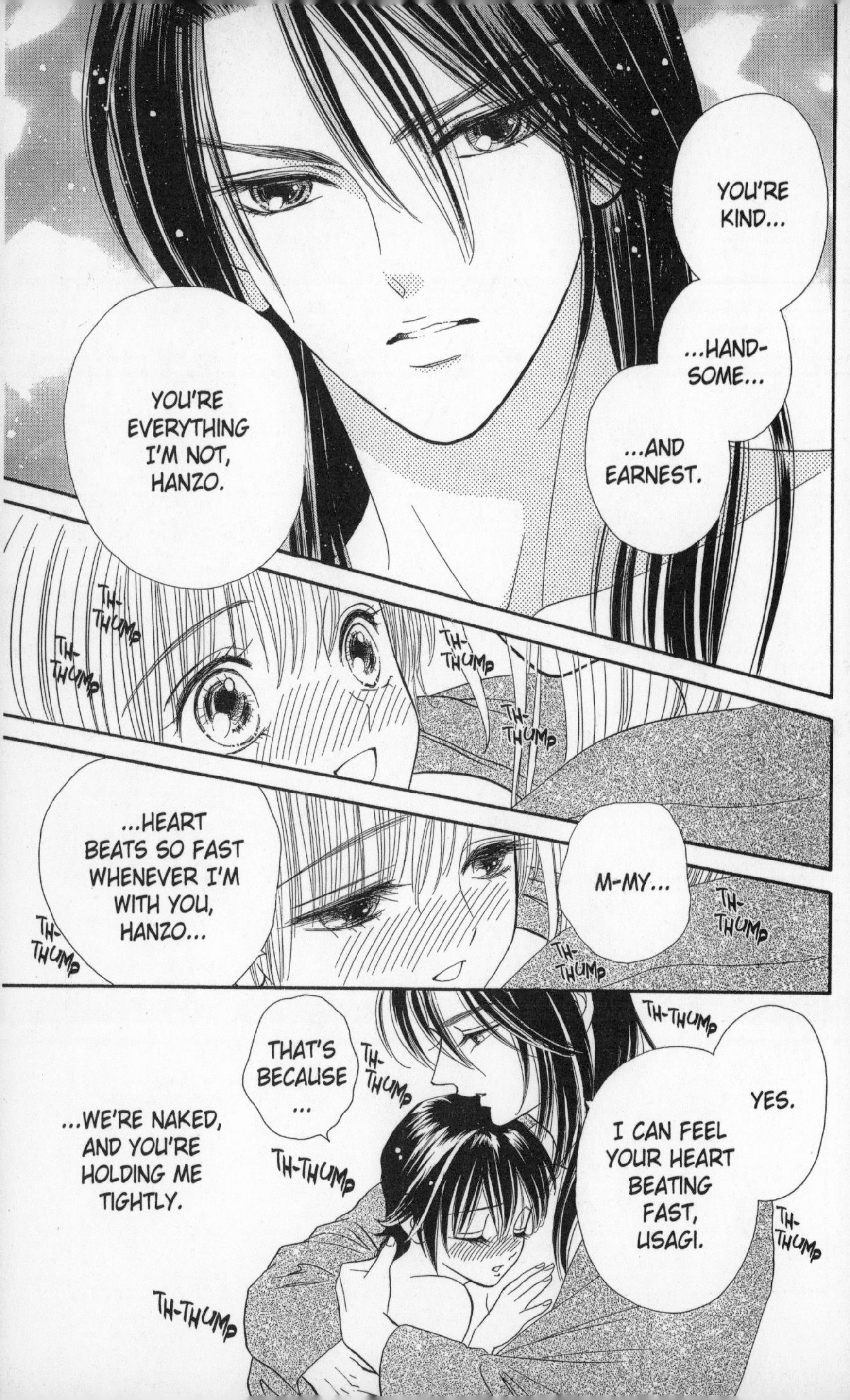
YOU'RE KIND...
...HAND-SOME...
...AND EARNEST.
YOU'RE EVERYTHING I'M NOT, HANZO.
TH-THUMP
TH-THUMP
TH-THUMP
TH-THUMP
M-MY...
...HEART BEATS SO FAST WHENEVER I'M WITH YOU, HANZO...
TH-THUMP
TH-THUMP
TH-THUMP
TH-THUMP
YES.
I CAN FEEL YOUR HEART BEATING FAST, USAGI.
TH-THUMP
TH-THUMP
THAT'S BECAUSE ...
...WE'RE NAKED, AND YOU'RE HOLDING ME TIGHTLY.
TH-THUMP
TH-THUMP

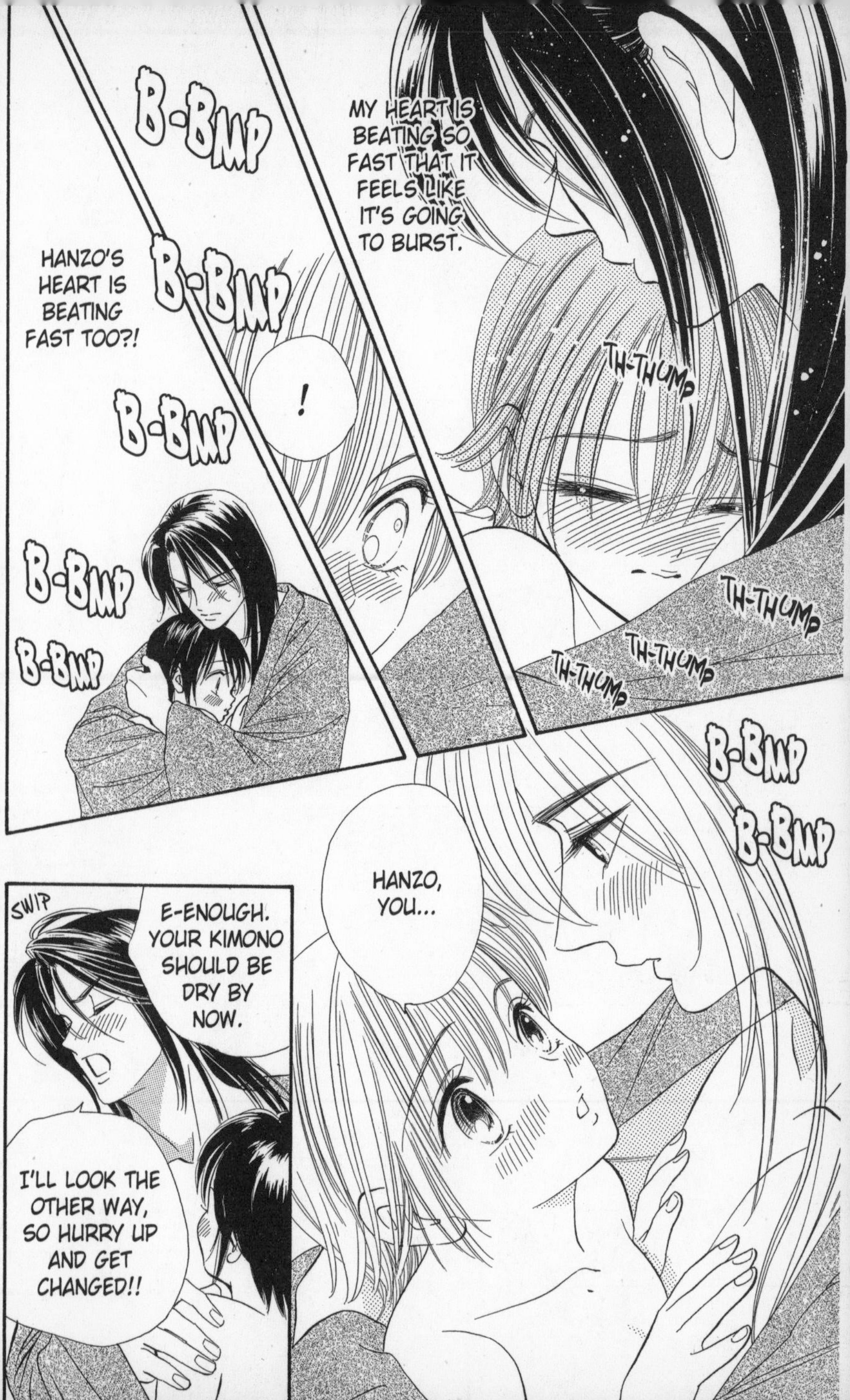
MY HEART IS BEATING SO FAST THAT IT FEELS LIKE IT'S GOING TO BURST.
TH-THUMP
TH-THUMP
TH-THUMP
TH-THUMP
!
B-BMP
B-BMP
HANZO'S HEART IS BEATING FAST TOO?!
B-BMP
B-BMP
B-BMP
B-BMP
B-BMP
HANZO, YOU...
SWIP
E-ENOUGH. YOUR KIMONO SHOULD BE DRY BY NOW.
I'LL LOOK THE OTHER WAY, SO HURRY UP AND GET CHANGED!!

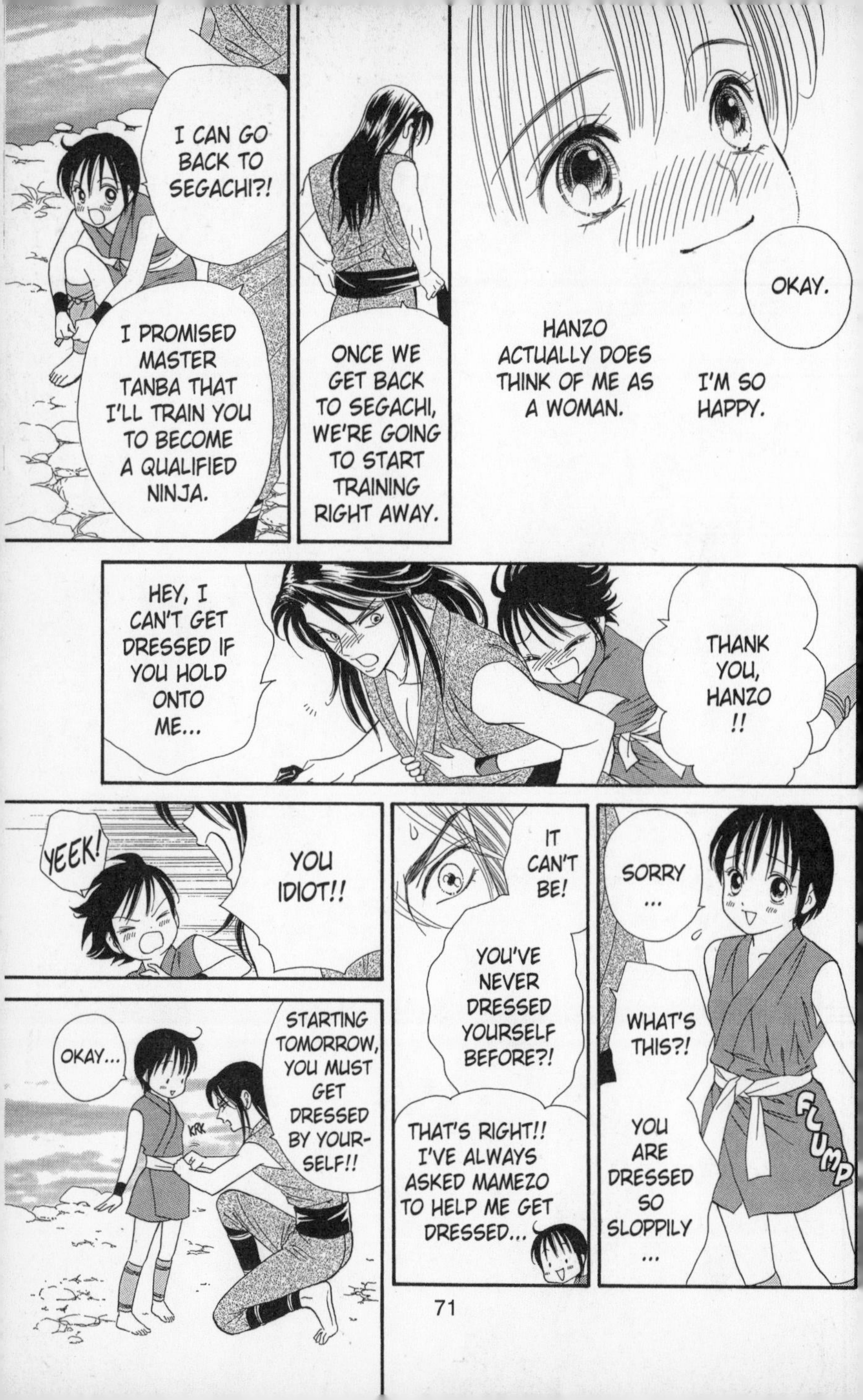
OKAY.
HANZO ACTUALLY DOES THINK OF ME AS A WOMAN.
I'M SO HAPPY.
ONCE WE GET BACK TO SEGACHI, WE'RE GOING TO START TRAINING RIGHT AWAY.
I CAN GO BACK TO SEGACHI?!
I PROMISED MASTER TANBA THAT I'LL TRAIN YOU TO BECOME A QUALIFIED NINJA.
THANK YOU, HANZO !!
HEY, I CAN'T GET DRESSED IF YOU HOLD ONTO ME...
FLUMP
WHAT'S THIS?!
YOU ARE DRESSED SO SLOPPILY ...
SORRY ...
IT CAN'T BE!
YOU'VE NEVER DRESSED YOURSELF BEFORE?!
THAT'S RIGHT!! I'VE ALWAYS ASKED MAMEZO TO HELP ME GET DRESSED...
YOU IDIOT!!
YEEK!
STARTING TOMORROW, YOU MUST GET DRESSED BY YOUR-SELF!!
KRK
OKAY...

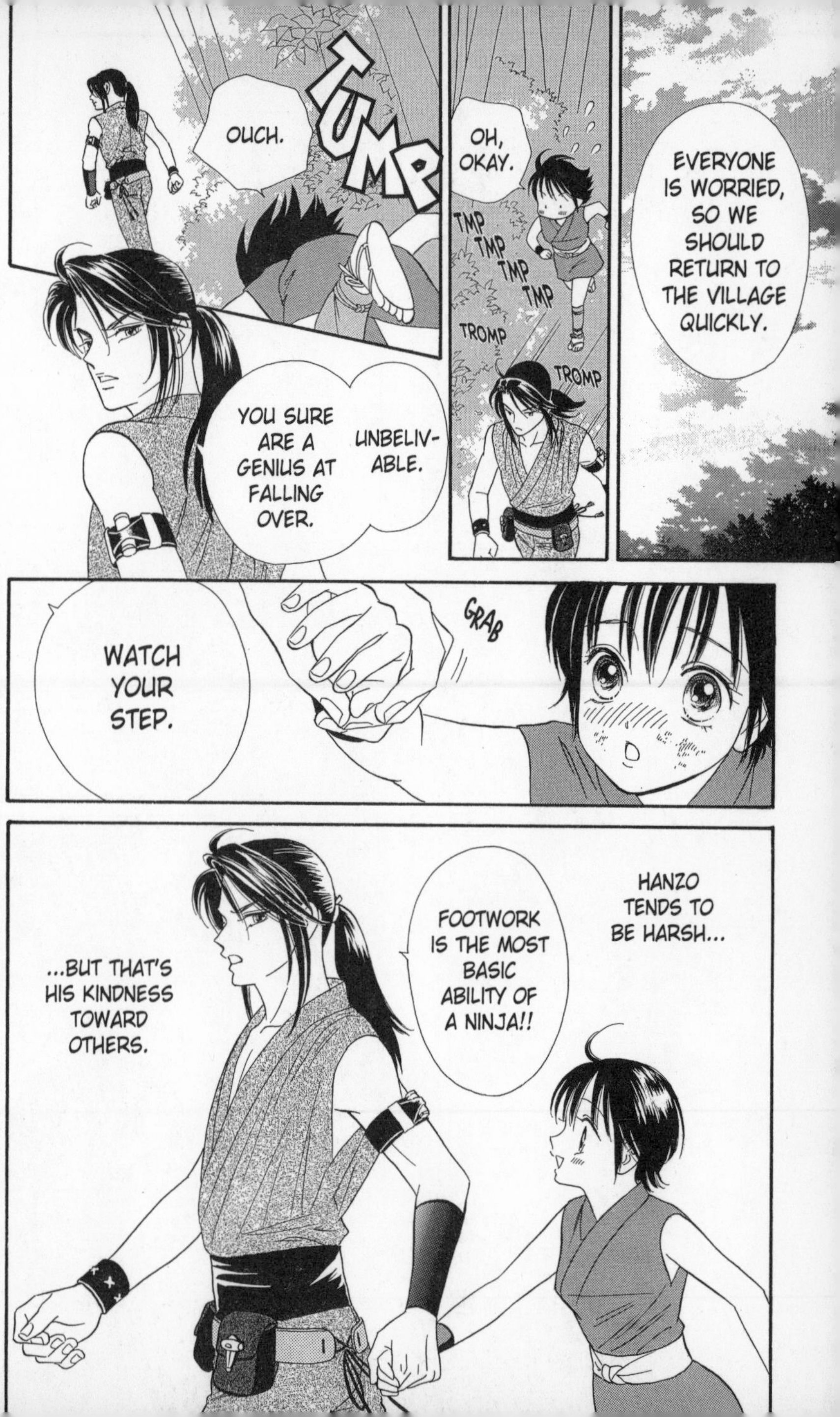
EVERYONE IS WORRIED, SO WE SHOULD RETURN TO THE VILLAGE QUICKLY.
OH, OKAY.
TMP TMP TMP TMP
TROMP
TROMP
TUMP
OUCH.
UNBELIV-ABLE.
YOU SURE ARE A GENIUS AT FALLING OVER.
GRAB
WATCH YOUR STEP.
HANZO TENDS TO BE HARSH...
FOOTWORK IS THE MOST BASIC ABILITY OF A NINJA!!
...BUT THAT'S HIS KINDNESS TOWARD OTHERS.

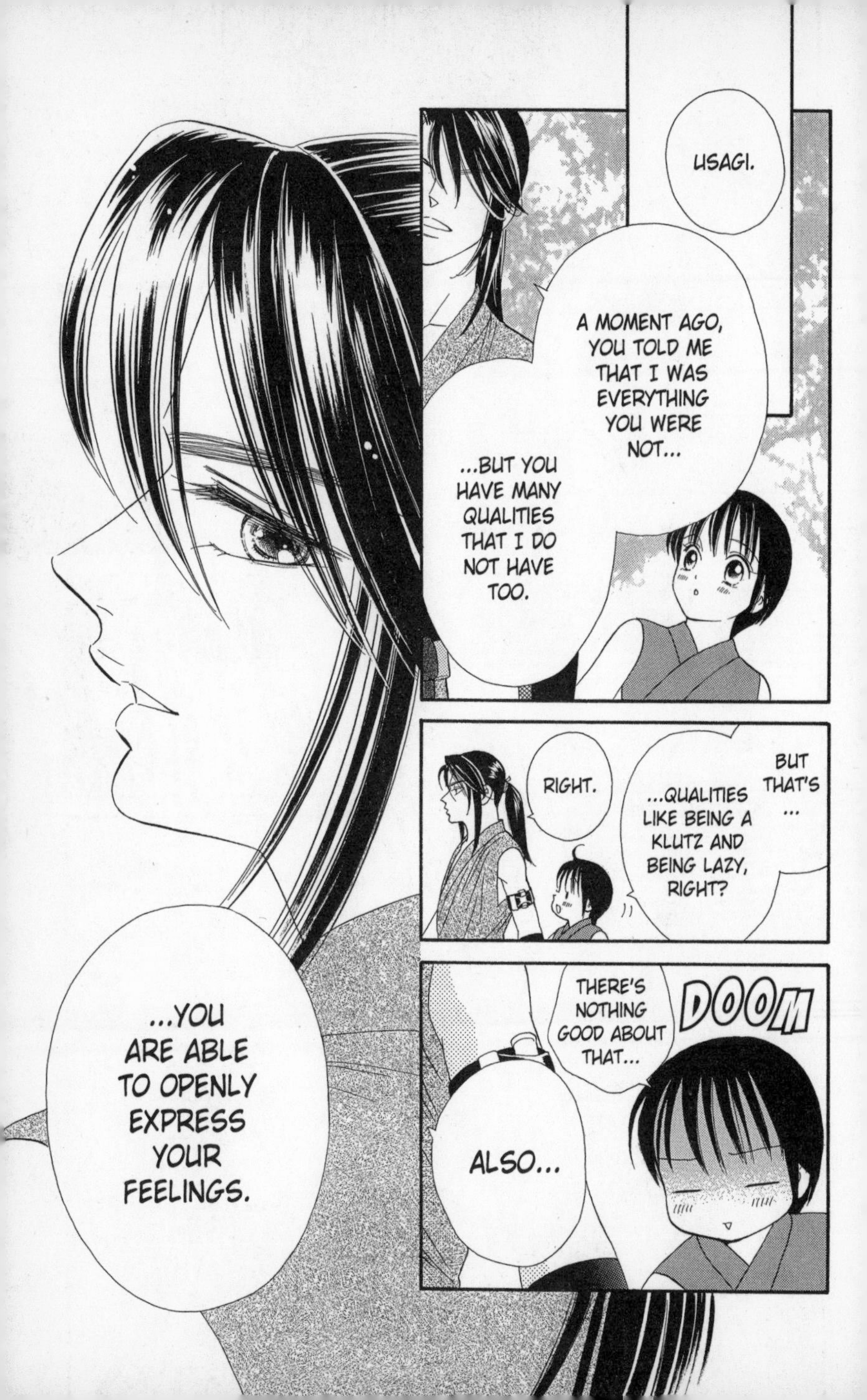
USAGI.
A MOMENT AGO, YOU TOLD ME THAT I WAS EVERYTHING YOU WERE NOT...
...BUT YOU HAVE MANY QUALITIES THAT I DO NOT HAVE TOO.
BUT THAT'S ...
...QUALITIES LIKE BEING A KLUTZ AND BEING LAZY, RIGHT?
RIGHT.
DOOM
THERE'S NOTHING GOOD ABOUT THAT...
ALSO...
...YOU ARE ABLE TO OPENLY EXPRESS YOUR FEELINGS.

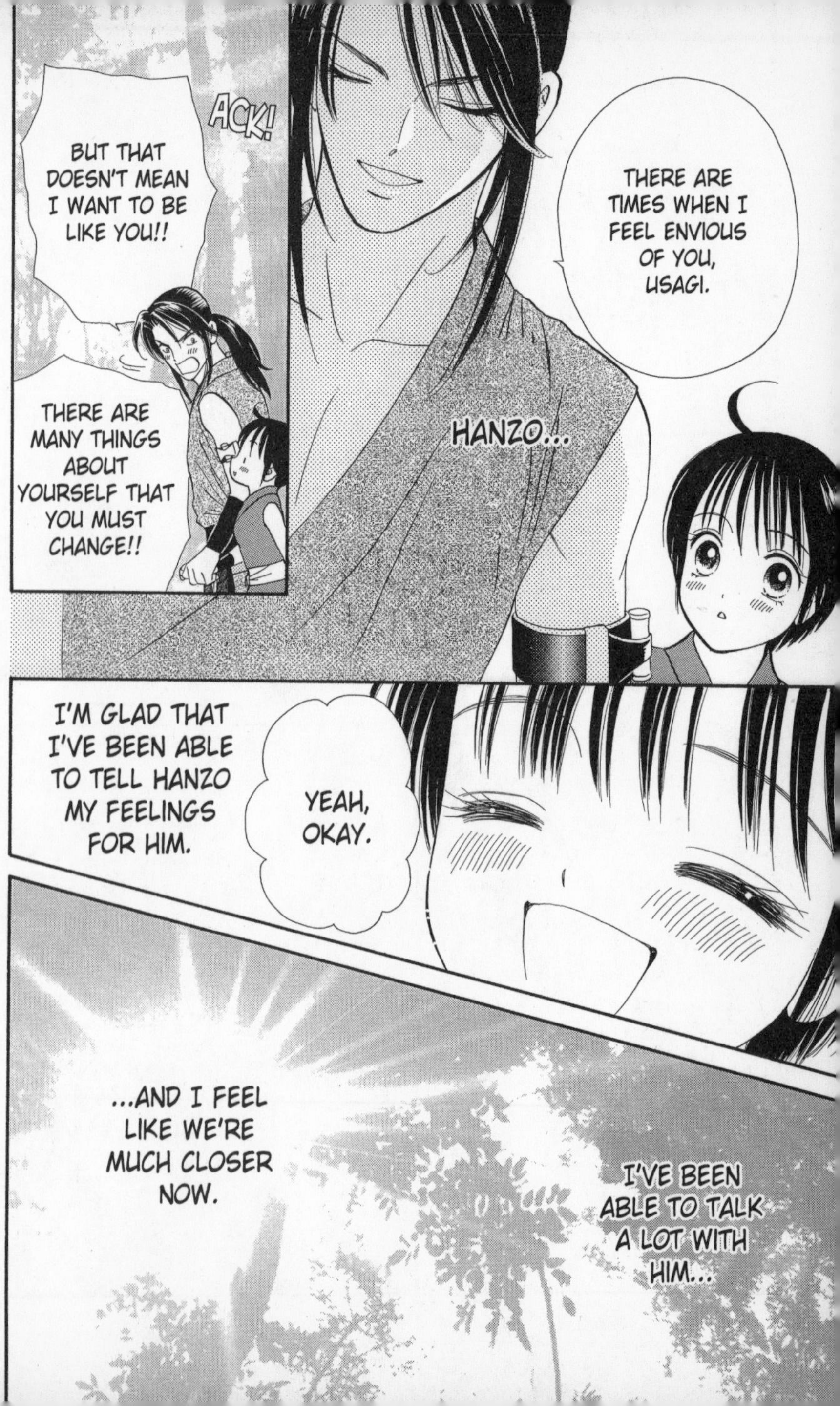
THERE ARE TIMES WHEN I FEEL ENVIOUS OF YOU, USAGI.
HANZO...
ACK!
BUT THAT DOESN'T MEAN I WANT TO BE LIKE YOU!!
THERE ARE MANY THINGS ABOUT YOURSELF THAT YOU MUST CHANGE!!
YEAH, OKAY.
I'M GLAD THAT I'VE BEEN ABLE TO TELL HANZO MY FEELINGS FOR HIM.
I'VE BEEN ABLE TO TALK A LOT WITH HIM...
...AND I FEEL LIKE WE'RE MUCH CLOSER NOW.

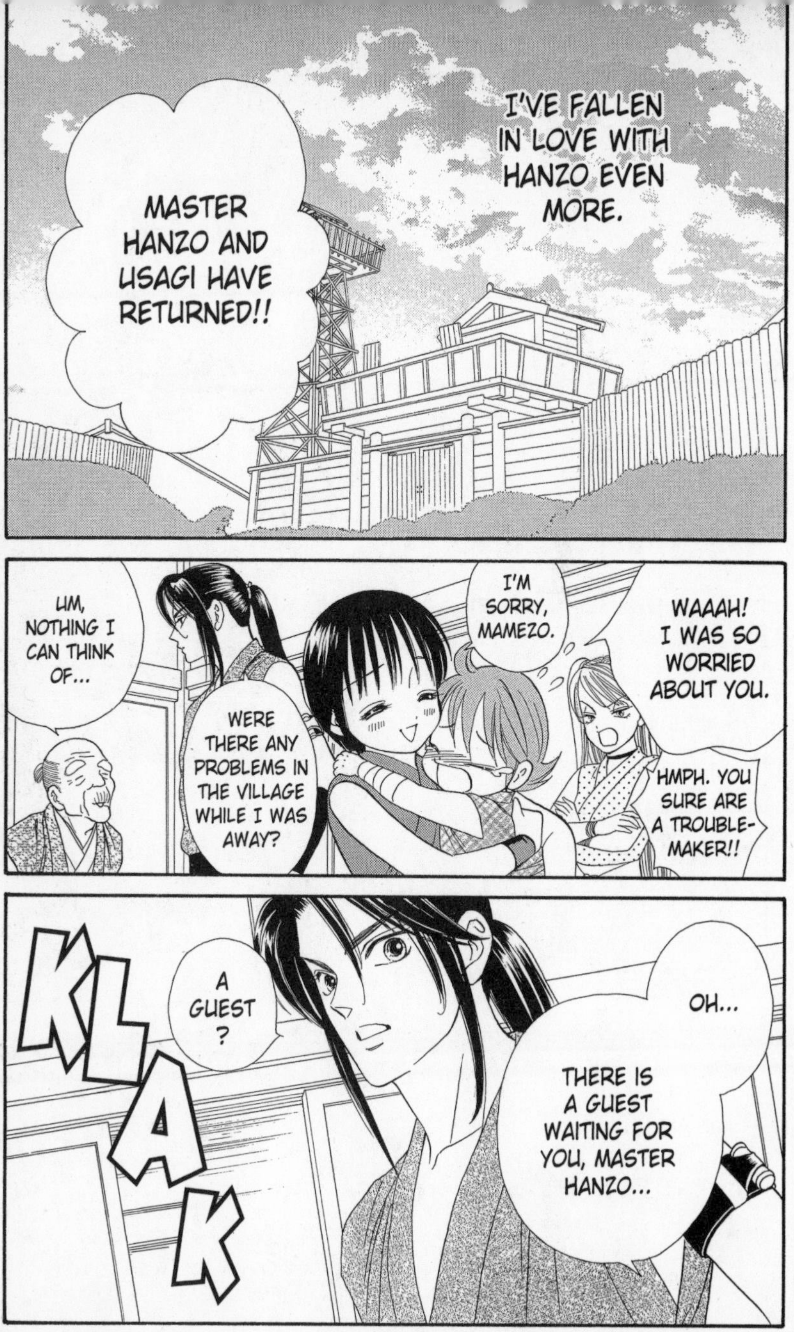
I'VE FALLEN IN LOVE WITH HANZO EVEN MORE.
MASTER HANZO AND USAGI HAVE RETURNED!!
WAAAH! I WAS SO WORRIED ABOUT YOU.
I'M SORRY, MAMEZO.
HMPH. YOU SURE ARE A TROUBLE-MAKER!!
WERE THERE ANY PROBLEMS IN THE VILLAGE WHILE I WAS AWAY?
UM, NOTHING I CAN THINK OF...
OH...
THERE IS A GUEST WAITING FOR YOU, MASTER HANZO...
A GUEST?
KLAK

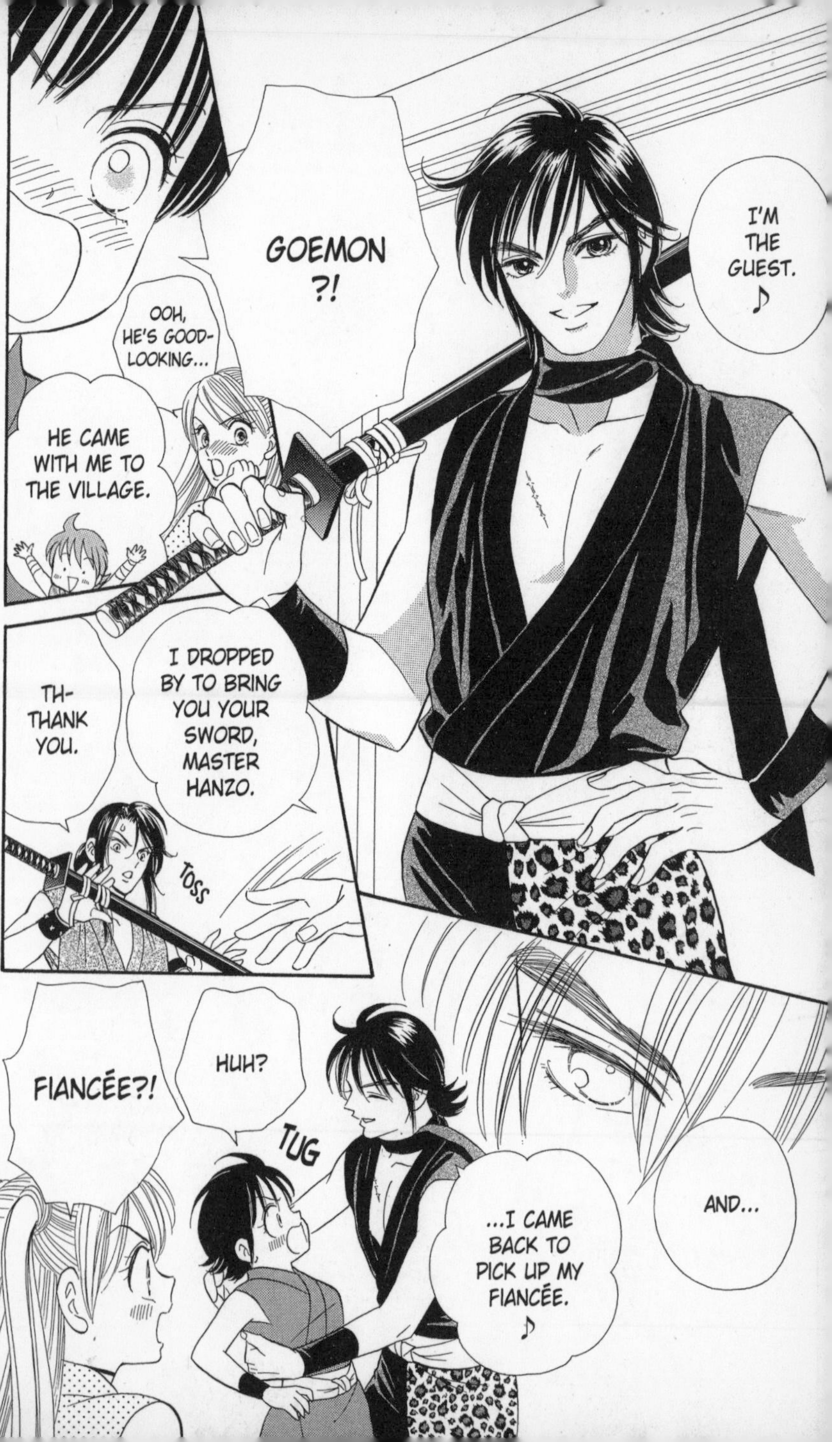
I'M THE GUEST. ♪
GOEMON ?!
OOH, HE'S GOOD-LOOKING...
HE CAME WITH ME TO THE VILLAGE.
I DROPPED BY TO BRING YOU YOUR SWORD, MASTER HANZO.
TH-THANK YOU.
TOSS
AND...
...I CAME BACK TO PICK UP MY FIANCÉE. ♪
TUG
HUH?
FIANCÉE?!

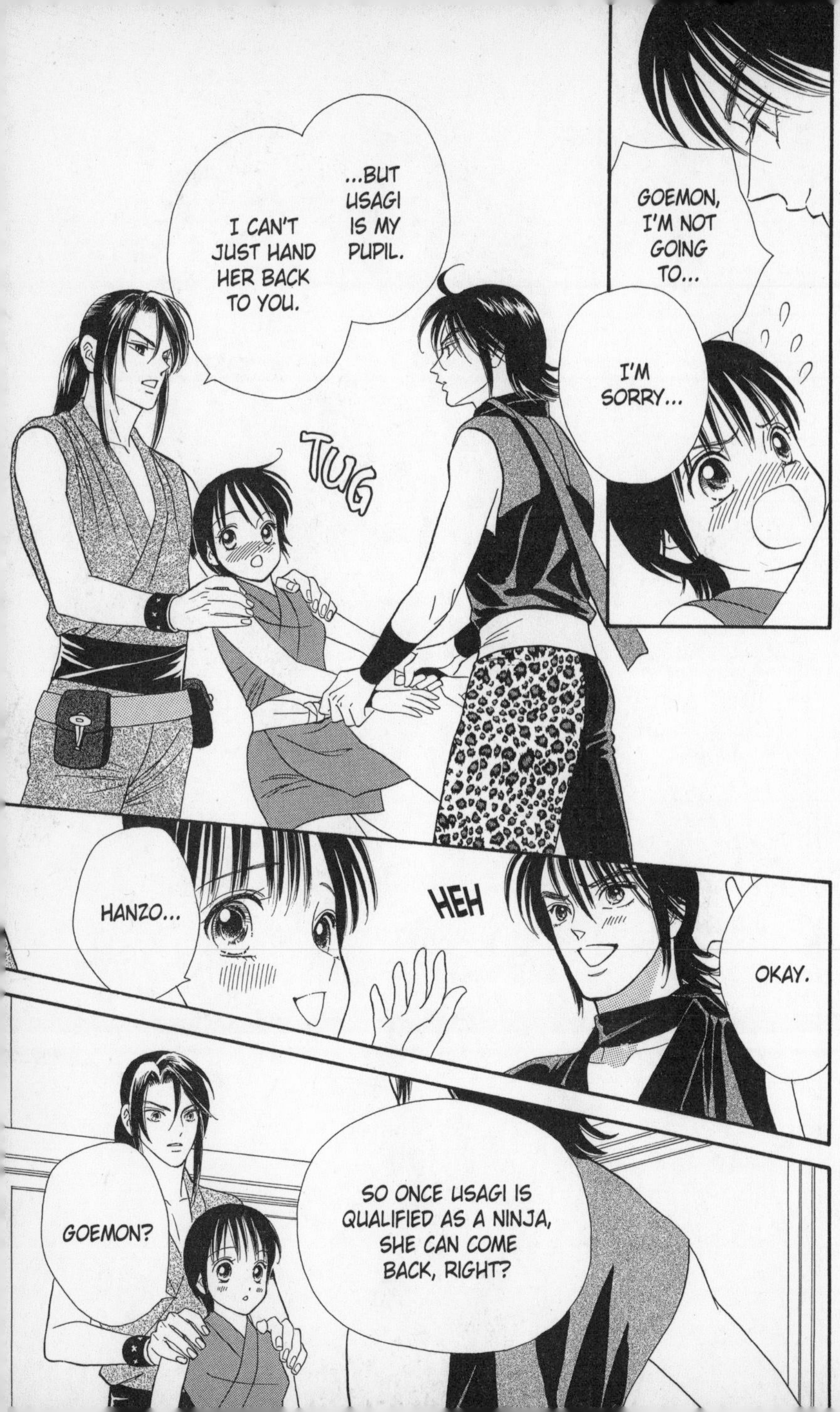
GOEMON, I'M NOT GOING TO...
I'M SORRY...
...BUT USAGI IS MY PUPIL.
I CAN'T JUST HAND HER BACK TO YOU.
TUG
OKAY.
HEH
HANZO...
SO ONCE USAGI IS QUALIFIED AS A NINJA, SHE CAN COME BACK, RIGHT?
GOEMON?

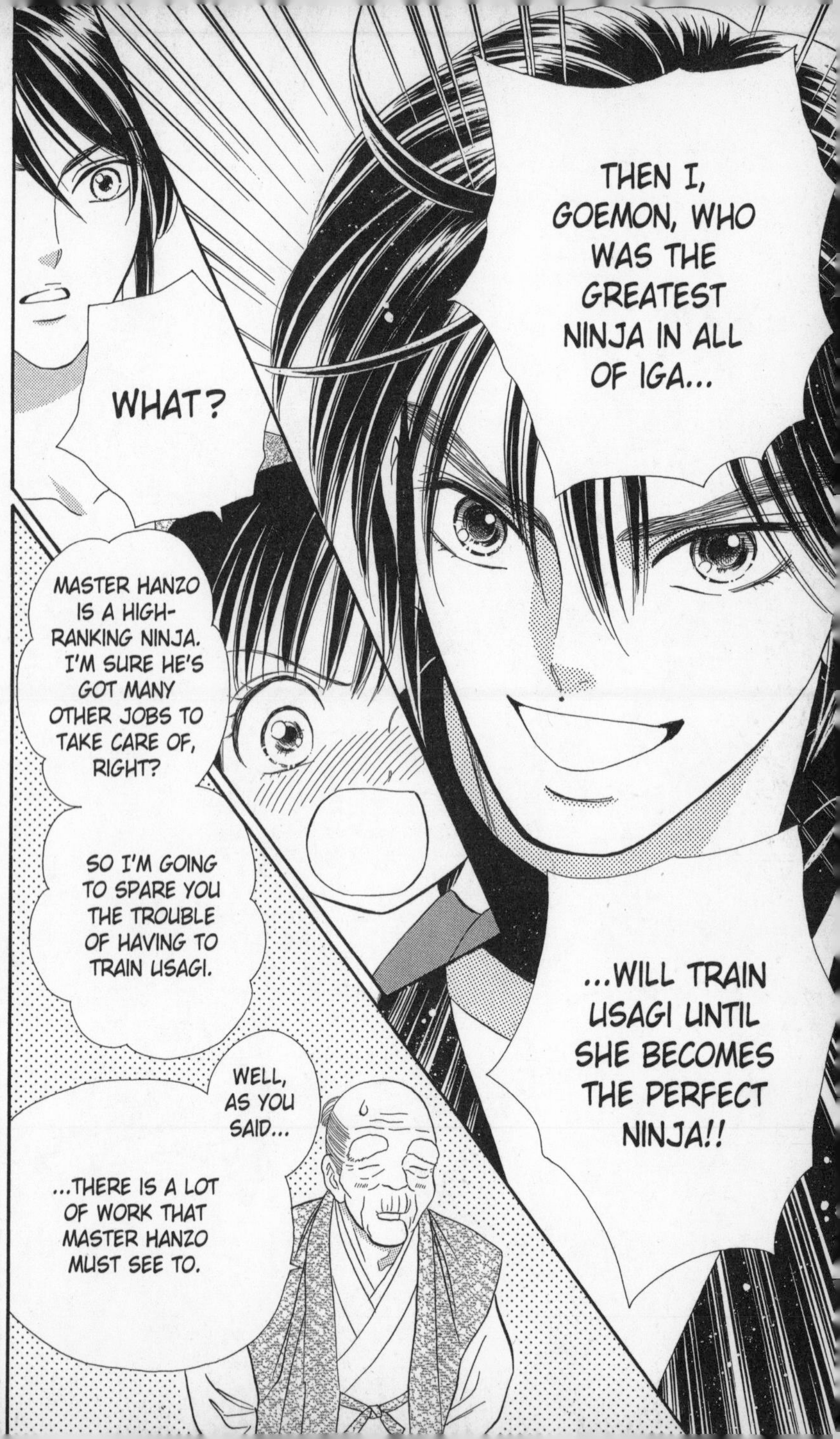
MASTER HANZO IS A HIGH-RANKING NINJA. I'M SURE HE'S GOT MANY OTHER JOBS TO TAKE CARE OF, RIGHT?
SO I'M GOING TO SPARE YOU THE TROUBLE OF HAVING TO TRAIN USAGI.
WELL, AS YOU SAID...
...THERE IS A LOT OF WORK THAT MASTER HANZO MUST SEE TO.
THEN I, GOEMON, WHO WAS THE GREATEST NINJA IN ALL OF IGA...
...WILL TRAIN USAGI UNTIL SHE BECOMES THE PERFECT NINJA!!
WHAT?

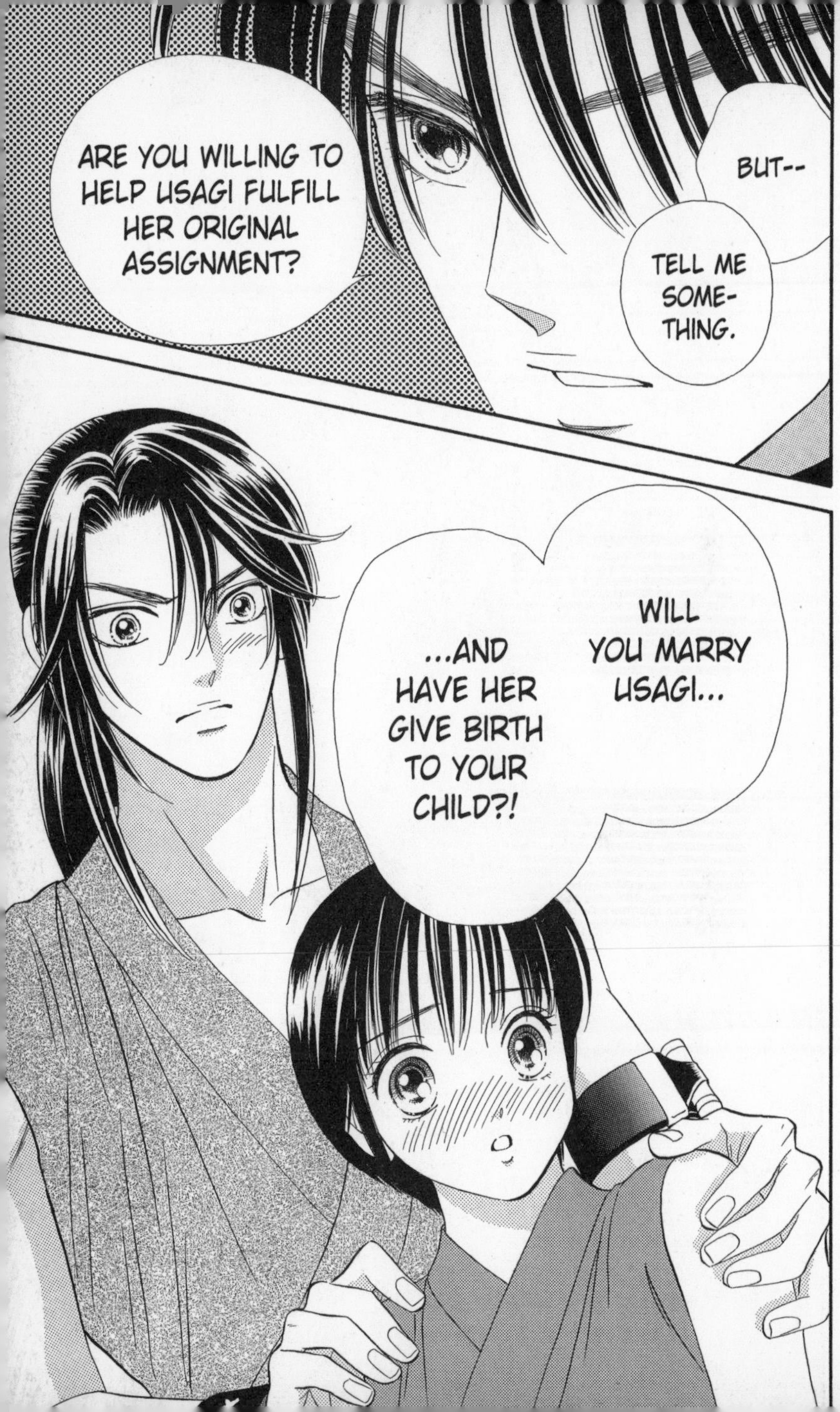
BUT--
TELL ME SOME-THING.
ARE YOU WILLING TO HELP USAGI FULFILL HER ORIGINAL ASSIGNMENT?
WILL YOU MARRY USAGI...
...AND HAVE HER GIVE BIRTH TO YOUR CHILD?!

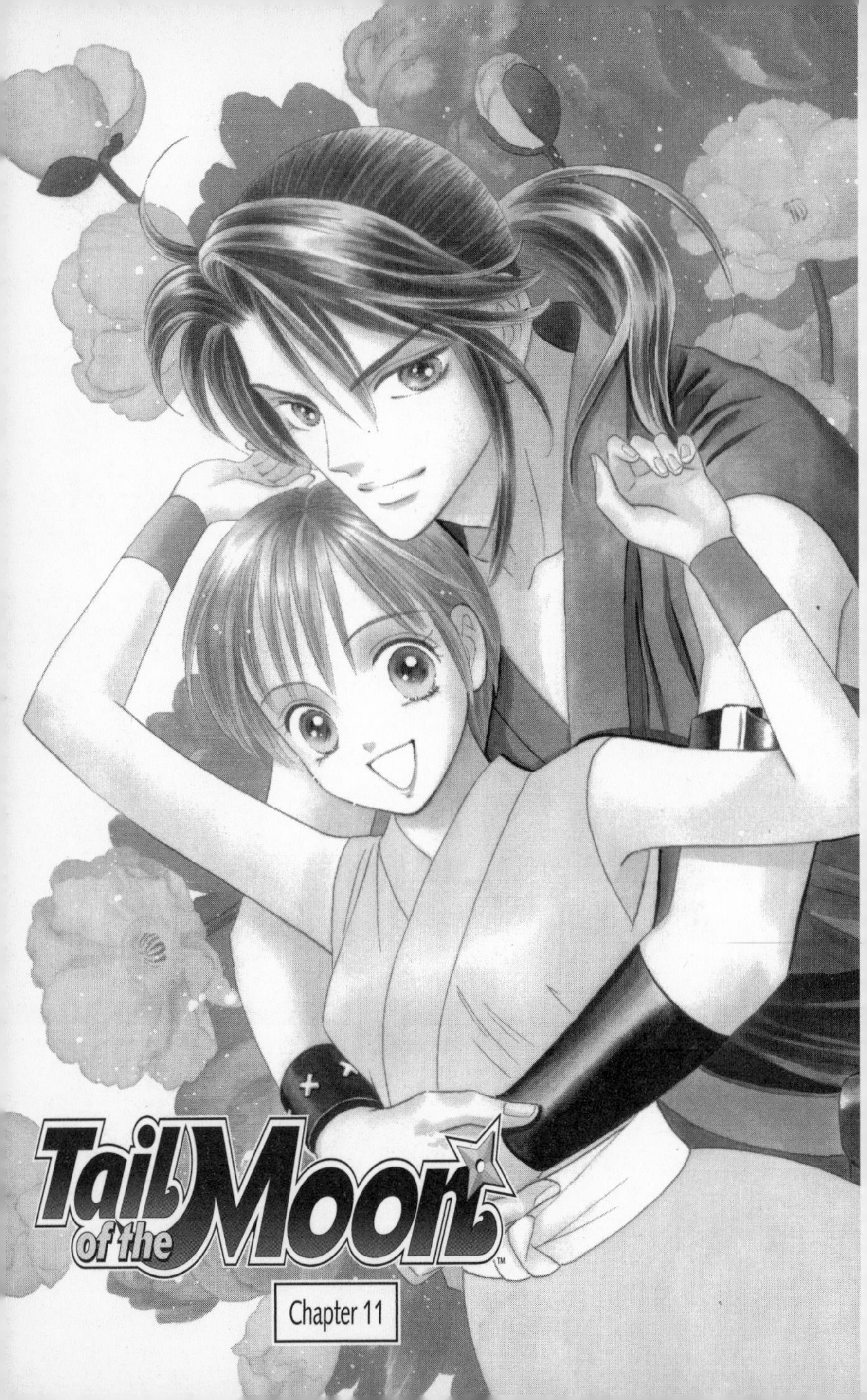
Tail of the Moon™
Chapter 11

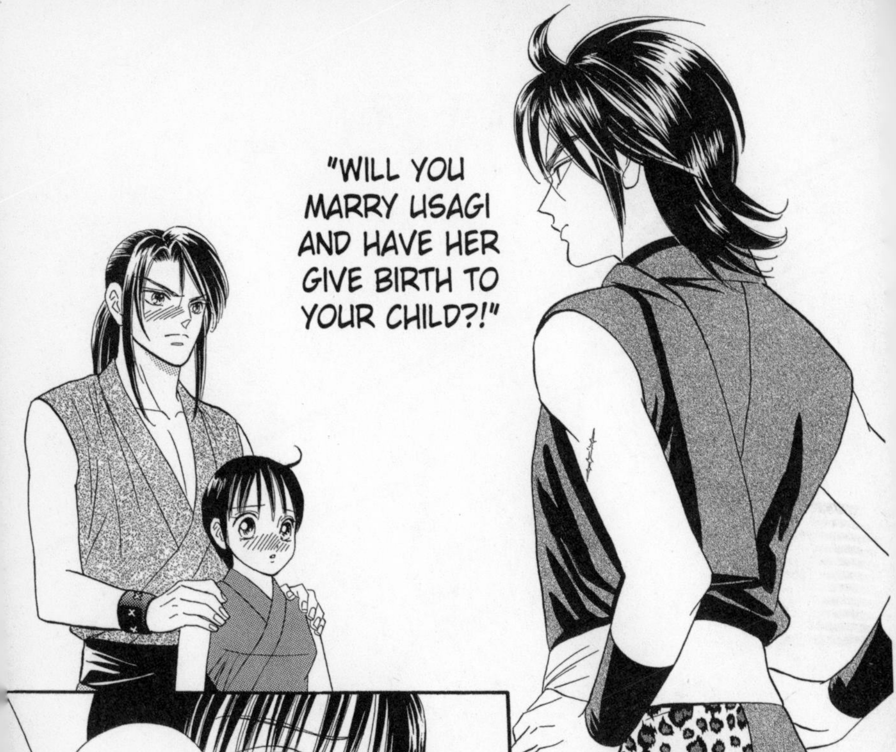
"WILL YOU MARRY USAGI AND HAVE HER GIVE BIRTH TO YOUR CHILD?!"
G-GOEMON ...
IF SHE CAN QUALIFY AS A NINJA...

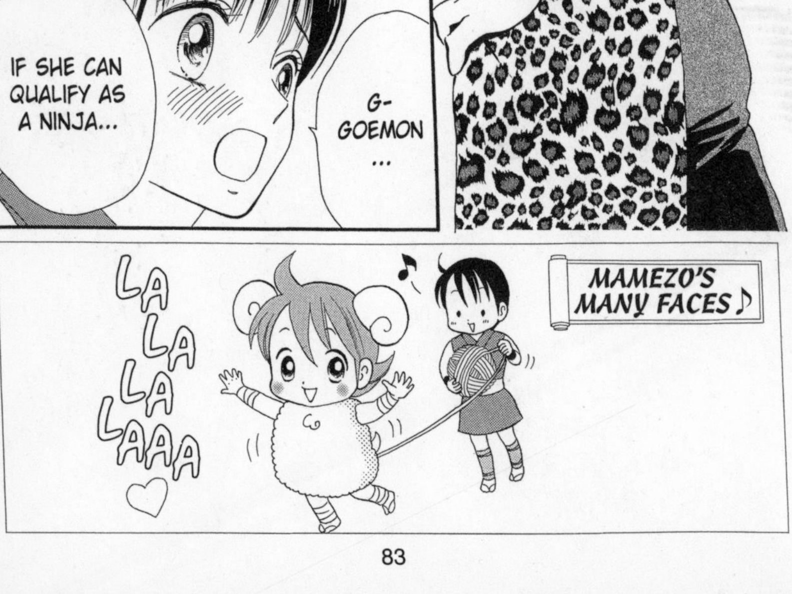
MAMEZO'S MANY FACES♪
LA LA LA LAAA

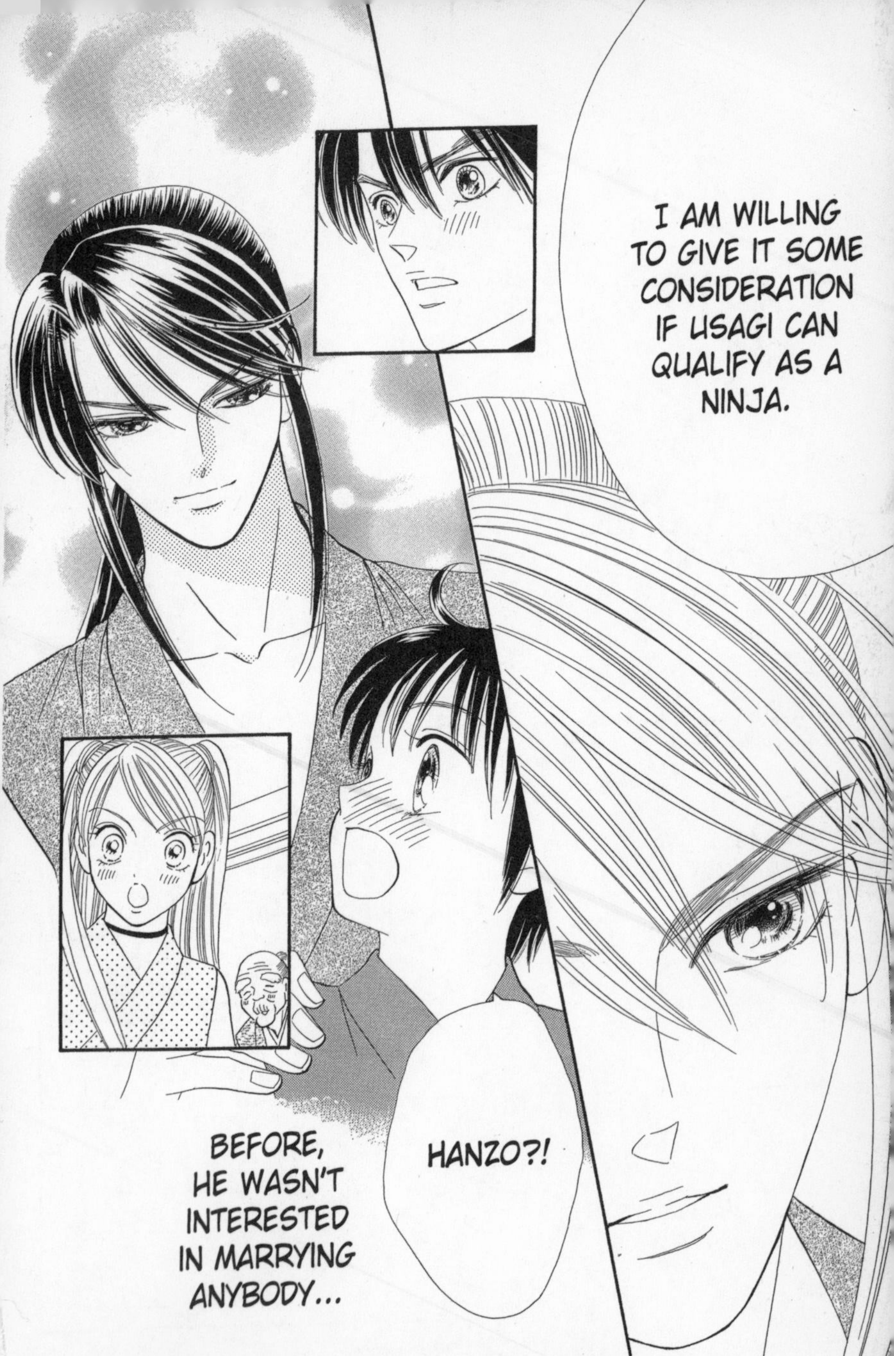
I AM WILLING TO GIVE IT SOME CONSIDERATION IF USAGI CAN QUALIFY AS A NINJA.
HANZO?!
BEFORE, HE WASN'T INTERESTED IN MARRYING ANYBODY...

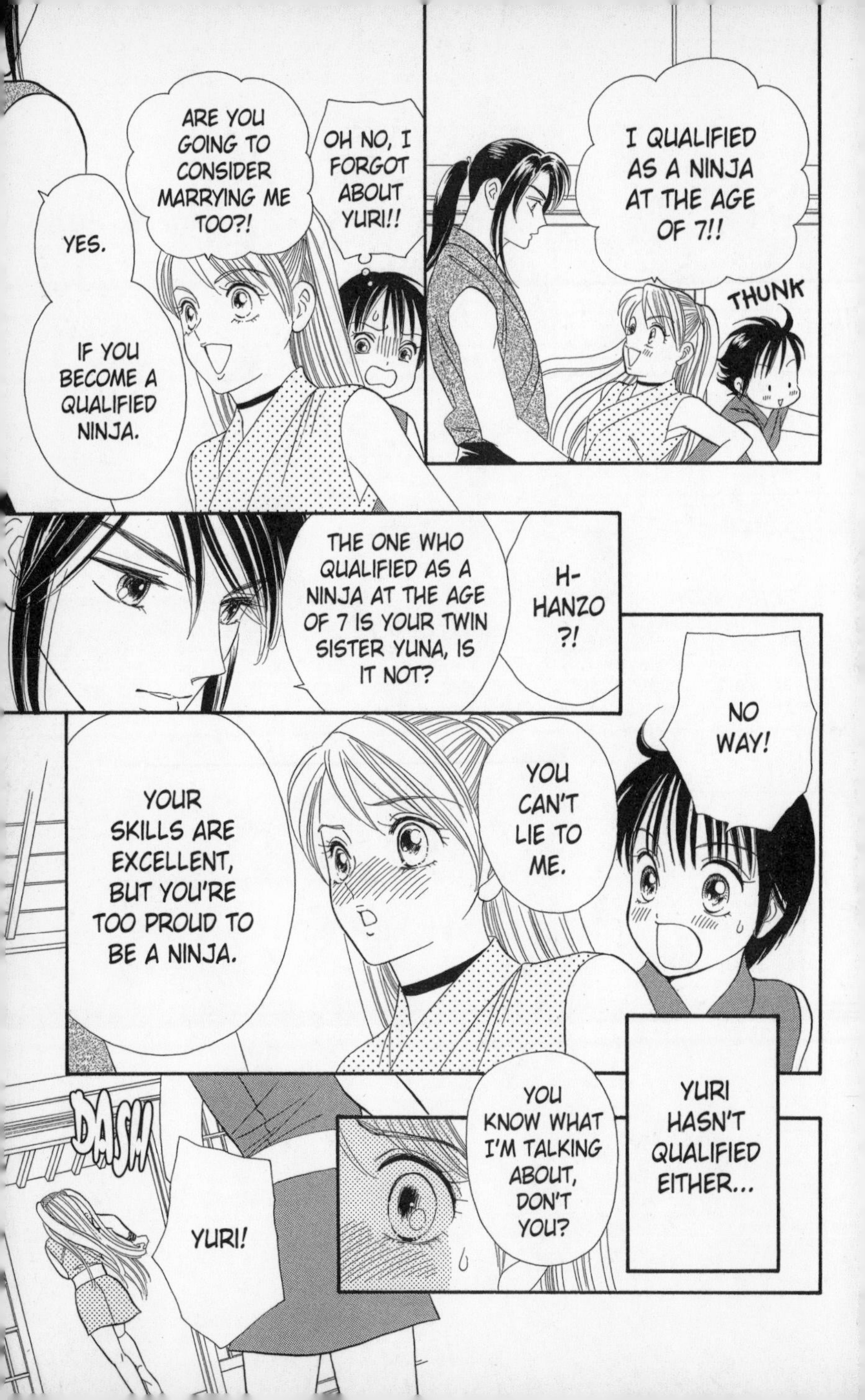
I QUALIFIED AS A NINJA AT THE AGE OF 7!!
THUNK
OH NO, I FORGOT ABOUT YURI!!
ARE YOU GOING TO CONSIDER MARRYING ME TOO?!
YES.
IF YOU BECOME A QUALIFIED NINJA.
H-HANZO?!
THE ONE WHO QUALIFIED AS A NINJA AT THE AGE OF 7 IS YOUR TWIN SISTER YUNA, IS IT NOT?
NO WAY!
YOU CAN'T LIE TO ME.
YOUR SKILLS ARE EXCELLENT, BUT YOU'RE TOO PROUD TO BE A NINJA.
YURI HASN'T QUALIFIED EITHER...
YOU KNOW WHAT I'M TALKING ABOUT, DON'T YOU?
DASH
YURI!

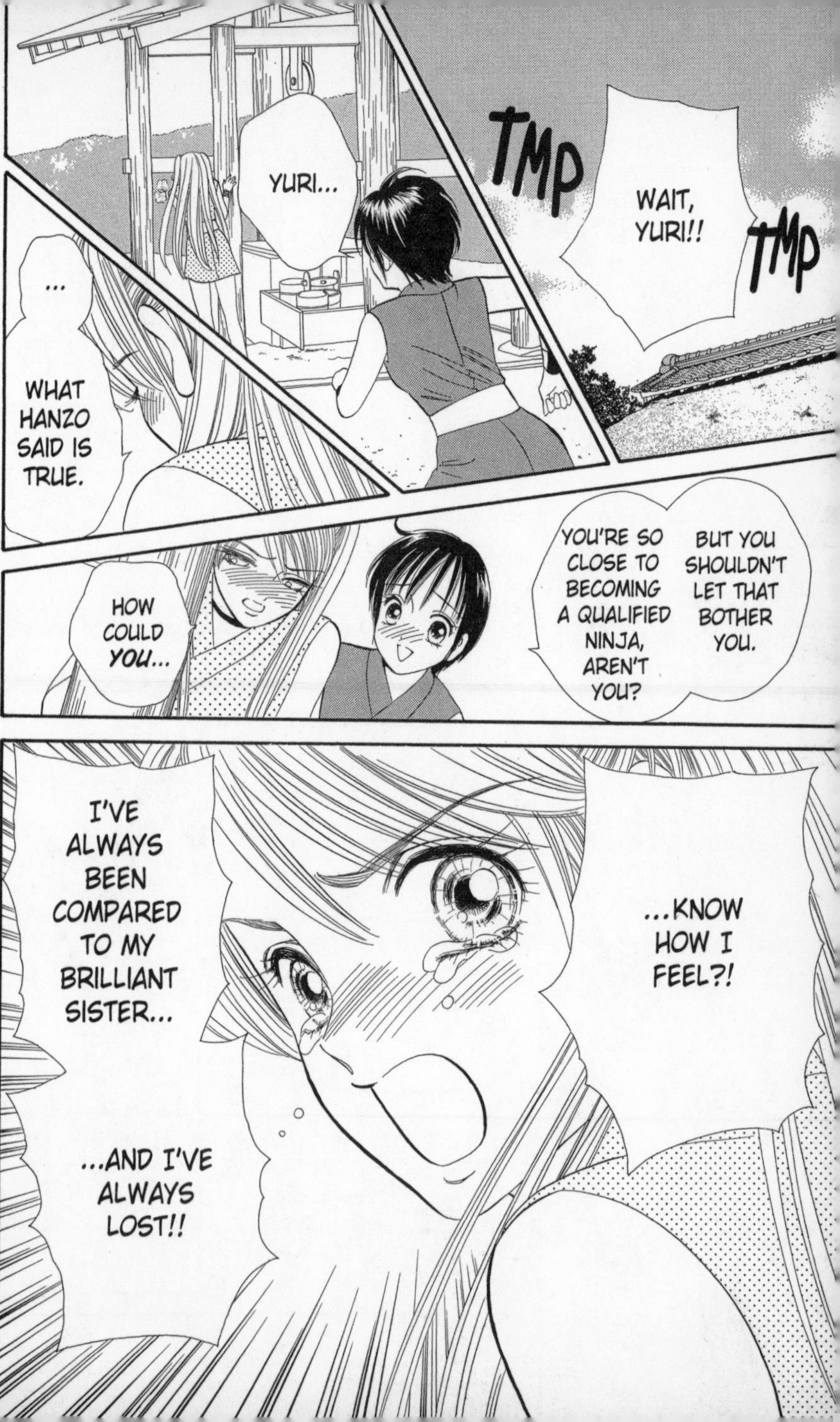
TMP
WAIT, YURI!!
TMP
YURI...
...
WHAT HANZO SAID IS TRUE.
BUT YOU SHOULDN'T LET THAT BOTHER YOU.
YOU'RE SO CLOSE TO BECOMING A QUALIFIED NINJA, AREN'T YOU?
HOW COULD *YOU*...
...KNOW HOW I FEEL?!
I'VE ALWAYS BEEN COMPARED TO MY BRILLIANT SISTER...
...AND I'VE ALWAYS LOST!!

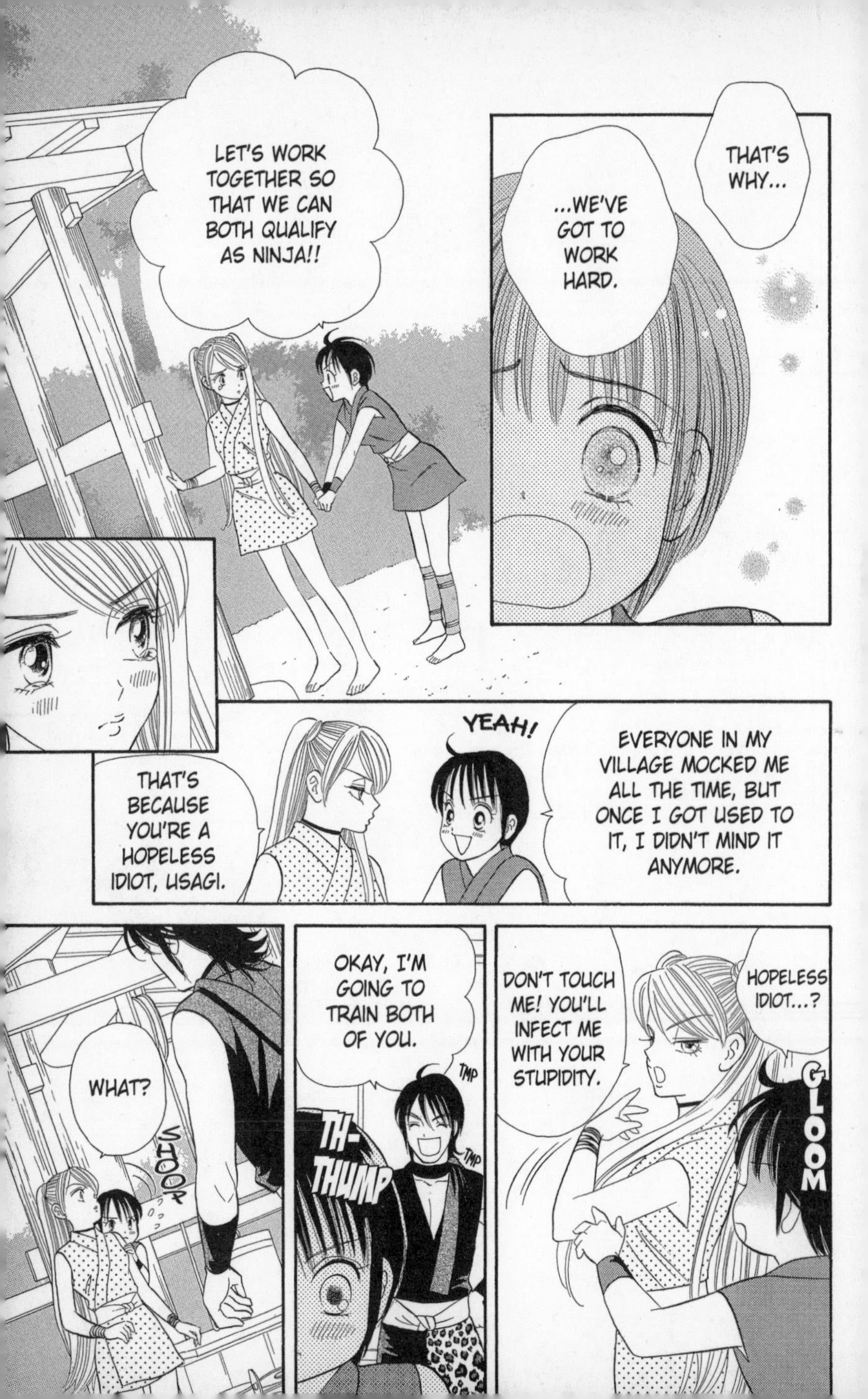
THAT'S WHY...
...WE'VE GOT TO WORK HARD.
LET'S WORK TOGETHER SO THAT WE CAN BOTH QUALIFY AS NINJA!!
YEAH!
EVERYONE IN MY VILLAGE MOCKED ME ALL THE TIME, BUT ONCE I GOT USED TO IT, I DIDN'T MIND IT ANYMORE.
THAT'S BECAUSE YOU'RE A HOPELESS IDIOT, USAGI.
HOPELESS IDIOT...?
GLOOM
DON'T TOUCH ME! YOU'LL INFECT ME WITH YOUR STUPIDITY.
OKAY, I'M GOING TO TRAIN BOTH OF YOU.
TMP
TMP
TH-THUMP
WHAT?
SHOOP

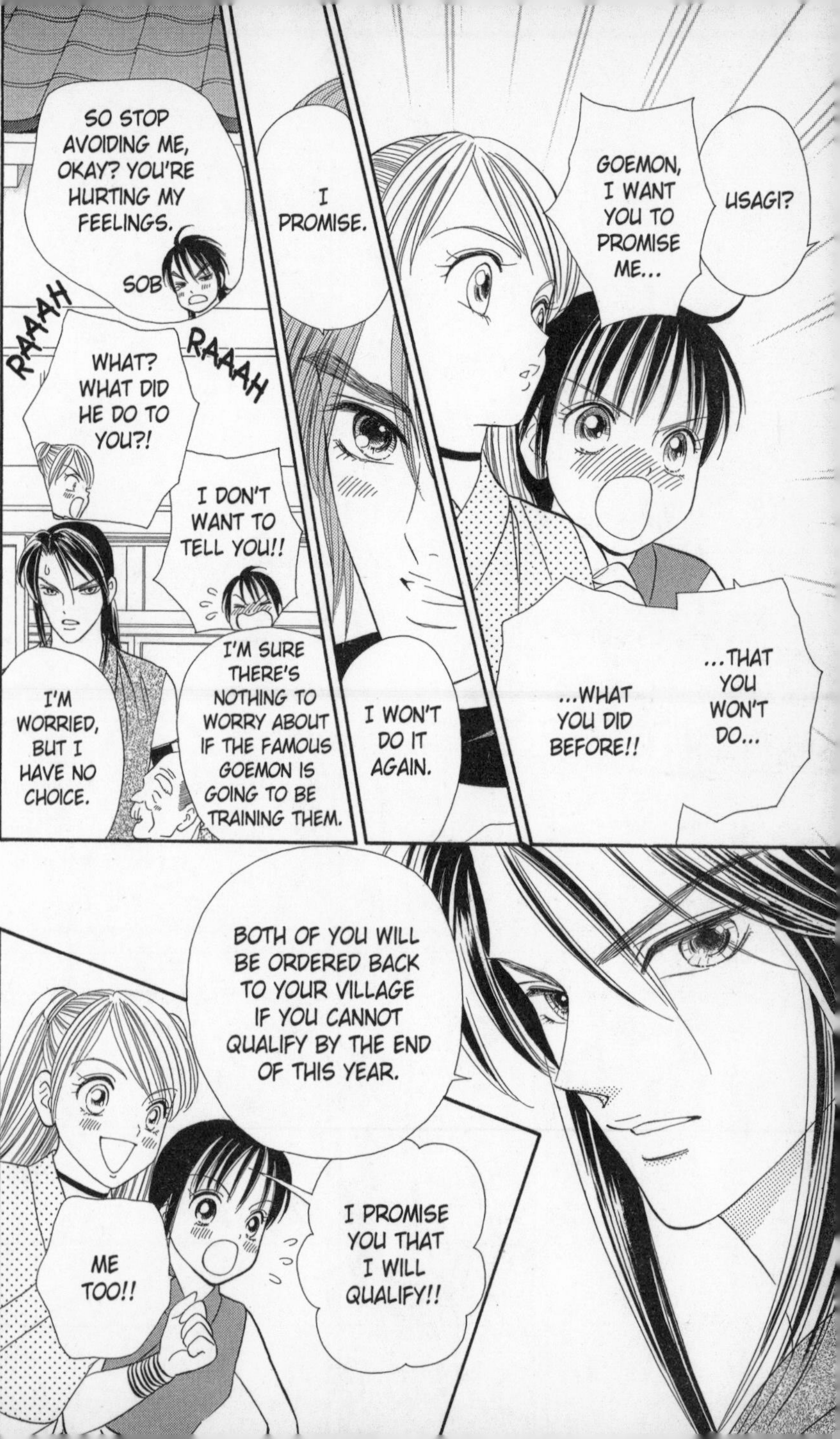
USAGI?
GOEMON, I WANT YOU TO PROMISE ME...
...THAT YOU WON'T DO...
...WHAT YOU DID BEFORE!!
I PROMISE.
I WON'T DO IT AGAIN.
SO STOP AVOIDING ME, OKAY? YOU'RE HURTING MY FEELINGS.
SOB
RAAAH
RAAAH
WHAT? WHAT DID HE DO TO YOU?!
I DON'T WANT TO TELL YOU!!
I'M SURE THERE'S NOTHING TO WORRY ABOUT IF THE FAMOUS GOEMON IS GOING TO BE TRAINING THEM.
I'M WORRIED, BUT I HAVE NO CHOICE.
BOTH OF YOU WILL BE ORDERED BACK TO YOUR VILLAGE IF YOU CANNOT QUALIFY BY THE END OF THIS YEAR.
I PROMISE YOU THAT I WILL QUALIFY!!
ME TOO!!

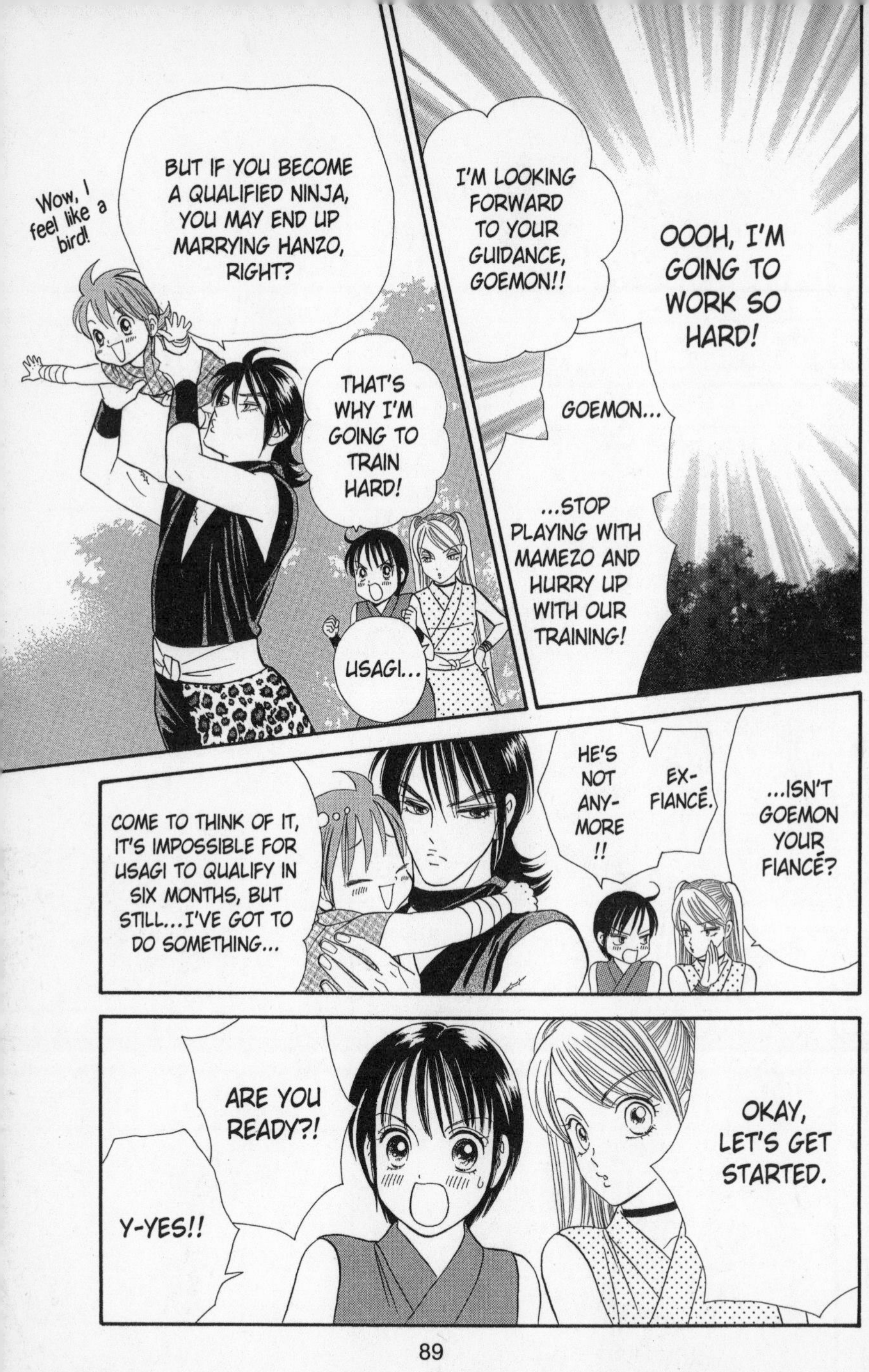
I'M LOOKING FORWARD TO YOUR GUIDANCE, GOEMON!!
OOOH, I'M GOING TO WORK SO HARD!
GOEMON...
...STOP PLAYING WITH MAMEZO AND HURRY UP WITH OUR TRAINING!
BUT IF YOU BECOME A QUALIFIED NINJA, YOU MAY END UP MARRYING HANZO, RIGHT?
Wow, I feel like a bird!
THAT'S WHY I'M GOING TO TRAIN HARD!
USAGI...
...ISN'T GOEMON YOUR FIANCÉ?
EX-FIANCÉ.
HE'S NOT ANY-MORE!!
COME TO THINK OF IT, IT'S IMPOSSIBLE FOR USAGI TO QUALIFY IN SIX MONTHS, BUT STILL...I'VE GOT TO DO SOMETHING...
OKAY, LET'S GET STARTED.
ARE YOU READY?!
Y-YES!!

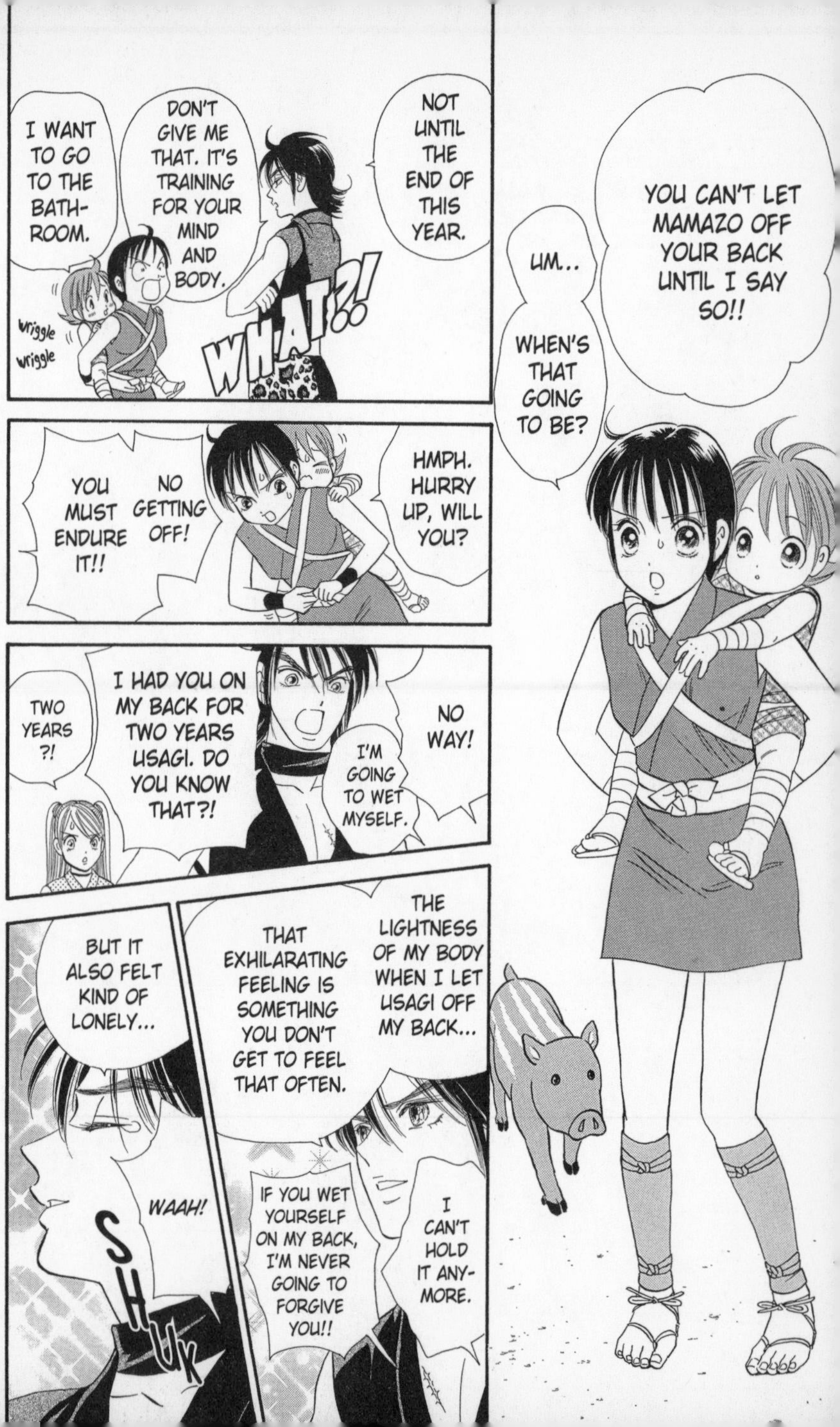

YOU CAN'T LET MAMAZO OFF YOUR BACK UNTIL I SAY SO!!
UM...
WHEN'S THAT GOING TO BE?
NOT UNTIL THE END OF THIS YEAR.
WHAT?!
DON'T GIVE ME THAT. IT'S TRAINING FOR YOUR MIND AND BODY.
I WANT TO GO TO THE BATHROOM.
wriggle wriggle
HMPH. HURRY UP, WILL YOU?
NO GETTING OFF!
YOU MUST ENDURE IT!!
NO WAY!
I'M GOING TO WET MYSELF.
I HAD YOU ON MY BACK FOR TWO YEARS USAGI. DO YOU KNOW THAT?!
TWO YEARS ?!
THE LIGHTNESS OF MY BODY WHEN I LET USAGI OFF MY BACK...
THAT EXHILARATING FEELING IS SOMETHING YOU DON'T GET TO FEEL THAT OFTEN.
I CAN'T HOLD IT ANY-MORE.
IF YOU WET YOURSELF ON MY BACK, I'M NEVER GOING TO FORGIVE YOU!!
BUT IT ALSO FELT KIND OF LONELY...
WAAH!
SHUK

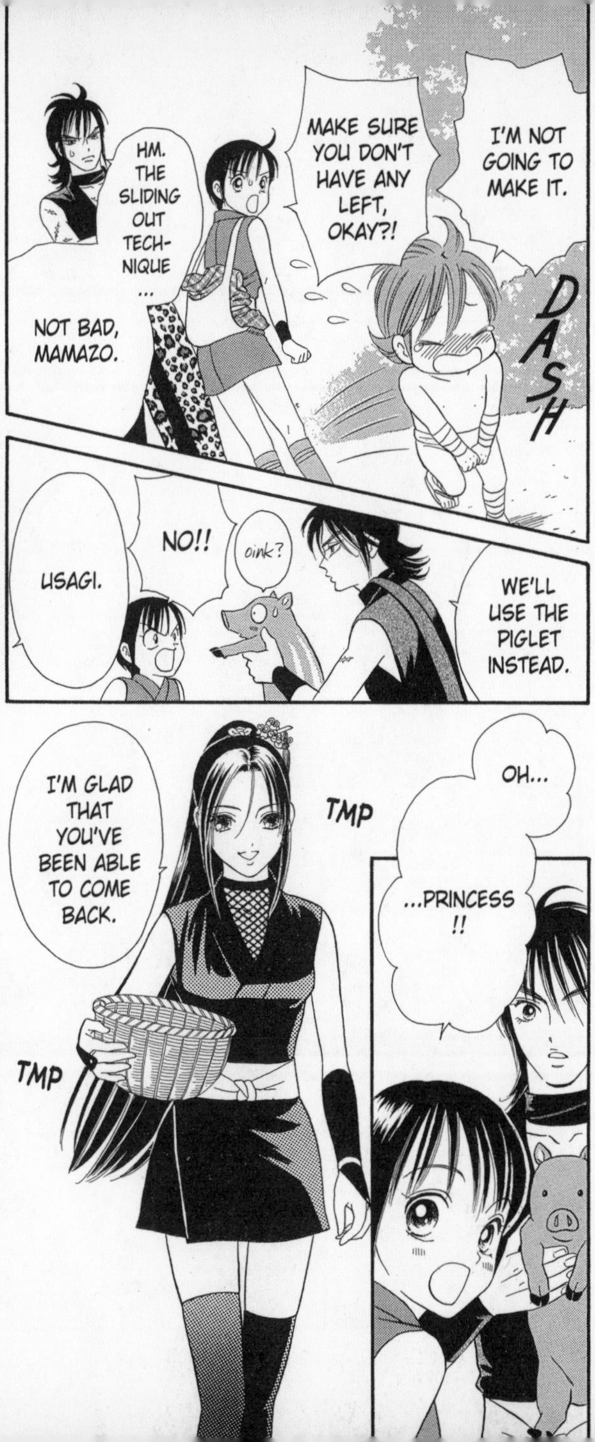
I'M NOT GOING TO MAKE IT.
DASH
MAKE SURE YOU DON'T HAVE ANY LEFT, OKAY?!
HM. THE SLIDING OUT TECHNIQUE ...
NOT BAD, MAMAZO.
WE'LL USE THE PIGLET INSTEAD.
oink?
NO!!
USAGI.
OH...
...PRINCESS !!
TMP
I'M GLAD THAT YOU'VE BEEN ABLE TO COME BACK.
TMP

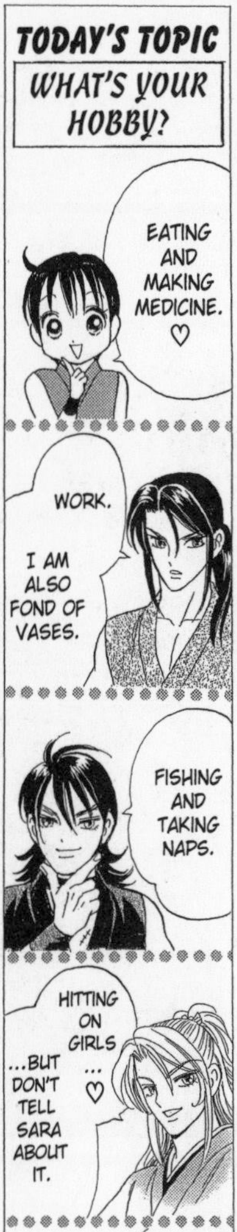
TODAY'S TOPIC
WHAT'S YOUR HOBBY?
EATING AND MAKING MEDICINE. ♡
WORK.
I AM ALSO FOND OF VASES.
FISHING AND TAKING NAPS.
HITTING ON GIRLS ... ♡
...BUT DON'T TELL SARA ABOUT IT.
PLAYING WITH MY PIGLET.

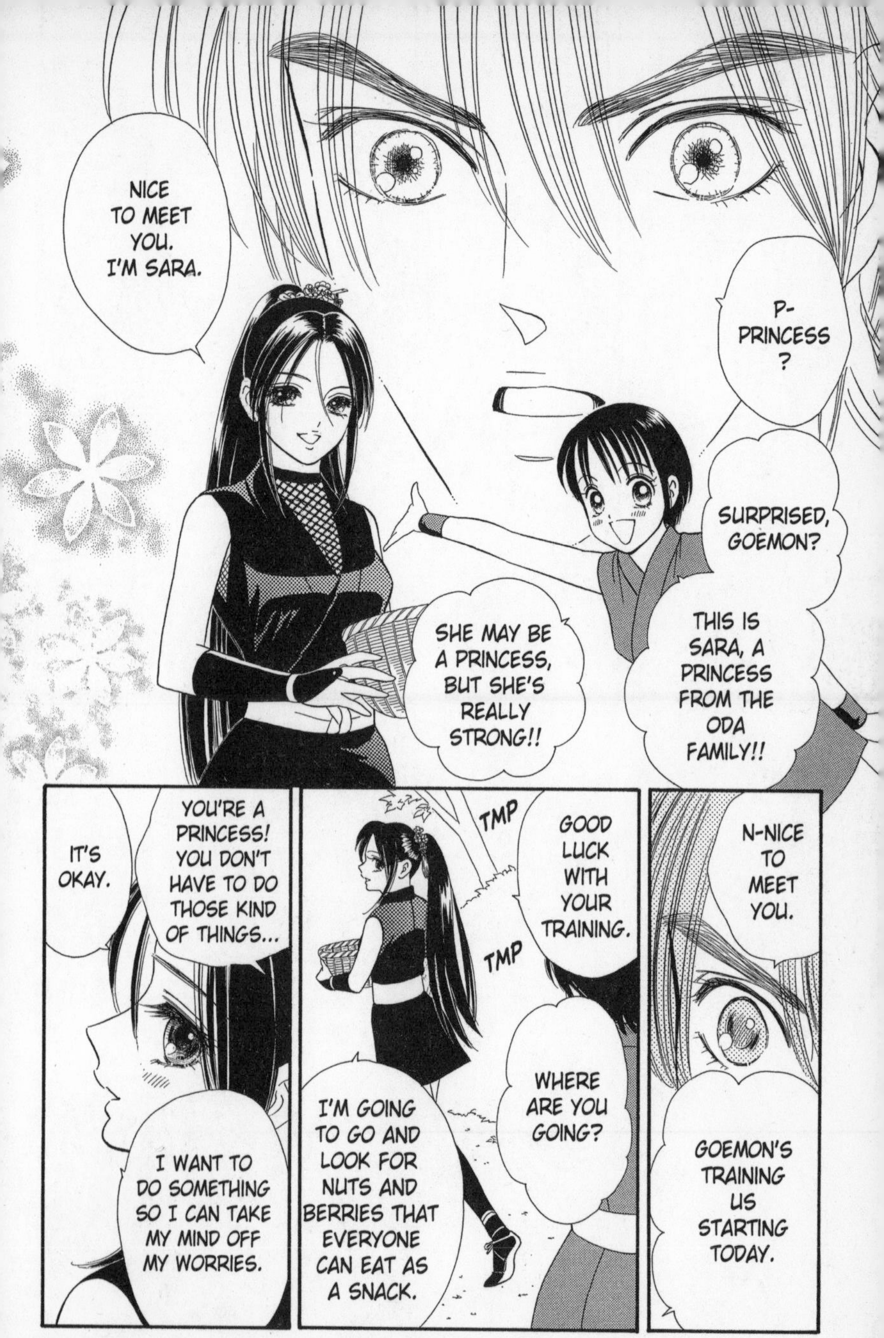
P-PRINCESS?
SURPRISED, GOEMON?
THIS IS SARA, A PRINCESS FROM THE ODA FAMILY!!
SHE MAY BE A PRINCESS, BUT SHE'S REALLY STRONG!!
NICE TO MEET YOU. I'M SARA.
N-NICE TO MEET YOU.
GOEMON'S TRAINING US STARTING TODAY.
GOOD LUCK WITH YOUR TRAINING.
TMP
TMP
WHERE ARE YOU GOING?
I'M GOING TO GO AND LOOK FOR NUTS AND BERRIES THAT EVERYONE CAN EAT AS A SNACK.
YOU'RE A PRINCESS! YOU DON'T HAVE TO DO THOSE KIND OF THINGS...
IT'S OKAY.
I WANT TO DO SOMETHING SO I CAN TAKE MY MIND OFF MY WORRIES.

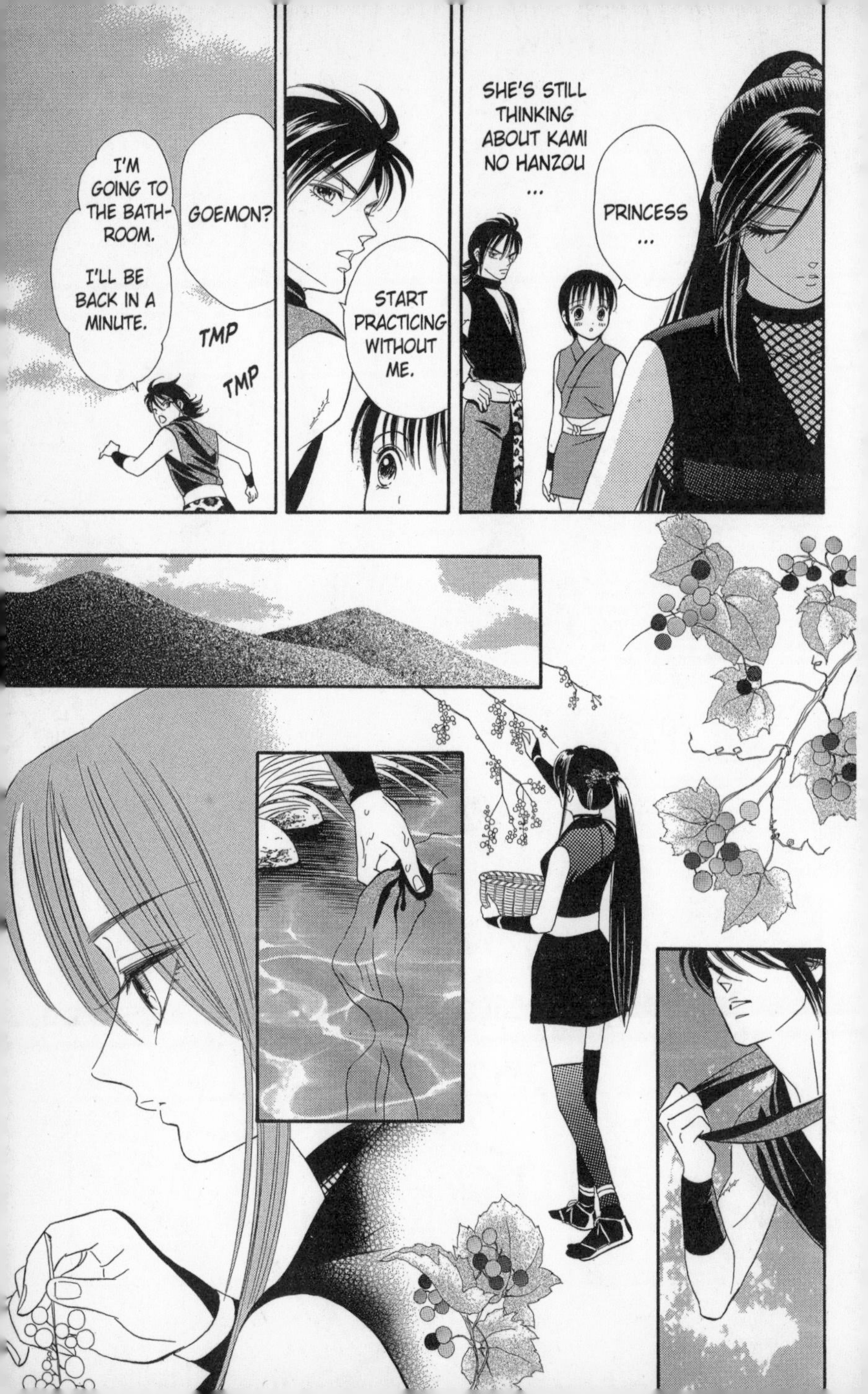
PRINCESS ...
SHE'S STILL THINKING ABOUT KAMI NO HANZOU ...
START PRACTICING WITHOUT ME.
GOEMON?
I'M GOING TO THE BATH-ROOM.
I'LL BE BACK IN A MINUTE.
TMP
TMP

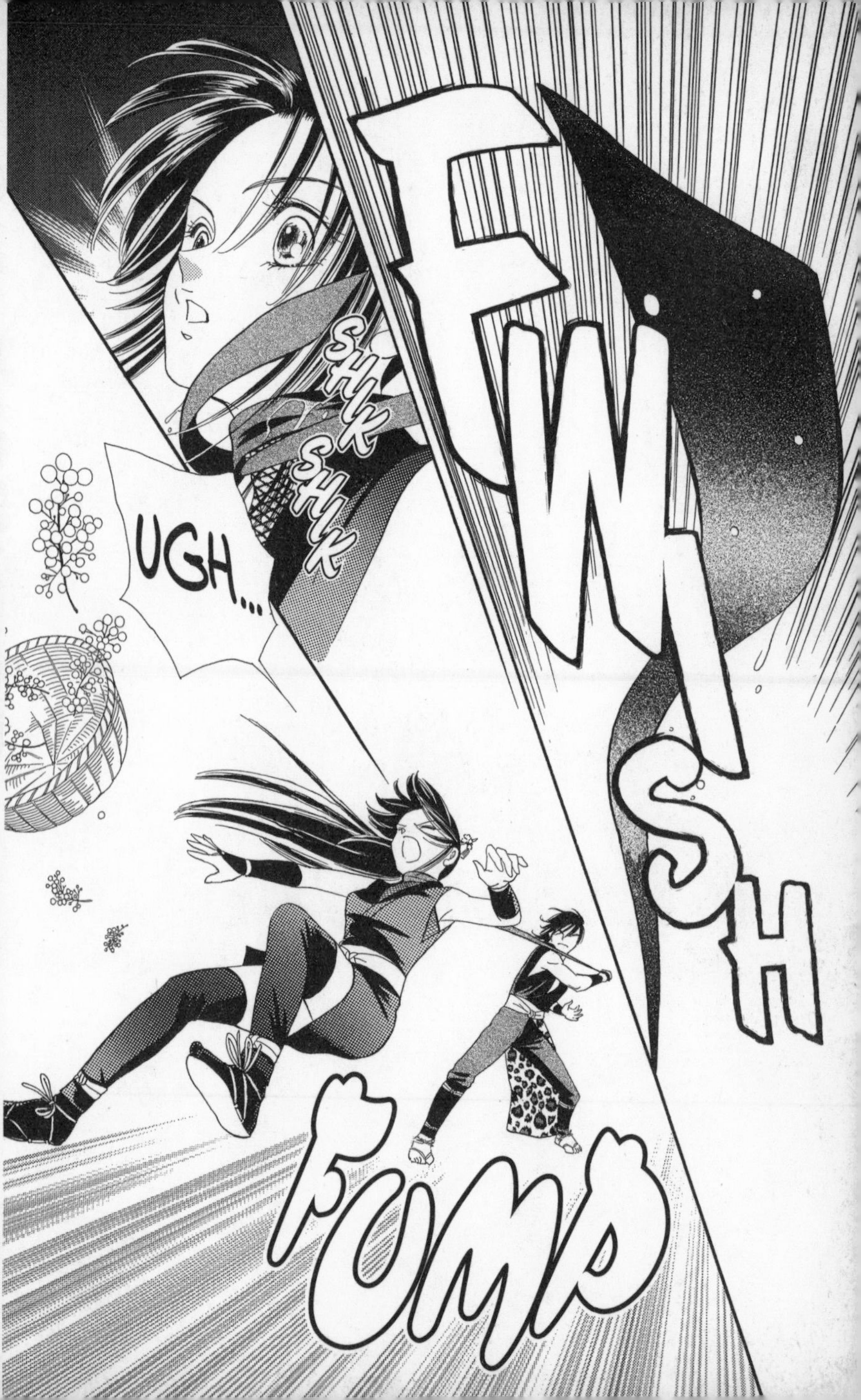
FWISH
SHIK SHIK
UGH...
FUMP

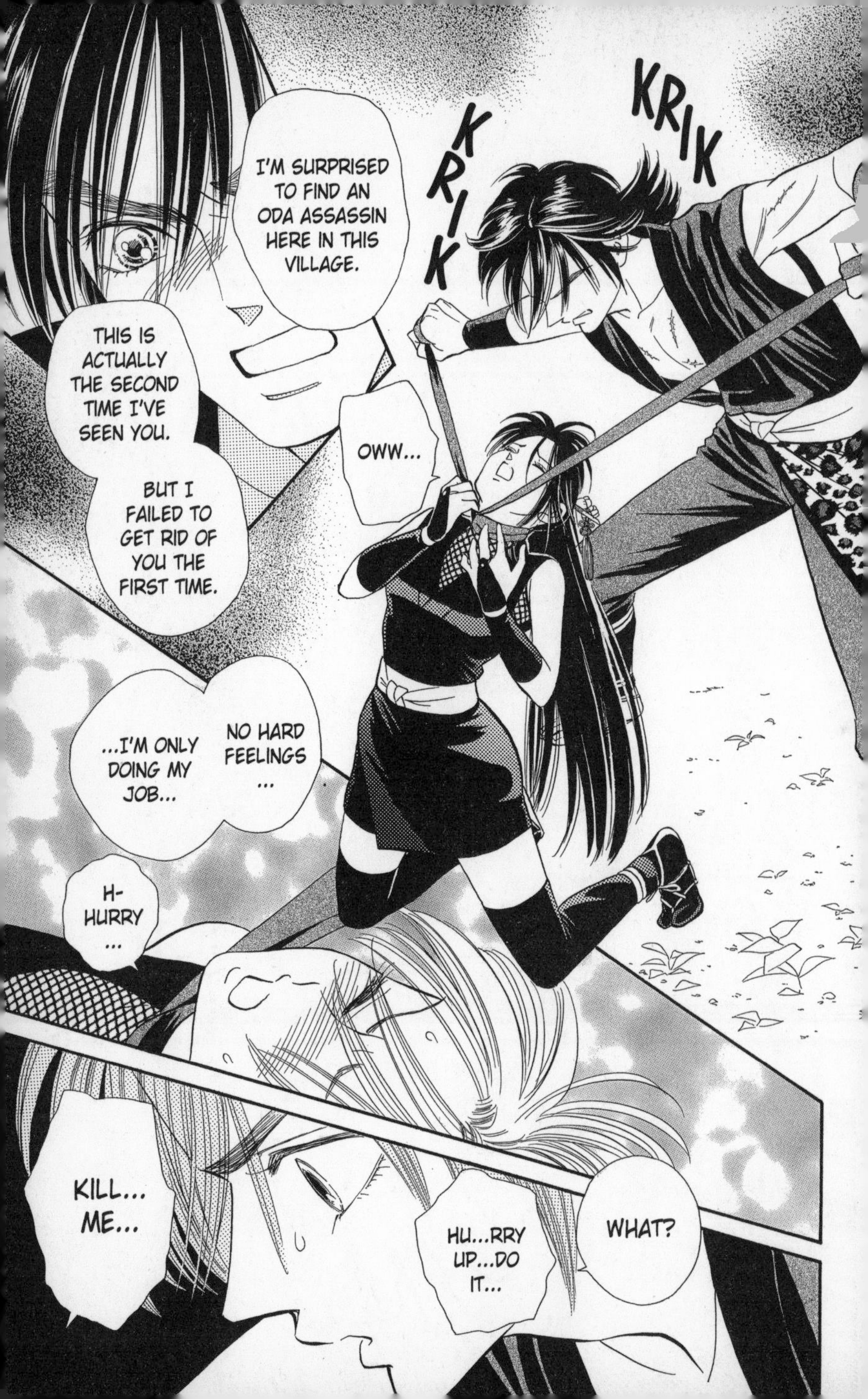
KRIK
KRIK
I'M SURPRISED TO FIND AN ODA ASSASSIN HERE IN THIS VILLAGE.
THIS IS ACTUALLY THE SECOND TIME I'VE SEEN YOU.
OWW...
BUT I FAILED TO GET RID OF YOU THE FIRST TIME.
NO HARD FEELINGS ...
...I'M ONLY DOING MY JOB...
H-HURRY ...
WHAT?
HU...RRY UP...DO IT...
KILL... ME...

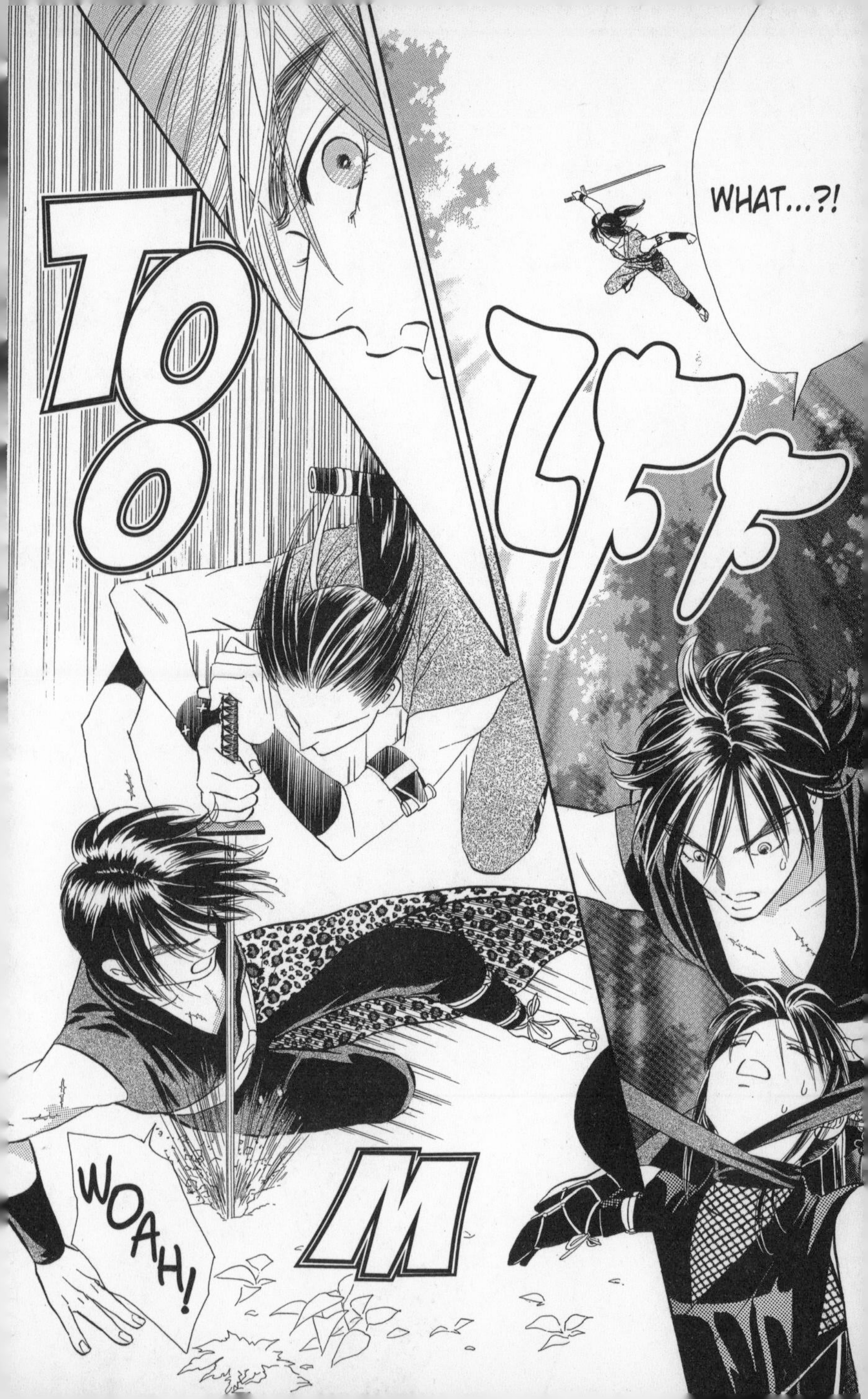
WHAT...?!
TOO
M
WOAH!

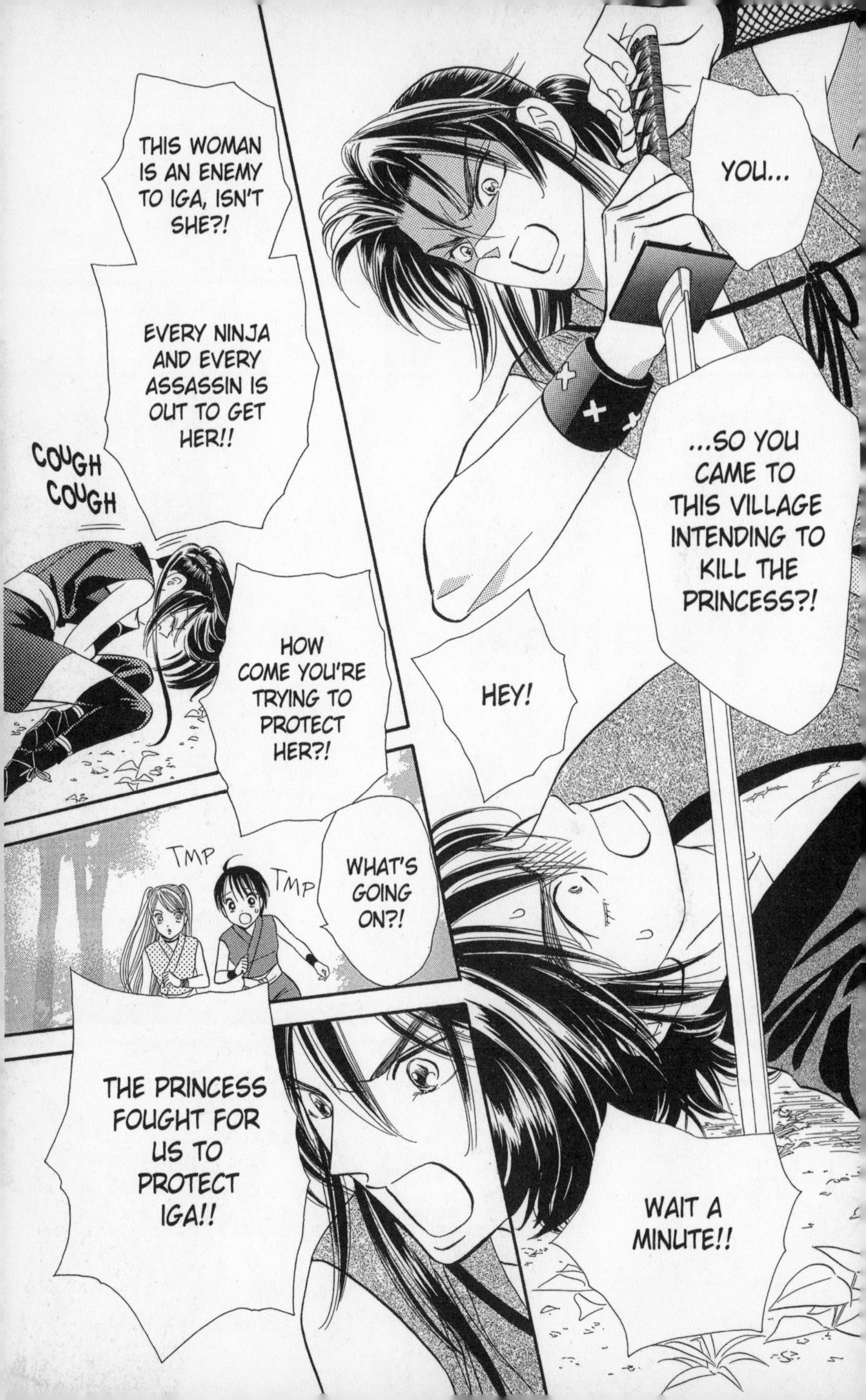
YOU...
...SO YOU CAME TO THIS VILLAGE INTENDING TO KILL THE PRINCESS?!
THIS WOMAN IS AN ENEMY TO IGA, ISN'T SHE?!
EVERY NINJA AND EVERY ASSASSIN IS OUT TO GET HER!!
COUGH COUGH
HOW COME YOU'RE TRYING TO PROTECT HER?!
HEY!
TMP
TMP
WHAT'S GOING ON?!
WAIT A MINUTE!!
THE PRINCESS FOUGHT FOR US TO PROTECT IGA!!

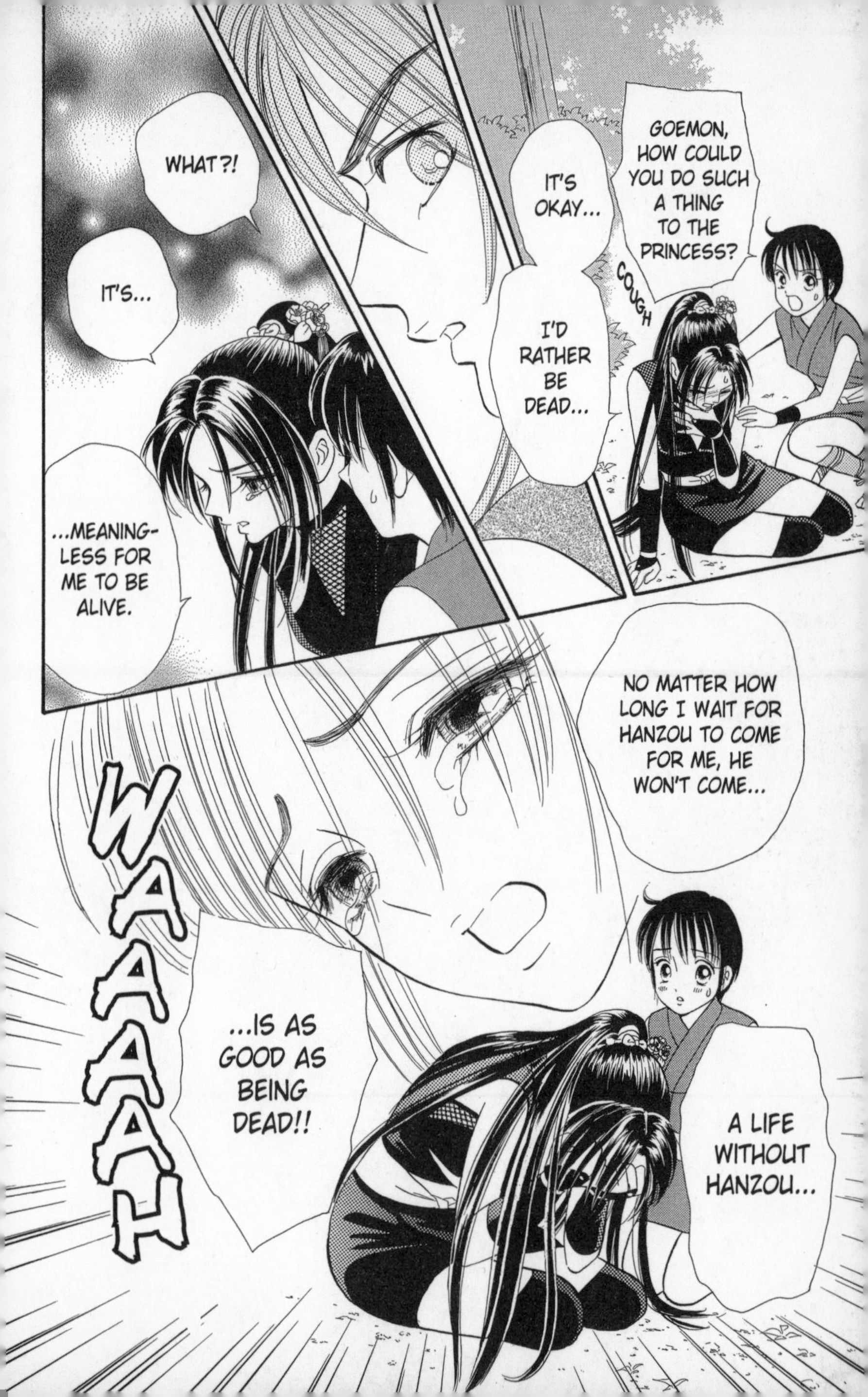
GOEMON, HOW COULD YOU DO SUCH A THING TO THE PRINCESS?
COUGH
IT'S OKAY...
I'D RATHER BE DEAD...
WHAT?!
IT'S...
...MEANING-LESS FOR ME TO BE ALIVE.
NO MATTER HOW LONG I WAIT FOR HANZOU TO COME FOR ME, HE WON'T COME...
A LIFE WITHOUT HANZOU...
...IS AS GOOD AS BEING DEAD!!
WAAAAH

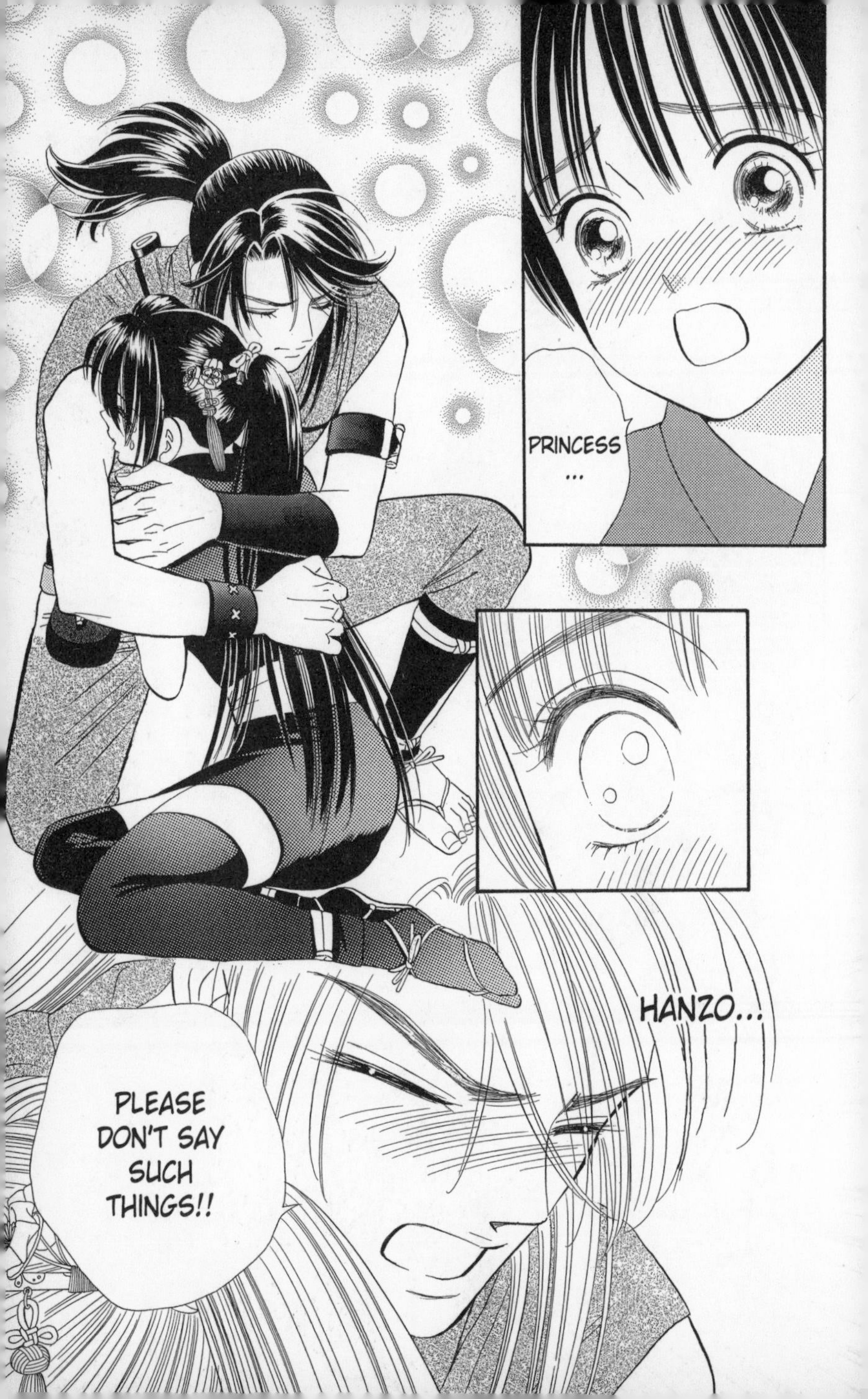
PRINCESS ...
HANZO...
PLEASE DON'T SAY SUCH THINGS!!

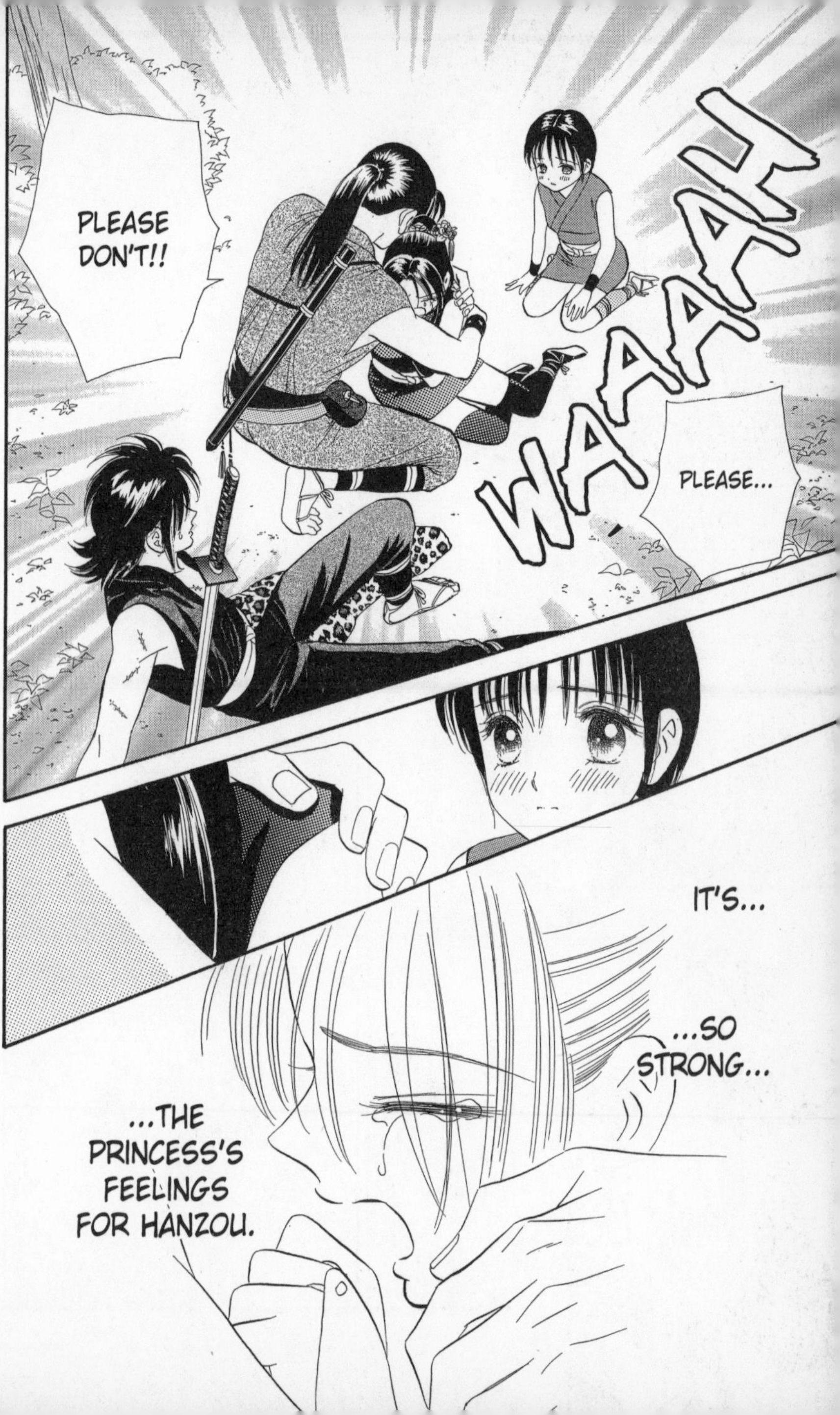
WAAAH
PLEASE...
PLEASE DON'T!!
IT'S...
...SO STRONG...
...THE PRINCESS'S FEELINGS FOR HANZOU.

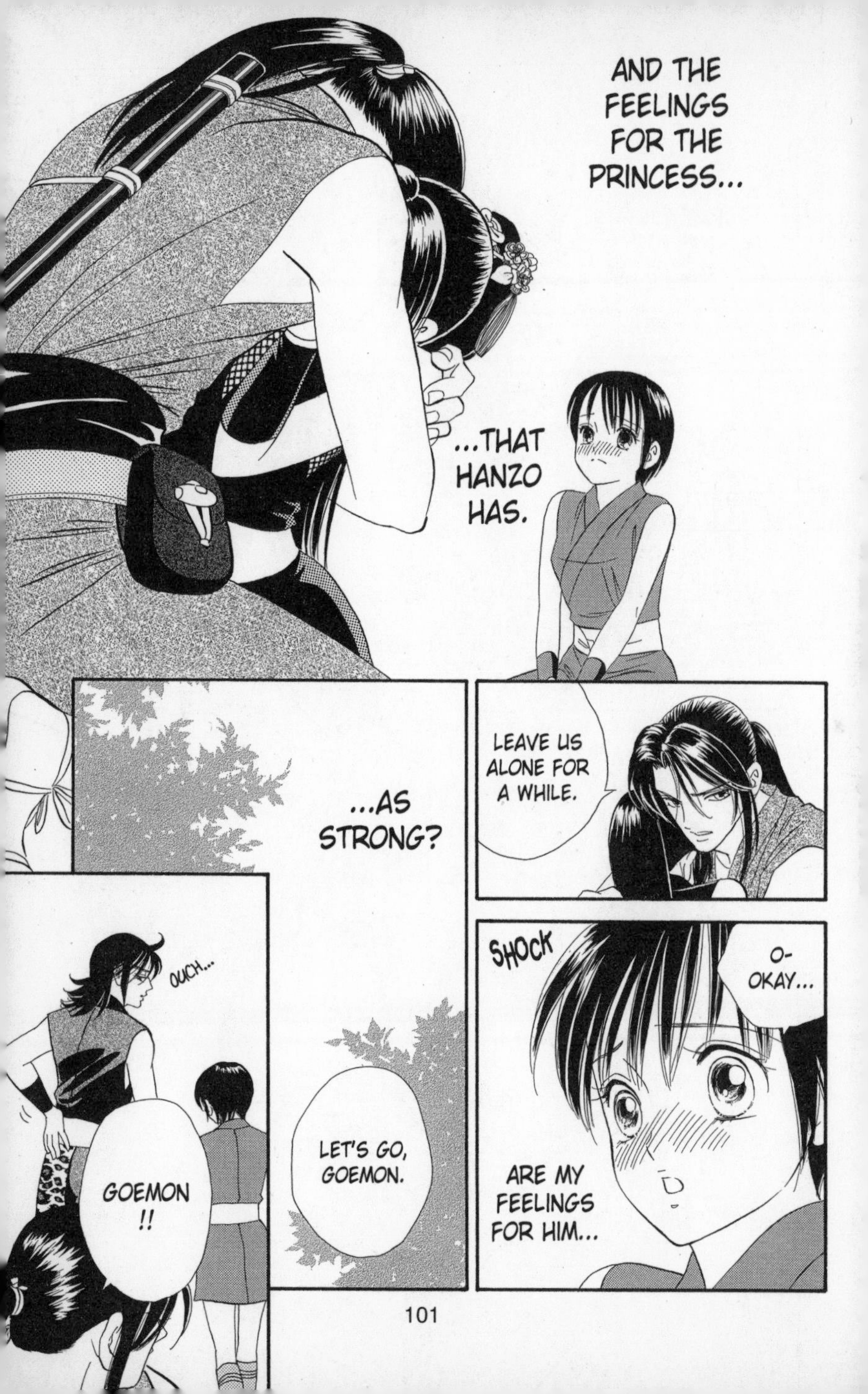
AND THE FEELINGS FOR THE PRINCESS...
...THAT HANZO HAS.
LEAVE US ALONE FOR A WHILE.
SHOCK
O-OKAY...
ARE MY FEELINGS FOR HIM...
...AS STRONG?
LET'S GO, GOEMON.
OUCH...
GOEMON !!

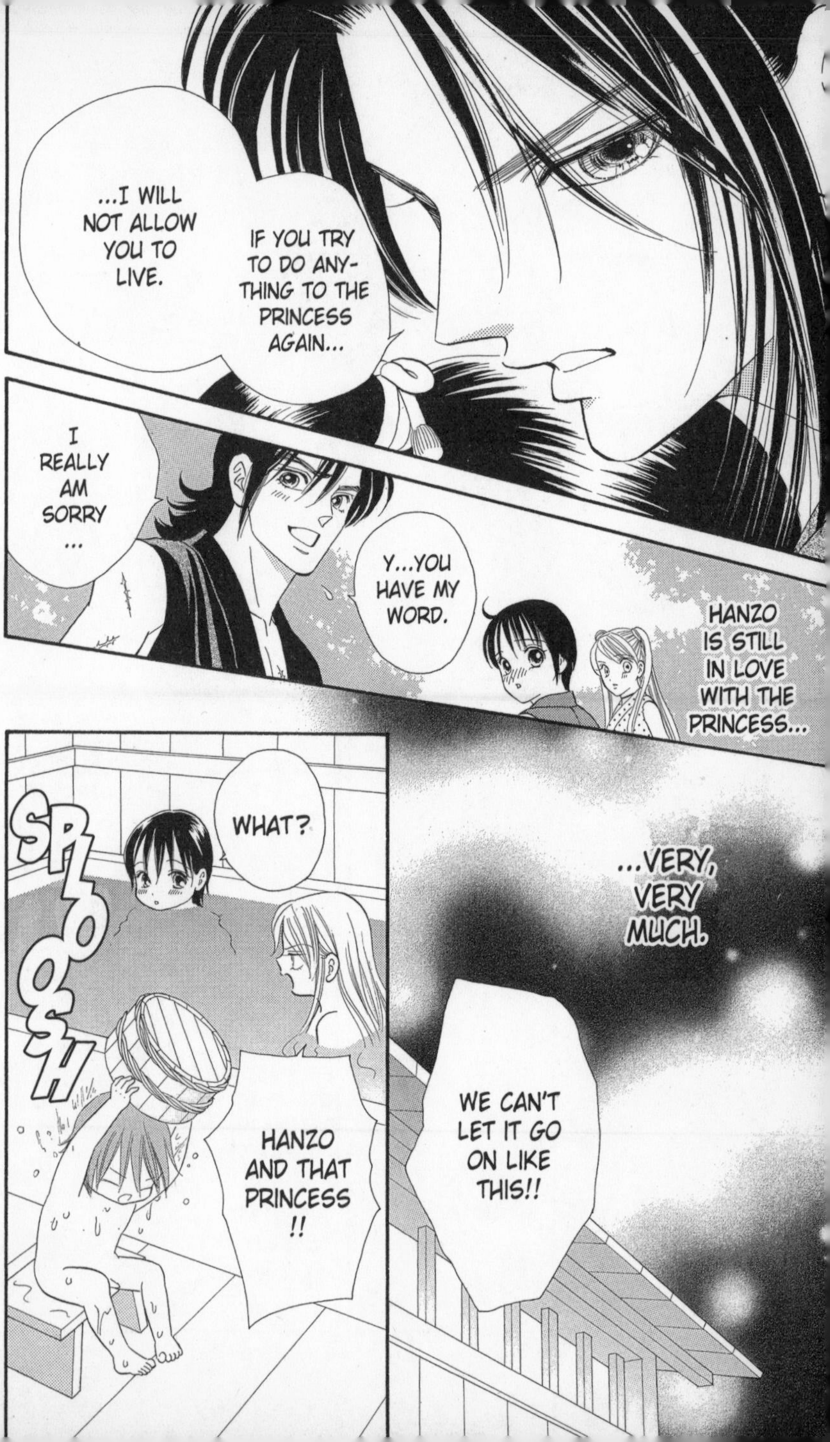

IF YOU TRY TO DO ANYTHING TO THE PRINCESS AGAIN...
...I WILL NOT ALLOW YOU TO LIVE.
I REALLY AM SORRY...
Y...YOU HAVE MY WORD.
HANZO IS STILL IN LOVE WITH THE PRINCESS...
...VERY, VERY MUCH.
SPLOOSH
HANZO AND THAT PRINCESS!!
WE CAN'T LET IT GO ON LIKE THIS!!
WHAT?

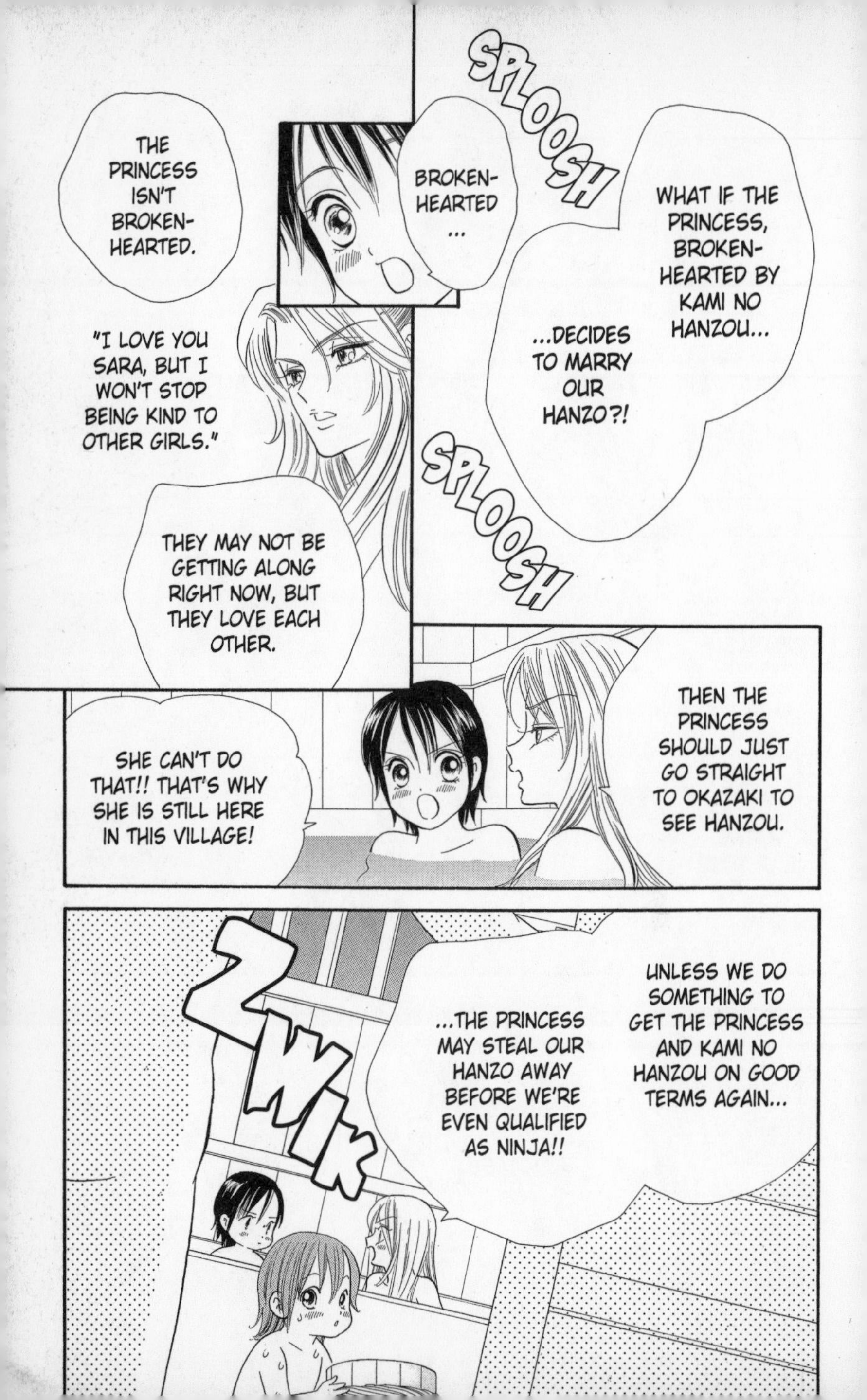
SPLOOSH
WHAT IF THE PRINCESS, BROKEN-HEARTED BY KAMI NO HANZOU...
...DECIDES TO MARRY OUR HANZO?!
SPLOOSH
BROKEN-HEARTED...
THE PRINCESS ISN'T BROKEN-HEARTED.
"I LOVE YOU SARA, BUT I WON'T STOP BEING KIND TO OTHER GIRLS."
THEY MAY NOT BE GETTING ALONG RIGHT NOW, BUT THEY LOVE EACH OTHER.
THEN THE PRINCESS SHOULD JUST GO STRAIGHT TO OKAZAKI TO SEE HANZOU.
SHE CAN'T DO THAT!! THAT'S WHY SHE IS STILL HERE IN THIS VILLAGE!
UNLESS WE DO SOMETHING TO GET THE PRINCESS AND KAMI NO HANZOU ON GOOD TERMS AGAIN...
...THE PRINCESS MAY STEAL OUR HANZO AWAY BEFORE WE'RE EVEN QUALIFIED AS NINJA!!
ZWIK

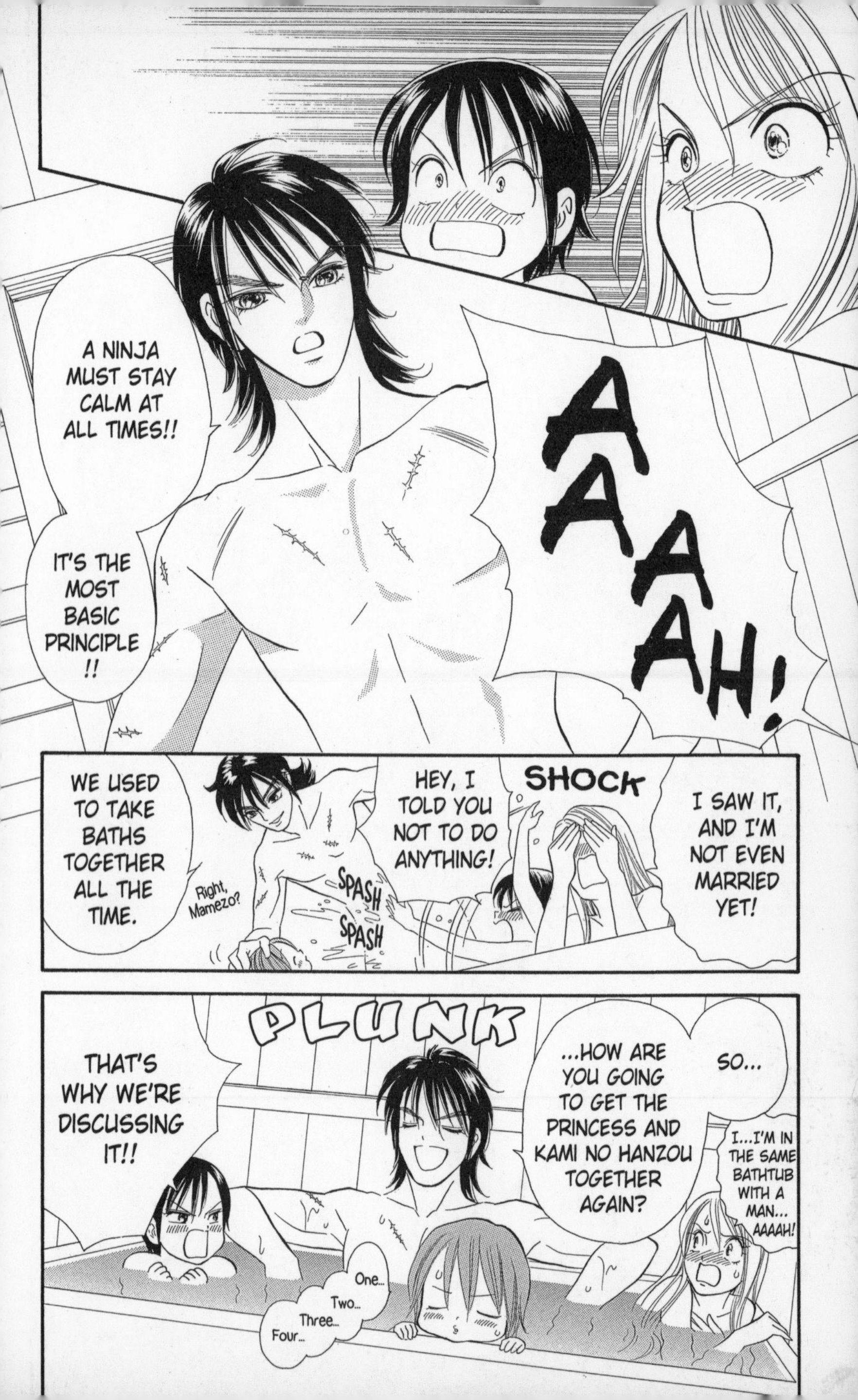
AAAAH!
A NINJA MUST STAY CALM AT ALL TIMES!!
IT'S THE MOST BASIC PRINCIPLE !!
I SAW IT, AND I'M NOT EVEN MARRIED YET!
SHOCK
HEY, I TOLD YOU NOT TO DO ANYTHING!
SPASH SPASH
Right, Mamezo?
WE USED TO TAKE BATHS TOGETHER ALL THE TIME.
SO...
...HOW ARE YOU GOING TO GET THE PRINCESS AND KAMI NO HANZOU TOGETHER AGAIN?
PLUNK
THAT'S WHY WE'RE DISCUSSING IT!!
I...I'M IN THE SAME BATHTUB WITH A MAN... AAAAH!
One... Two... Three... Four...

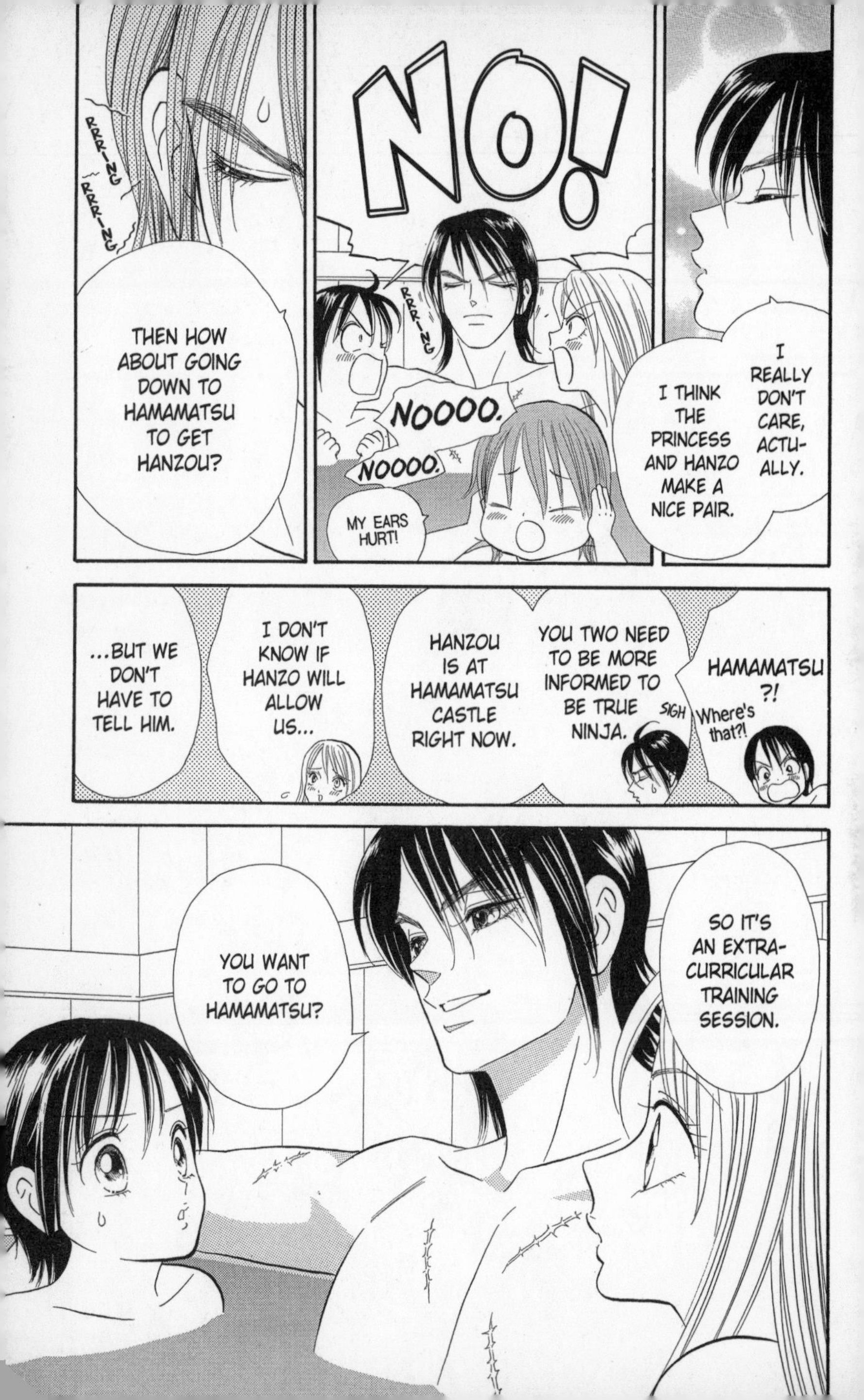
I REALLY DON'T CARE, ACTUALLY.
I THINK THE PRINCESS AND HANZO MAKE A NICE PAIR.
NO!
RRRING
NOOOO.
NOOOO.
MY EARS HURT!
RRRING RRRING
THEN HOW ABOUT GOING DOWN TO HAMAMATSU TO GET HANZOU?
HAMAMATSU?!
Where's that?!
SIGH
YOU TWO NEED TO BE MORE INFORMED TO BE TRUE NINJA.
HANZOU IS AT HAMAMATSU CASTLE RIGHT NOW.
I DON'T KNOW IF HANZO WILL ALLOW US...
...BUT WE DON'T HAVE TO TELL HIM.
SO IT'S AN EXTRA-CURRICULAR TRAINING SESSION.
YOU WANT TO GO TO HAMAMATSU?

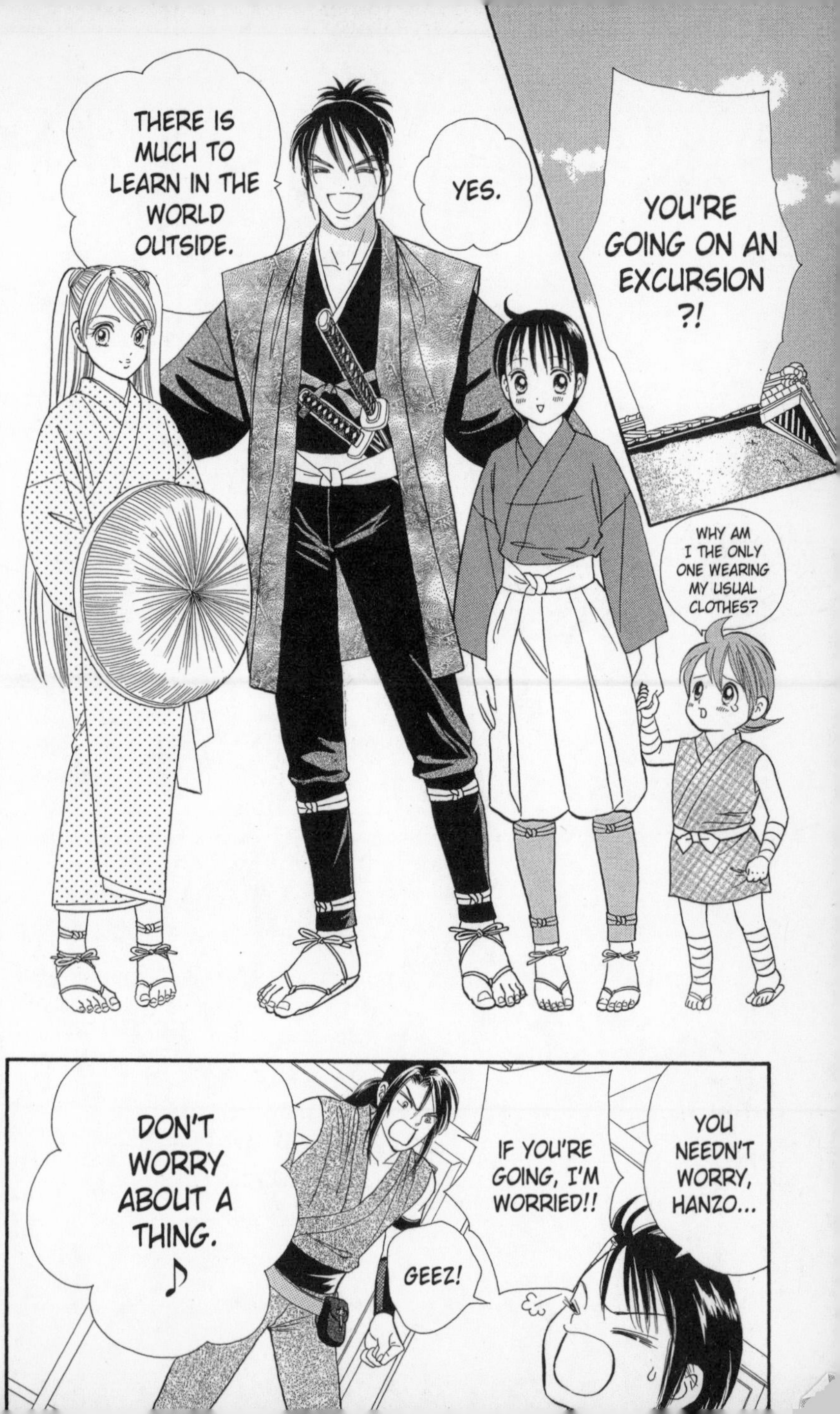
YOU'RE GOING ON AN EXCURSION ?!
THERE IS MUCH TO LEARN IN THE WORLD OUTSIDE.
YES.
WHY AM I THE ONLY ONE WEARING MY USUAL CLOTHES?
YOU NEEDN'T WORRY, HANZO...
IF YOU'RE GOING, I'M WORRIED!!
GEEZ!
DON'T WORRY ABOUT A THING. ♪

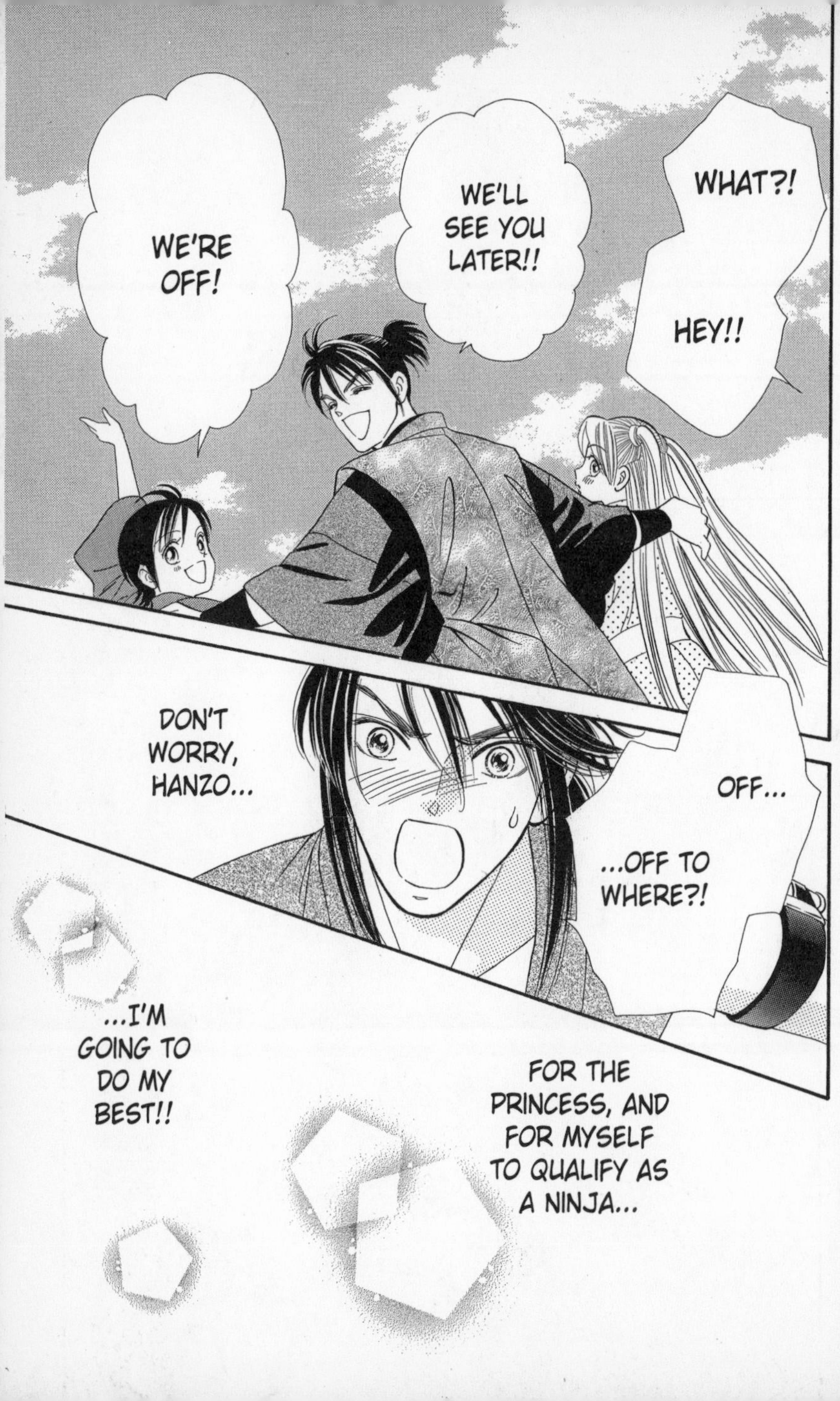
WHAT?!
HEY!!
WE'LL SEE YOU LATER!!
WE'RE OFF!
OFF...
...OFF TO WHERE?!
DON'T WORRY, HANZO...
FOR THE PRINCESS, AND FOR MYSELF TO QUALIFY AS A NINJA...
...I'M GOING TO DO MY BEST!!

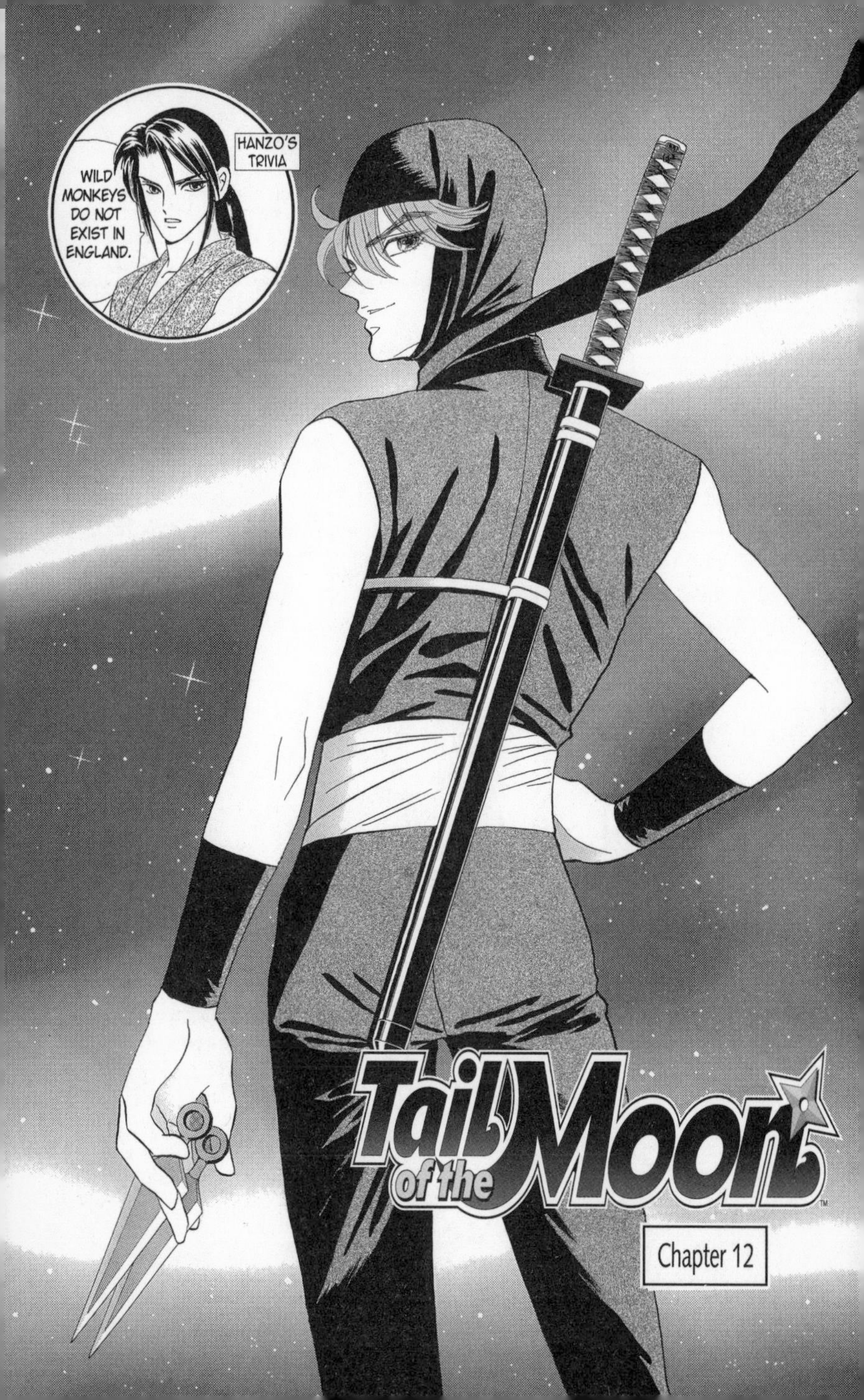
HANZO'S TRIVIA
WILD MONKEYS DO NOT EXIST IN ENGLAND.
Tail of the Moon™
Chapter 12

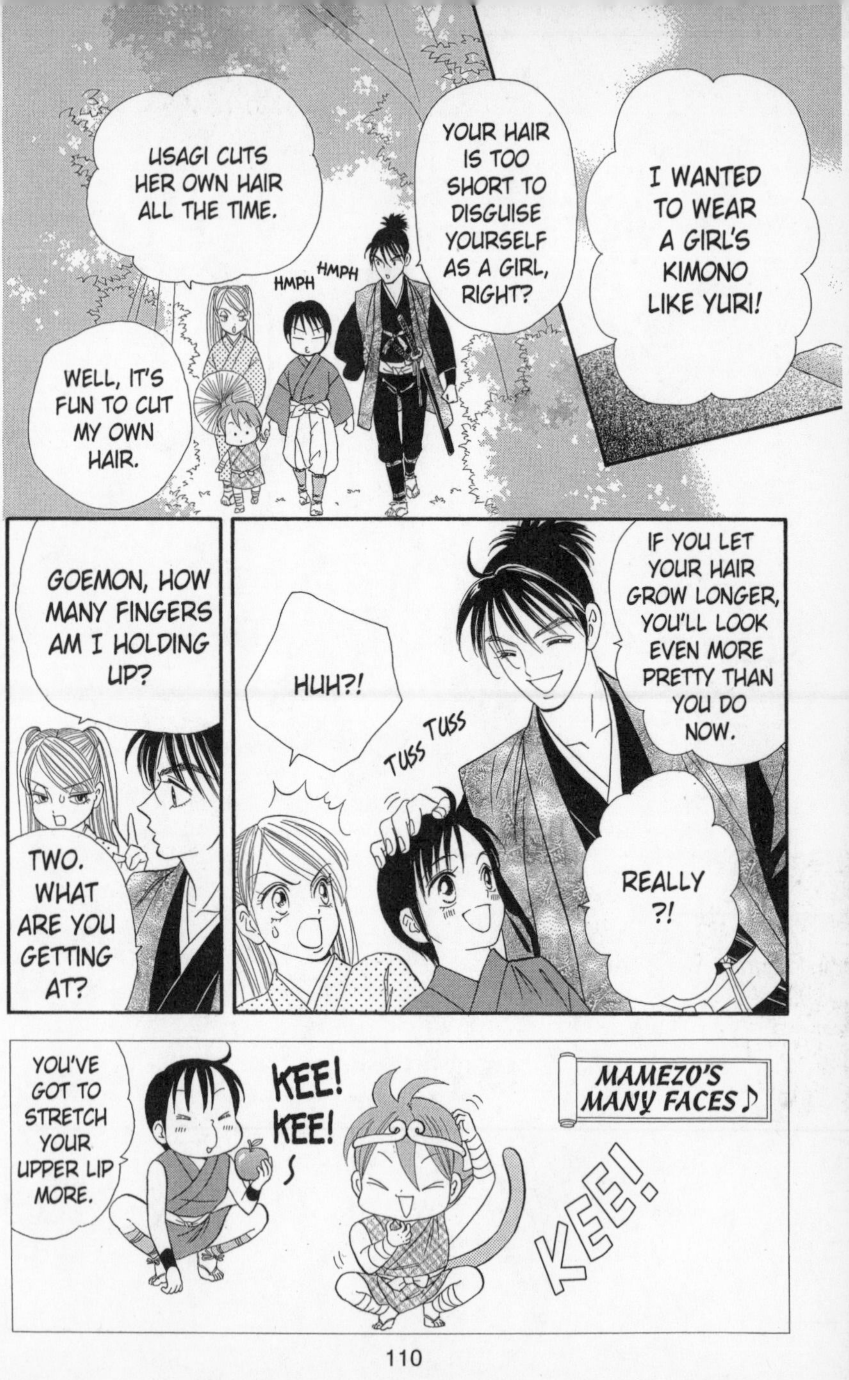
I WANTED TO WEAR A GIRL'S KIMONO LIKE YURI!
YOUR HAIR IS TOO SHORT TO DISGUISE YOURSELF AS A GIRL, RIGHT?
HMPH HMPH
USAGI CUTS HER OWN HAIR ALL THE TIME.
WELL, IT'S FUN TO CUT MY OWN HAIR.
IF YOU LET YOUR HAIR GROW LONGER, YOU'LL LOOK EVEN MORE PRETTY THAN YOU DO NOW.
TUSS TUSS
REALLY?!
HUH?!
GOEMON, HOW MANY FINGERS AM I HOLDING UP?
TWO. WHAT ARE YOU GETTING AT?
MAMEZO'S MANY FACES♪
KEE!
KEE! KEE!
YOU'VE GOT TO STRETCH YOUR UPPER LIP MORE.

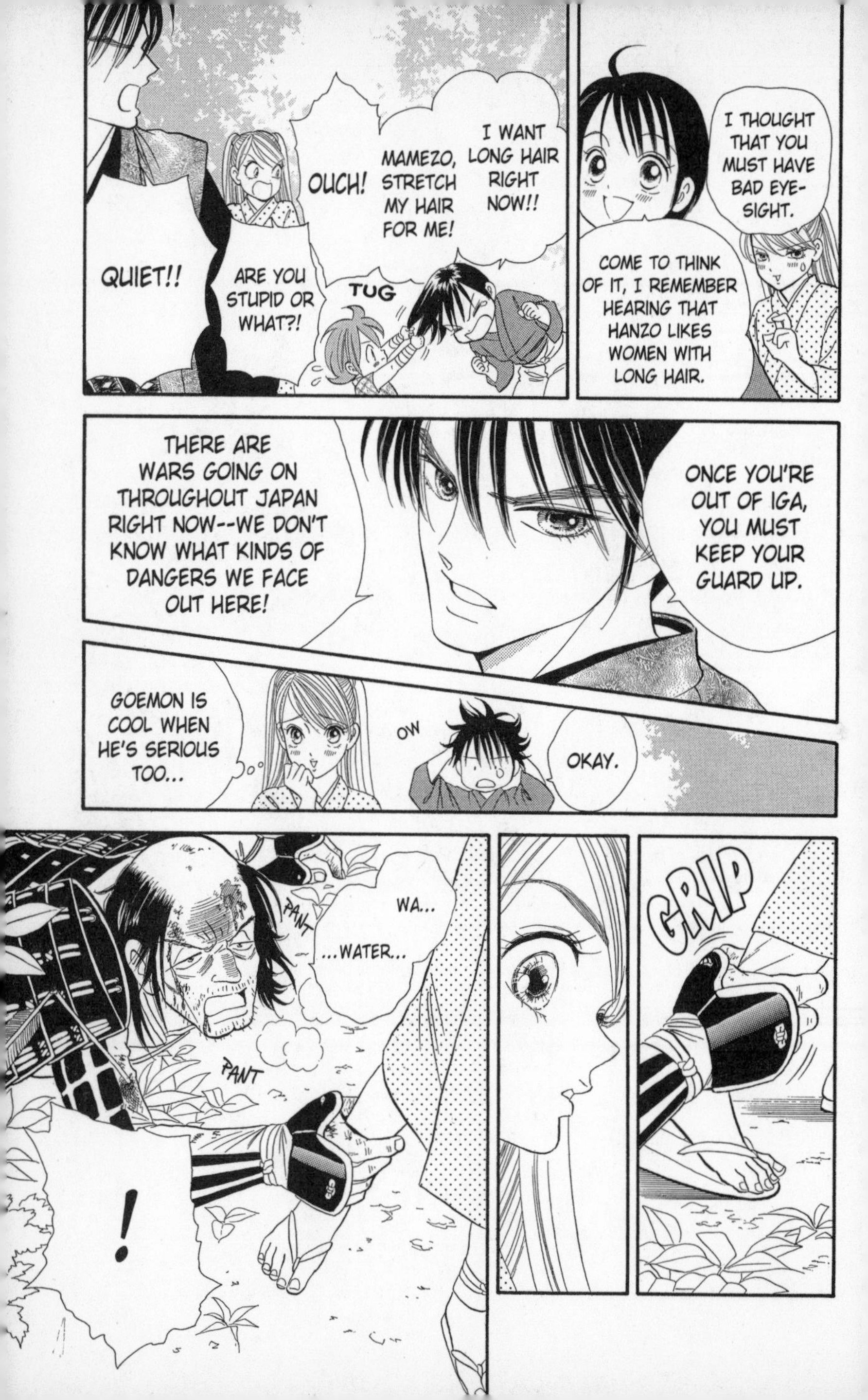
I THOUGHT THAT YOU MUST HAVE BAD EYE-SIGHT.
COME TO THINK OF IT, I REMEMBER HEARING THAT HANZO LIKES WOMEN WITH LONG HAIR.
I WANT LONG HAIR RIGHT NOW!!
MAMEZO, STRETCH MY HAIR FOR ME!
OUCH!
TUG
ARE YOU STUPID OR WHAT?!
QUIET!!
ONCE YOU'RE OUT OF IGA, YOU MUST KEEP YOUR GUARD UP.
THERE ARE WARS GOING ON THROUGHOUT JAPAN RIGHT NOW--WE DON'T KNOW WHAT KINDS OF DANGERS WE FACE OUT HERE!
OKAY.
OW
GOEMON IS COOL WHEN HE'S SERIOUS TOO...
GRIP
WA...
...WATER...
PANT
PANT
!

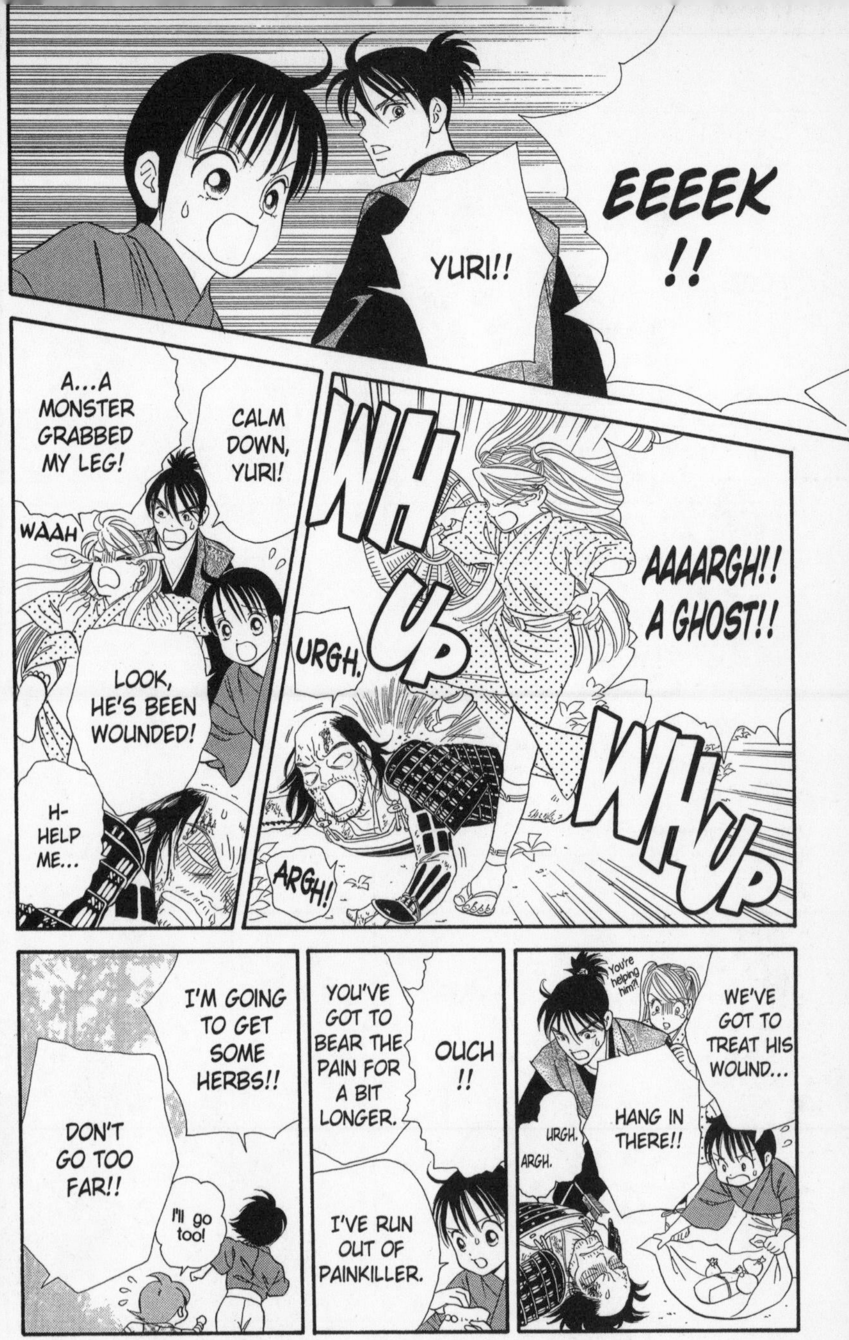
EEEEK!!
YURI!!
AAAARGH!! A GHOST!!
WH UP
URGH.
WHUP
ARGH!
CALM DOWN, YURI!
A...A MONSTER GRABBED MY LEG!
WAAH
LOOK, HE'S BEEN WOUNDED!
H-HELP ME...
WE'VE GOT TO TREAT HIS WOUND...
You're helping him?!
HANG IN THERE!!
URGH.
ARGH.
OUCH!!
YOU'VE GOT TO BEAR THE PAIN FOR A BIT LONGER.
I'VE RUN OUT OF PAINKILLER.
I'M GOING TO GET SOME HERBS!!
DON'T GO TOO FAR!!
I'll go too!

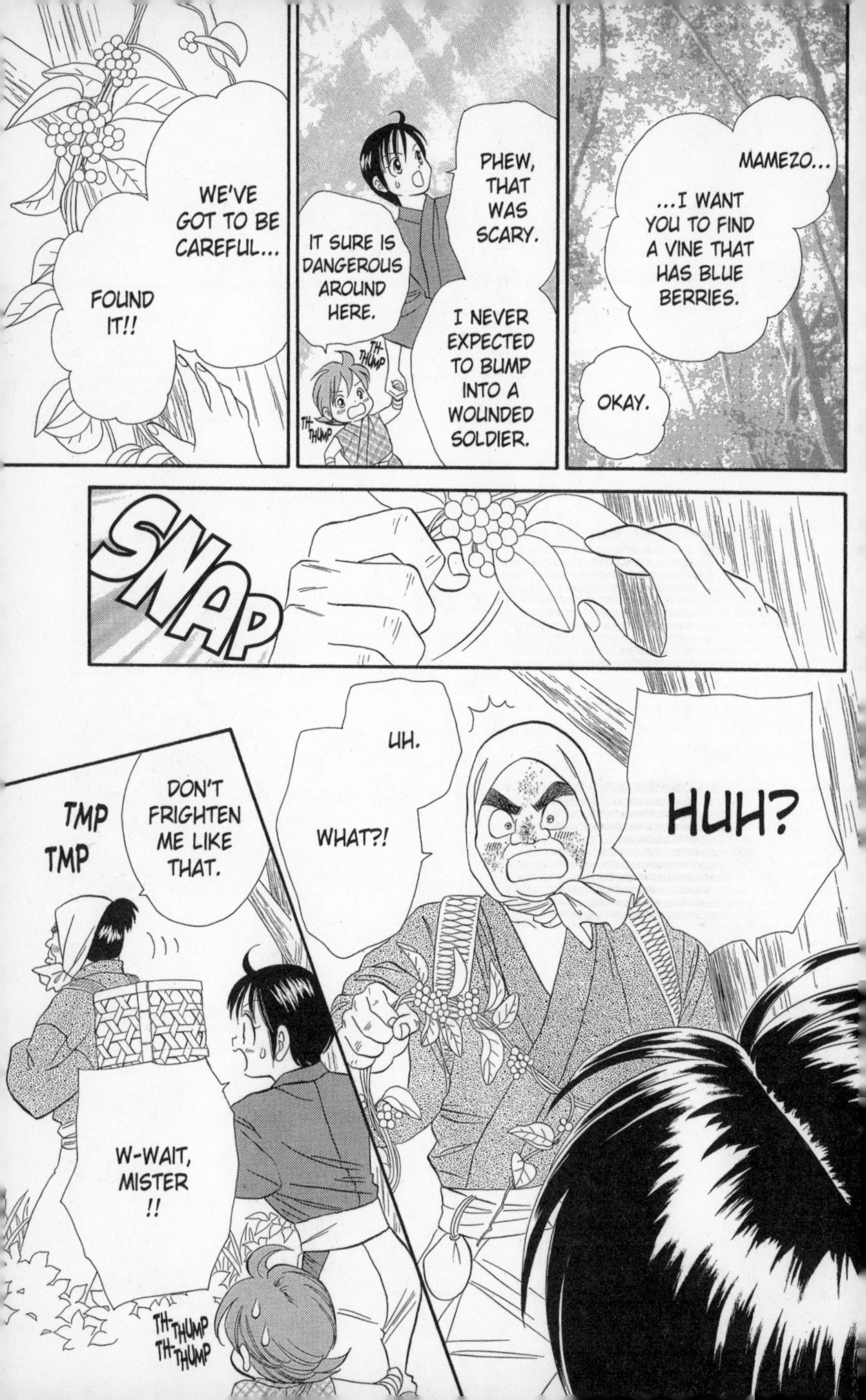
MAMEZO...
...I WANT YOU TO FIND A VINE THAT HAS BLUE BERRIES.
OKAY.
PHEW, THAT WAS SCARY.
I NEVER EXPECTED TO BUMP INTO A WOUNDED SOLDIER.
IT SURE IS DANGEROUS AROUND HERE.
TH-THUMP
TH-THUMP
WE'VE GOT TO BE CAREFUL...
FOUND IT!!
SNAP
HUH?
UH.
WHAT?!
DON'T FRIGHTEN ME LIKE THAT.
TMP TMP
W-WAIT, MISTER!!
TH-THUMP TH-THUMP

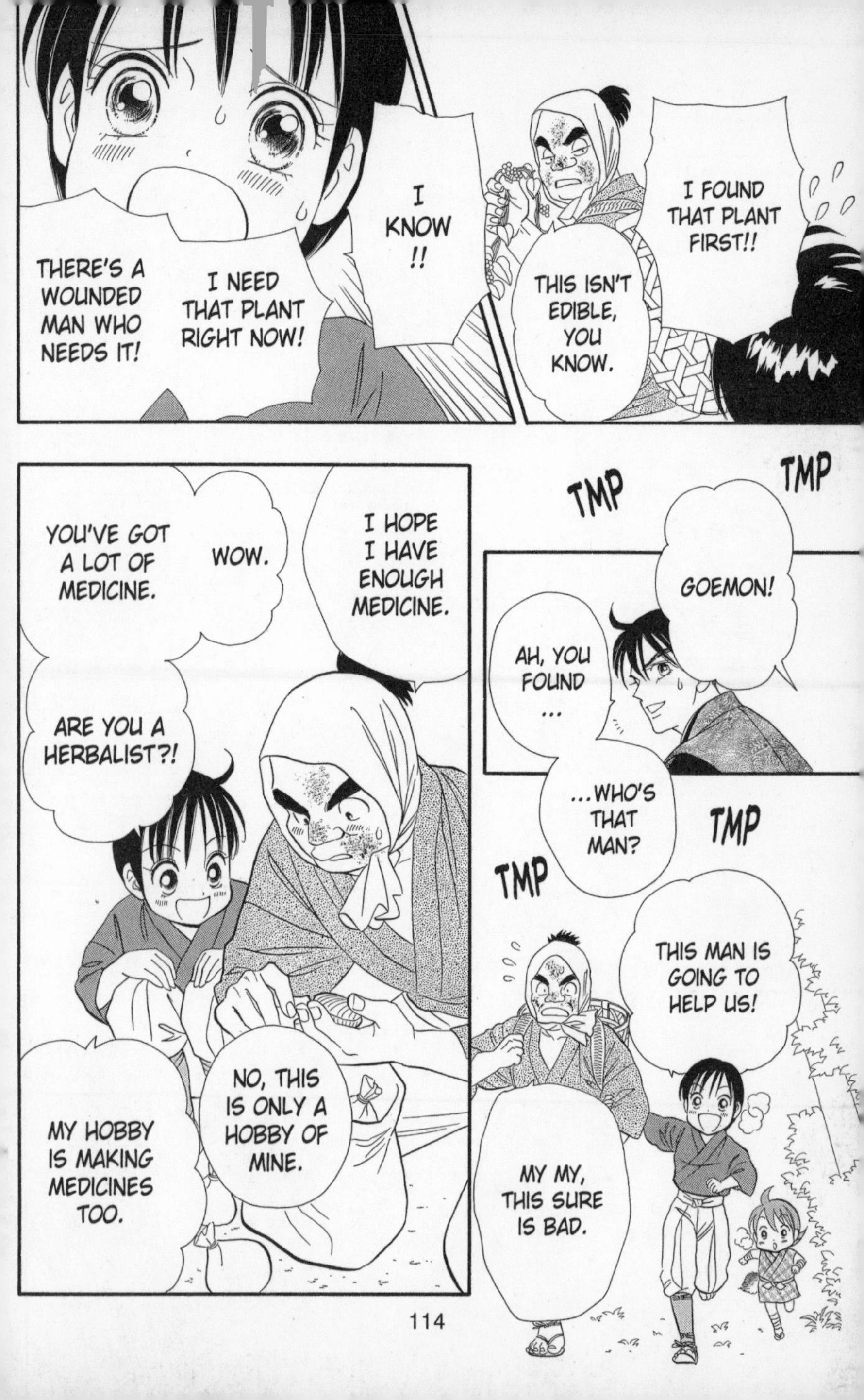
I FOUND THAT PLANT FIRST!!
THIS ISN'T EDIBLE, YOU KNOW.
I KNOW !!
I NEED THAT PLANT RIGHT NOW!
THERE'S A WOUNDED MAN WHO NEEDS IT!
TMP
TMP
GOEMON!
AH, YOU FOUND ...
...WHO'S THAT MAN?
TMP
TMP
THIS MAN IS GOING TO HELP US!
MY MY, THIS SURE IS BAD.
I HOPE I HAVE ENOUGH MEDICINE.
WOW.
YOU'VE GOT A LOT OF MEDICINE.
ARE YOU A HERBALIST?!
NO, THIS IS ONLY A HOBBY OF MINE.
MY HOBBY IS MAKING MEDICINES TOO.

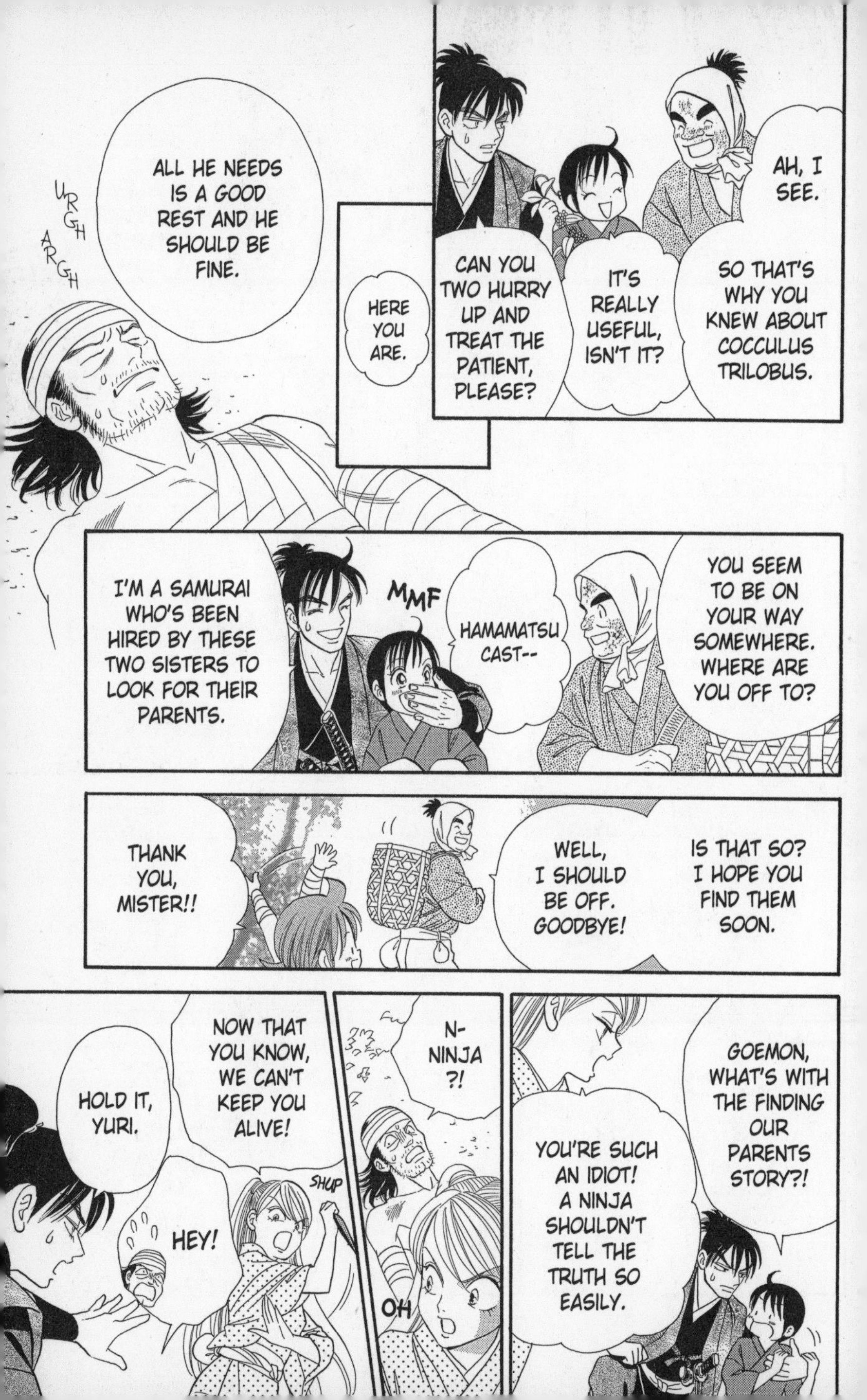
AH, I SEE.
SO THAT'S WHY YOU KNEW ABOUT COCCULUS TRILOBUS.
IT'S REALLY USEFUL, ISN'T IT?
CAN YOU TWO HURRY UP AND TREAT THE PATIENT, PLEASE?
HERE YOU ARE.
ALL HE NEEDS IS A GOOD REST AND HE SHOULD BE FINE.
URGH
ARGH
YOU SEEM TO BE ON YOUR WAY SOMEWHERE. WHERE ARE YOU OFF TO?
HAMAMATSU CAST--
MMF
I'M A SAMURAI WHO'S BEEN HIRED BY THESE TWO SISTERS TO LOOK FOR THEIR PARENTS.
IS THAT SO? I HOPE YOU FIND THEM SOON.
WELL, I SHOULD BE OFF. GOODBYE!
THANK YOU, MISTER!!
GOEMON, WHAT'S WITH THE FINDING OUR PARENTS STORY?!
YOU'RE SUCH AN IDIOT! A NINJA SHOULDN'T TELL THE TRUTH SO EASILY.
N-NINJA?!
OH
NOW THAT YOU KNOW, WE CAN'T KEEP YOU ALIVE!
SHUP
HOLD IT, YURI.
HEY!

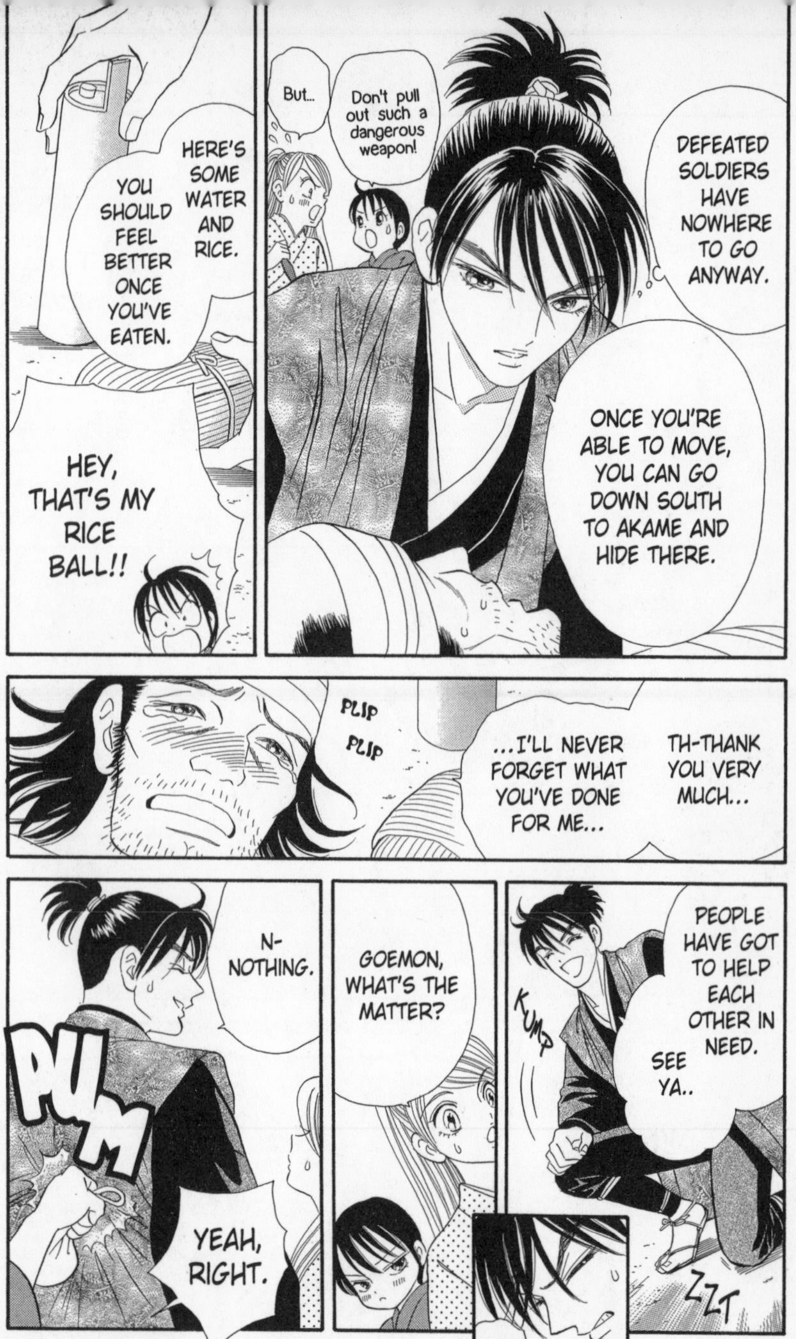
DEFEATED SOLDIERS HAVE NOWHERE TO GO ANYWAY.
Don't pull out such a dangerous weapon!
But...
ONCE YOU'RE ABLE TO MOVE, YOU CAN GO DOWN SOUTH TO AKAME AND HIDE THERE.
HERE'S SOME WATER AND RICE.
YOU SHOULD FEEL BETTER ONCE YOU'VE EATEN.
HEY, THAT'S MY RICE BALL!!
TH-THANK YOU VERY MUCH...
...I'LL NEVER FORGET WHAT YOU'VE DONE FOR ME...
PLIP
PLIP
PEOPLE HAVE GOT TO HELP EACH OTHER IN NEED.
SEE YA..
KUMP
ZZZT
Ouch...
GOEMON, WHAT'S THE MATTER?
N-NOTHING.
PUM
YEAH, RIGHT.

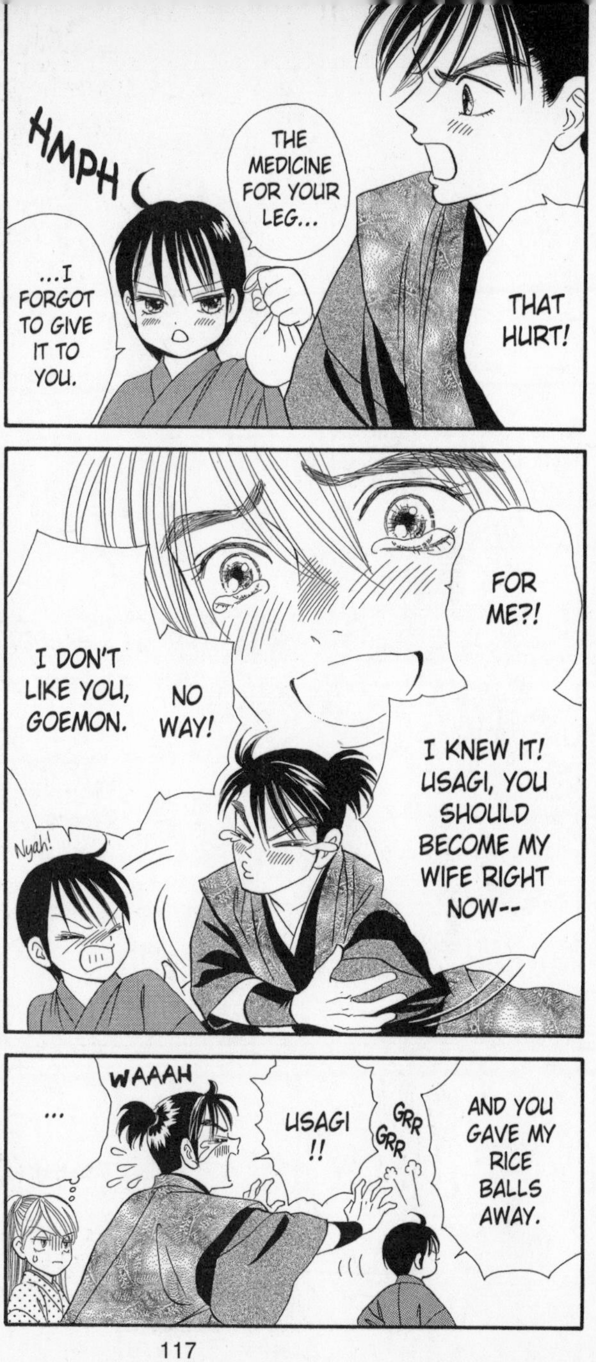
THAT HURT!
THE MEDICINE FOR YOUR LEG...
HMPH
...I FORGOT TO GIVE IT TO YOU.
FOR ME?!
I KNEW IT! USAGI, YOU SHOULD BECOME MY WIFE RIGHT NOW--
NO WAY!
I DON'T LIKE YOU, GOEMON.
Nyah!
AND YOU GAVE MY RICE BALLS AWAY.
GRR GRR
USAGI !!
WAAAH
...

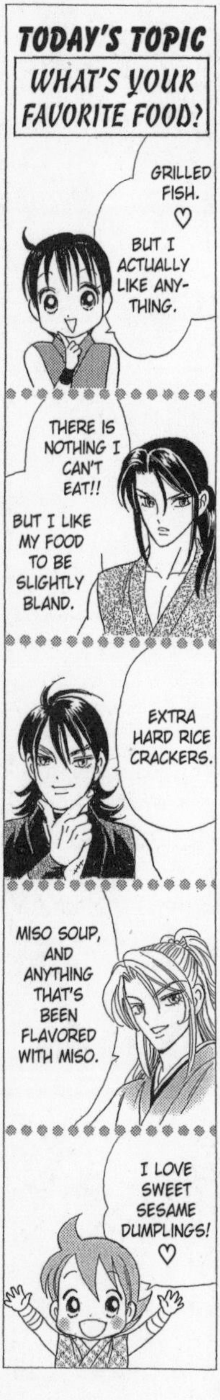
TODAY'S TOPIC
WHAT'S YOUR FAVORITE FOOD?
GRILLED FISH. ♡
BUT I ACTUALLY LIKE ANYTHING.
THERE IS NOTHING I CAN'T EAT!!
BUT I LIKE MY FOOD TO BE SLIGHTLY BLAND.
EXTRA HARD RICE CRACKERS.
MISO SOUP, AND ANYTHING THAT'S BEEN FLAVORED WITH MISO.
I LOVE SWEET SESAME DUMPLINGS! ♡

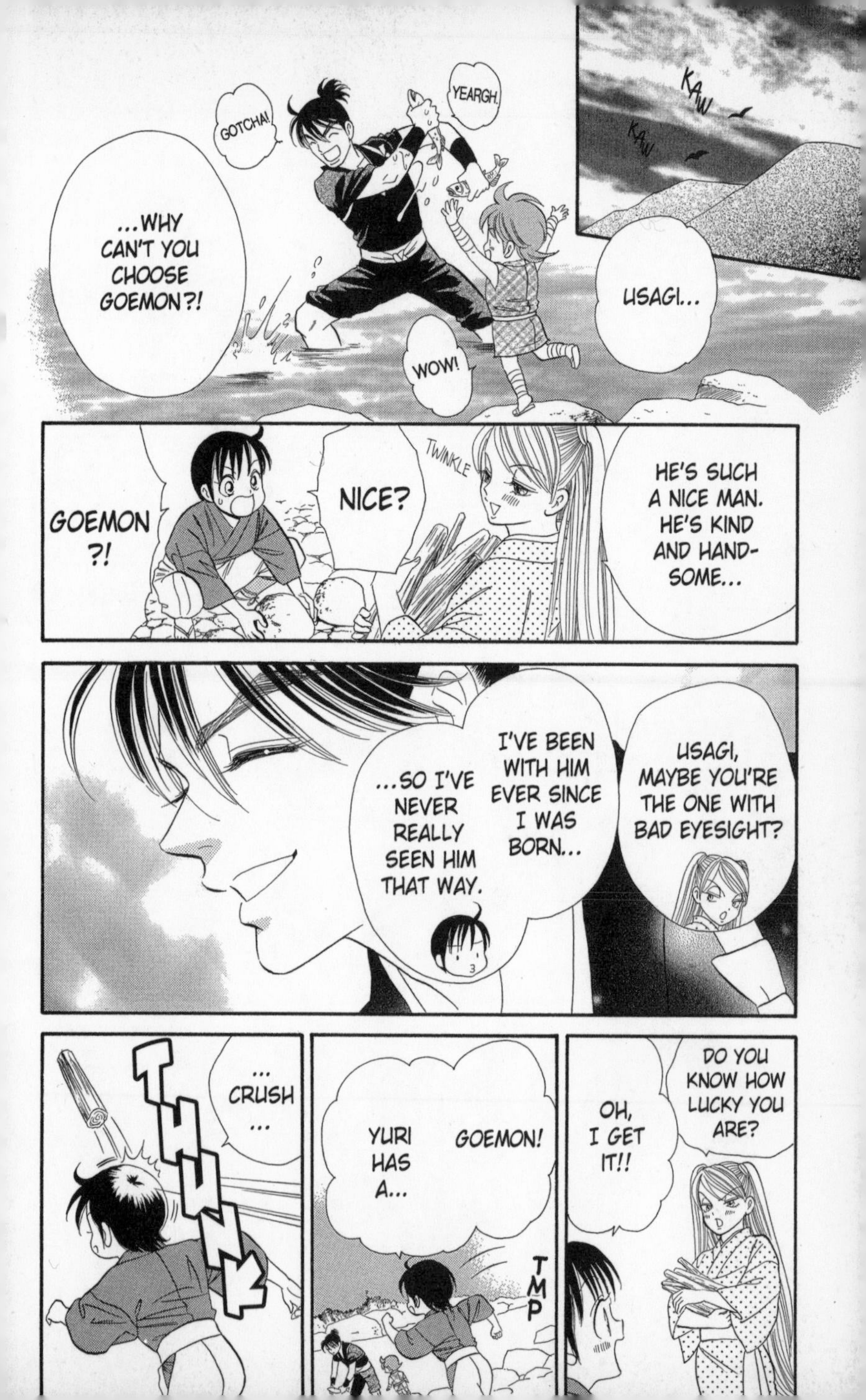
KAW
KAW
USAGI...
YEARGH.
GOTCHA!
WOW!
...WHY CAN'T YOU CHOOSE GOEMON?!
HE'S SUCH A NICE MAN. HE'S KIND AND HAND-SOME...
TWINKLE
NICE?
GOEMON ?!
USAGI, MAYBE YOU'RE THE ONE WITH BAD EYESIGHT?
I'VE BEEN WITH HIM EVER SINCE I WAS BORN...
...SO I'VE NEVER REALLY SEEN HIM THAT WAY.
DO YOU KNOW HOW LUCKY YOU ARE?
OH, I GET IT!!
GOEMON!
YURI HAS A...
TMP
... CRUSH ...
THUNK

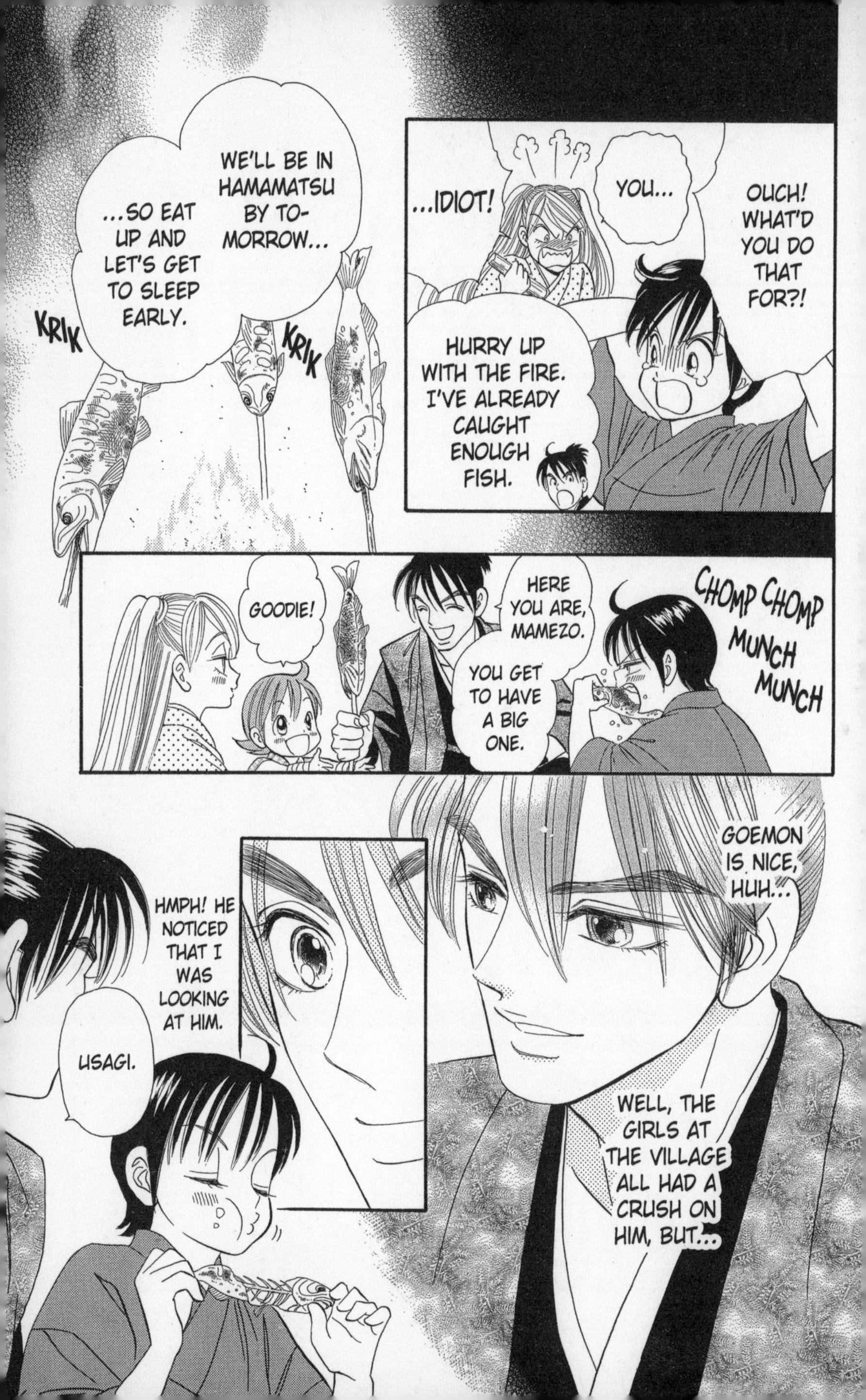
OUCH! WHAT'D YOU DO THAT FOR?!
YOU...
...IDIOT!
HURRY UP WITH THE FIRE. I'VE ALREADY CAUGHT ENOUGH FISH.
WE'LL BE IN HAMAMATSU BY TO-MORROW...
...SO EAT UP AND LET'S GET TO SLEEP EARLY.
KRIK
KRIK
CHOMP CHOMP
MUNCH MUNCH
HERE YOU ARE, MAMEZO.
YOU GET TO HAVE A BIG ONE.
GOODIE!
GOEMON IS NICE, HUH...
WELL, THE GIRLS AT THE VILLAGE ALL HAD A CRUSH ON HIM, BUT...
HMPH! HE NOTICED THAT I WAS LOOKING AT HIM.
USAGI.

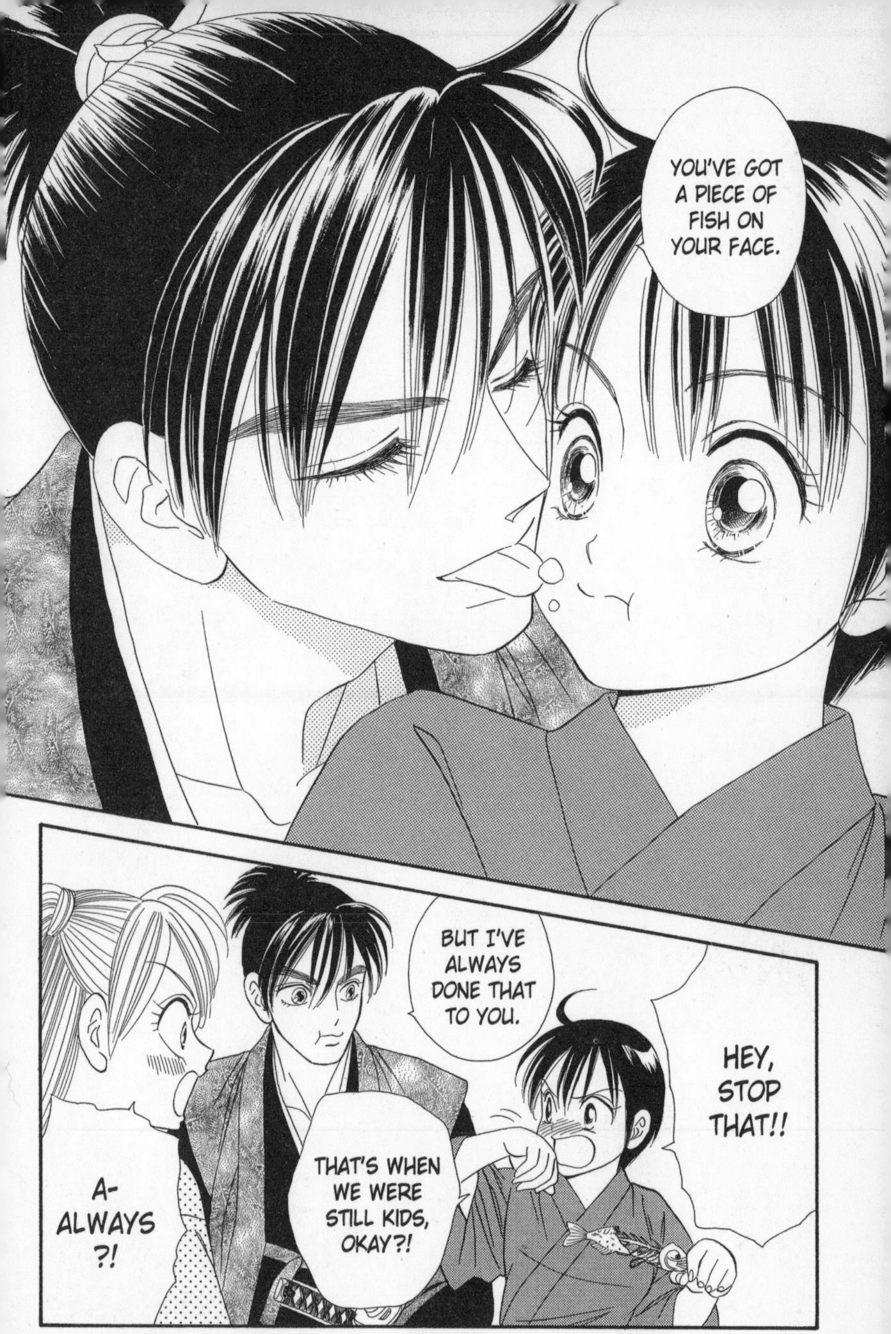
YOU'VE GOT A PIECE OF FISH ON YOUR FACE.
HEY, STOP THAT!!
BUT I'VE ALWAYS DONE THAT TO YOU.
THAT'S WHEN WE WERE STILL KIDS, OKAY?!
A- ALWAYS?!

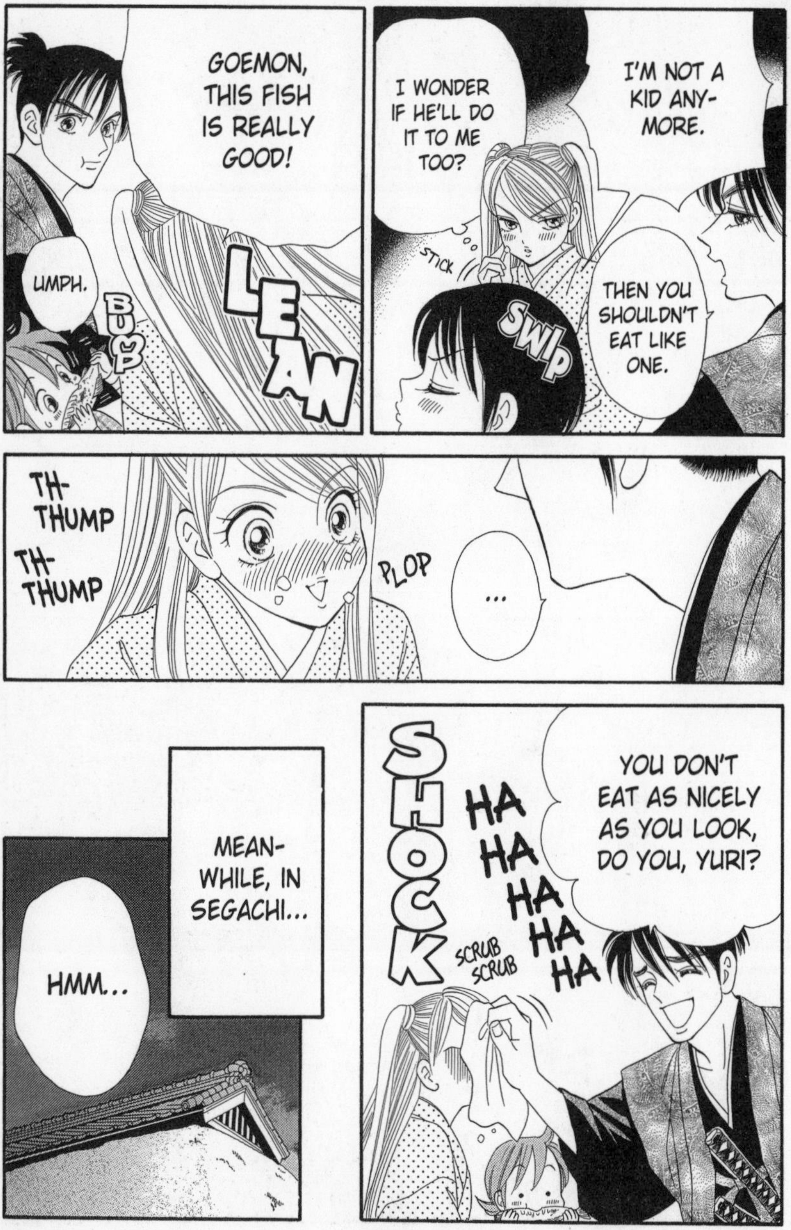
I'M NOT A KID ANY-MORE.
THEN YOU SHOULDN'T EAT LIKE ONE.
SWIP
I WONDER IF HE'LL DO IT TO ME TOO?
STICK
GOEMON, THIS FISH IS REALLY GOOD!
LEAN
UMPH.
BUMP
...
PLOP
TH-THUMP
TH-THUMP
YOU DON'T EAT AS NICELY AS YOU LOOK, DO YOU, YURI?
HA HA HA HA HA
SCRUB SCRUB
SHOCK
MEAN-WHILE, IN SEGACHI...
HMM...

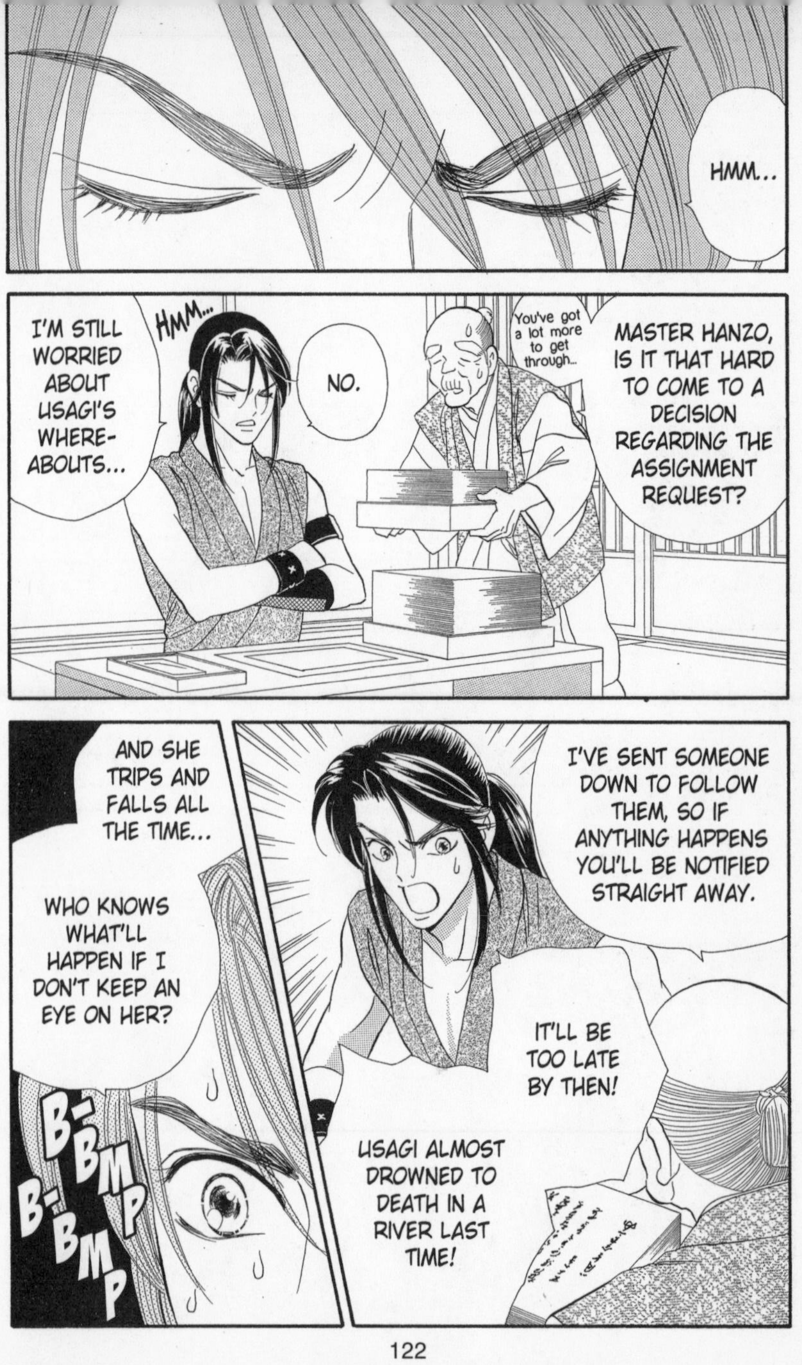
HMM...
MASTER HANZO, IS IT THAT HARD TO COME TO A DECISION REGARDING THE ASSIGNMENT REQUEST?
You've got a lot more to get through...
NO.
HMM...
I'M STILL WORRIED ABOUT USAGI'S WHERE-ABOUTS...
I'VE SENT SOMEONE DOWN TO FOLLOW THEM, SO IF ANYTHING HAPPENS YOU'LL BE NOTIFIED STRAIGHT AWAY.
IT'LL BE TOO LATE BY THEN!
USAGI ALMOST DROWNED TO DEATH IN A RIVER LAST TIME!
AND SHE TRIPS AND FALLS ALL THE TIME...
WHO KNOWS WHAT'LL HAPPEN IF I DON'T KEEP AN EYE ON HER?
B-BMP B-BMP

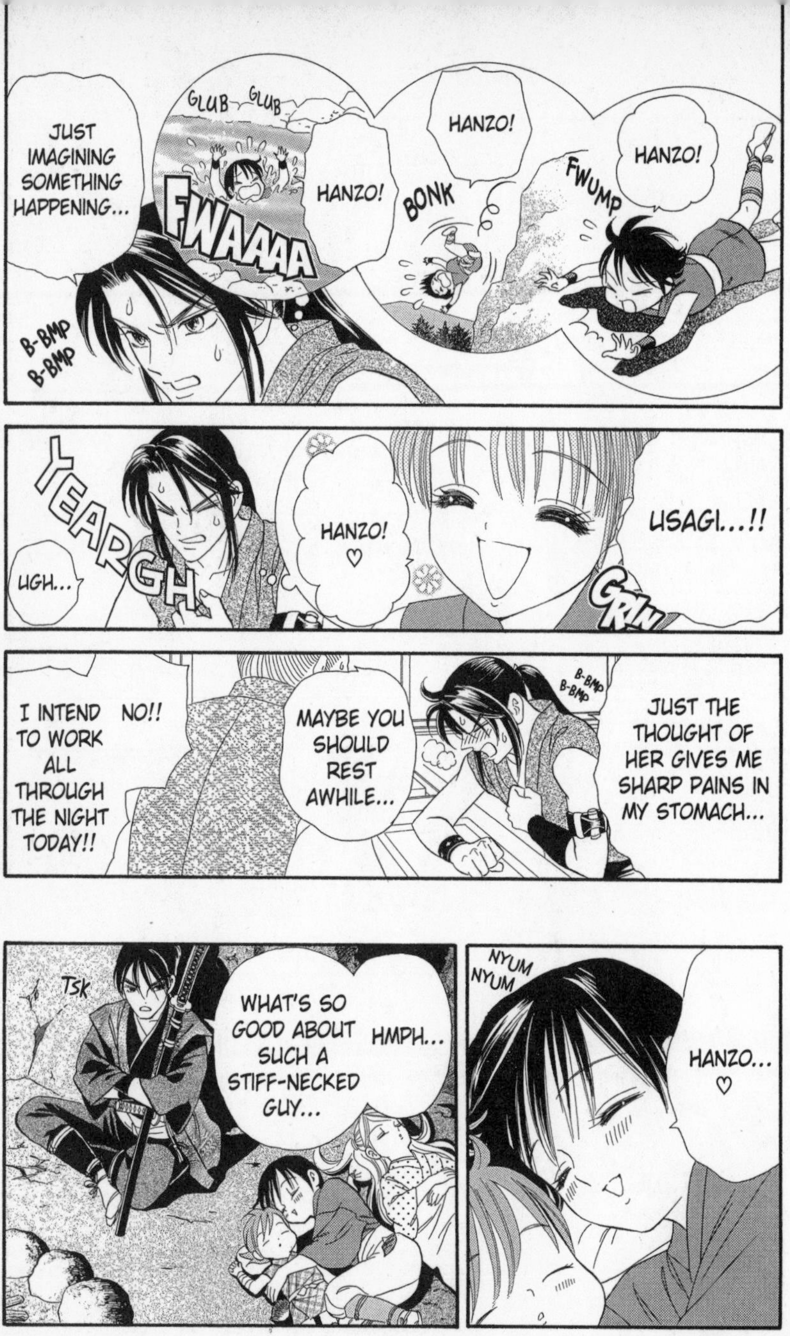
HANZO!
FWUMP
HANZO!
BONK
HANZO!
GLUB GLUB
FWAAAA
JUST IMAGINING SOMETHING HAPPENING...
B-BMP B-BMP
USAGI...!!
GRIN
HANZO! ♡
YEARGH
UGH...
JUST THE THOUGHT OF HER GIVES ME SHARP PAINS IN MY STOMACH...
B-BMP B-BMP
MAYBE YOU SHOULD REST AWHILE...
NO!!
I INTEND TO WORK ALL THROUGH THE NIGHT TODAY!!
HANZO... ♡
NYUM NYUM
HMPH...
WHAT'S SO GOOD ABOUT SUCH A STIFF-NECKED GUY...
TSK

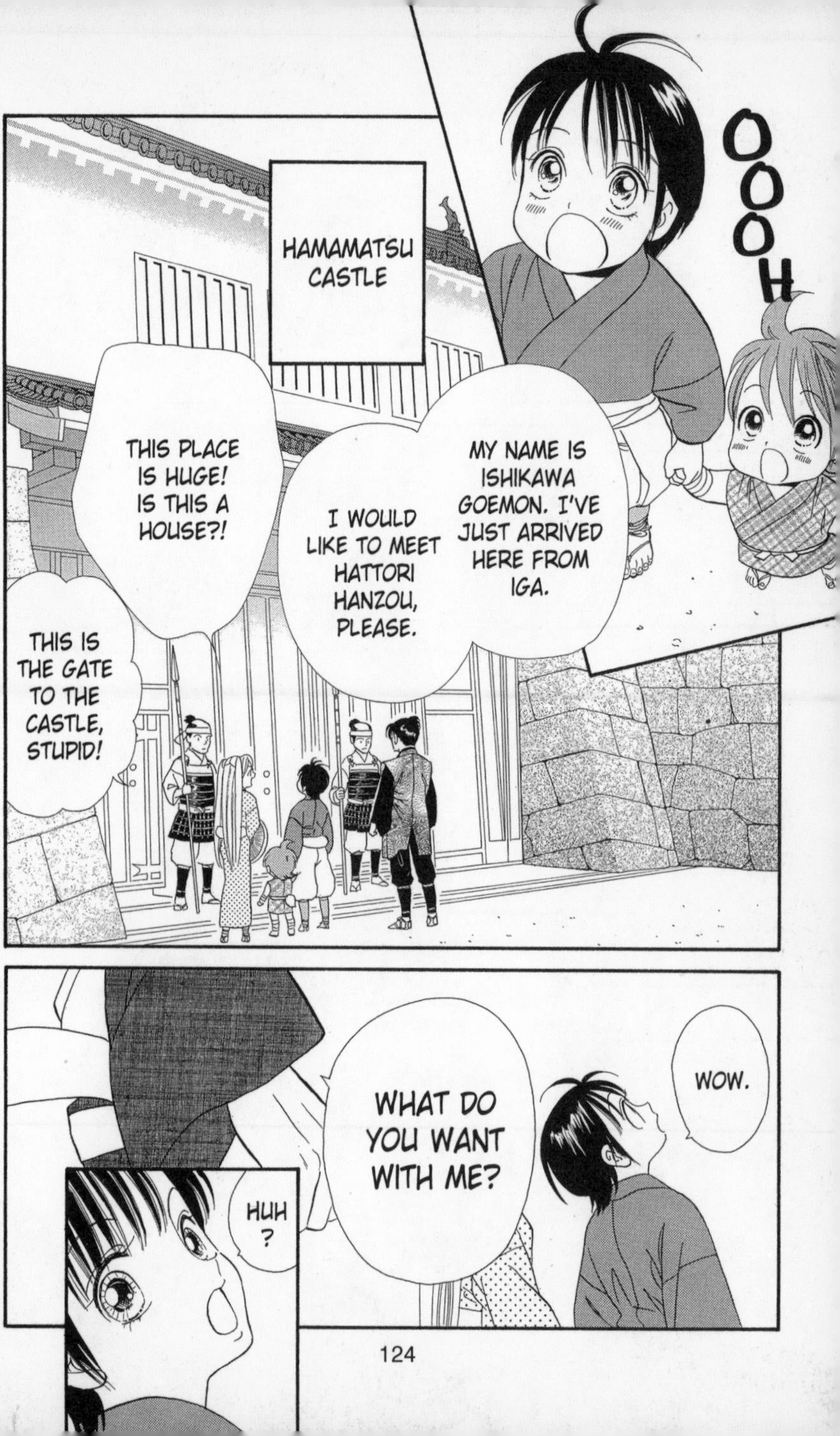
OOOH
HAMAMATSU CASTLE
MY NAME IS ISHIKAWA GOEMON. I'VE JUST ARRIVED HERE FROM IGA.
I WOULD LIKE TO MEET HATTORI HANZOU, PLEASE.
THIS PLACE IS HUGE! IS THIS A HOUSE?!
THIS IS THE GATE TO THE CASTLE, STUPID!
WOW.
WHAT DO YOU WANT WITH ME?
HUH?

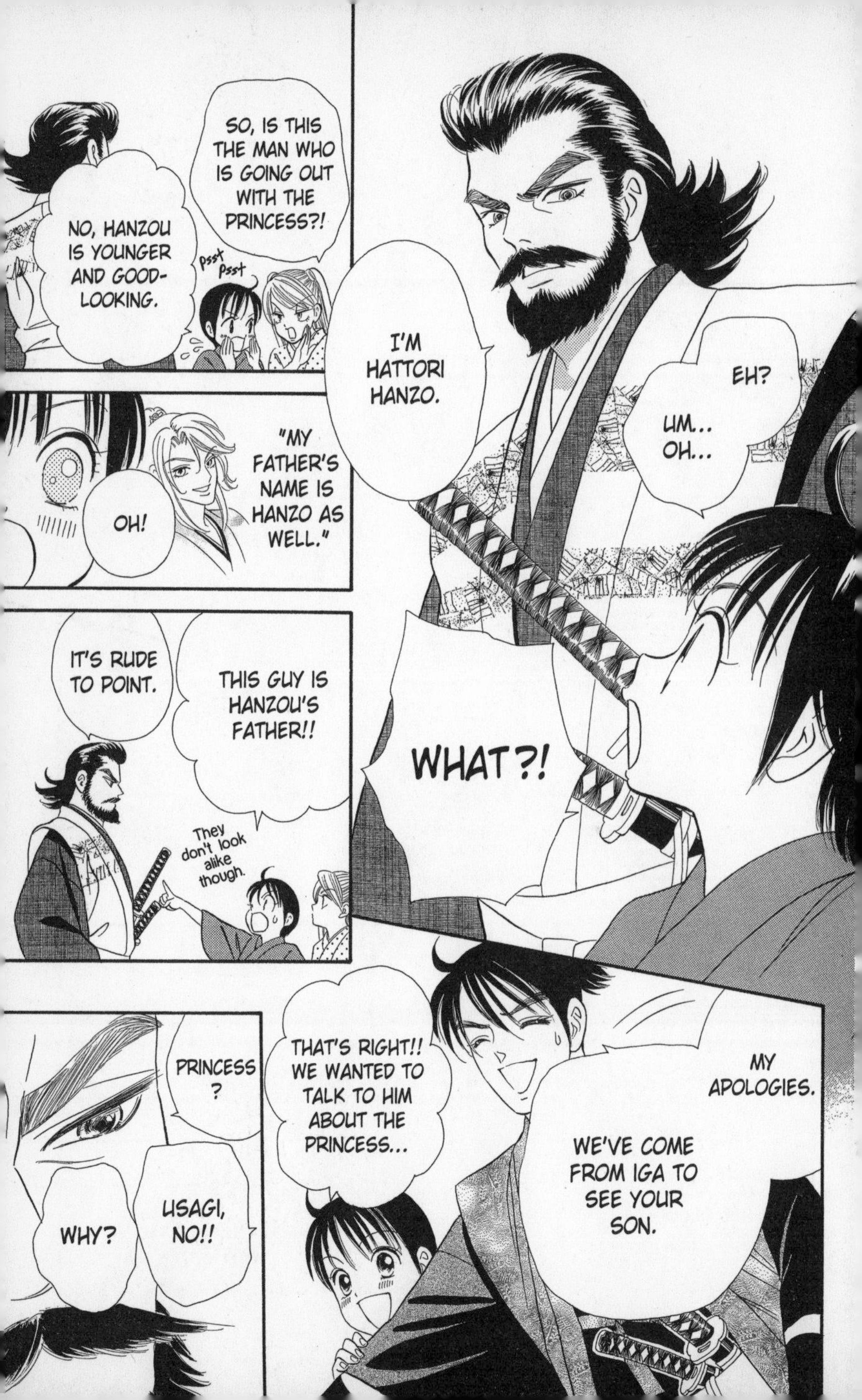
I'M HATTORI HANZO.
EH?
UM... OH...
WHAT?!
SO, IS THIS THE MAN WHO IS GOING OUT WITH THE PRINCESS?!
psst psst
NO, HANZOU IS YOUNGER AND GOOD-LOOKING.
"MY FATHER'S NAME IS HANZO AS WELL."
OH!
THIS GUY IS HANZOU'S FATHER!!
IT'S RUDE TO POINT.
They don't look alike though.
MY APOLOGIES.
WE'VE COME FROM IGA TO SEE YOUR SON.
THAT'S RIGHT!! WE WANTED TO TALK TO HIM ABOUT THE PRINCESS...
PRINCESS?
USAGI, NO!!
WHY?

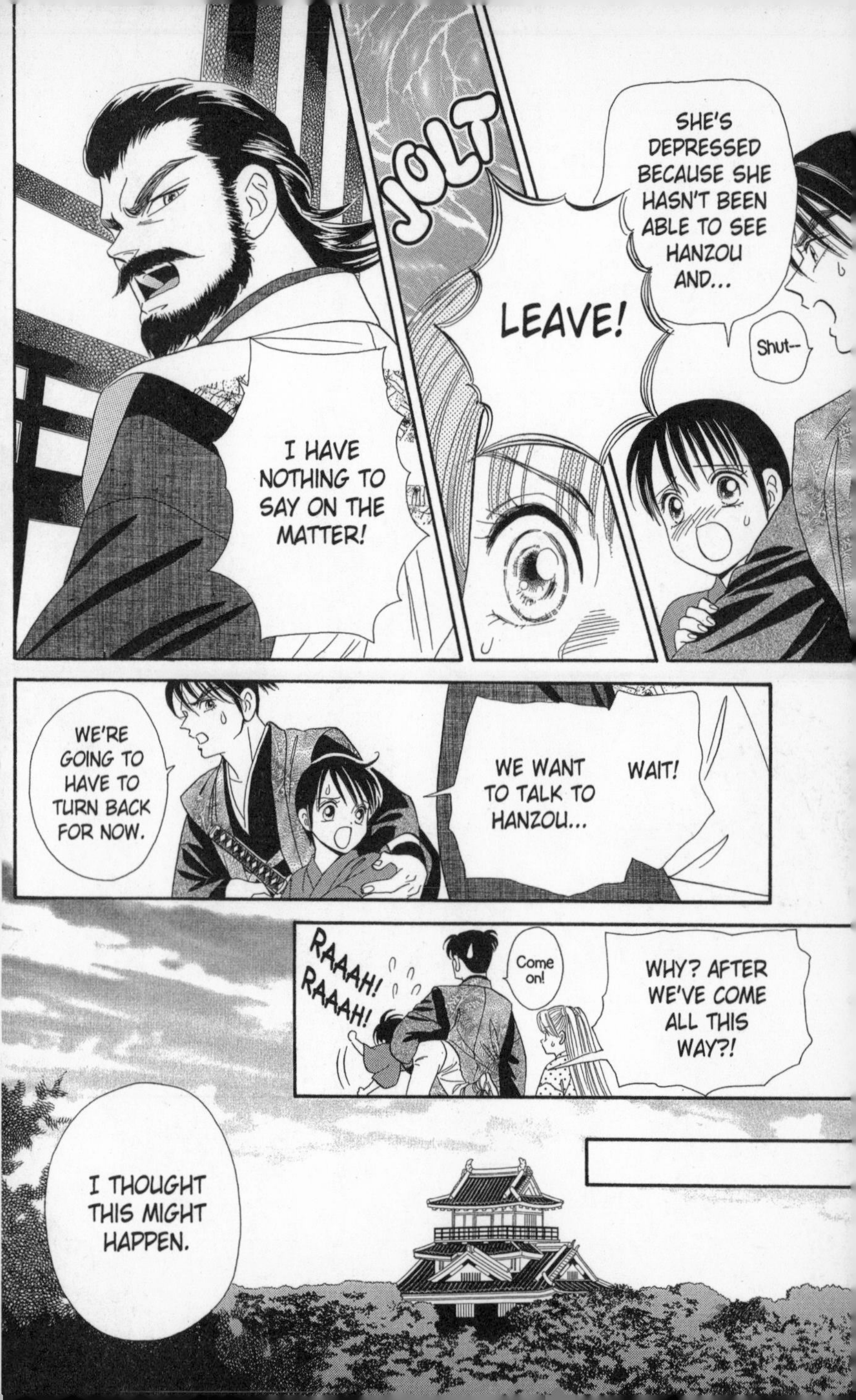
SHE'S DEPRESSED BECAUSE SHE HASN'T BEEN ABLE TO SEE HANZOU AND...
Shut--
JOLT
LEAVE!
I HAVE NOTHING TO SAY ON THE MATTER!
WAIT!
WE WANT TO TALK TO HANZOU...
WE'RE GOING TO HAVE TO TURN BACK FOR NOW.
WHY? AFTER WE'VE COME ALL THIS WAY?!
Come on!
RAAAH! RAAAH!
I THOUGHT THIS MIGHT HAPPEN.

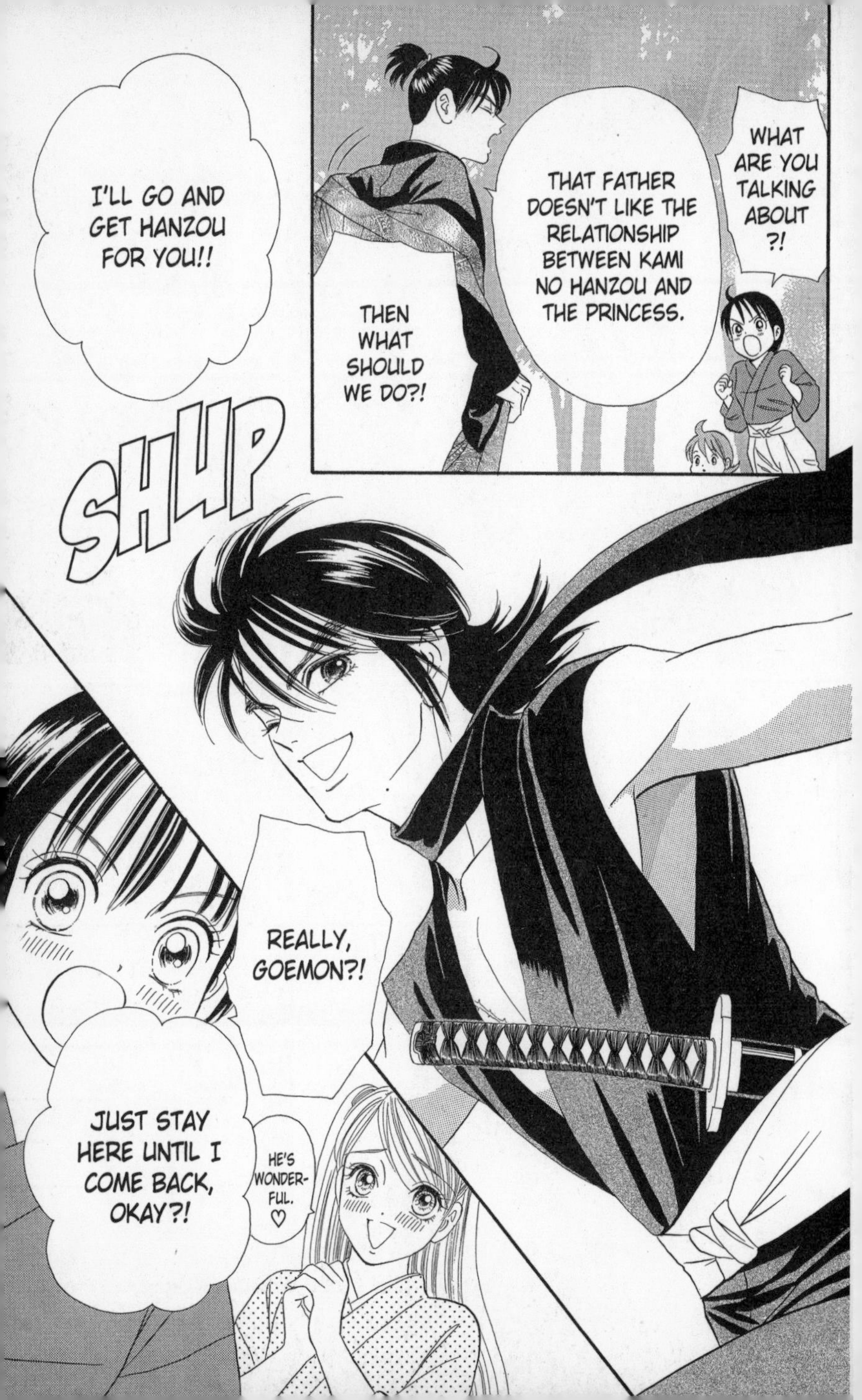
WHAT ARE YOU TALKING ABOUT ?!
THAT FATHER DOESN'T LIKE THE RELATIONSHIP BETWEEN KAMI NO HANZOU AND THE PRINCESS.
THEN WHAT SHOULD WE DO?!
I'LL GO AND GET HANZOU FOR YOU!!
SHUP
REALLY, GOEMON?!
JUST STAY HERE UNTIL I COME BACK, OKAY?!
HE'S WONDER-FUL. ♡

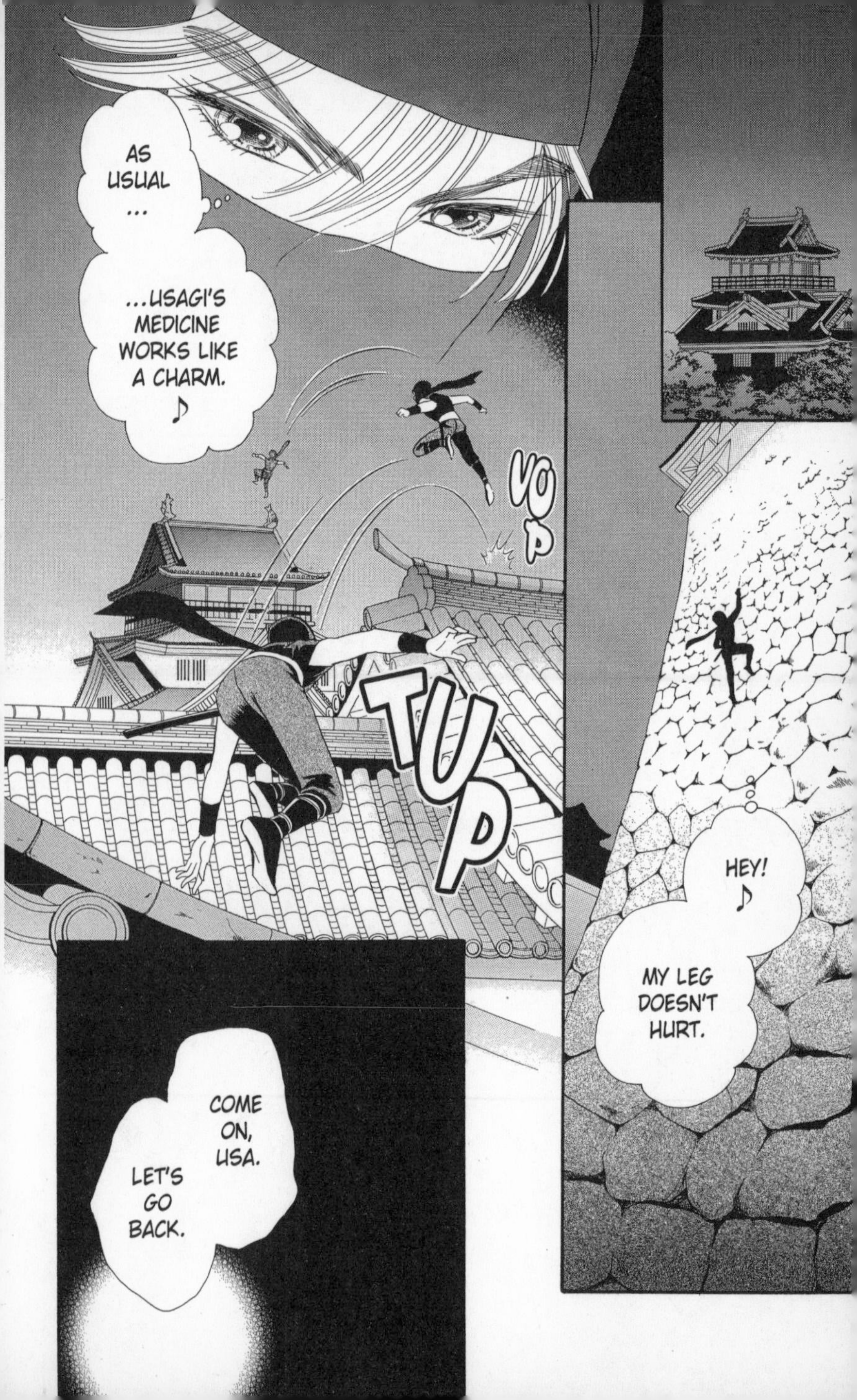
HEY! ♪
MY LEG DOESN'T HURT.
AS USUAL...
...USAGI'S MEDICINE WORKS LIKE A CHARM. ♪
VOP
TUP
COME ON, USA.
LET'S GO BACK.

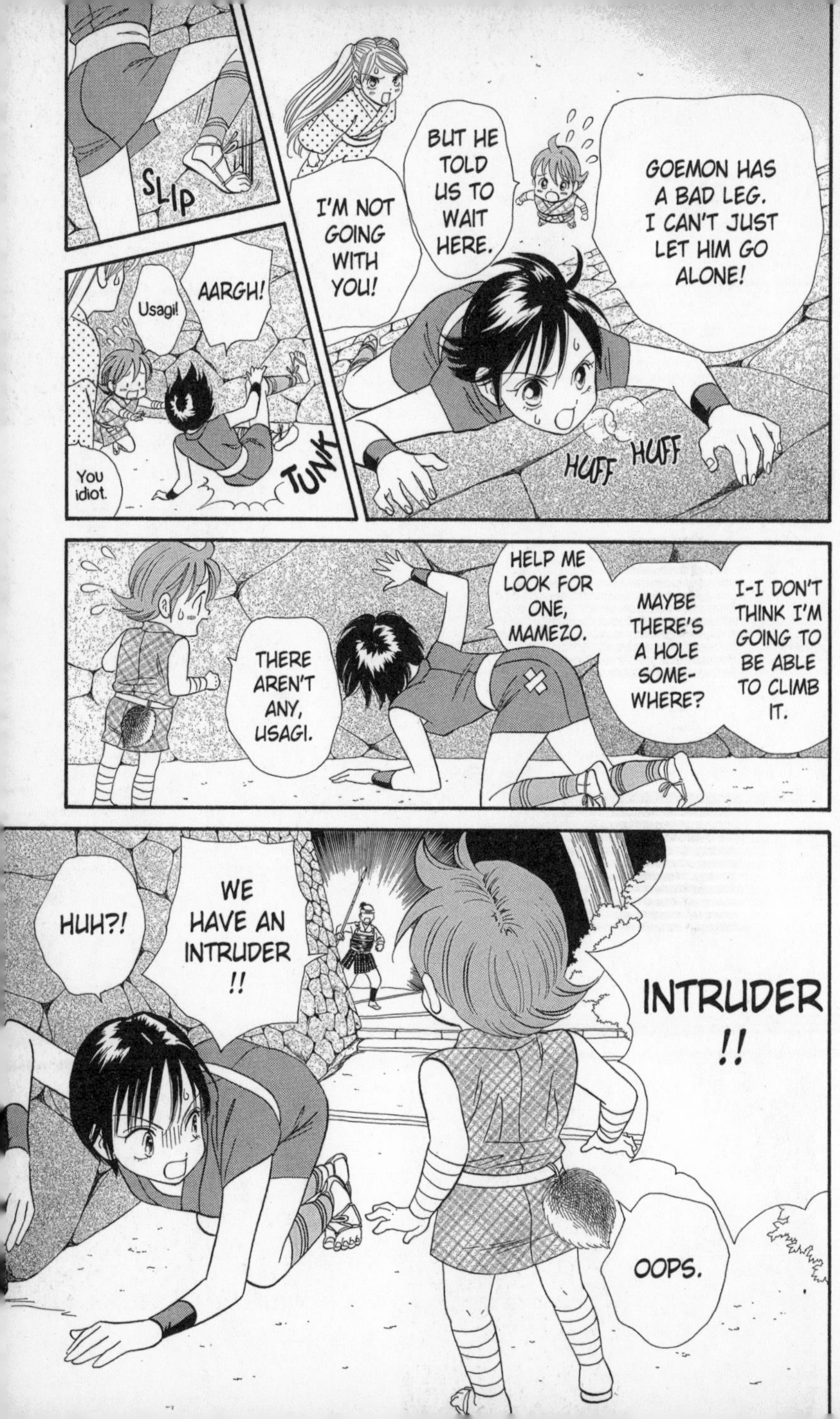
GOEMON HAS A BAD LEG. I CAN'T JUST LET HIM GO ALONE!
BUT HE TOLD US TO WAIT HERE.
I'M NOT GOING WITH YOU!
HUFF HUFF
SLIP
AARGH!
Usagi!
TUNK
You idiot.
I-I DON'T THINK I'M GOING TO BE ABLE TO CLIMB IT.
MAYBE THERE'S A HOLE SOMEWHERE?
HELP ME LOOK FOR ONE, MAMEZO.
THERE AREN'T ANY, USAGI.
WE HAVE AN INTRUDER!!
INTRUDER!!
HUH?!
OOPS.

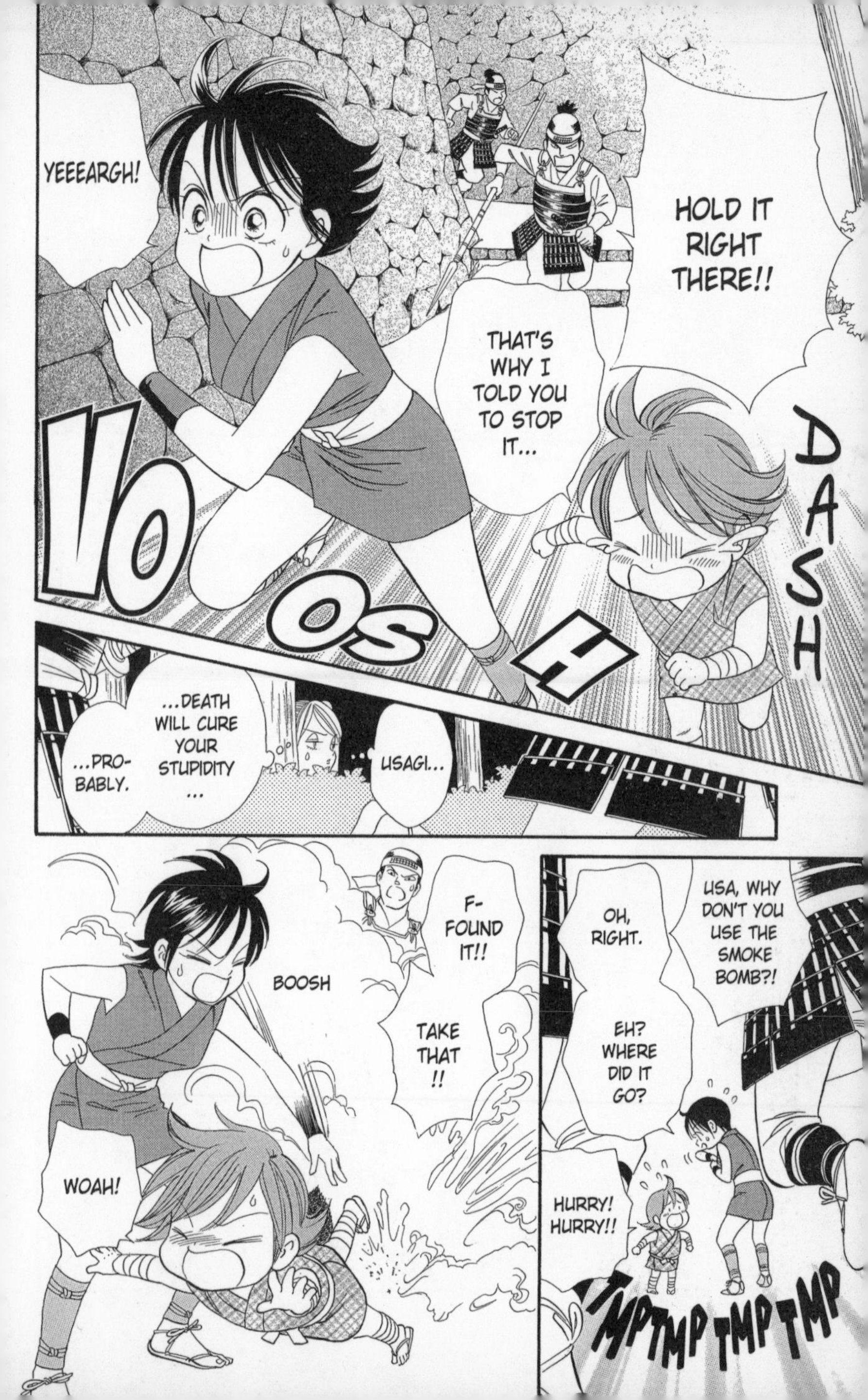
HOLD IT RIGHT THERE!!
THAT'S WHY I TOLD YOU TO STOP IT...
YEEEARGH!
DASH
WOOSH
USAGI...
...DEATH WILL CURE YOUR STUPIDITY ...
...PRO-BABLY.
USA, WHY DON'T YOU USE THE SMOKE BOMB?!
OH, RIGHT.
EH? WHERE DID IT GO?
HURRY! HURRY!!
TMPTMP TMP TMP
F-FOUND IT!!
TAKE THAT !!
BOOSH
WOAH!

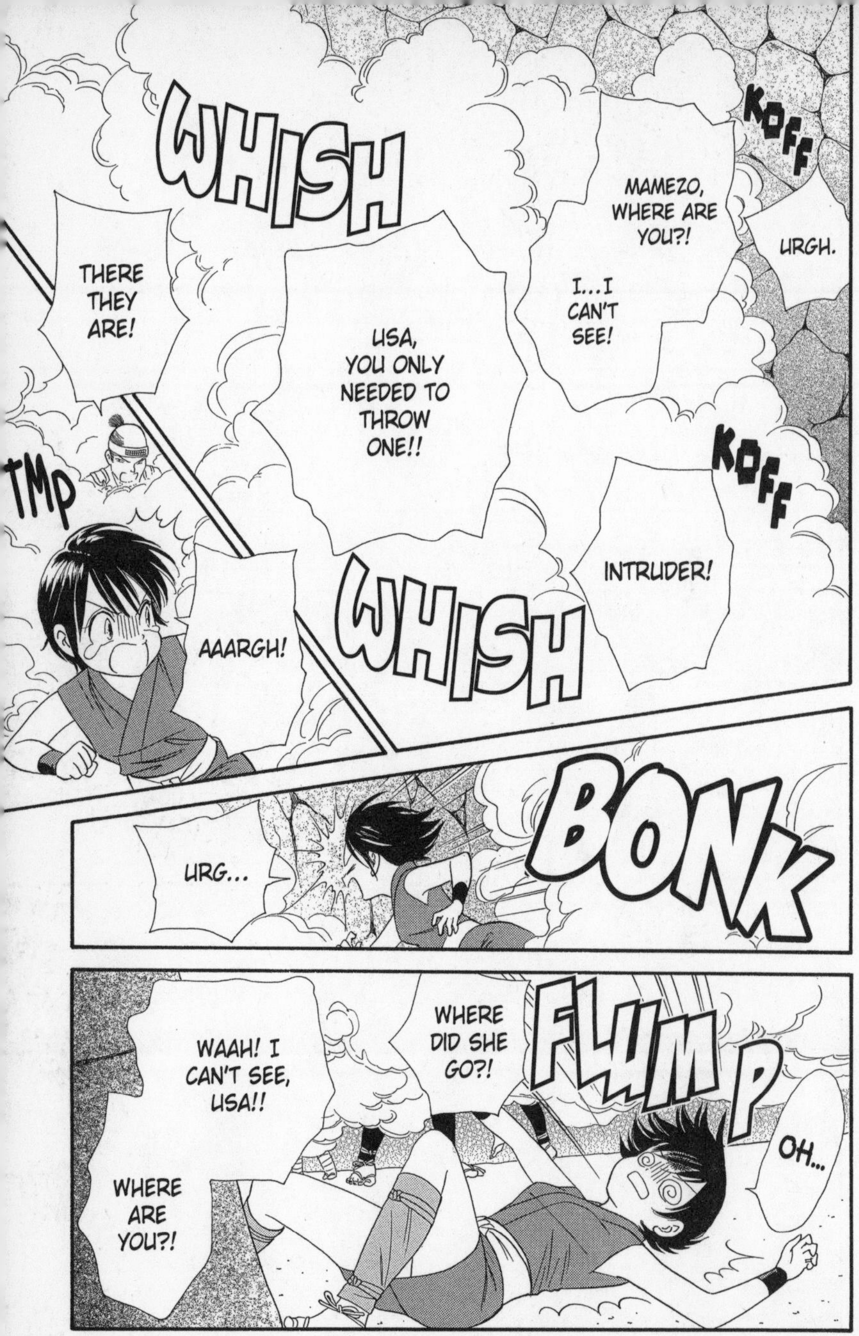

KOFF
URGH.
MAMEZO, WHERE ARE YOU?!
I...I CAN'T SEE!
WHISH
USA, YOU ONLY NEEDED TO THROW ONE!!
THERE THEY ARE!
KOFF
INTRUDER!
WHISH
AAARGH!
TMP
BONK
URG...
FLUMP
OH...
WHERE DID SHE GO?!
WAAH! I CAN'T SEE, USA!!
WHERE ARE YOU?!

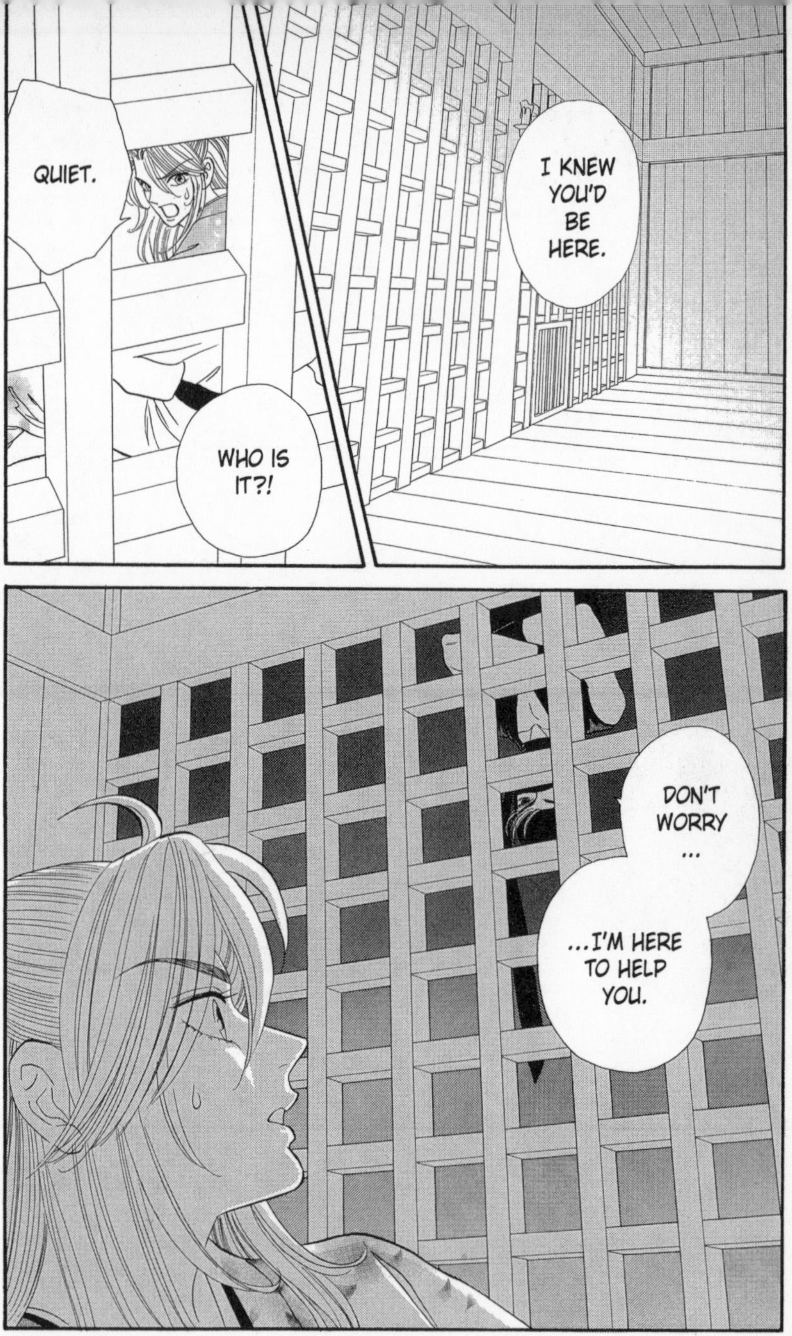
I KNEW YOU'D BE HERE.
WHO IS IT?!
QUIET.
DON'T WORRY ...
...I'M HERE TO HELP YOU.

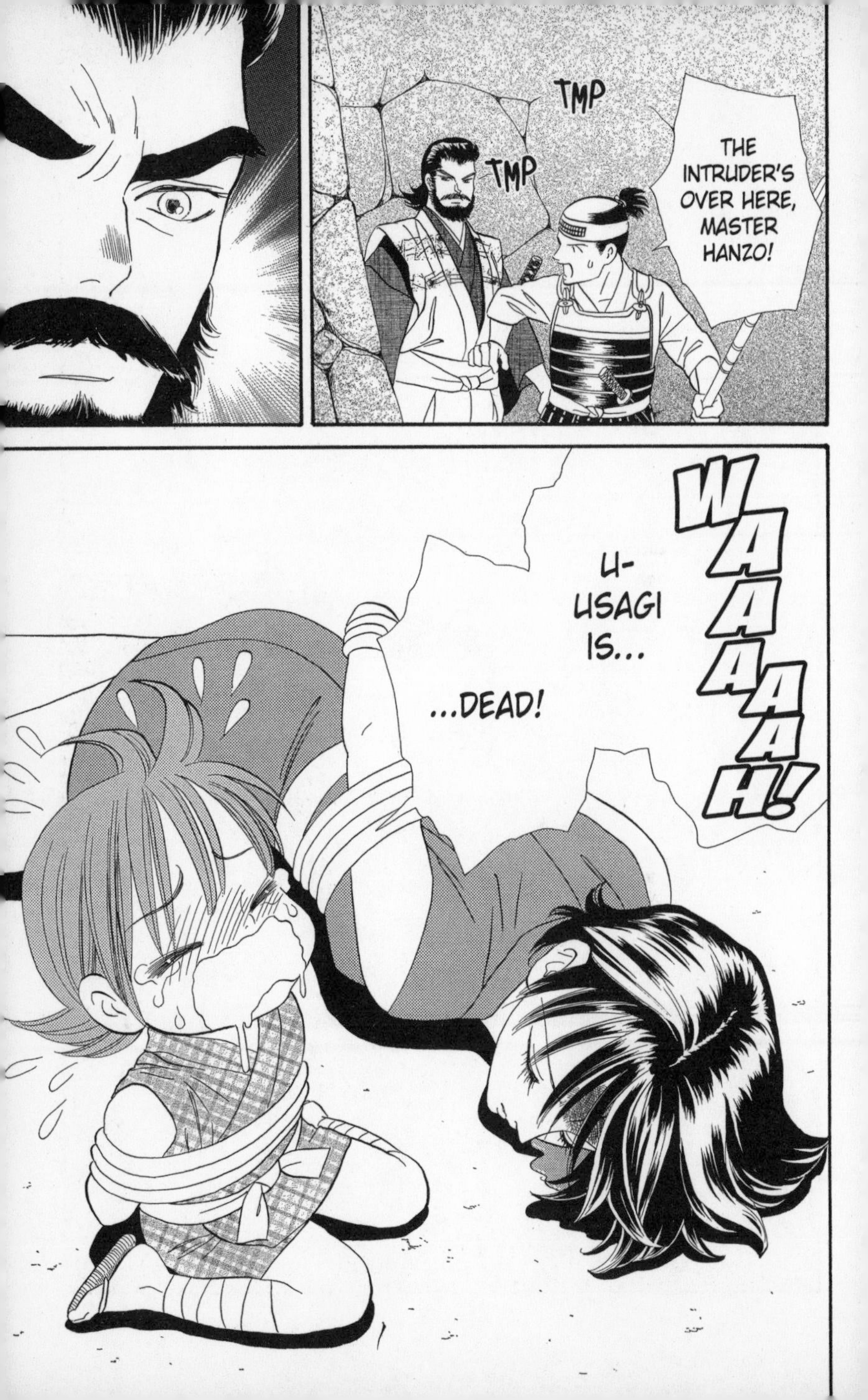
TMP
TMP
THE INTRUDER'S OVER HERE, MASTER HANZO!
WAAAAAAH!
U-USAGI IS...
...DEAD!

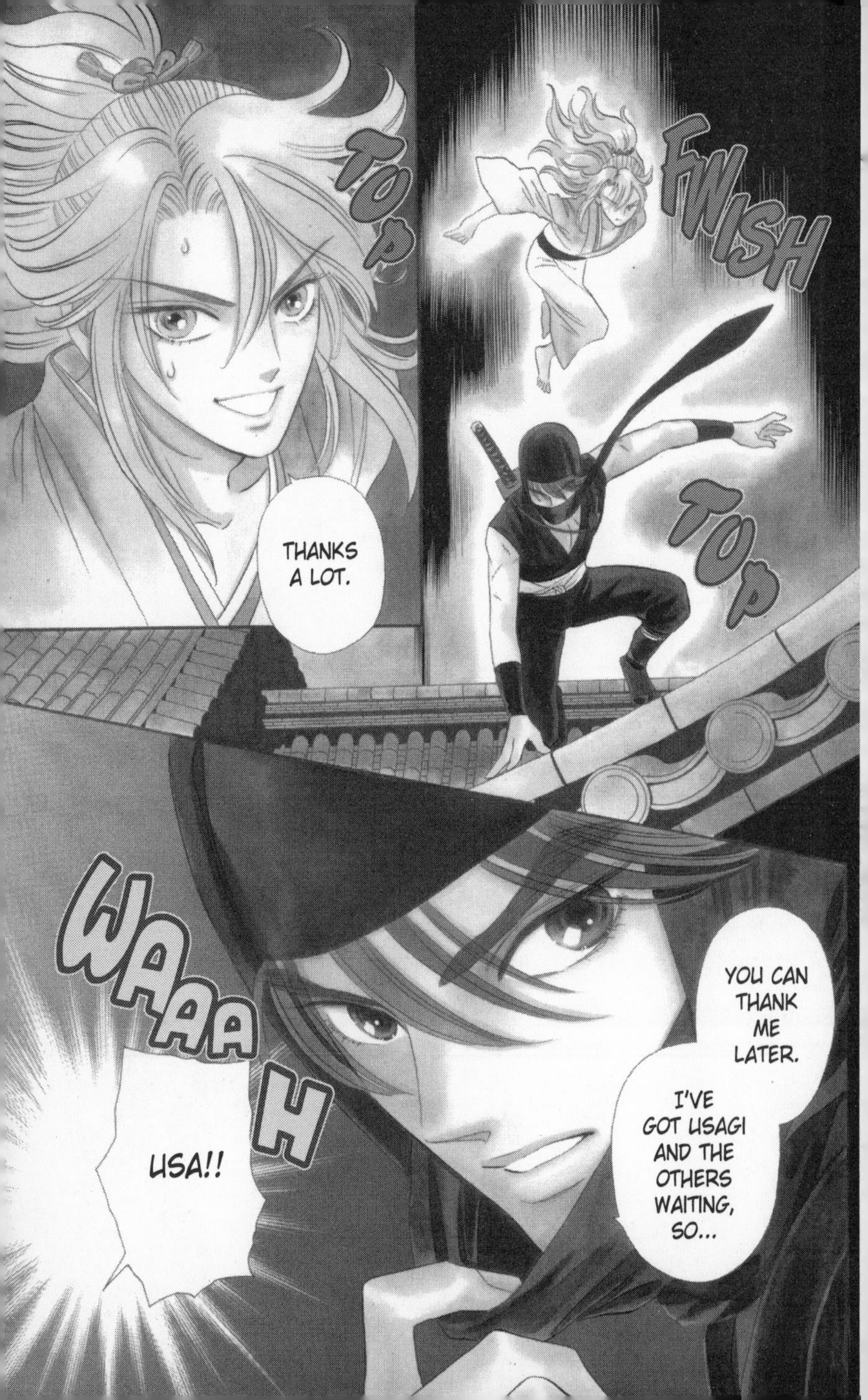
FWISH
TOP
TOP
THANKS A LOT.
YOU CAN THANK ME LATER.
I'VE GOT USAGI AND THE OTHERS WAITING, SO...
WAAAH
USA!!

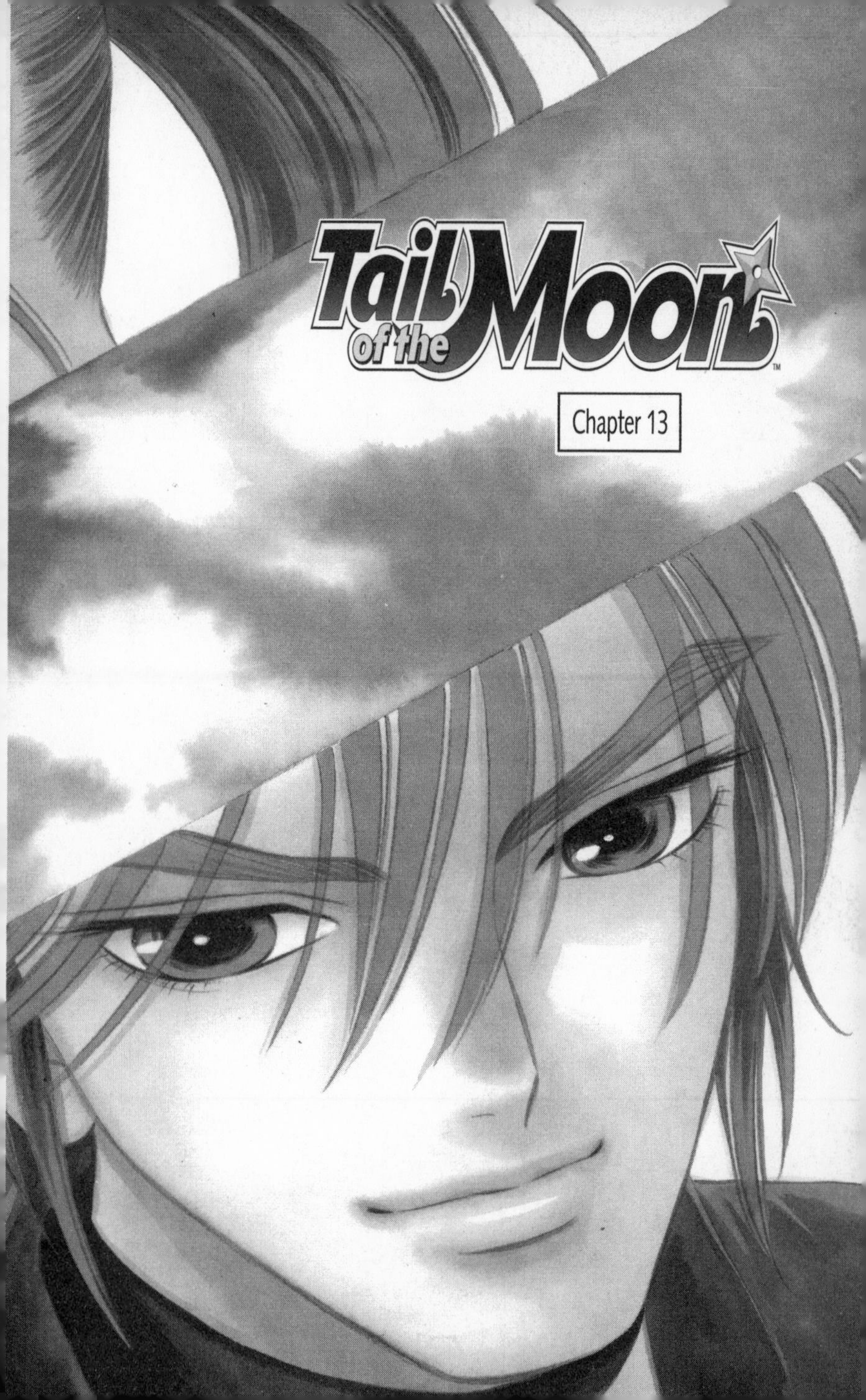
Tail of the Moon™
Chapter 13

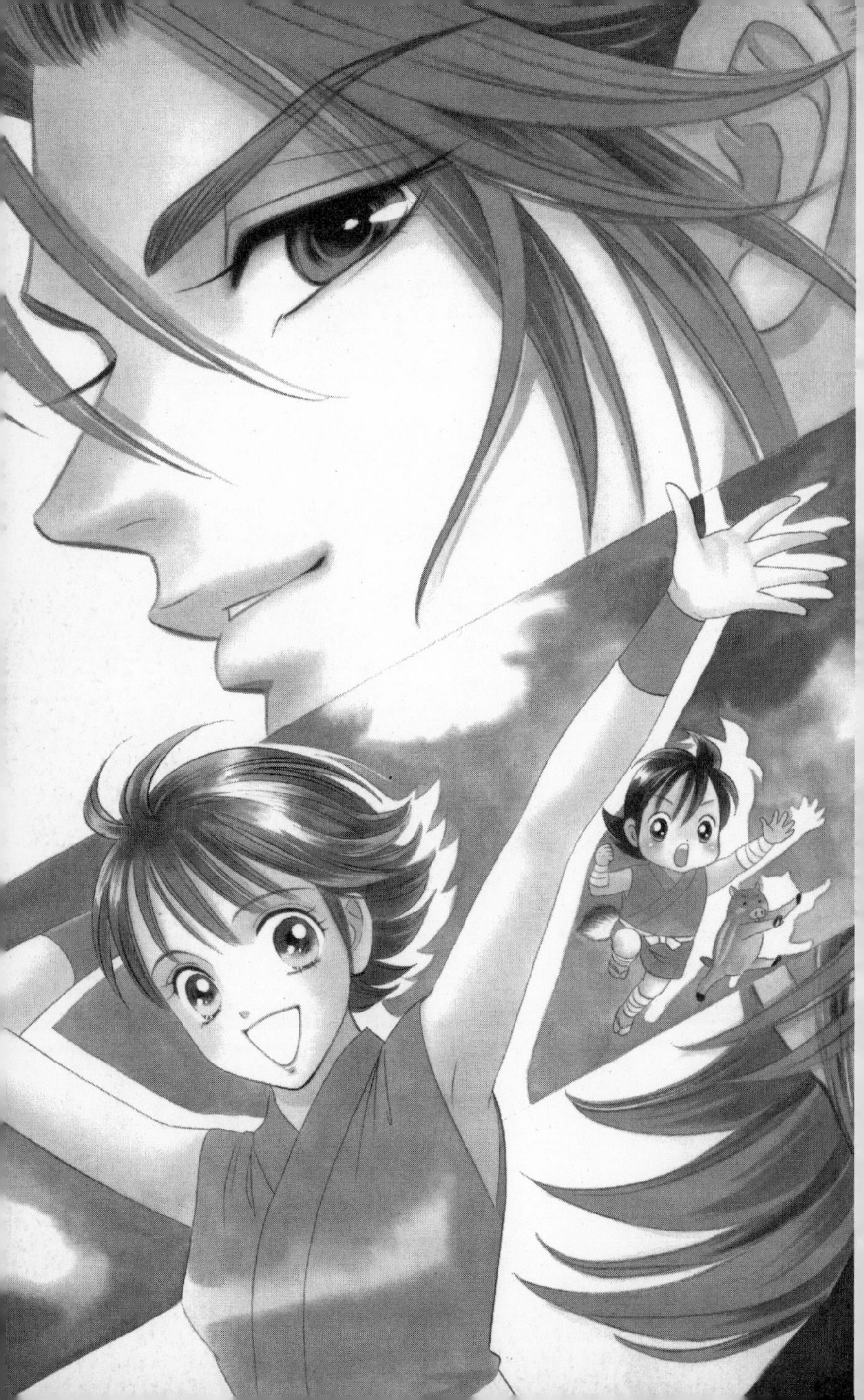

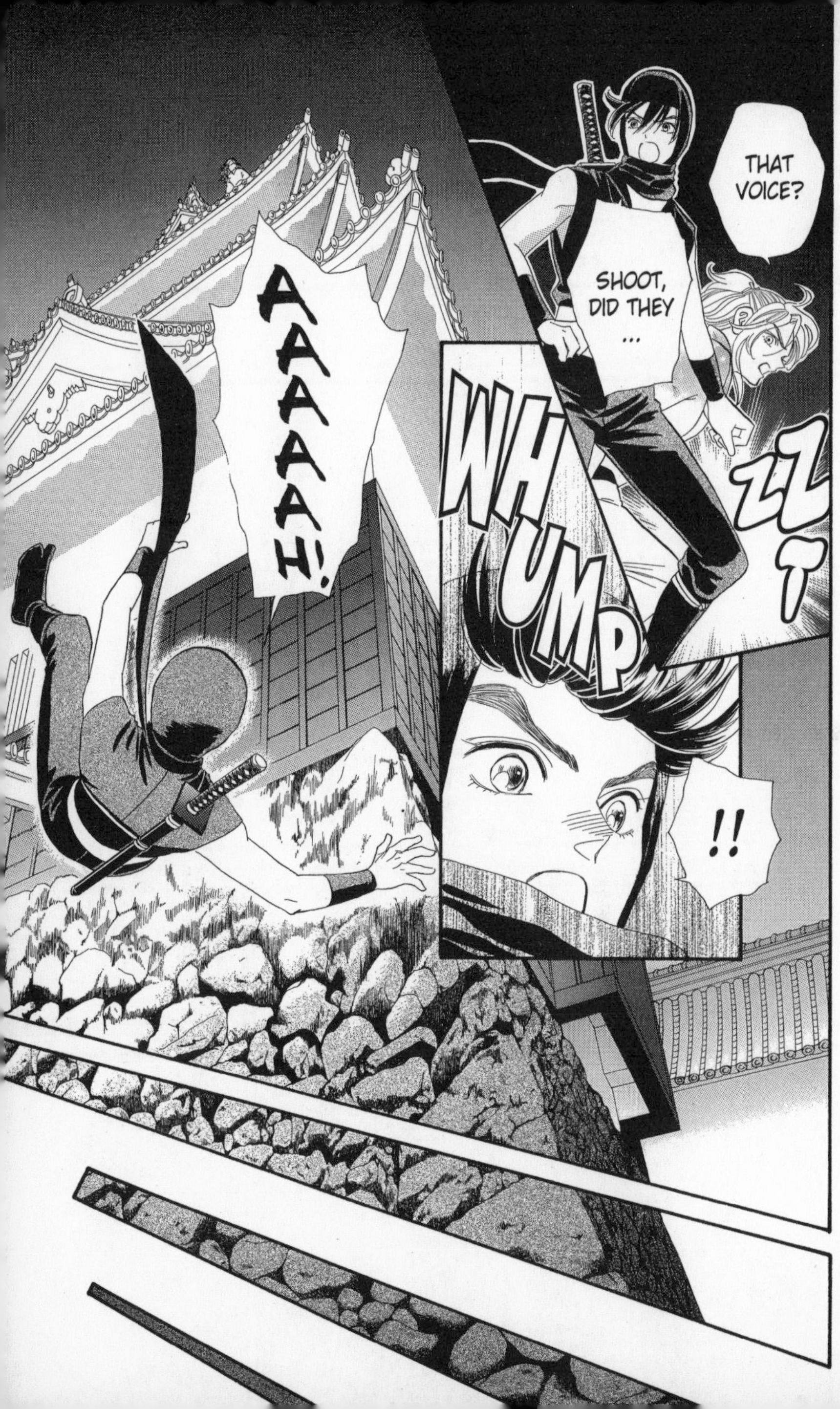
THAT VOICE?
SHOOT, DID THEY ...
ZZT
WHUMP
!!
AAAAAH!

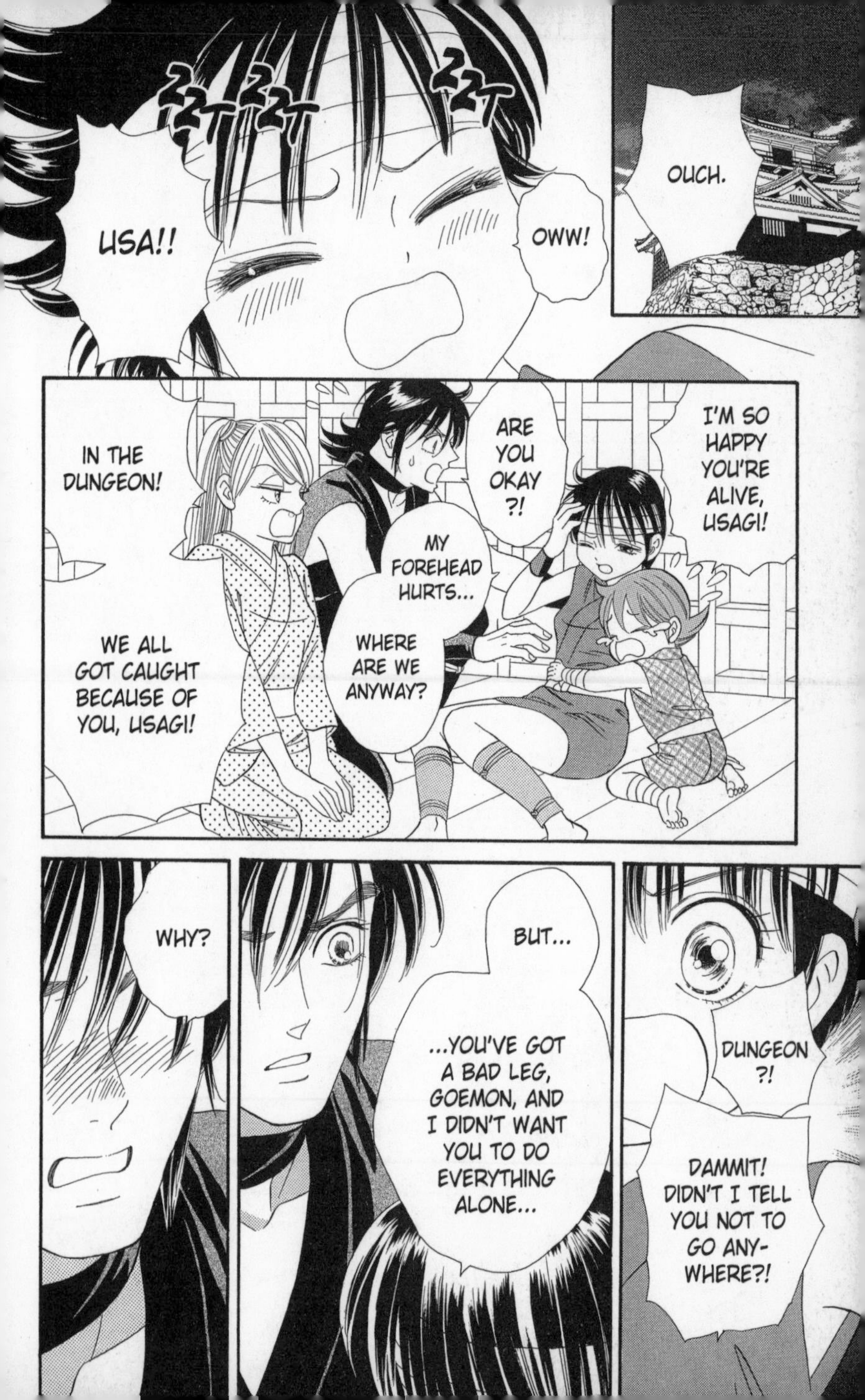
OUCH.
ZZT
ZZT
ZZT
OWW!
USA!!
I'M SO HAPPY YOU'RE ALIVE, USAGI!
ARE YOU OKAY?!
MY FOREHEAD HURTS...
WHERE ARE WE ANYWAY?
IN THE DUNGEON!
WE ALL GOT CAUGHT BECAUSE OF YOU, USAGI!
DUNGEON?!
DAMMIT! DIDN'T I TELL YOU NOT TO GO ANY-WHERE?!
BUT...
...YOU'VE GOT A BAD LEG, GOEMON, AND I DIDN'T WANT YOU TO DO EVERYTHING ALONE...
WHY?

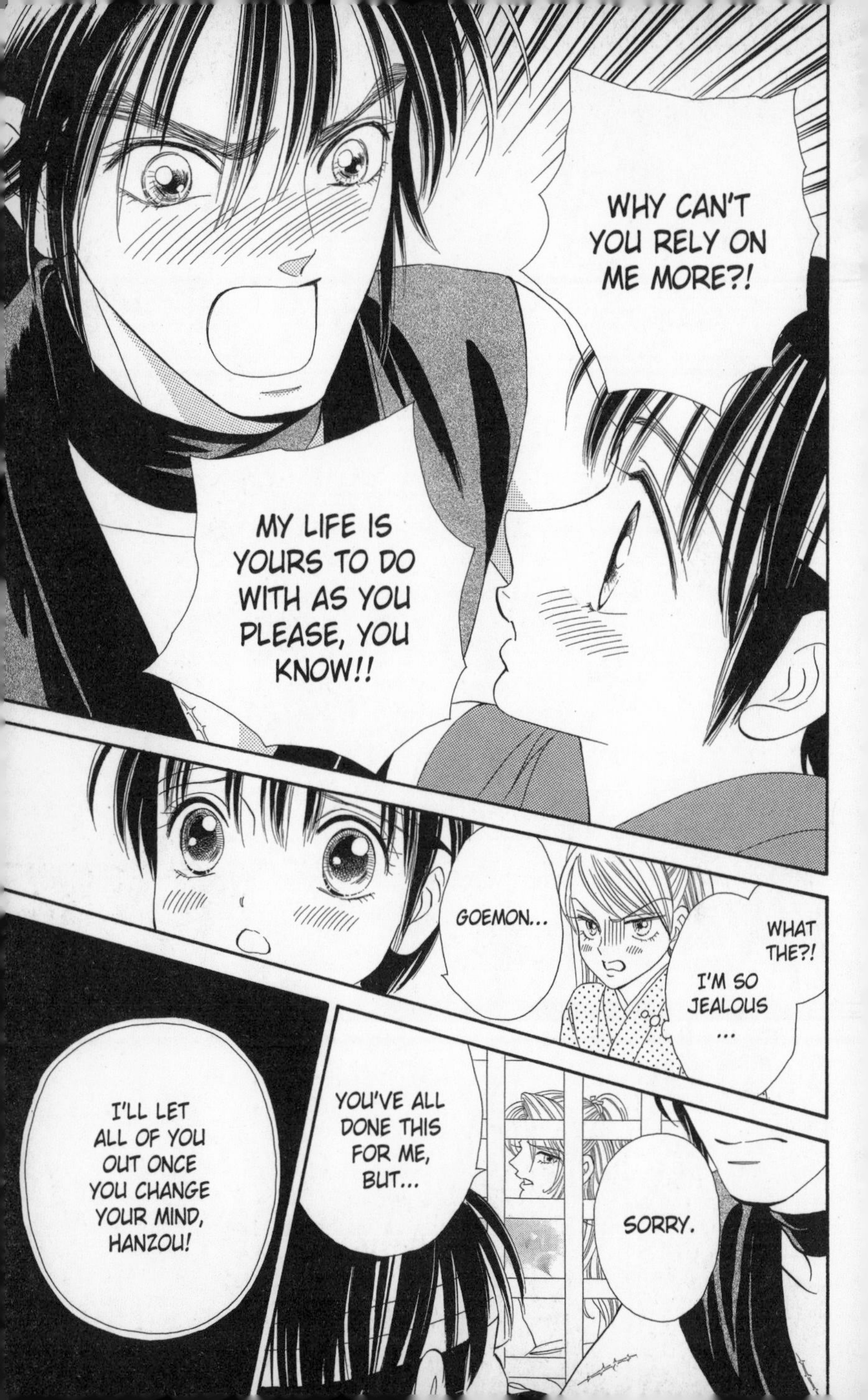
WHY CAN'T YOU RELY ON ME MORE?!
MY LIFE IS YOURS TO DO WITH AS YOU PLEASE, YOU KNOW!!
WHAT THE?!
I'M SO JEALOUS ...
GOEMON...
YOU'VE ALL DONE THIS FOR ME, BUT...
SORRY.
I'LL LET ALL OF YOU OUT ONCE YOU CHANGE YOUR MIND, HANZOU!

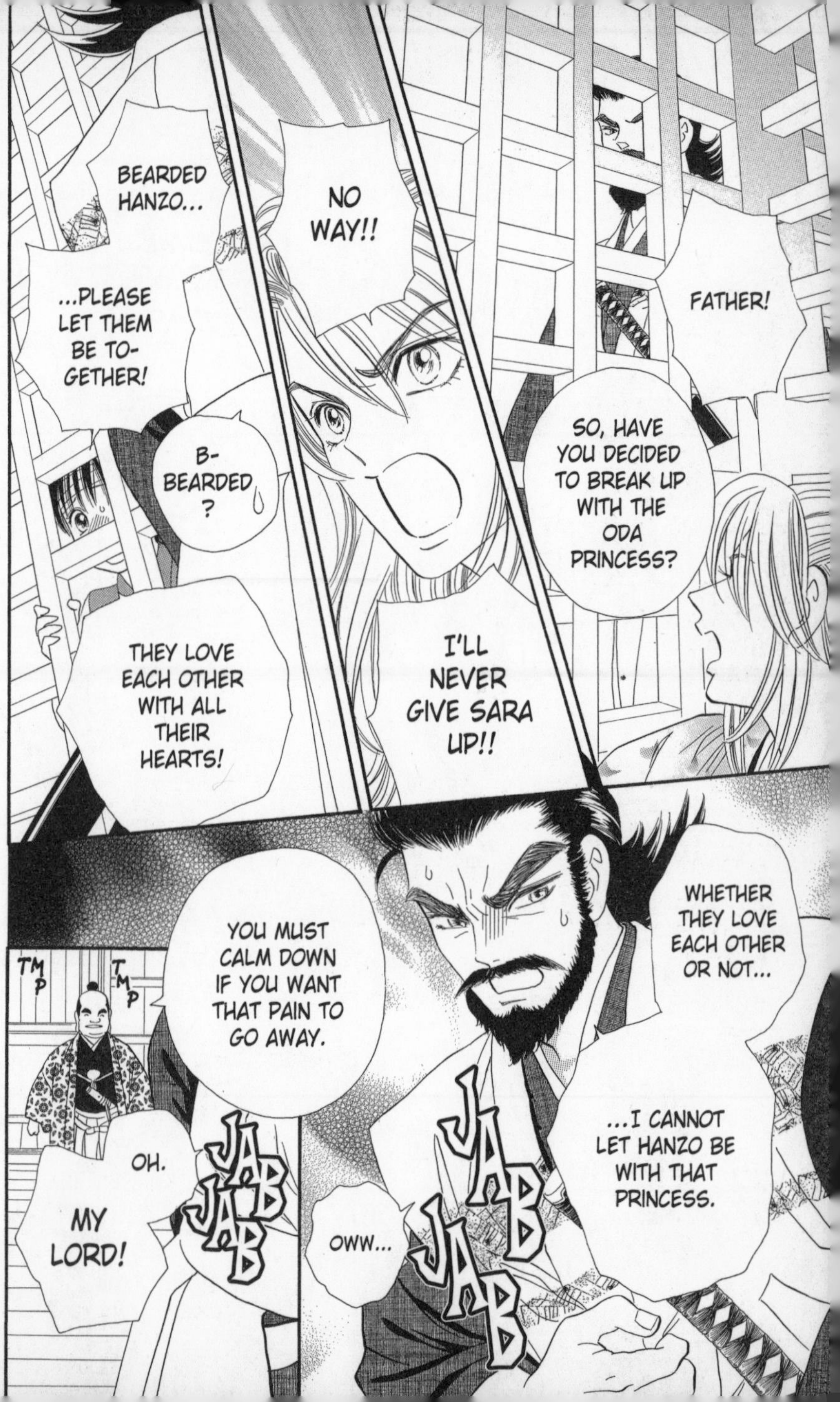
FATHER!
SO, HAVE YOU DECIDED TO BREAK UP WITH THE ODA PRINCESS?
NO WAY!!
I'LL NEVER GIVE SARA UP!!
BEARDED HANZO...
...PLEASE LET THEM BE TO-GETHER!
B-BEARDED?
THEY LOVE EACH OTHER WITH ALL THEIR HEARTS!
WHETHER THEY LOVE EACH OTHER OR NOT...
...I CANNOT LET HANZO BE WITH THAT PRINCESS.
YOU MUST CALM DOWN IF YOU WANT THAT PAIN TO GO AWAY.
JAB JAB
OWW...
TMP TMP
OH.
MY LORD!
JAB JAB

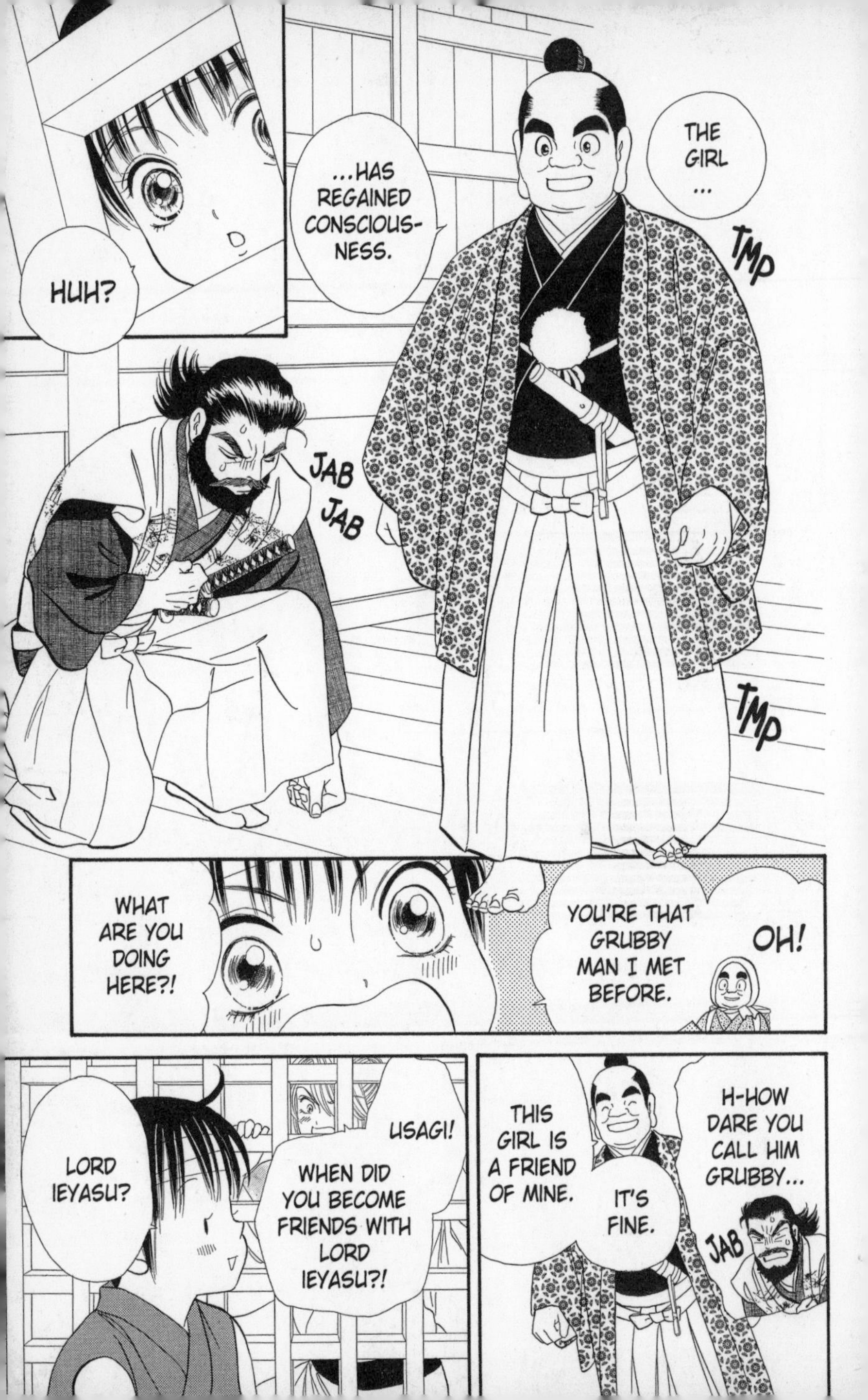
THE GIRL ...
TMP
...HAS REGAINED CONSCIOUS-NESS.
HUH?
TMP
JAB JAB
OH!
YOU'RE THAT GRUBBY MAN I MET BEFORE.
WHAT ARE YOU DOING HERE?!
H-HOW DARE YOU CALL HIM GRUBBY...
JAB
THIS GIRL IS A FRIEND OF MINE.
IT'S FINE.
USAGI!
WHEN DID YOU BECOME FRIENDS WITH LORD IEYASU?!
LORD IEYASU?

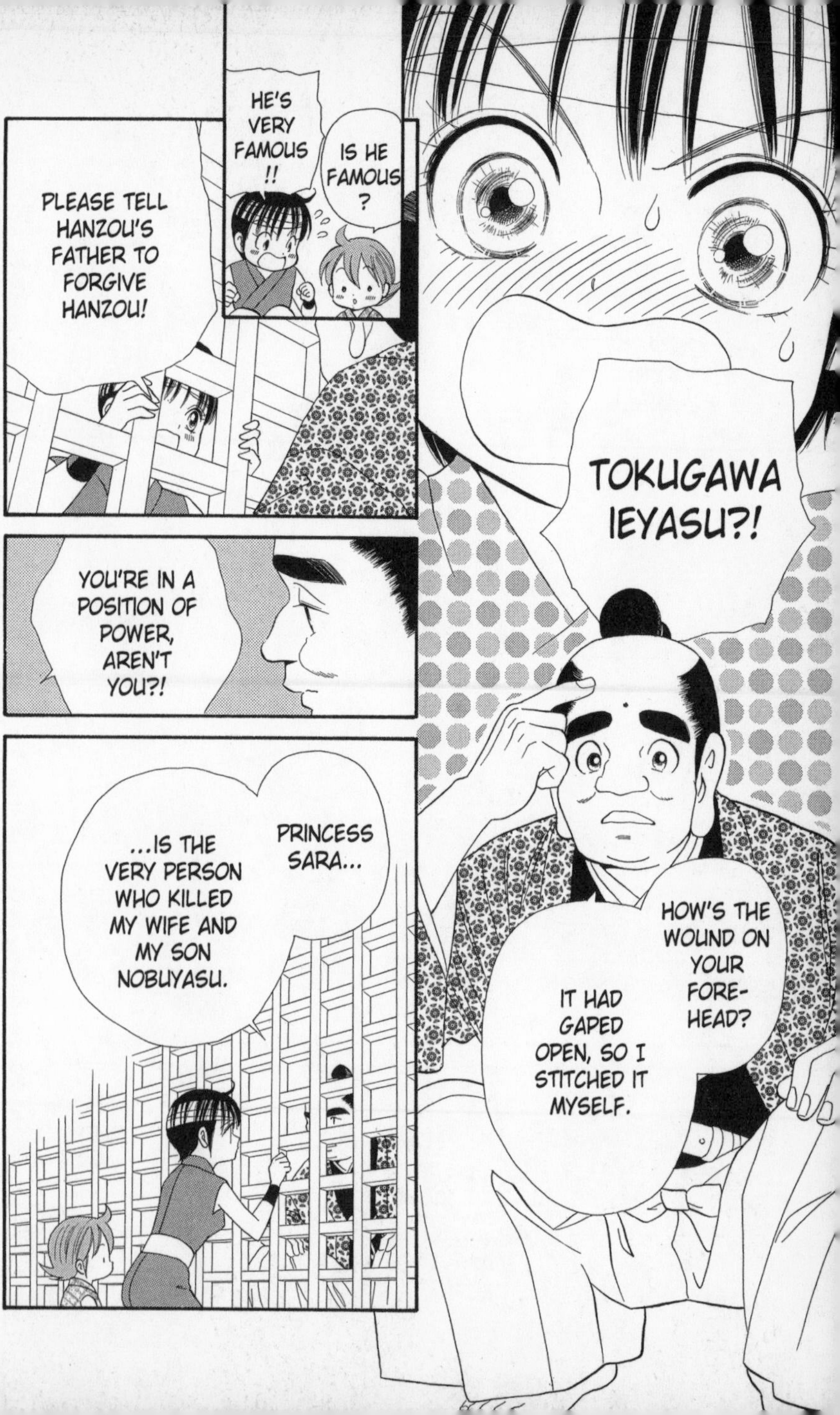
TOKUGAWA IEYASU?!
HOW'S THE WOUND ON YOUR FOREHEAD?
IT HAD GAPED OPEN, SO I STITCHED IT MYSELF.
IS HE FAMOUS?
HE'S VERY FAMOUS!!
PLEASE TELL HANZOU'S FATHER TO FORGIVE HANZOU!
YOU'RE IN A POSITION OF POWER, AREN'T YOU?!
PRINCESS SARA...
...IS THE VERY PERSON WHO KILLED MY WIFE AND MY SON NOBUYASU.

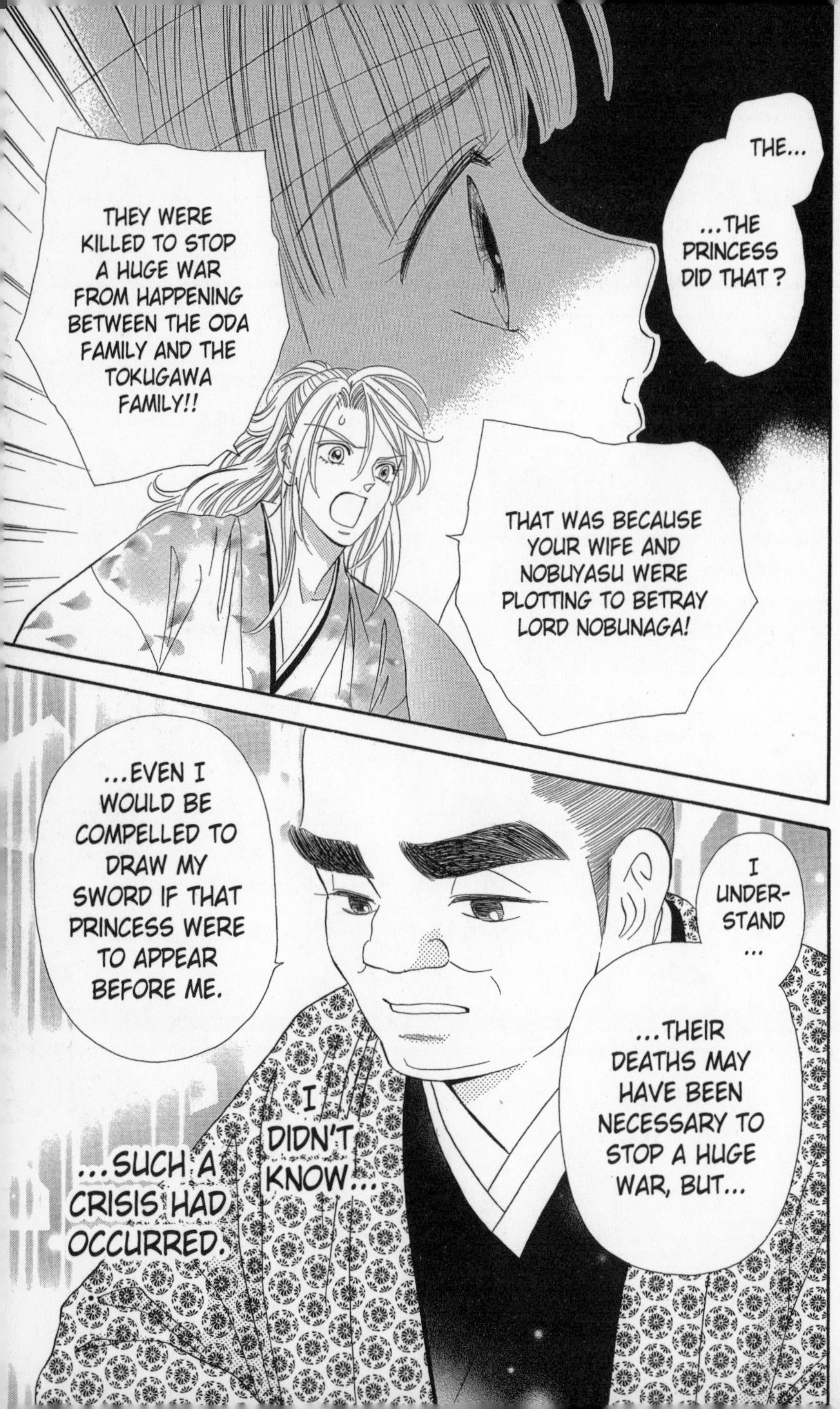
THE...
...THE PRINCESS DID THAT?
THAT WAS BECAUSE YOUR WIFE AND NOBUYASU WERE PLOTTING TO BETRAY LORD NOBUNAGA!
THEY WERE KILLED TO STOP A HUGE WAR FROM HAPPENING BETWEEN THE ODA FAMILY AND THE TOKUGAWA FAMILY!!
I UNDER-STAND...
...THEIR DEATHS MAY HAVE BEEN NECESSARY TO STOP A HUGE WAR, BUT...
...EVEN I WOULD BE COMPELLED TO DRAW MY SWORD IF THAT PRINCESS WERE TO APPEAR BEFORE ME.
I DIDN'T KNOW...
...SUCH A CRISIS HAD OCCURRED.

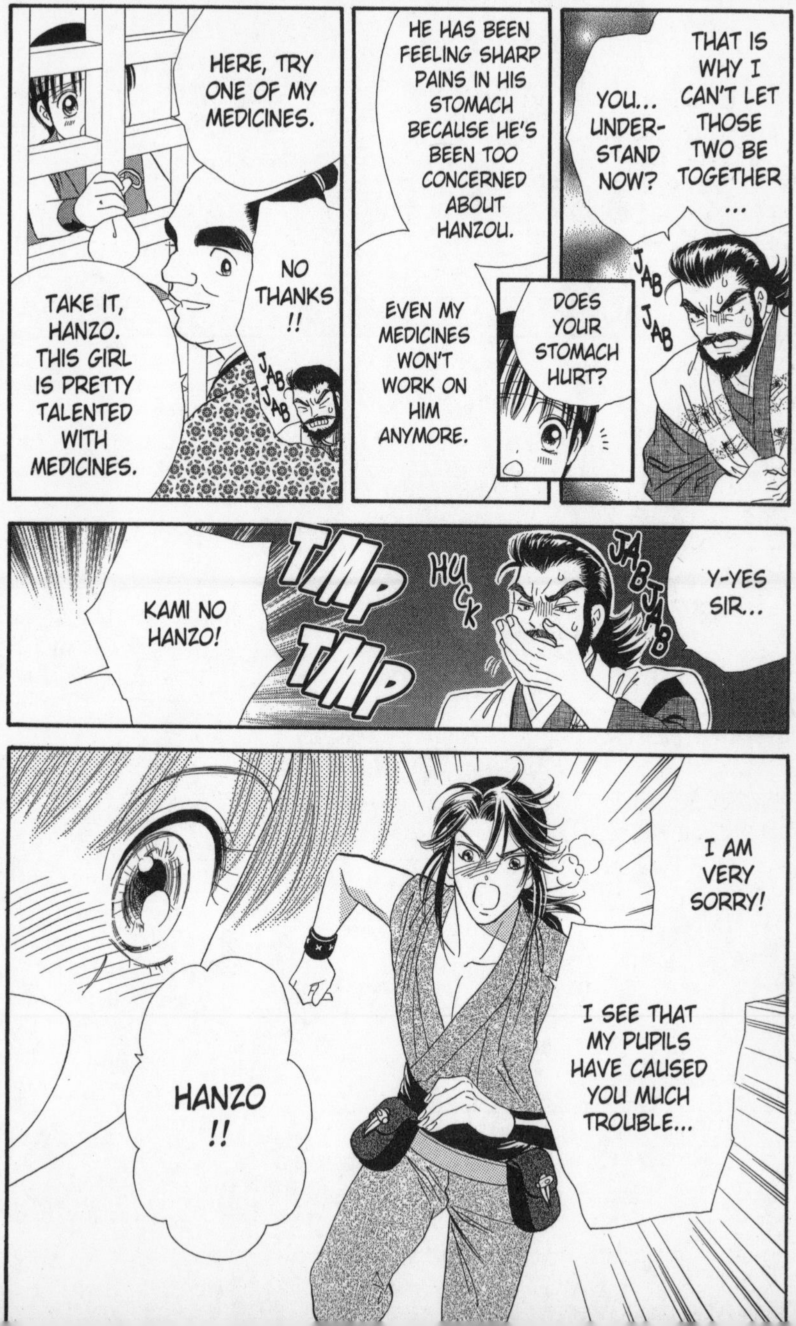
THAT IS WHY I CAN'T LET THOSE TWO BE TOGETHER...
YOU... UNDER-STAND NOW?
JAB JAB
HE HAS BEEN FEELING SHARP PAINS IN HIS STOMACH BECAUSE HE'S BEEN TOO CONCERNED ABOUT HANZOU.
EVEN MY MEDICINES WON'T WORK ON HIM ANYMORE.
DOES YOUR STOMACH HURT?
HERE, TRY ONE OF MY MEDICINES.
NO THANKS!!
JAB JAB
TAKE IT, HANZO. THIS GIRL IS PRETTY TALENTED WITH MEDICINES.
Y-YES SIR...
JAB JAB
HUCK
TMP TMP
KAMI NO HANZO!
I AM VERY SORRY!
I SEE THAT MY PUPILS HAVE CAUSED YOU MUCH TROUBLE...
HANZO!!

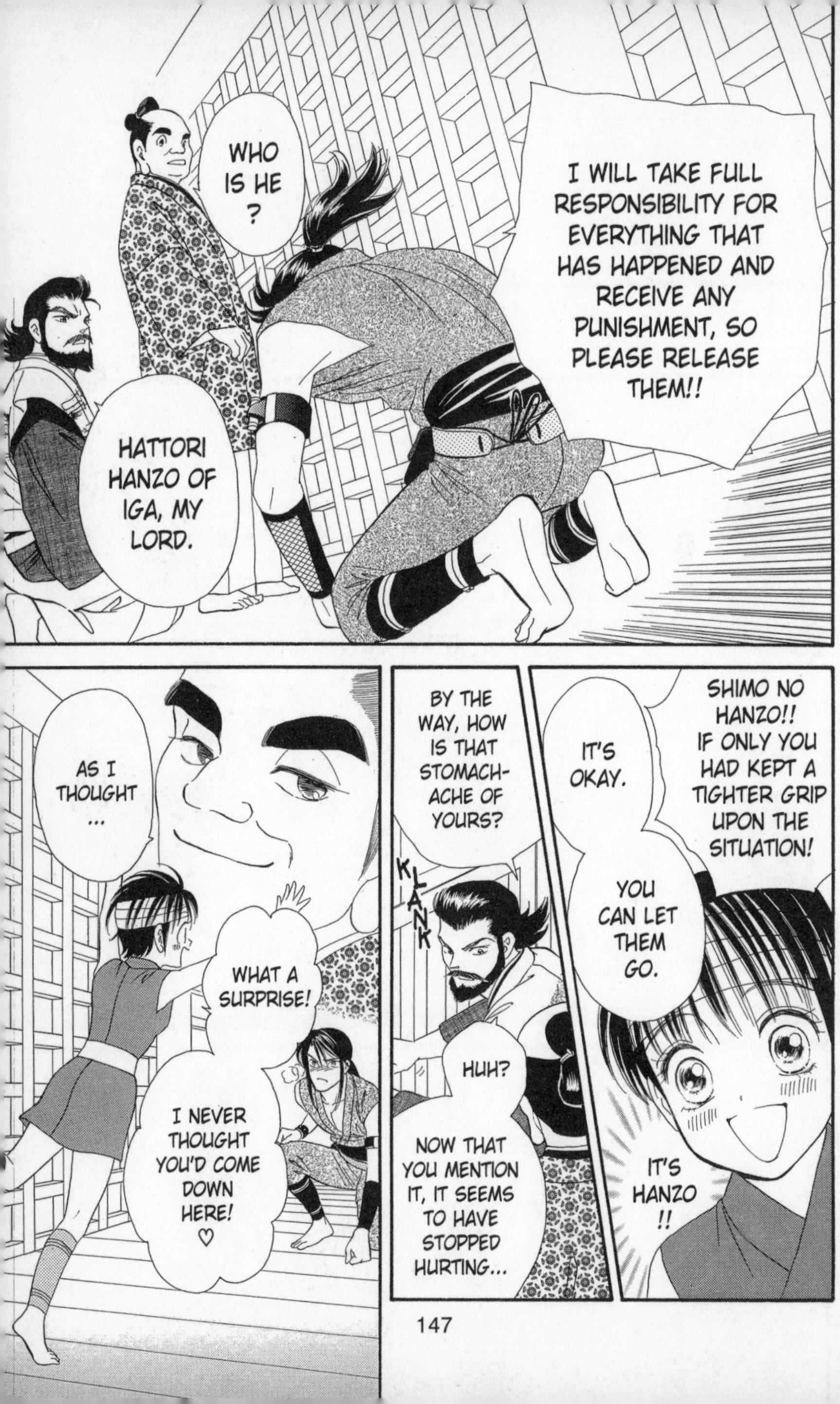
I WILL TAKE FULL RESPONSIBILITY FOR EVERYTHING THAT HAS HAPPENED AND RECEIVE ANY PUNISHMENT, SO PLEASE RELEASE THEM!!
WHO IS HE ?
HATTORI HANZO OF IGA, MY LORD.
SHIMO NO HANZO!! IF ONLY YOU HAD KEPT A TIGHTER GRIP UPON THE SITUATION!
IT'S OKAY.
YOU CAN LET THEM GO.
IT'S HANZO !!
BY THE WAY, HOW IS THAT STOMACH-ACHE OF YOURS?
KLANK
HUH?
NOW THAT YOU MENTION IT, IT SEEMS TO HAVE STOPPED HURTING...
AS I THOUGHT ...
WHAT A SURPRISE!
I NEVER THOUGHT YOU'D COME DOWN HERE! ♡

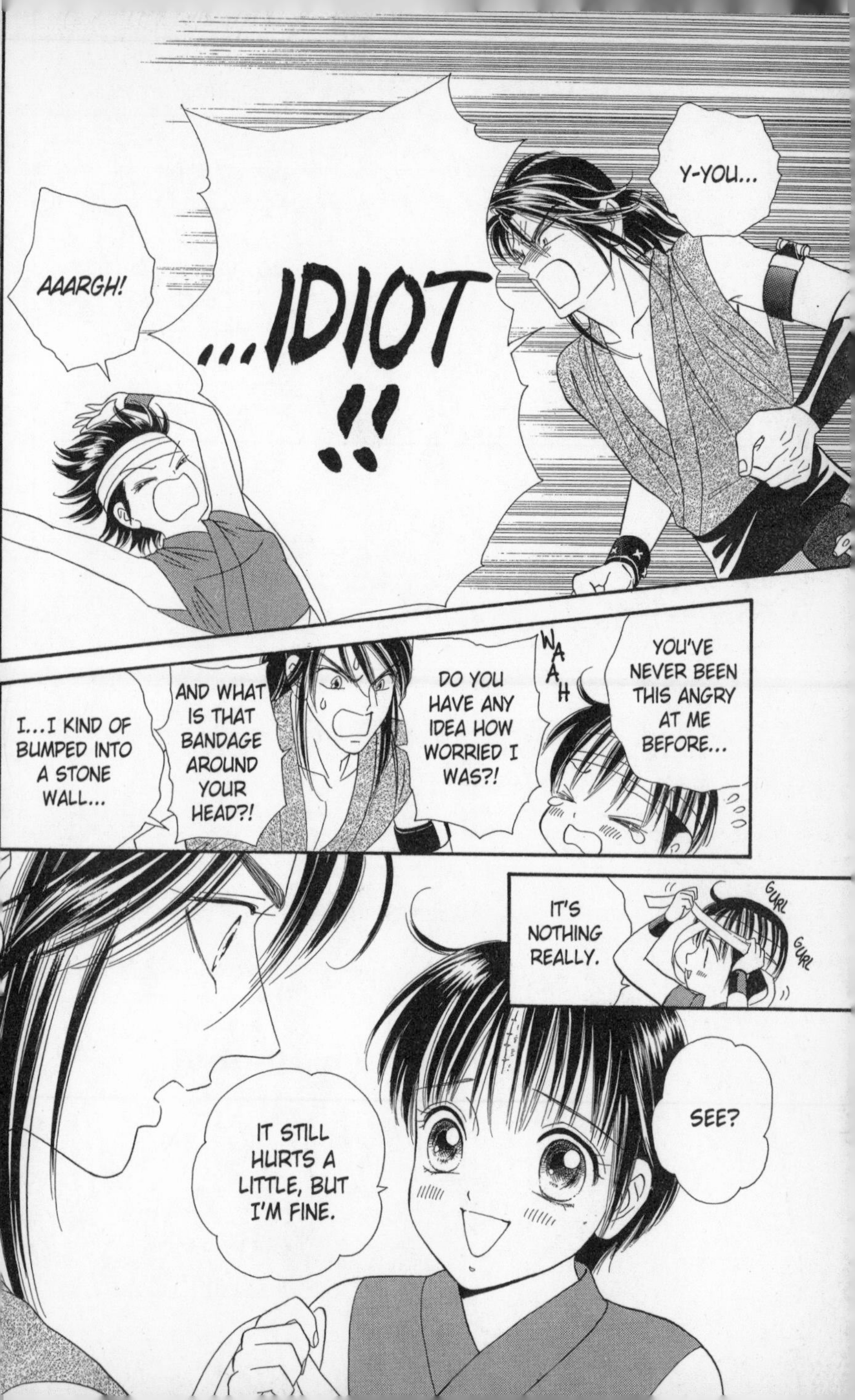
Y-YOU...
...IDIOT!!
AAARGH!
YOU'VE NEVER BEEN THIS ANGRY AT ME BEFORE...
WAAH
DO YOU HAVE ANY IDEA HOW WORRIED I WAS?!
AND WHAT IS THAT BANDAGE AROUND YOUR HEAD?!
I...I KIND OF BUMPED INTO A STONE WALL...
GURL GURL
IT'S NOTHING REALLY.
SEE?
IT STILL HURTS A LITTLE, BUT I'M FINE.

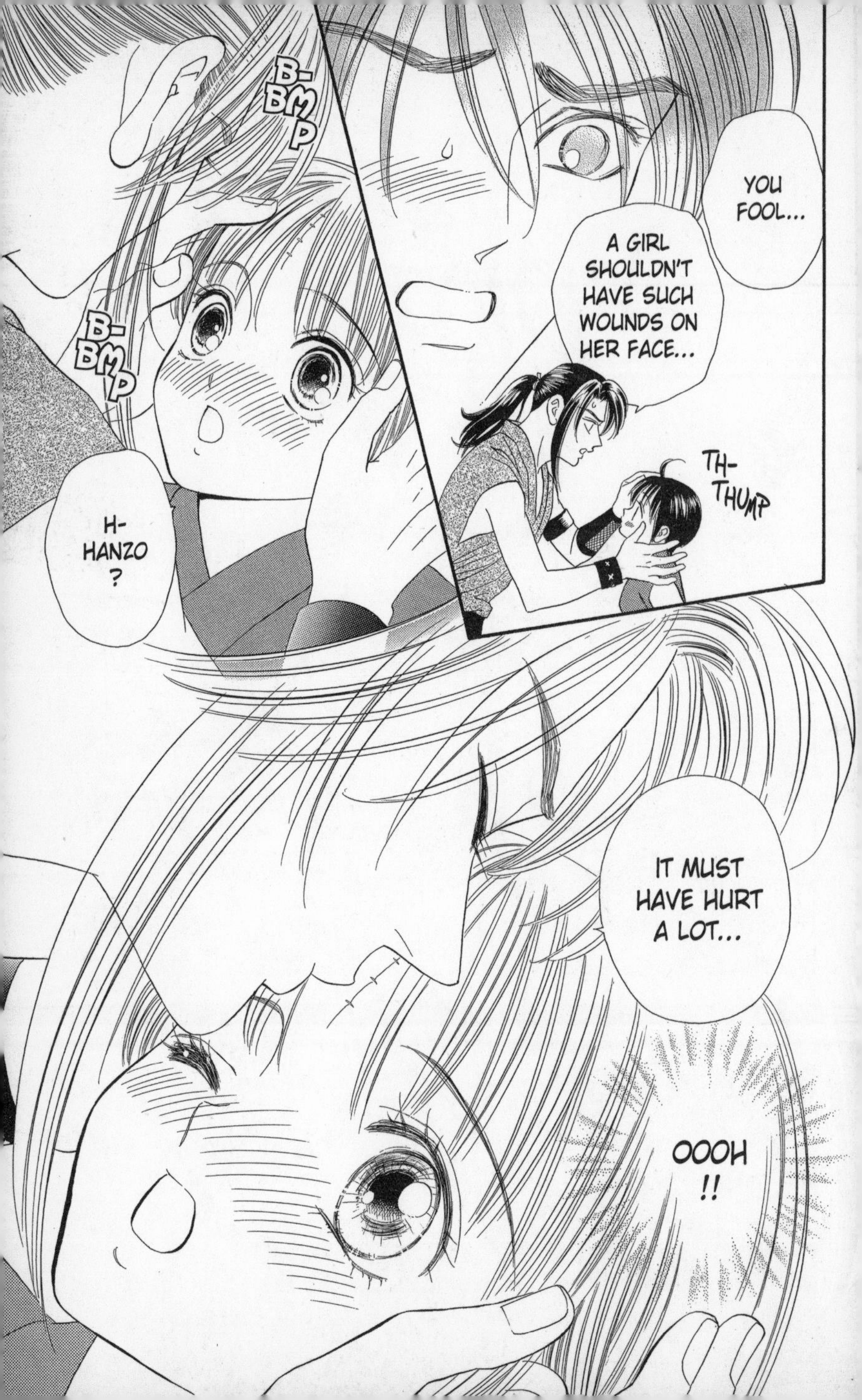
YOU FOOL...
A GIRL SHOULDN'T HAVE SUCH WOUNDS ON HER FACE...
TH-THUMP
B-BMP
B-BMP
H-HANZO?
IT MUST HAVE HURT A LOT...
OOOH!!

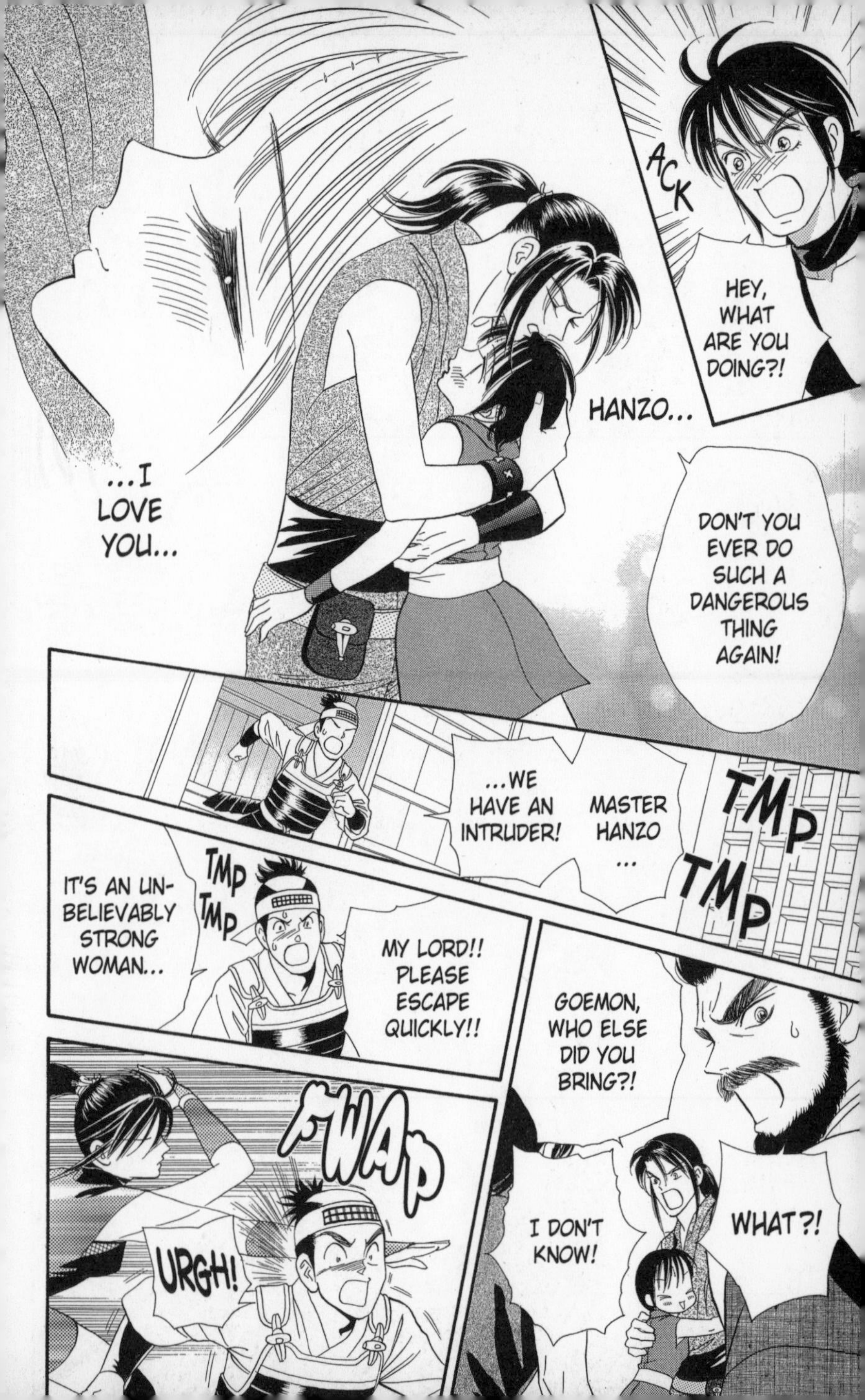
ACK
HEY, WHAT ARE YOU DOING?!
HANZO...
DON'T YOU EVER DO SUCH A DANGEROUS THING AGAIN!
...I LOVE YOU...
TMP
TMP
MASTER HANZO ...
...WE HAVE AN INTRUDER!
GOEMON, WHO ELSE DID YOU BRING?!
WHAT?!
I DON'T KNOW!
MY LORD!! PLEASE ESCAPE QUICKLY!!
IT'S AN UN-BELIEVABLY STRONG WOMAN...
TMP
TMP
FWAP
URGH!

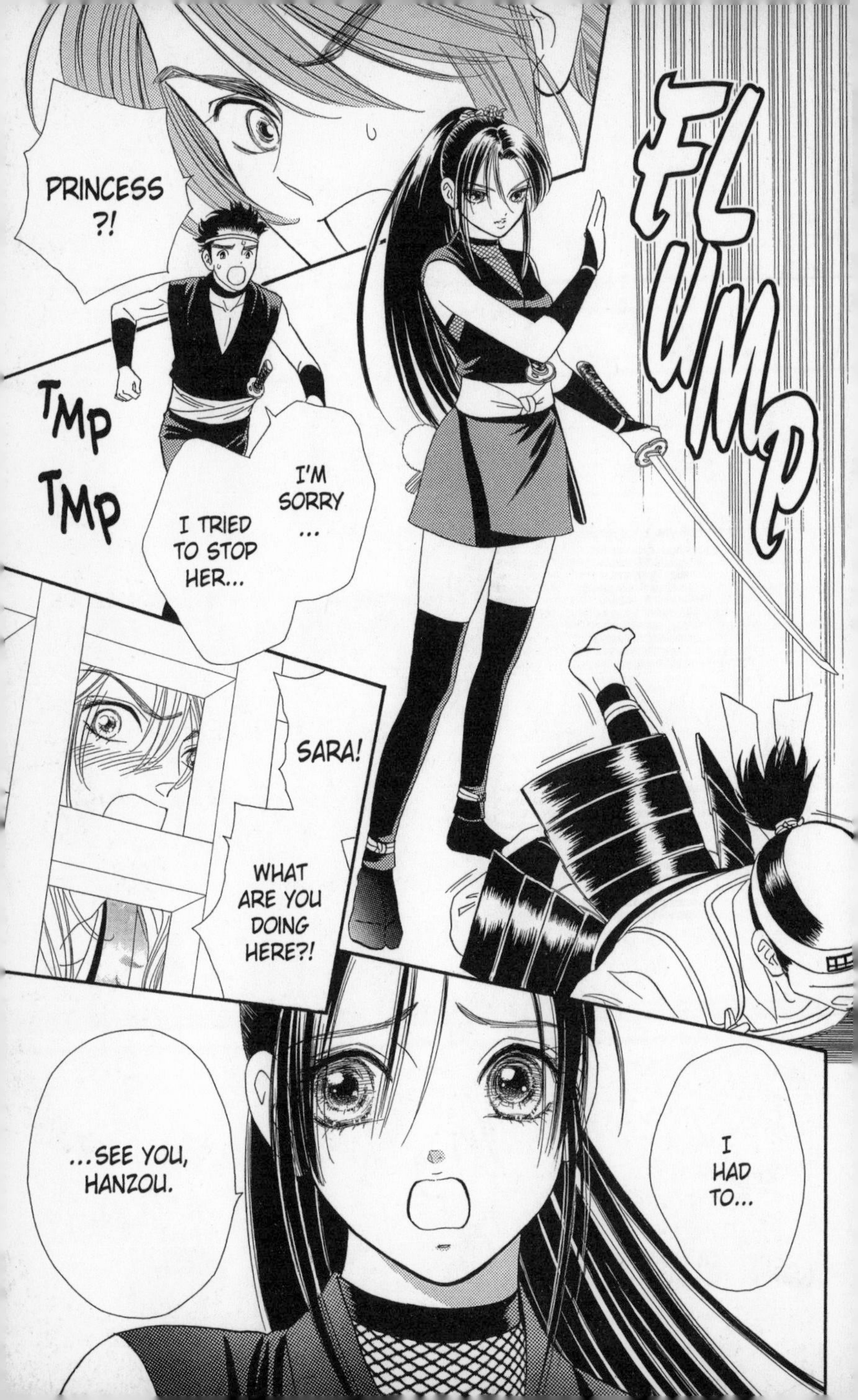
FLUMP
PRINCESS?!
TMP TMP
I'M SORRY...
I TRIED TO STOP HER...
SARA!
WHAT ARE YOU DOING HERE?!
I HAD TO...
...SEE YOU, HANZOU.

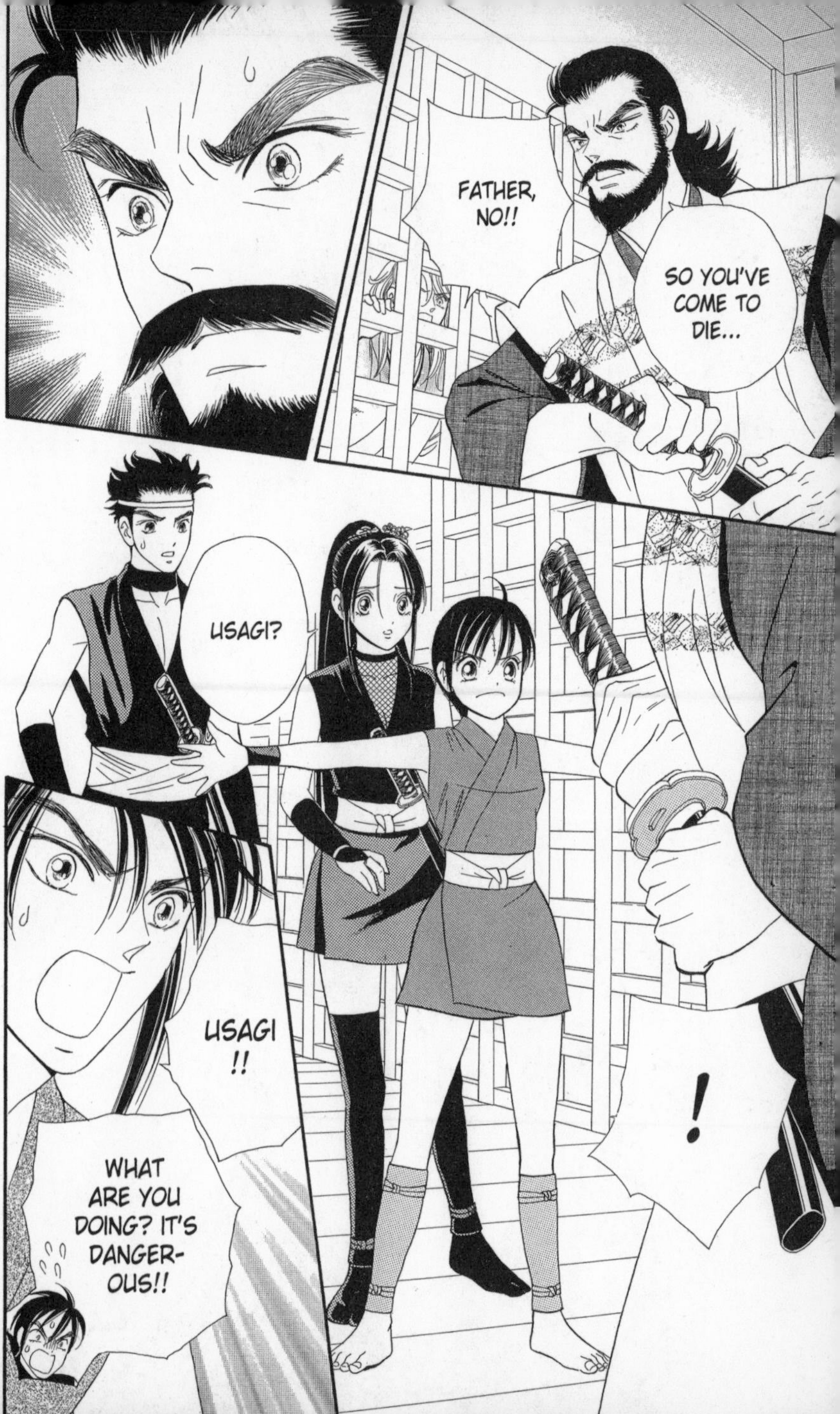
SO YOU'VE COME TO DIE...
FATHER, NO!!
!
USAGI?
USAGI !!
WHAT ARE YOU DOING? IT'S DANGER-OUS!!

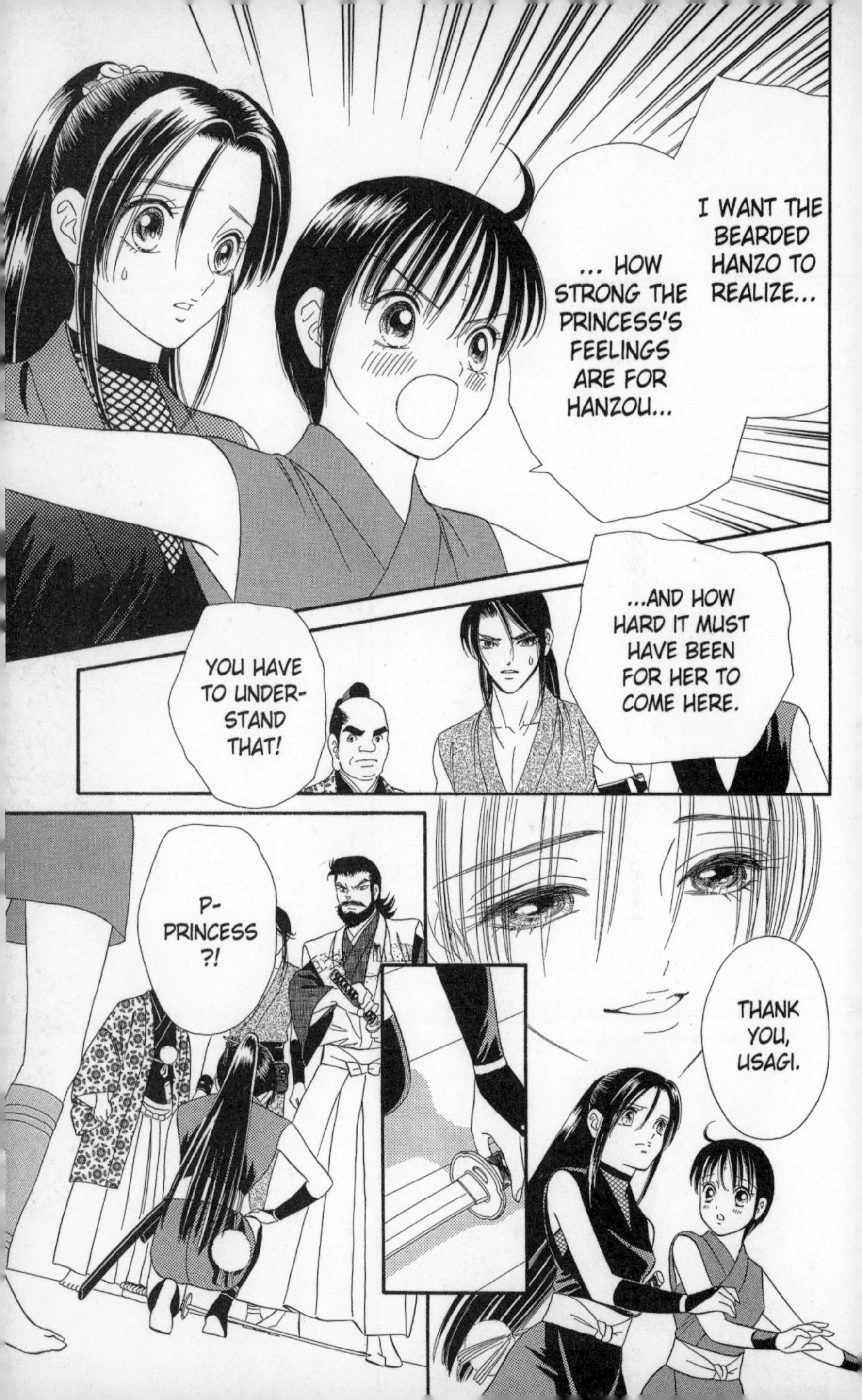
I WANT THE BEARDED HANZO TO REALIZE...
... HOW STRONG THE PRINCESS'S FEELINGS ARE FOR HANZOU...
...AND HOW HARD IT MUST HAVE BEEN FOR HER TO COME HERE.
YOU HAVE TO UNDER-STAND THAT!
THANK YOU, USAGI.
P-PRINCESS?!

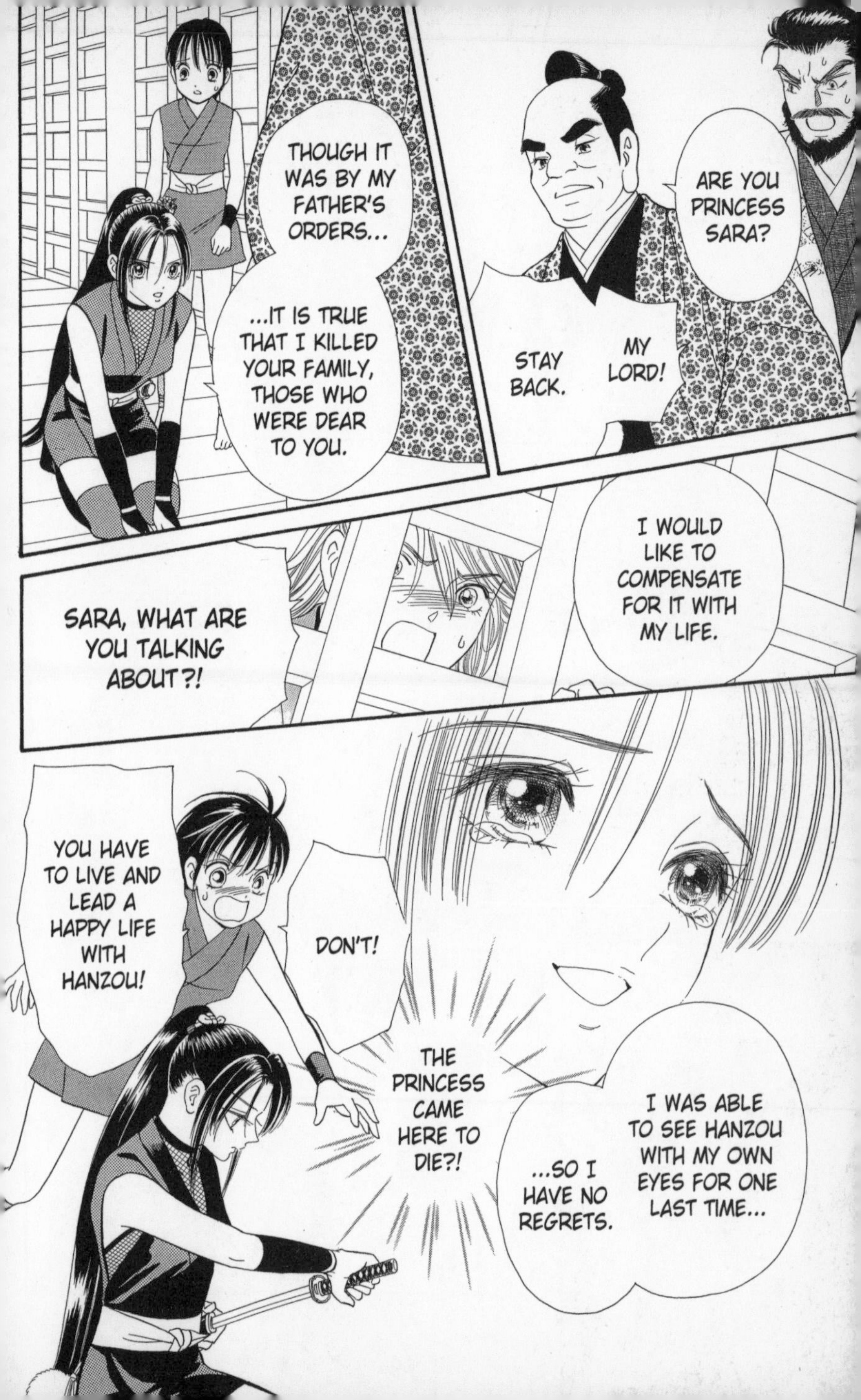

ARE YOU PRINCESS SARA?
MY LORD!
STAY BACK.
THOUGH IT WAS BY MY FATHER'S ORDERS...
...IT IS TRUE THAT I KILLED YOUR FAMILY, THOSE WHO WERE DEAR TO YOU.
I WOULD LIKE TO COMPENSATE FOR IT WITH MY LIFE.
SARA, WHAT ARE YOU TALKING ABOUT?!
I WAS ABLE TO SEE HANZOU WITH MY OWN EYES FOR ONE LAST TIME...
...SO I HAVE NO REGRETS.
THE PRINCESS CAME HERE TO DIE?!
DON'T!
YOU HAVE TO LIVE AND LEAD A HAPPY LIFE WITH HANZOU!

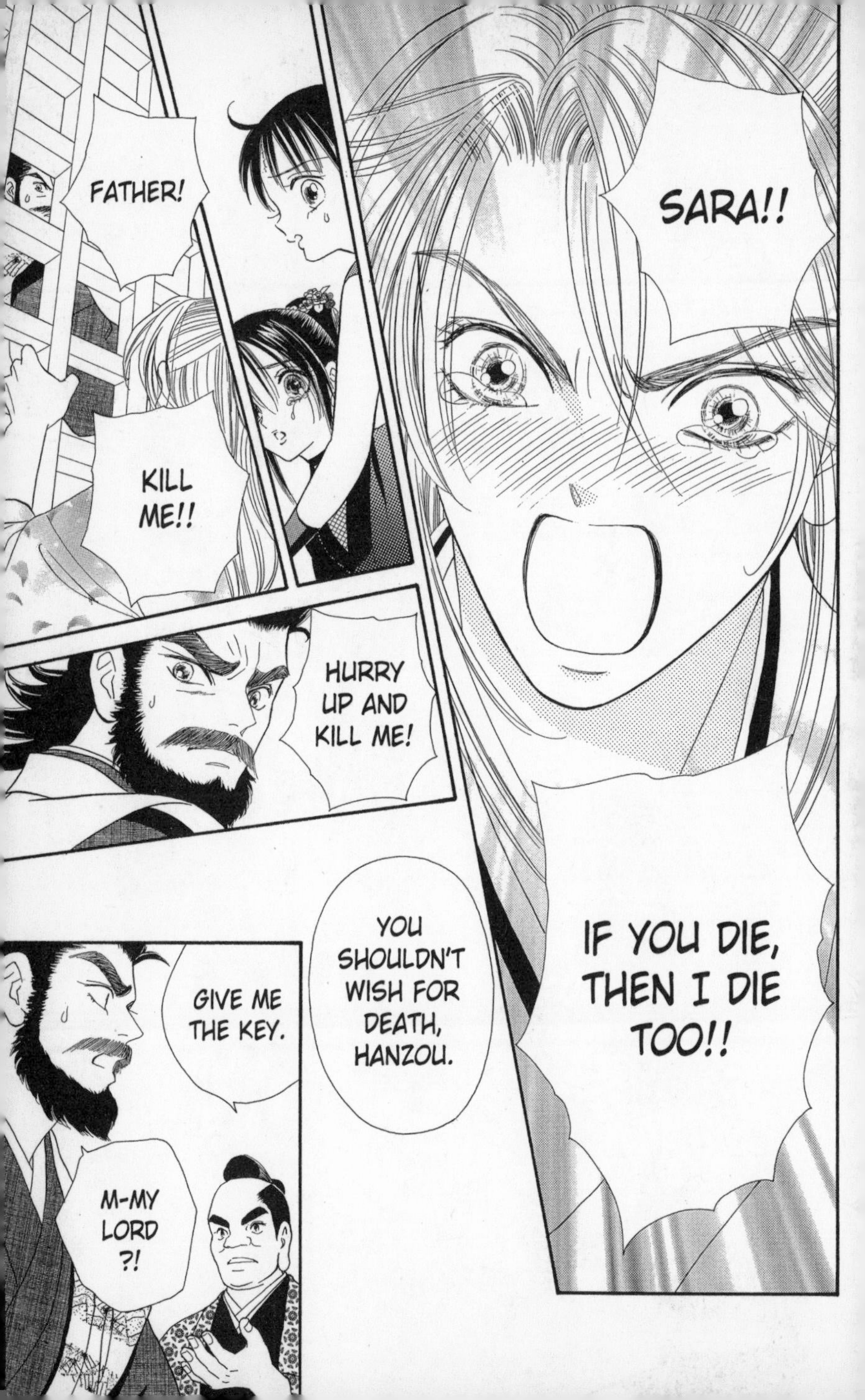
SARA!!
IF YOU DIE, THEN I DIE TOO!!
FATHER!
KILL ME!!
HURRY UP AND KILL ME!
YOU SHOULDN'T WISH FOR DEATH, HANZOU.
GIVE ME THE KEY.
M-MY LORD ?!

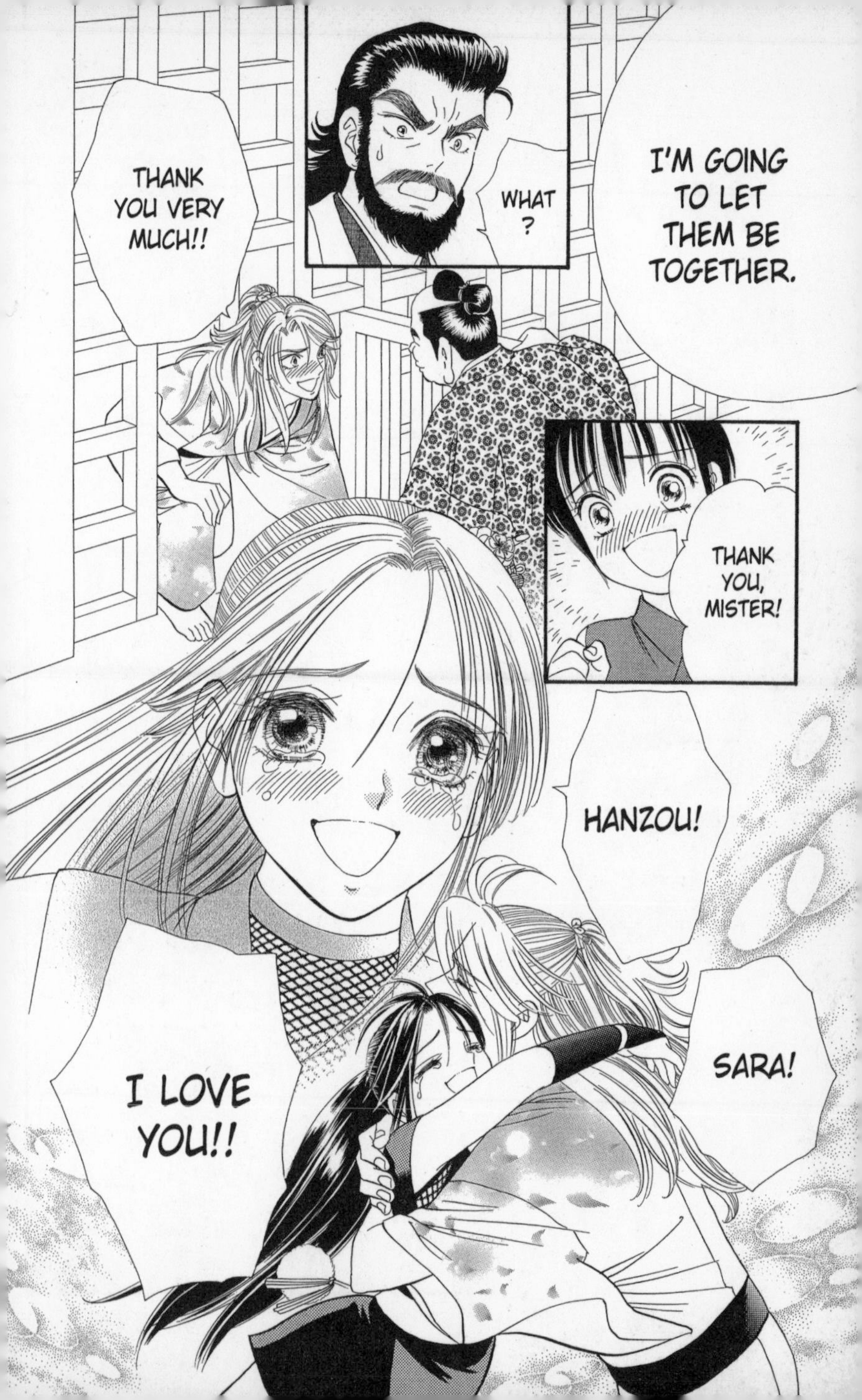
I'M GOING TO LET THEM BE TOGETHER.
WHAT ?
THANK YOU VERY MUCH!!
THANK YOU, MISTER!
HANZOU!
SARA!
I LOVE YOU!!

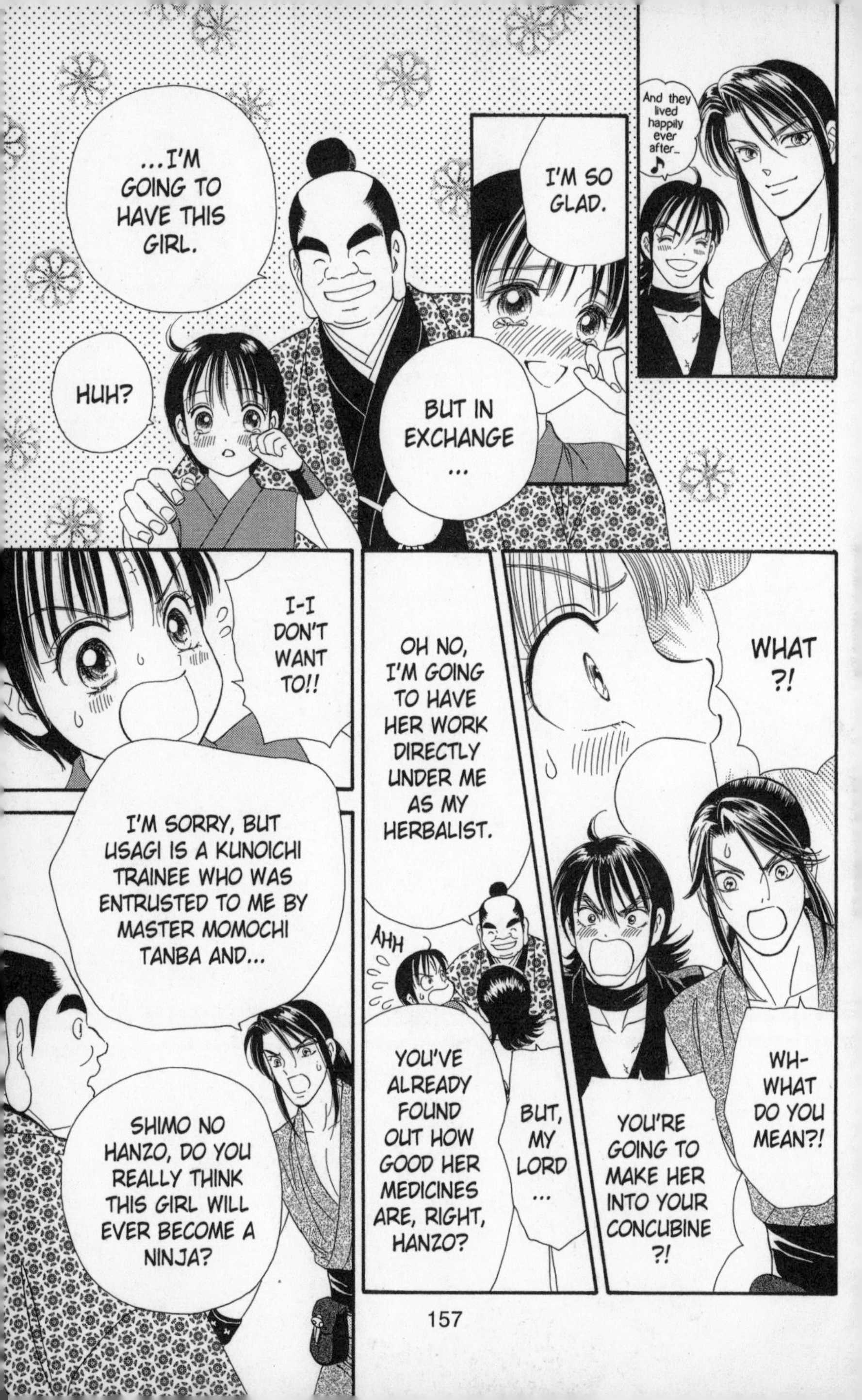

And they lived happily ever after... ♪
I'M SO GLAD.
BUT IN EXCHANGE...
...I'M GOING TO HAVE THIS GIRL.
HUH?
WHAT?!
WH-WHAT DO YOU MEAN?!
YOU'RE GOING TO MAKE HER INTO YOUR CONCUBINE?!
OH NO, I'M GOING TO HAVE HER WORK DIRECTLY UNDER ME AS MY HERBALIST.
AHH
BUT, MY LORD...
YOU'VE ALREADY FOUND OUT HOW GOOD HER MEDICINES ARE, RIGHT, HANZO?
I-I DON'T WANT TO!!
I'M SORRY, BUT USAGI IS A KUNOICHI TRAINEE WHO WAS ENTRUSTED TO ME BY MASTER MOMOCHI TANBA AND...
SHIMO NO HANZO, DO YOU REALLY THINK THIS GIRL WILL EVER BECOME A NINJA?

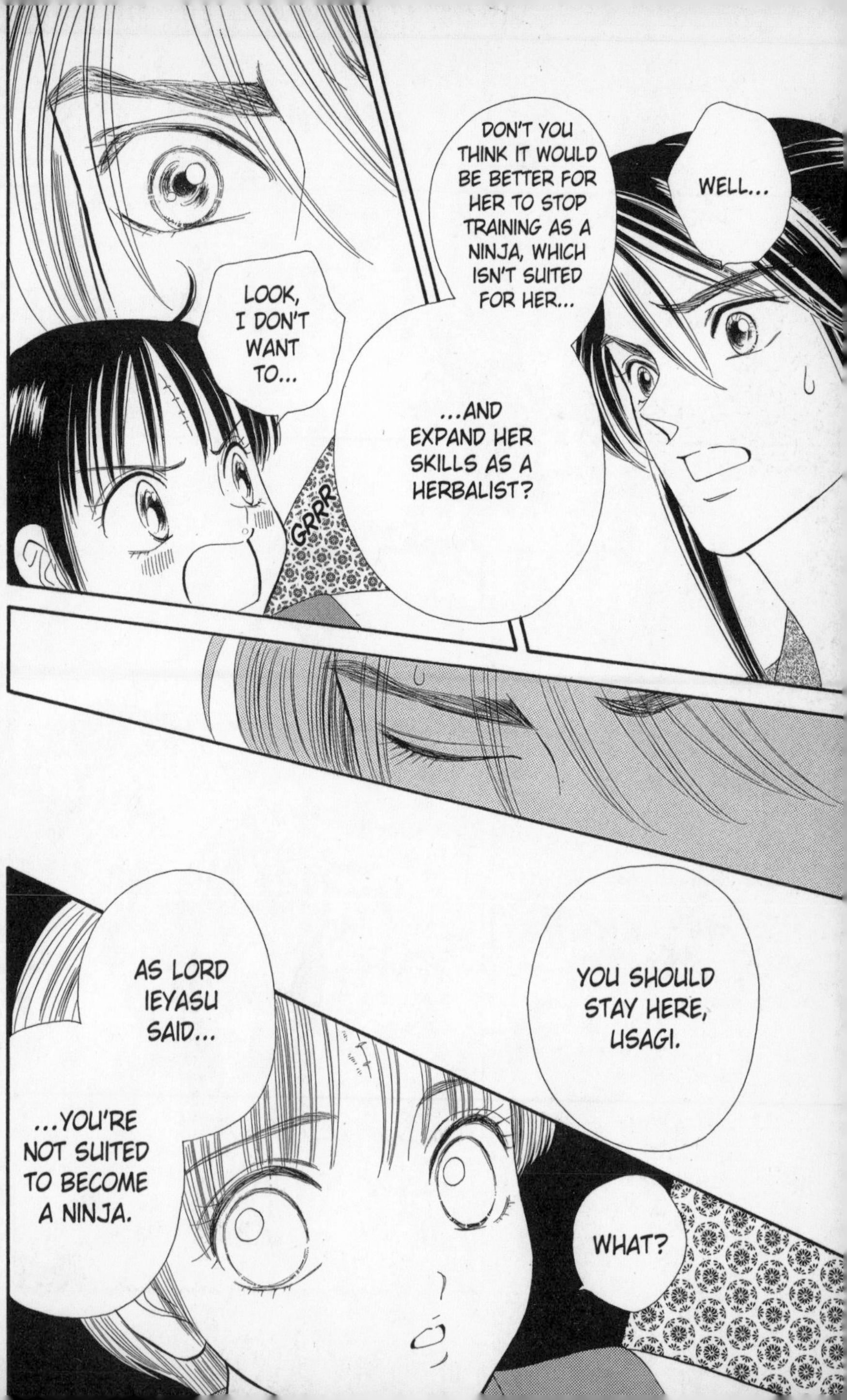
WELL...
DON'T YOU THINK IT WOULD BE BETTER FOR HER TO STOP TRAINING AS A NINJA, WHICH ISN'T SUITED FOR HER...
...AND EXPAND HER SKILLS AS A HERBALIST?
LOOK, I DON'T WANT TO...
GRRR
YOU SHOULD STAY HERE, USAGI.
AS LORD IEYASU SAID...
...YOU'RE NOT SUITED TO BECOME A NINJA.
WHAT?

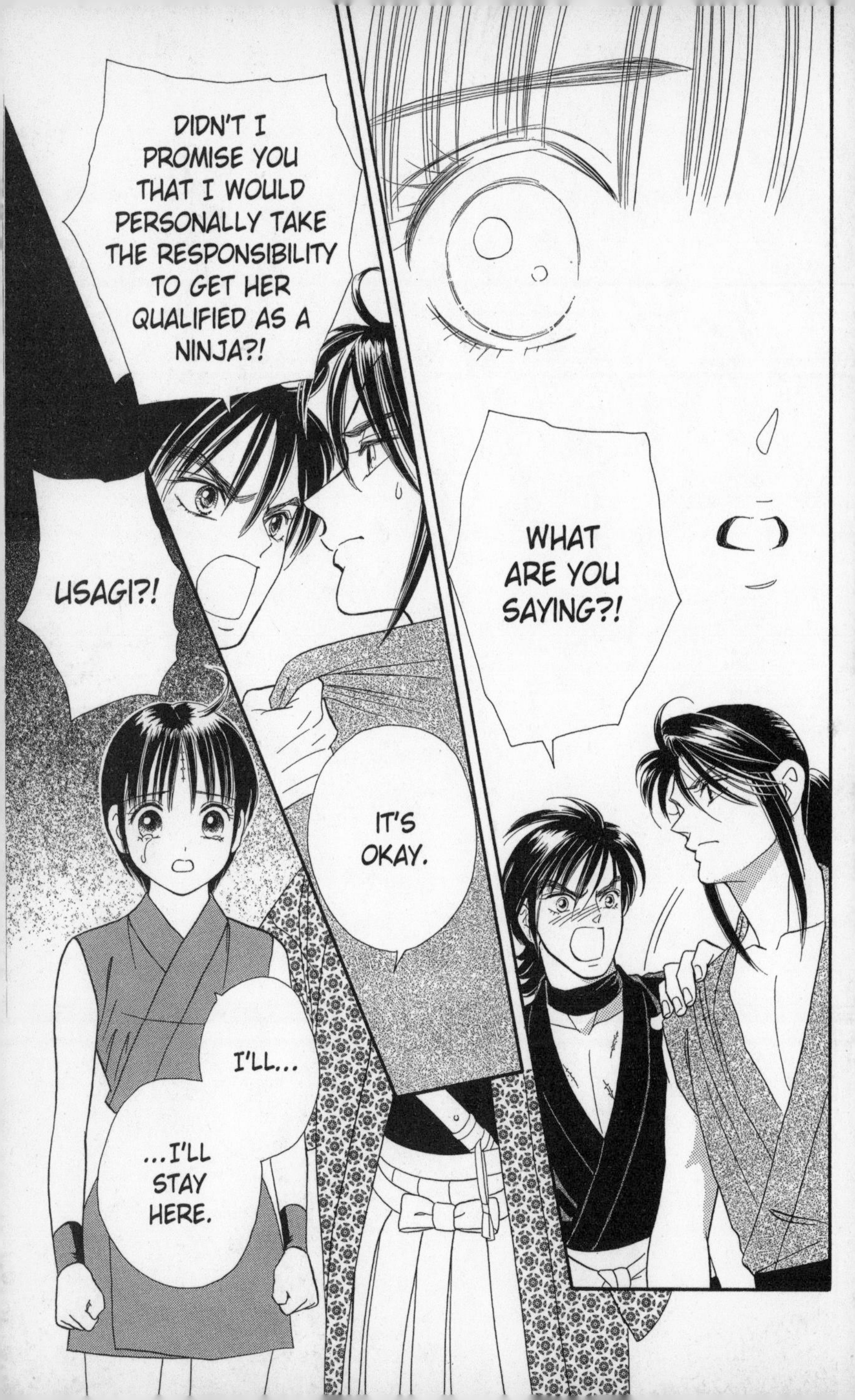
WHAT ARE YOU SAYING?!
DIDN'T I PROMISE YOU THAT I WOULD PERSONALLY TAKE THE RESPONSIBILITY TO GET HER QUALIFIED AS A NINJA?!
USAGI?!
IT'S OKAY.
I'LL...
...I'LL STAY HERE.

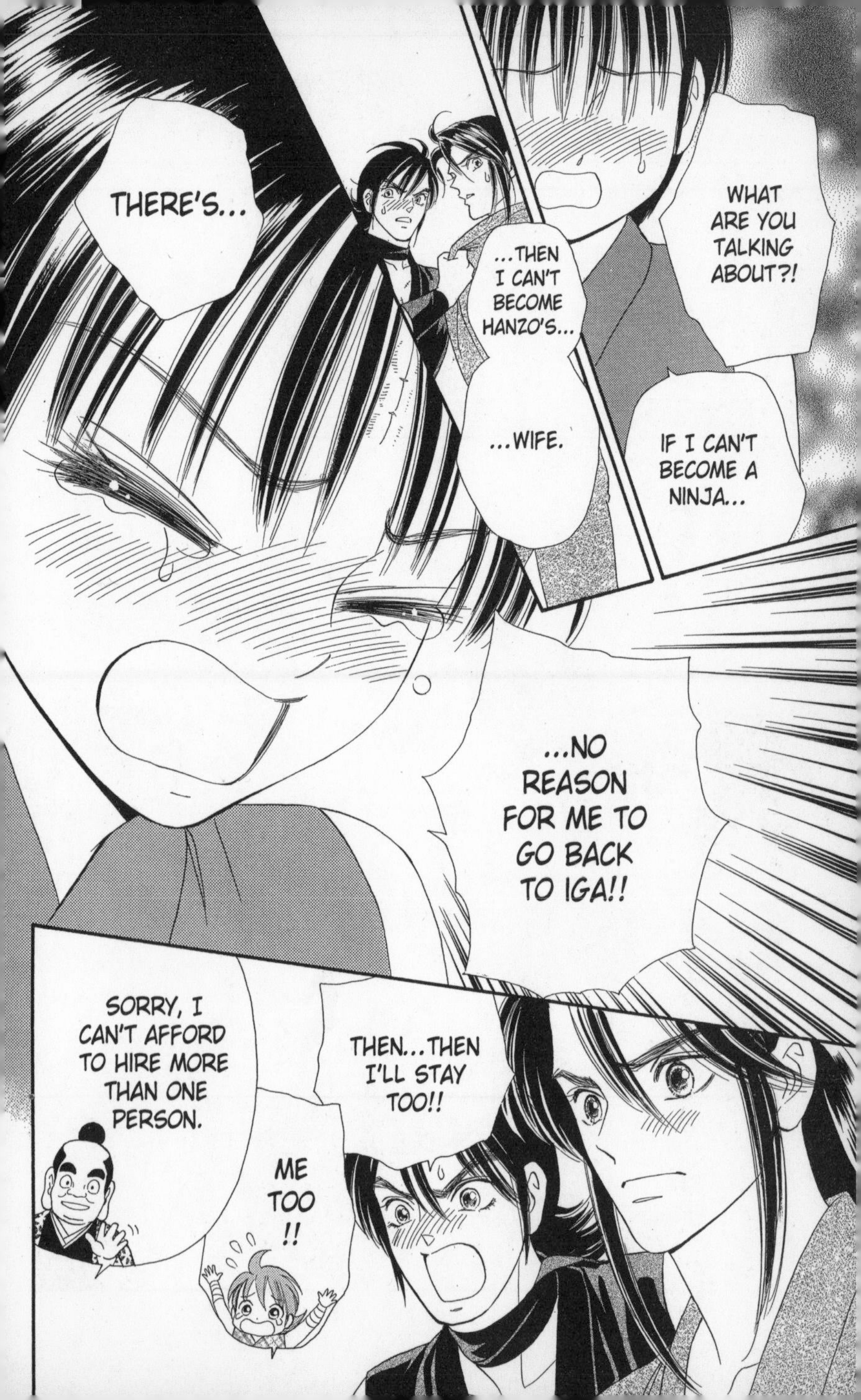
WHAT ARE YOU TALKING ABOUT?!
IF I CAN'T BECOME A NINJA...
...THEN I CAN'T BECOME HANZO'S...
...WIFE.
THERE'S...
...NO REASON FOR ME TO GO BACK TO IGA!!
THEN...THEN I'LL STAY TOO!!
ME TOO !!
SORRY, I CAN'T AFFORD TO HIRE MORE THAN ONE PERSON.

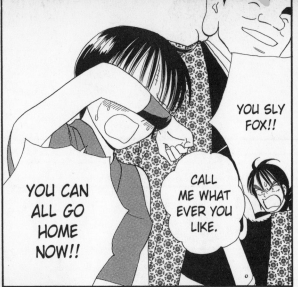

YOU SLY FOX!!
CALL ME WHAT EVER YOU LIKE.
YOU CAN ALL GO HOME NOW!!
LEAVE!
USAGI!
RIGHT ON. ♡
Now I can have Goemon all to myself. ♡

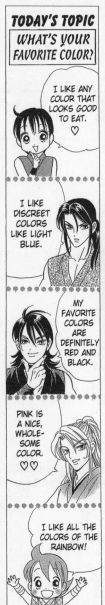

TODAY'S TOPIC
WHAT'S YOUR FAVORITE COLOR?
I LIKE ANY COLOR THAT LOOKS GOOD TO EAT. ♡
I LIKE DISCREET COLORS LIKE LIGHT BLUE.
MY FAVORITE COLORS ARE DEFINITELY RED AND BLACK.
PINK IS A NICE, WHOLE-SOME COLOR. ♡♡
I LIKE ALL THE COLORS OF THE RAINBOW!

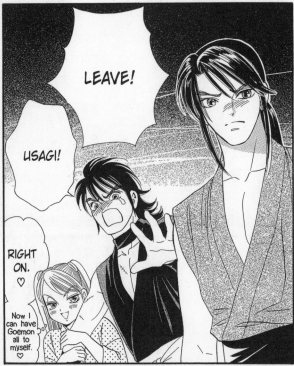

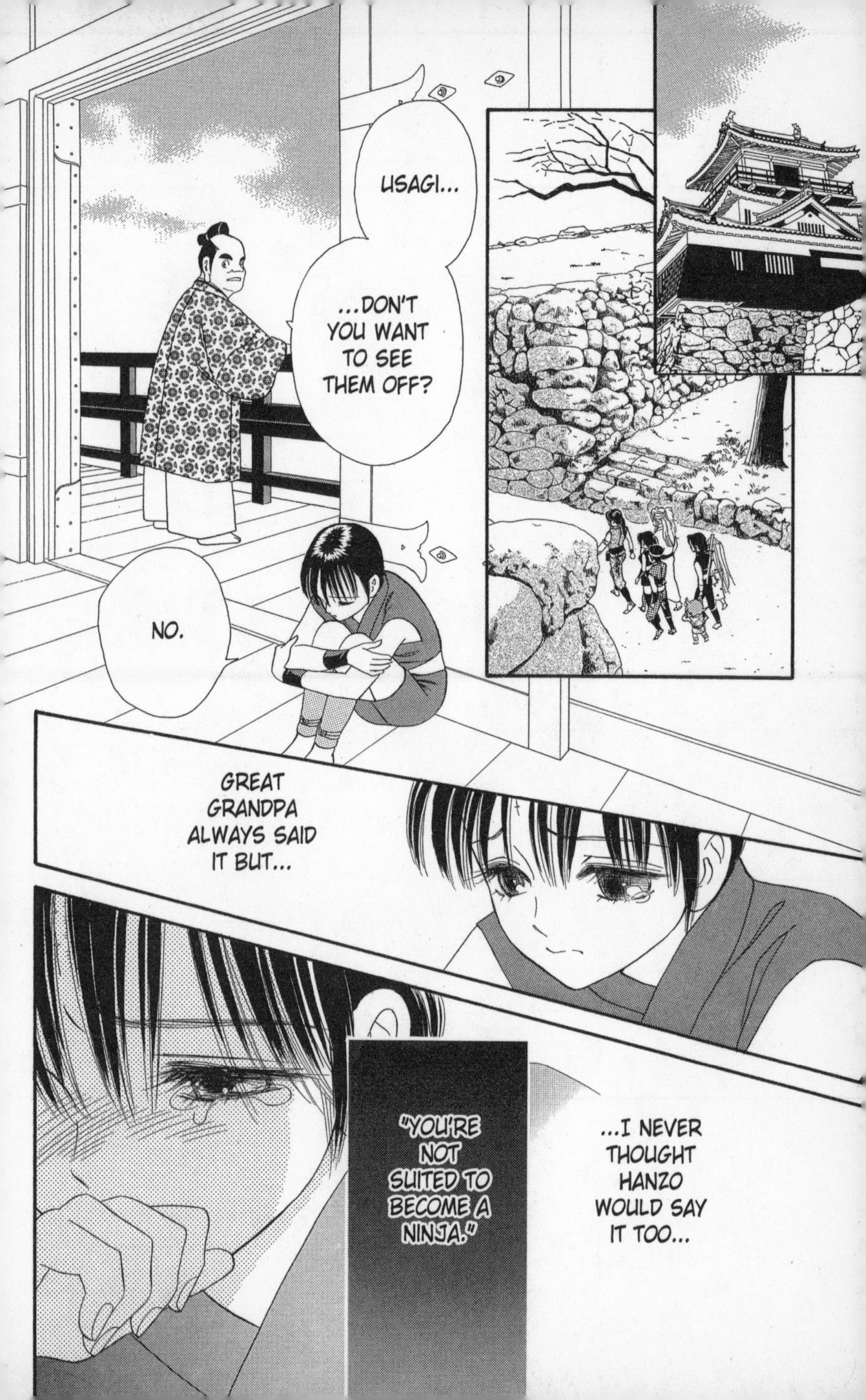
USAGI...
...DON'T YOU WANT TO SEE THEM OFF?
NO.
GREAT GRANDPA ALWAYS SAID IT BUT...
...I NEVER THOUGHT HANZO WOULD SAY IT TOO...
"YOU'RE NOT SUITED TO BECOME A NINJA."

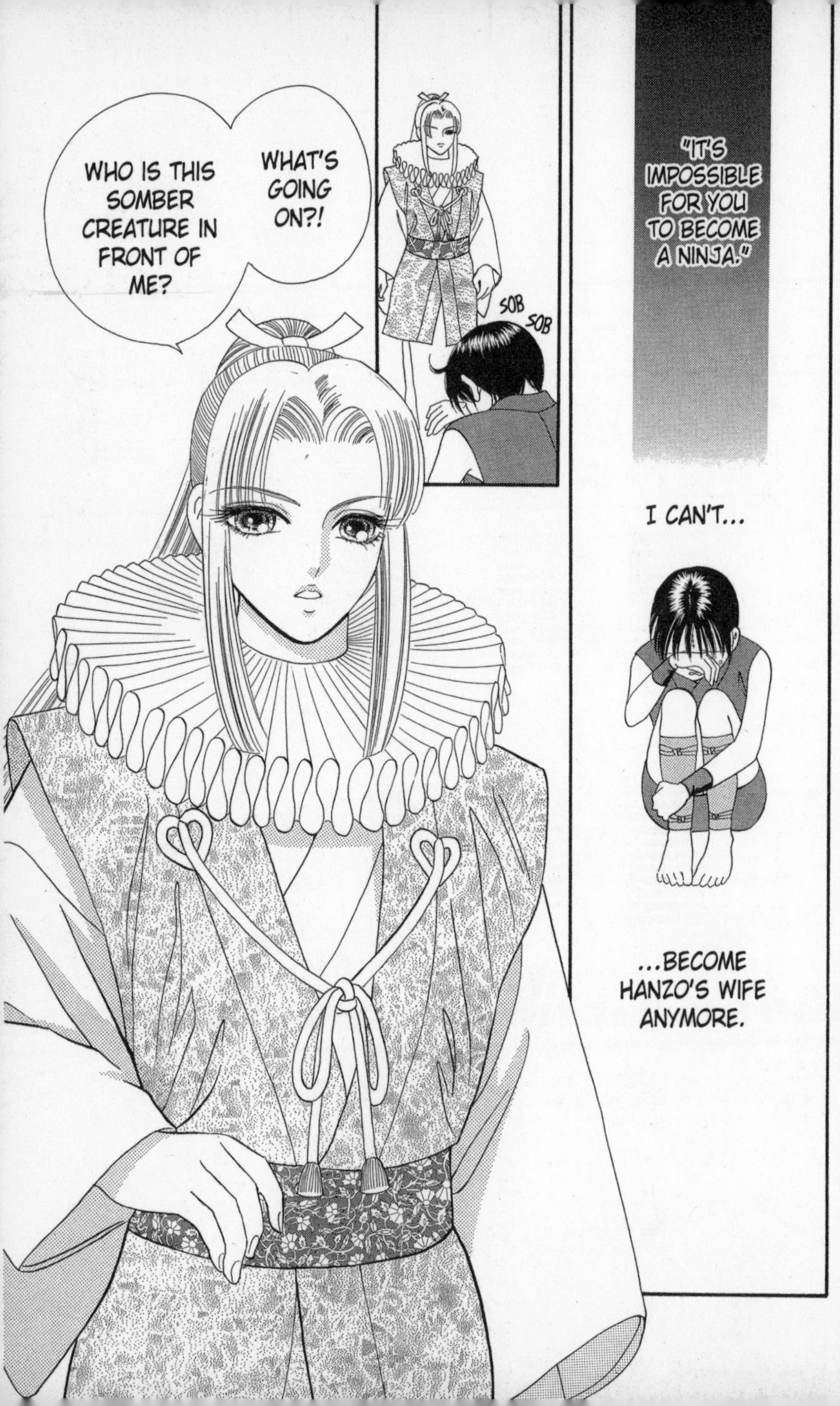
"IT'S IMPOSSIBLE FOR YOU TO BECOME A NINJA."
I CAN'T...
...BECOME HANZO'S WIFE ANYMORE.
SOB SOB
WHAT'S GOING ON?!
WHO IS THIS SOMBER CREATURE IN FRONT OF ME?

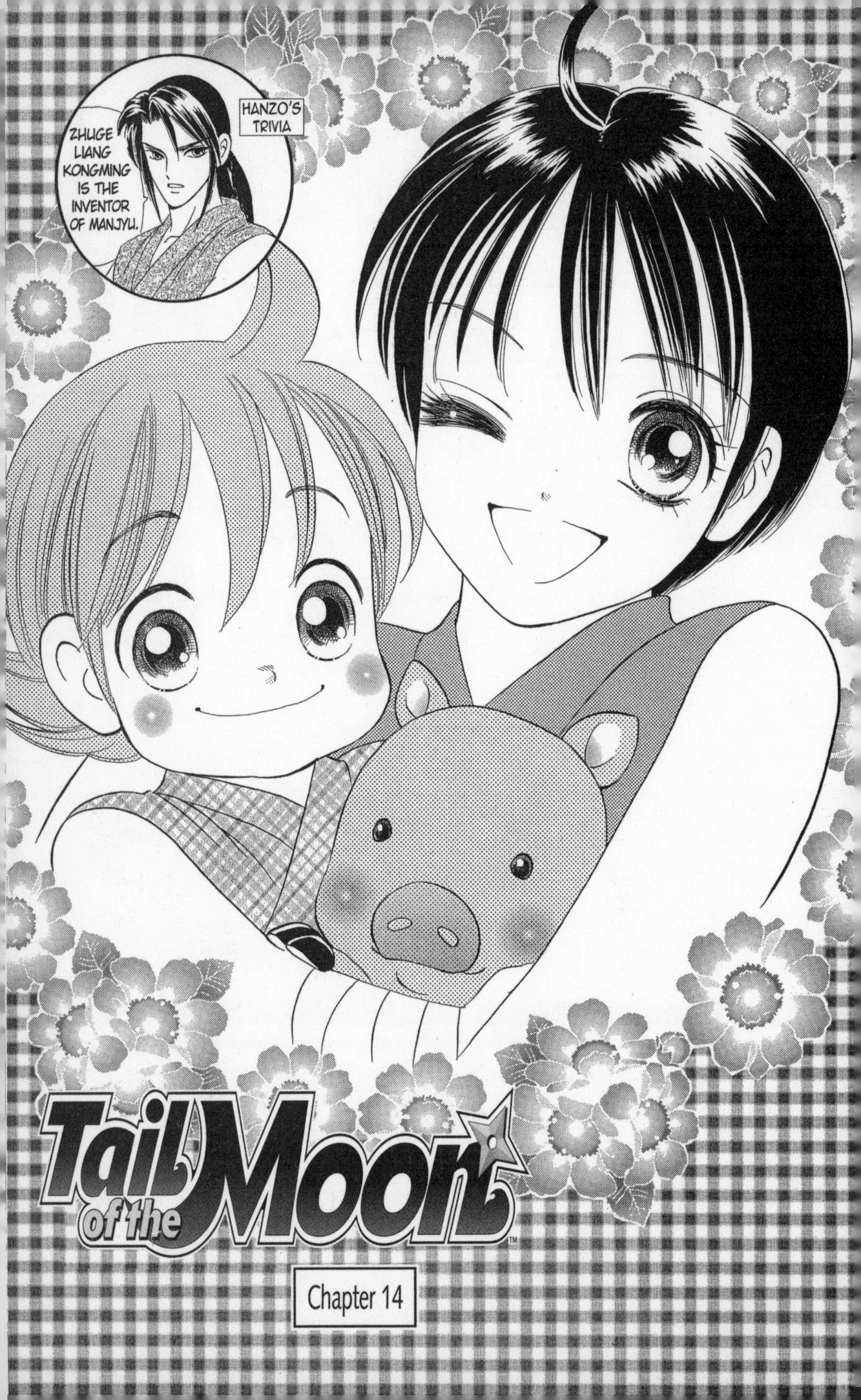
HANZO'S TRIVIA
ZHUGE LIANG KONGMING IS THE INVENTOR OF MANJYU.
Tail of the Moon™
Chapter 14

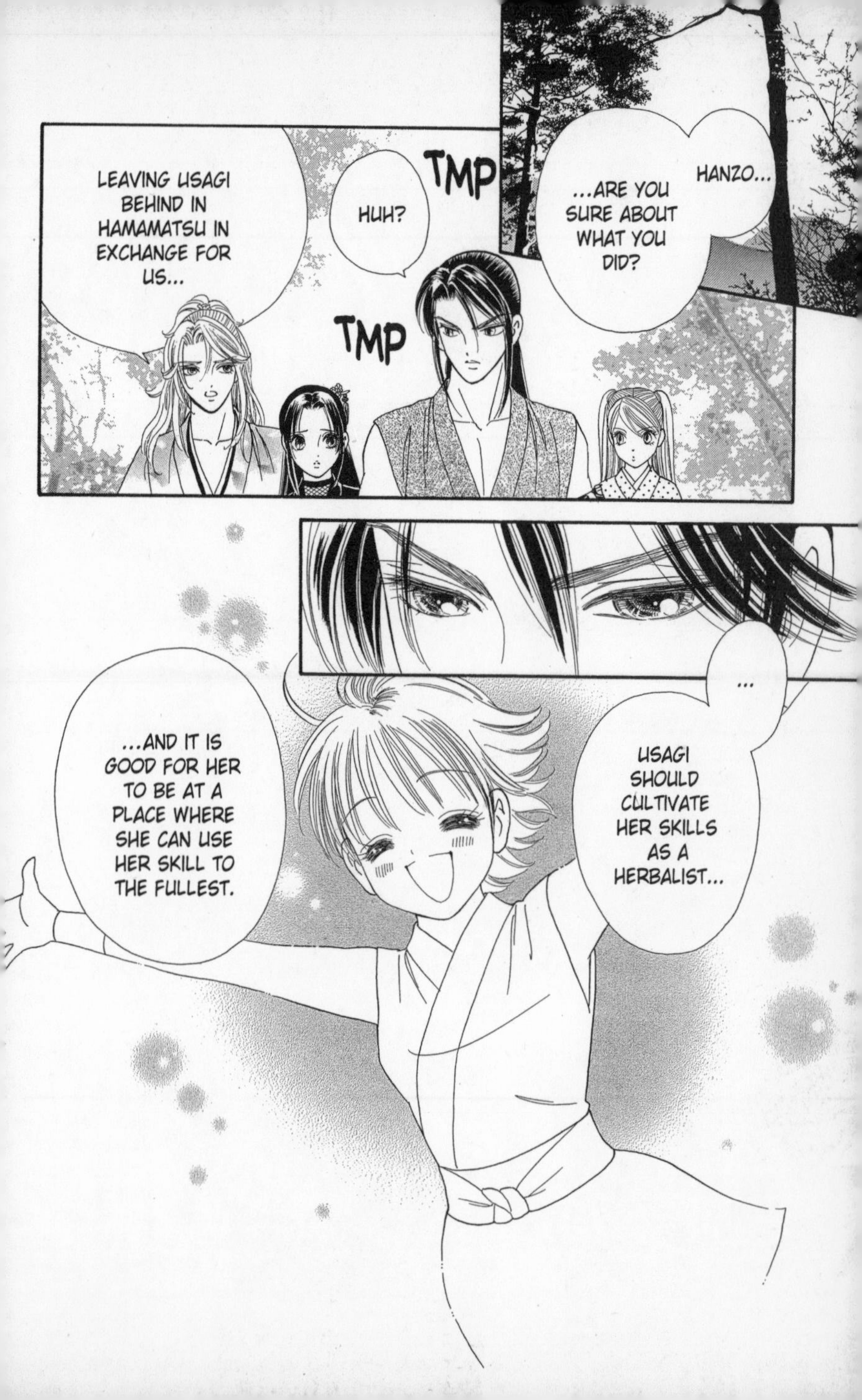
HANZO...
...ARE YOU SURE ABOUT WHAT YOU DID?
TMP
HUH?
LEAVING USAGI BEHIND IN HAMAMATSU IN EXCHANGE FOR US...
TMP
...
USAGI SHOULD CULTIVATE HER SKILLS AS A HERBALIST...
...AND IT IS GOOD FOR HER TO BE AT A PLACE WHERE SHE CAN USE HER SKILL TO THE FULLEST.

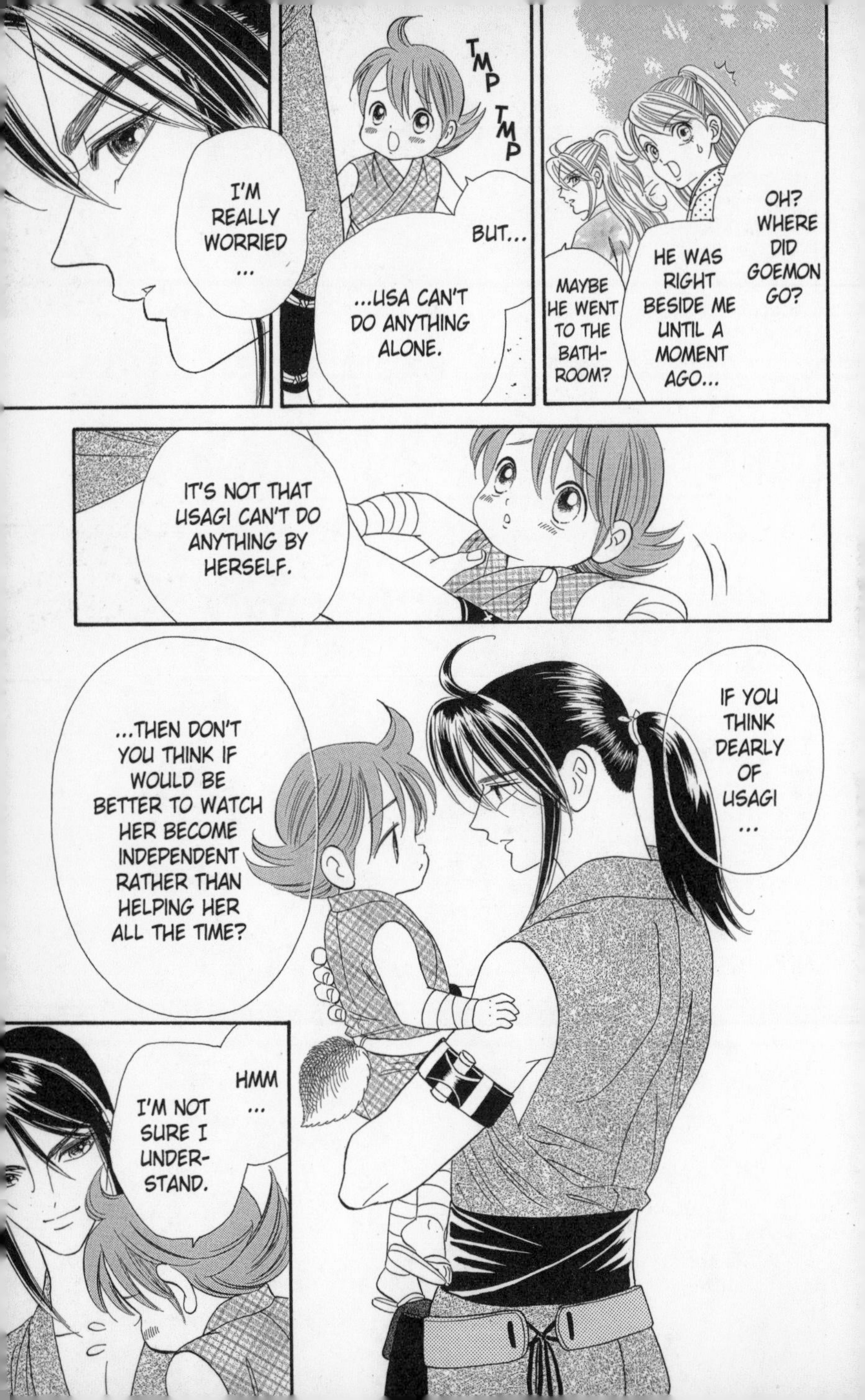
OH? WHERE DID GOEMON GO?
HE WAS RIGHT BESIDE ME UNTIL A MOMENT AGO...
MAYBE HE WENT TO THE BATH-ROOM?
TMP TMP
BUT...
...USA CAN'T DO ANYTHING ALONE.
I'M REALLY WORRIED ...
IT'S NOT THAT USAGI CAN'T DO ANYTHING BY HERSELF.
IF YOU THINK DEARLY OF USAGI ...
...THEN DON'T YOU THINK IF WOULD BE BETTER TO WATCH HER BECOME INDEPENDENT RATHER THAN HELPING HER ALL THE TIME?
HMM ...
I'M NOT SURE I UNDER-STAND.

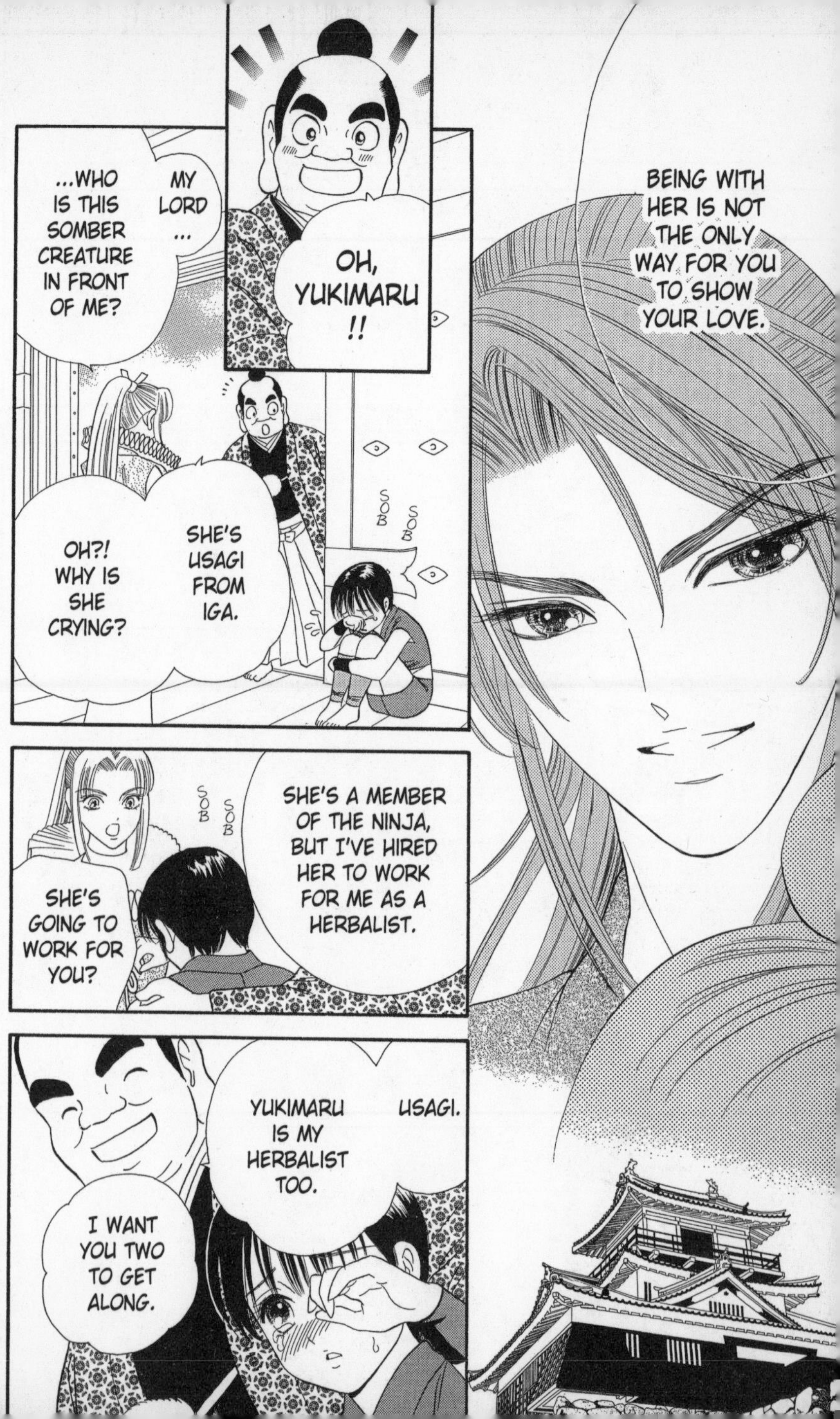
BEING WITH HER IS NOT THE ONLY WAY FOR YOU TO SHOW YOUR LOVE.
OH, YUKIMARU !!
MY LORD ...
...WHO IS THIS SOMBER CREATURE IN FRONT OF ME?
SOB SOB
SHE'S USAGI FROM IGA.
OH?! WHY IS SHE CRYING?
SOB SOB
SHE'S A MEMBER OF THE NINJA, BUT I'VE HIRED HER TO WORK FOR ME AS A HERBALIST.
SHE'S GOING TO WORK FOR YOU?
USAGI.
YUKIMARU IS MY HERBALIST TOO.
I WANT YOU TWO TO GET ALONG.

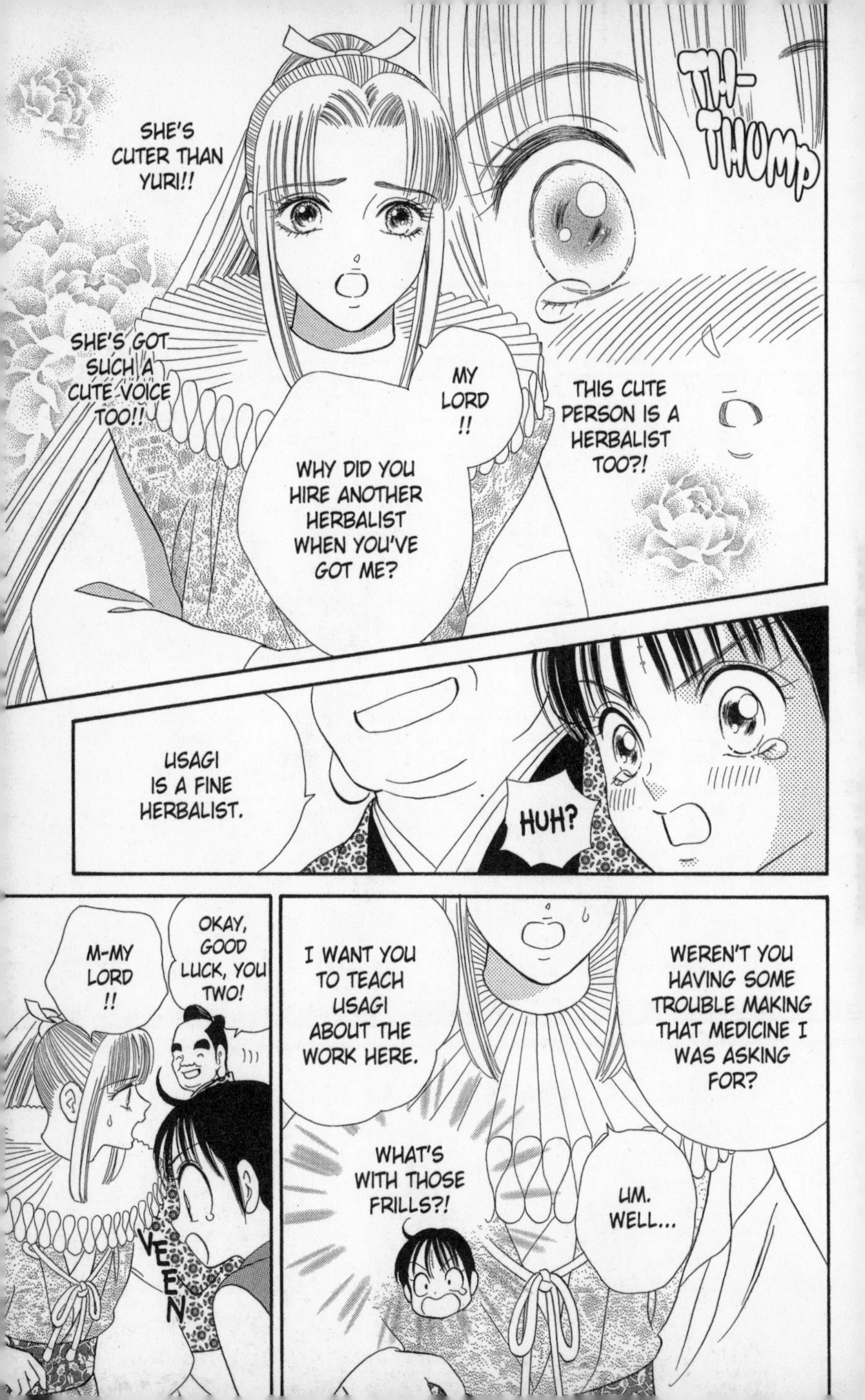
TH-THUMP
MY LORD!!
THIS CUTE PERSON IS A HERBALIST TOO?!
WHY DID YOU HIRE ANOTHER HERBALIST WHEN YOU'VE GOT ME?
SHE'S CUTER THAN YURI!!
SHE'S GOT SUCH A CUTE VOICE TOO!!
HUH?
USAGI IS A FINE HERBALIST.
WEREN'T YOU HAVING SOME TROUBLE MAKING THAT MEDICINE I WAS ASKING FOR?
UM. WELL...
I WANT YOU TO TEACH USAGI ABOUT THE WORK HERE.
WHAT'S WITH THOSE FRILLS?!
OKAY, GOOD LUCK, YOU TWO!
M-MY LORD!!
VEEEN

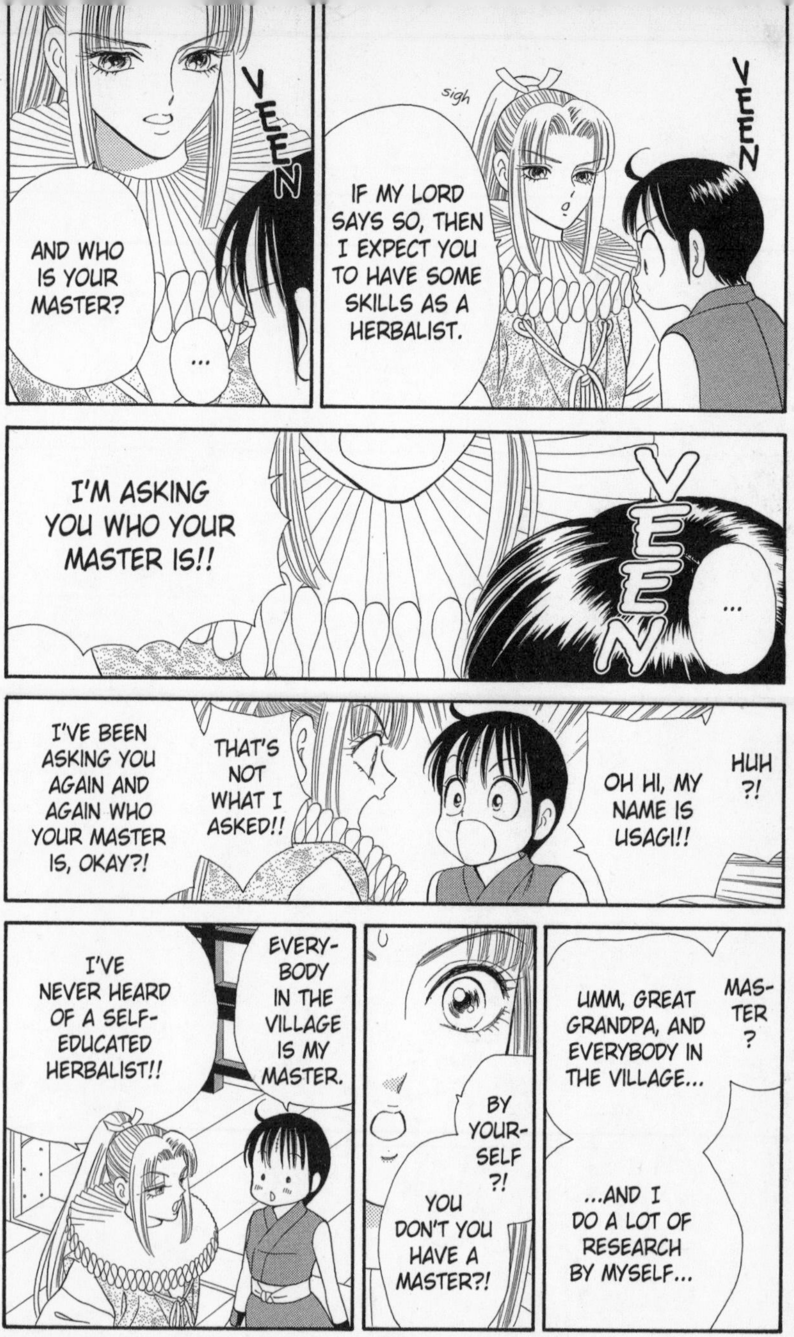
sigh
VEEN
IF MY LORD SAYS SO, THEN I EXPECT YOU TO HAVE SOME SKILLS AS A HERBALIST.
VEEN
AND WHO IS YOUR MASTER?
...
VEEN
I'M ASKING YOU WHO YOUR MASTER IS!!
...
HUH?!
OH HI, MY NAME IS USAGI!!
THAT'S NOT WHAT I ASKED!!
I'VE BEEN ASKING YOU AGAIN AND AGAIN WHO YOUR MASTER IS, OKAY?!
MASTER?
UMM, GREAT GRANDPA, AND EVERYBODY IN THE VILLAGE...
...AND I DO A LOT OF RESEARCH BY MYSELF...
BY YOURSELF?!
YOU DON'T YOU HAVE A MASTER?!
EVERYBODY IN THE VILLAGE IS MY MASTER.
I'VE NEVER HEARD OF A SELF-EDUCATED HERBALIST!!

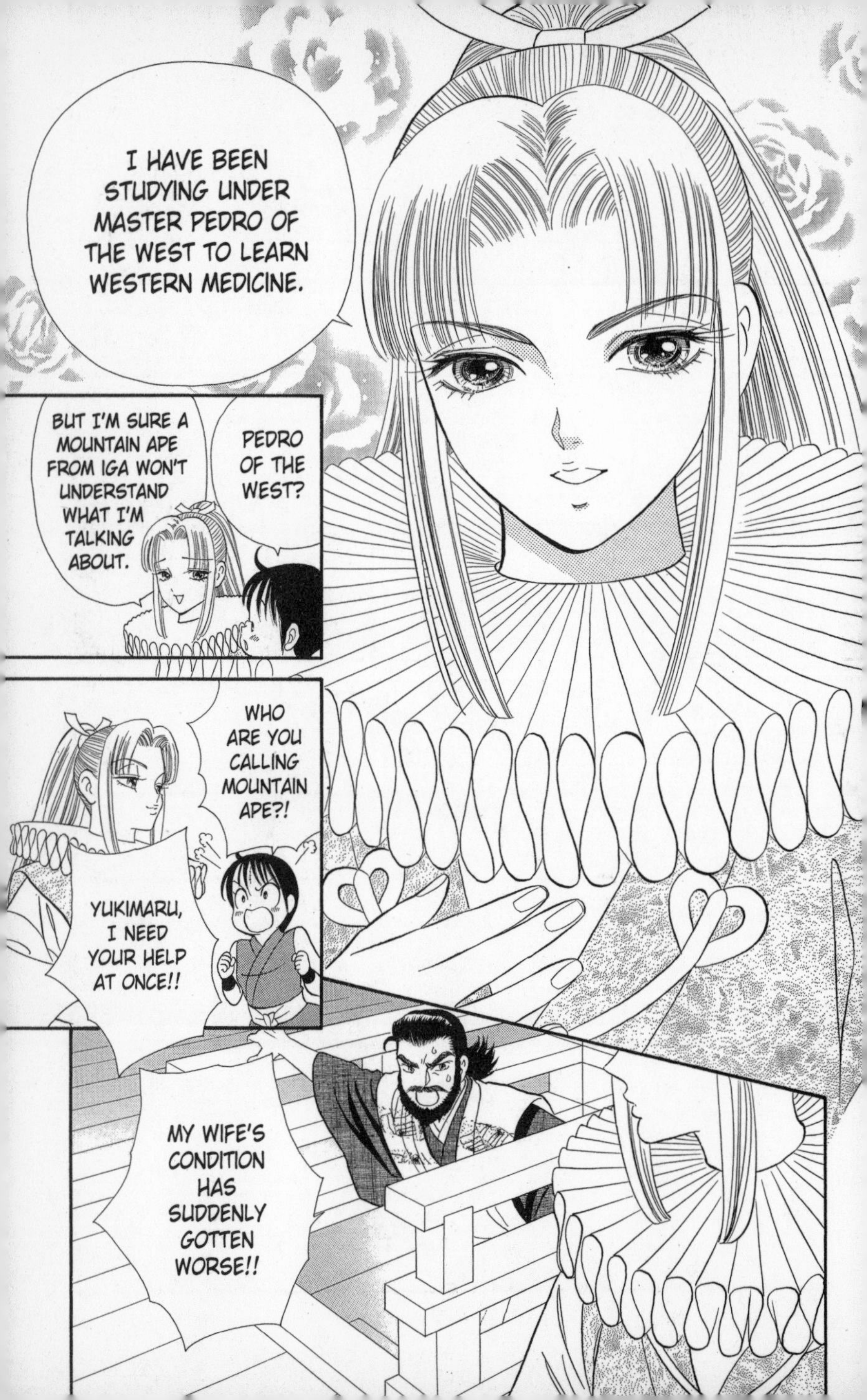
I HAVE BEEN STUDYING UNDER MASTER PEDRO OF THE WEST TO LEARN WESTERN MEDICINE.
PEDRO OF THE WEST?
BUT I'M SURE A MOUNTAIN APE FROM IGA WON'T UNDERSTAND WHAT I'M TALKING ABOUT.
WHO ARE YOU CALLING MOUNTAIN APE?!
YUKIMARU, I NEED YOUR HELP AT ONCE!!
MY WIFE'S CONDITION HAS SUDDENLY GOTTEN WORSE!!

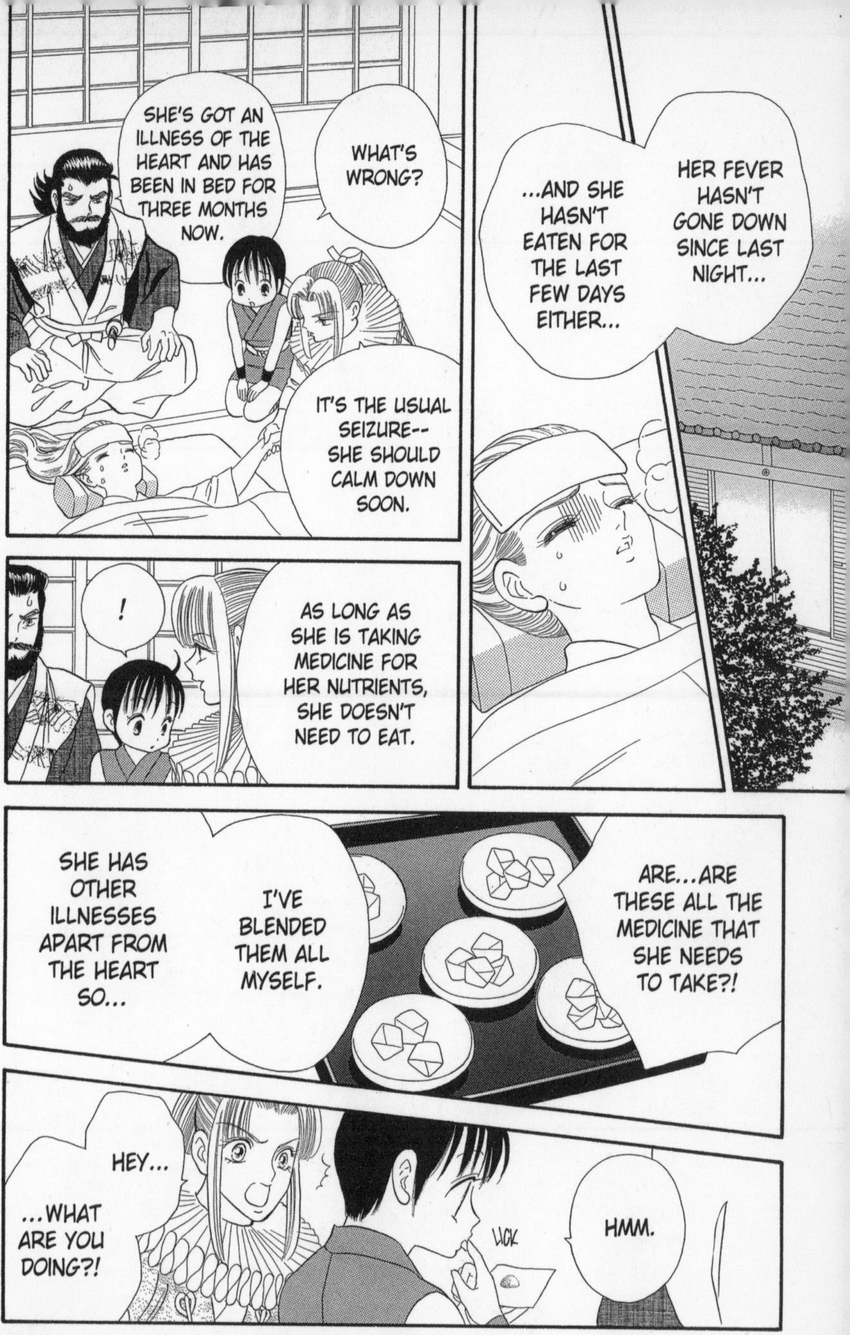
HER FEVER HASN'T GONE DOWN SINCE LAST NIGHT...
...AND SHE HASN'T EATEN FOR THE LAST FEW DAYS EITHER...
WHAT'S WRONG?
SHE'S GOT AN ILLNESS OF THE HEART AND HAS BEEN IN BED FOR THREE MONTHS NOW.
IT'S THE USUAL SEIZURE-- SHE SHOULD CALM DOWN SOON.
AS LONG AS SHE IS TAKING MEDICINE FOR HER NUTRIENTS, SHE DOESN'T NEED TO EAT.
!
ARE...ARE THESE ALL THE MEDICINE THAT SHE NEEDS TO TAKE?!
I'VE BLENDED THEM ALL MYSELF.
SHE HAS OTHER ILLNESSES APART FROM THE HEART SO...
HMM.
LICK
HEY...
...WHAT ARE YOU DOING?!

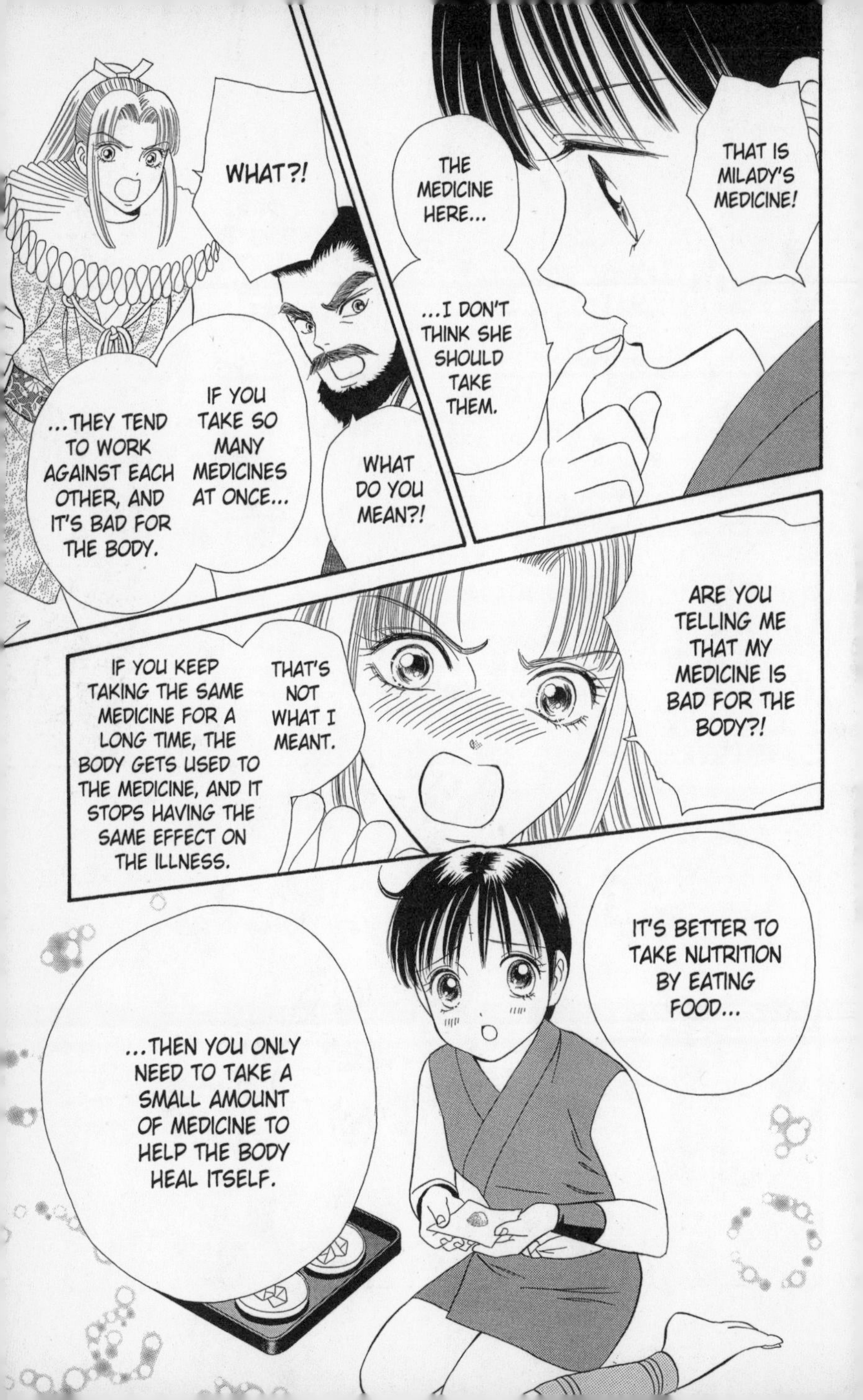
THAT IS MILADY'S MEDICINE!
THE MEDICINE HERE...
...I DON'T THINK SHE SHOULD TAKE THEM.
WHAT?!
WHAT DO YOU MEAN?!
IF YOU TAKE SO MANY MEDICINES AT ONCE...
...THEY TEND TO WORK AGAINST EACH OTHER, AND IT'S BAD FOR THE BODY.
ARE YOU TELLING ME THAT MY MEDICINE IS BAD FOR THE BODY?!
THAT'S NOT WHAT I MEANT.
IF YOU KEEP TAKING THE SAME MEDICINE FOR A LONG TIME, THE BODY GETS USED TO THE MEDICINE, AND IT STOPS HAVING THE SAME EFFECT ON THE ILLNESS.
IT'S BETTER TO TAKE NUTRITION BY EATING FOOD...
...THEN YOU ONLY NEED TO TAKE A SMALL AMOUNT OF MEDICINE TO HELP THE BODY HEAL ITSELF.

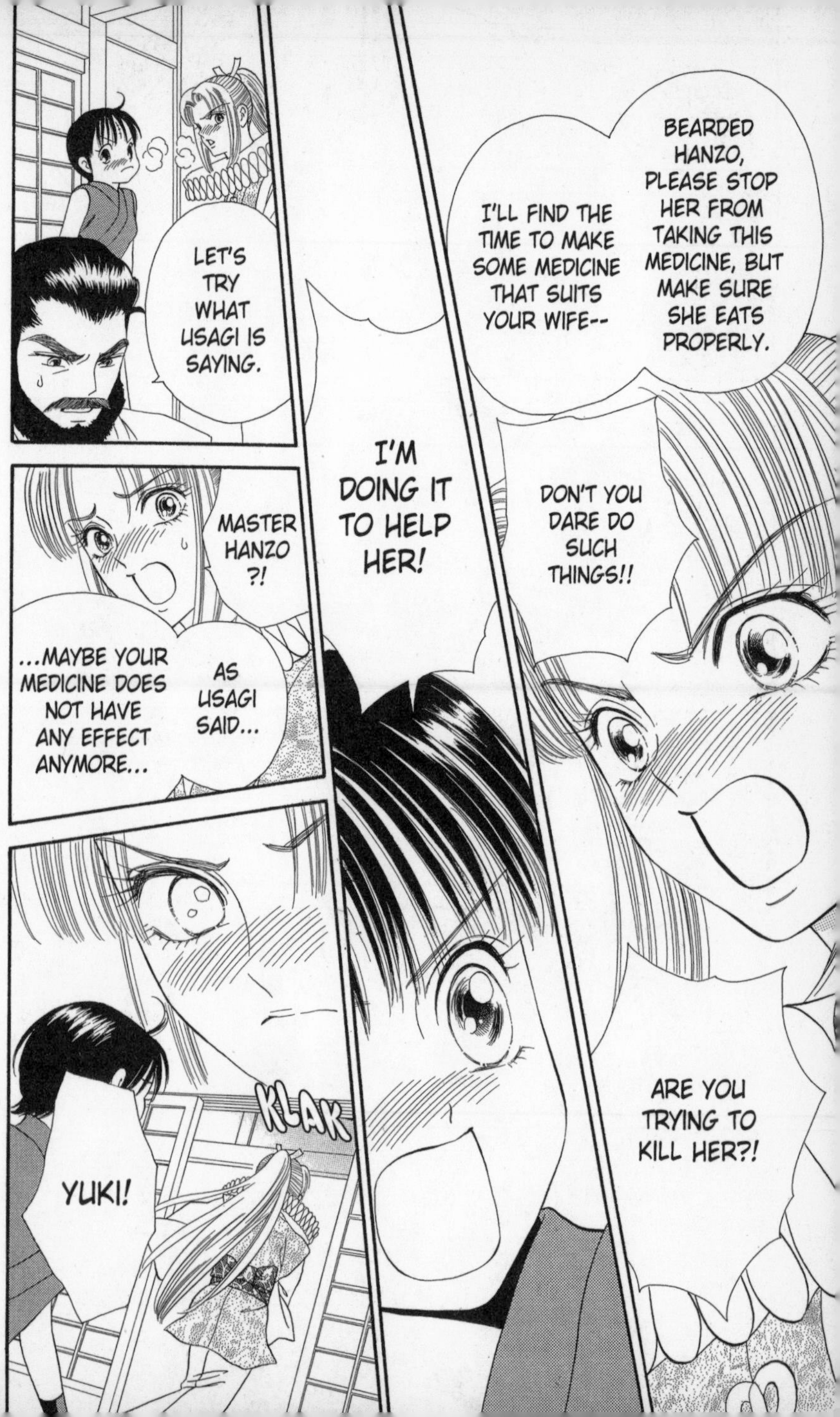

BEARDED HANZO, PLEASE STOP HER FROM TAKING THIS MEDICINE, BUT MAKE SURE SHE EATS PROPERLY.
I'LL FIND THE TIME TO MAKE SOME MEDICINE THAT SUITS YOUR WIFE--
DON'T YOU DARE DO SUCH THINGS!!
ARE YOU TRYING TO KILL HER?!
I'M DOING IT TO HELP HER!
LET'S TRY WHAT USAGI IS SAYING.
MASTER HANZO ?!
AS USAGI SAID...
...MAYBE YOUR MEDICINE DOES NOT HAVE ANY EFFECT ANYMORE...
KLAK
YUKI!

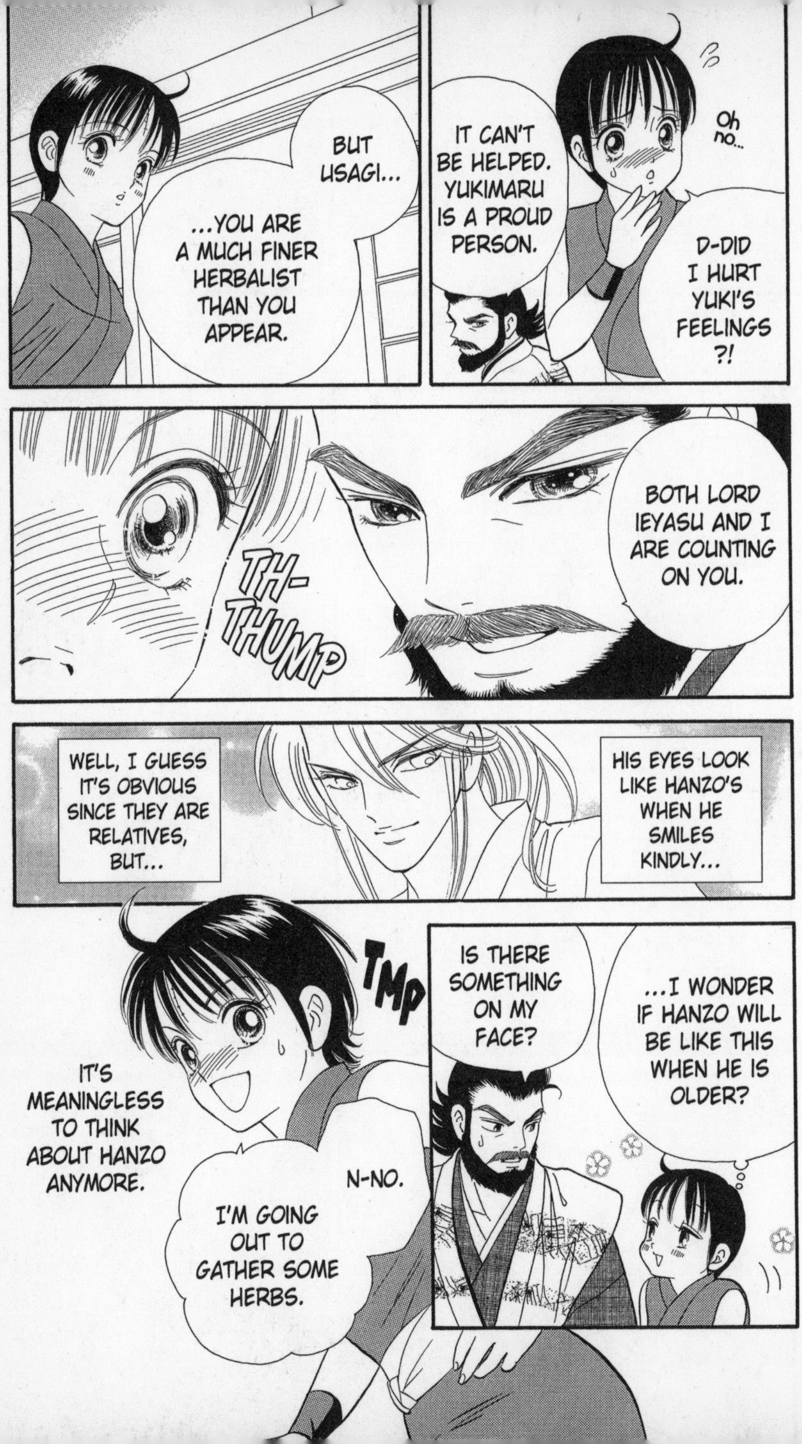
Oh no...
D-DID I HURT YUKI'S FEELINGS ?!
IT CAN'T BE HELPED. YUKIMARU IS A PROUD PERSON.
BUT USAGI...
...YOU ARE A MUCH FINER HERBALIST THAN YOU APPEAR.
BOTH LORD IEYASU AND I ARE COUNTING ON YOU.
TH-THUMP
HIS EYES LOOK LIKE HANZO'S WHEN HE SMILES KINDLY...
WELL, I GUESS IT'S OBVIOUS SINCE THEY ARE RELATIVES, BUT...
...I WONDER IF HANZO WILL BE LIKE THIS WHEN HE IS OLDER?
IS THERE SOMETHING ON MY FACE?
TMP
N-NO.
I'M GOING OUT TO GATHER SOME HERBS.
IT'S MEANINGLESS TO THINK ABOUT HANZO ANYMORE.

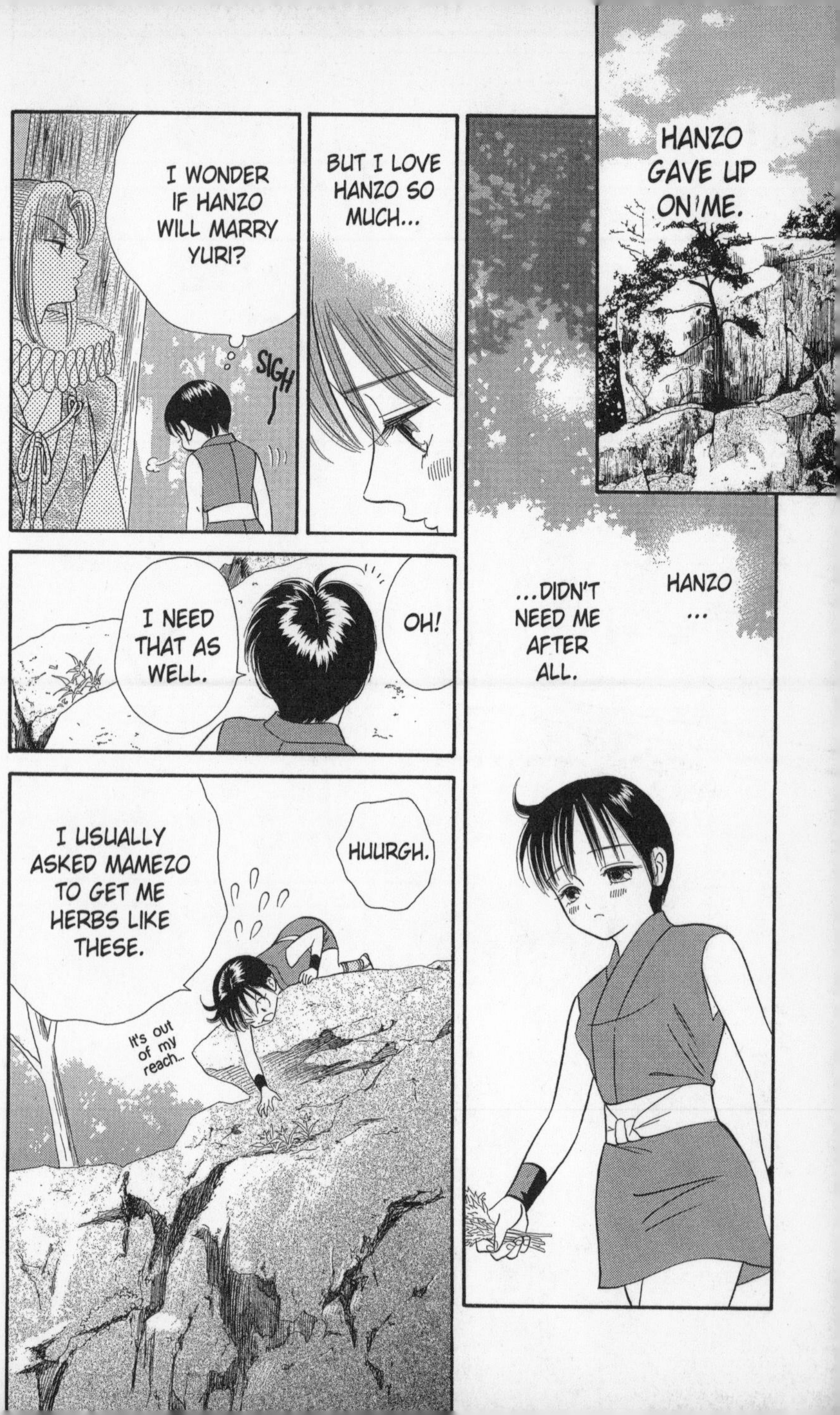
HANZO GAVE UP ON ME.
HANZO ...
...DIDN'T NEED ME AFTER ALL.
BUT I LOVE HANZO SO MUCH...
I WONDER IF HANZO WILL MARRY YURI?
SIGH
OH!
I NEED THAT AS WELL.
HUURGH.
I USUALLY ASKED MAMEZO TO GET ME HERBS LIKE THESE.
It's out of my reach...

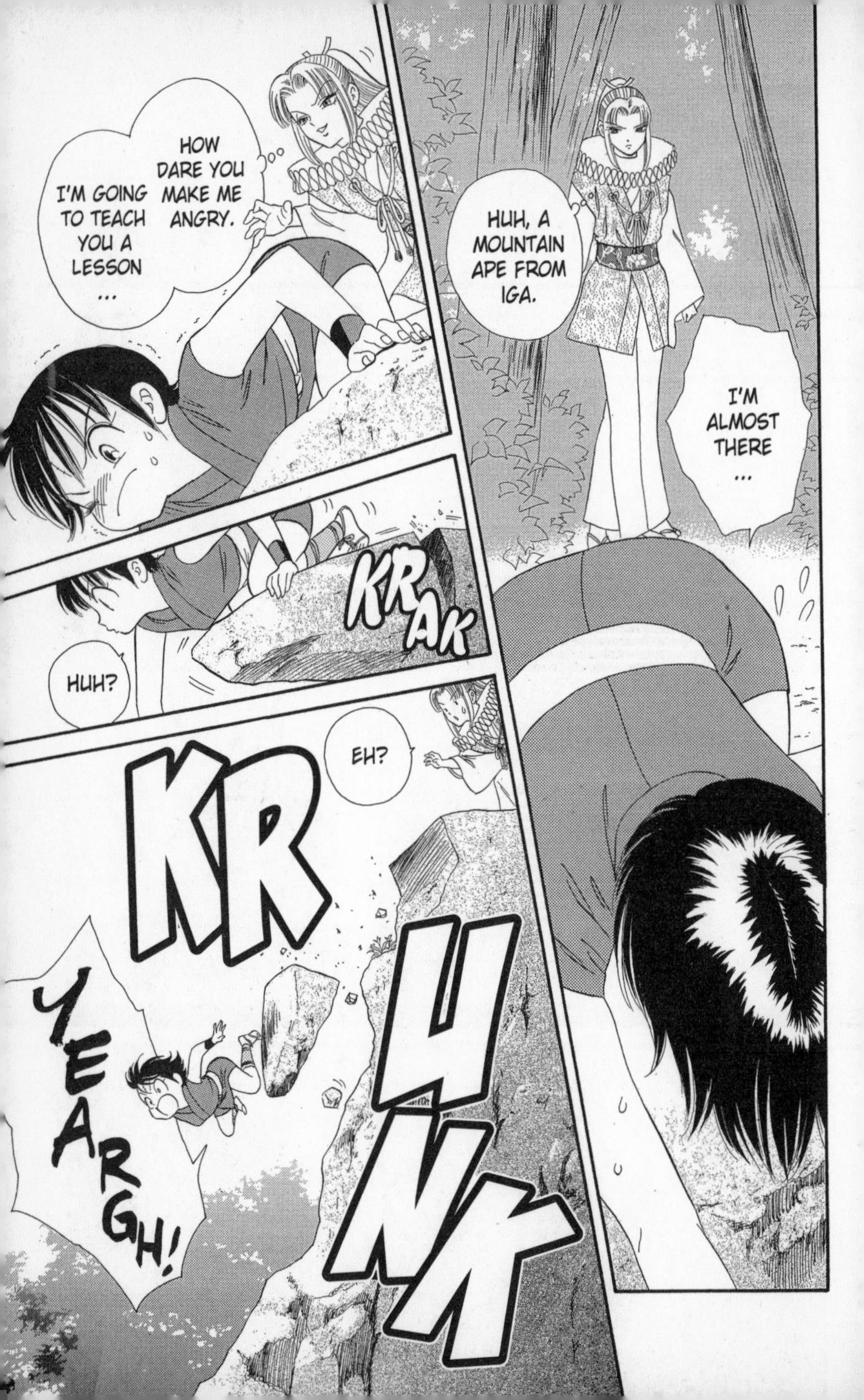
HUH, A MOUNTAIN APE FROM IGA.
I'M ALMOST THERE ...
HOW DARE YOU MAKE ME ANGRY.
I'M GOING TO TEACH YOU A LESSON ...
KRAK
HUH?
EH?
KRUNK
YEARGH!

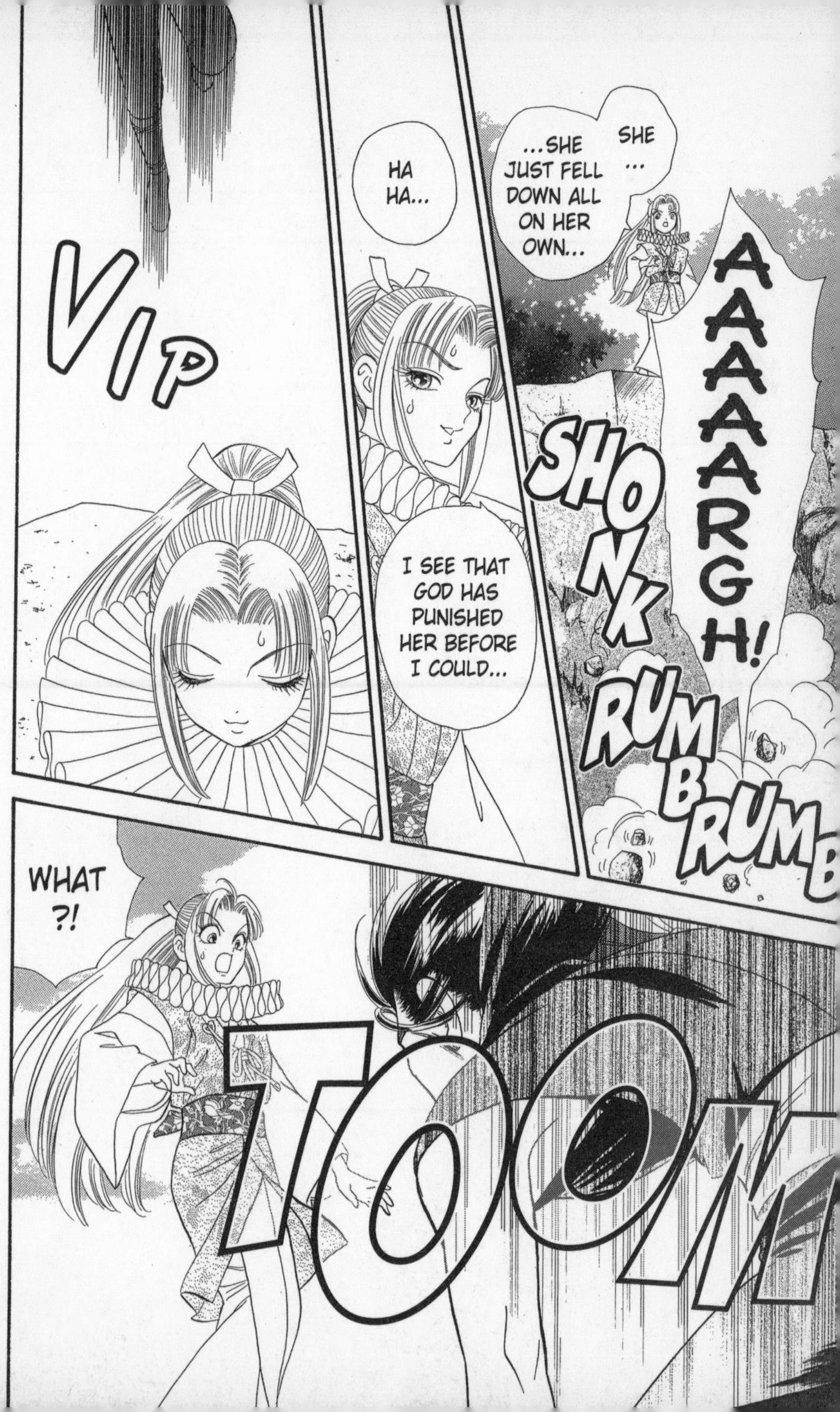
SHE ...
...SHE JUST FELL DOWN ALL ON HER OWN...
AAAAARGH!
SHONK
RUMBRUMB
HA HA...
I SEE THAT GOD HAS PUNISHED HER BEFORE I COULD...
VIP
WHAT ?!
TOOM

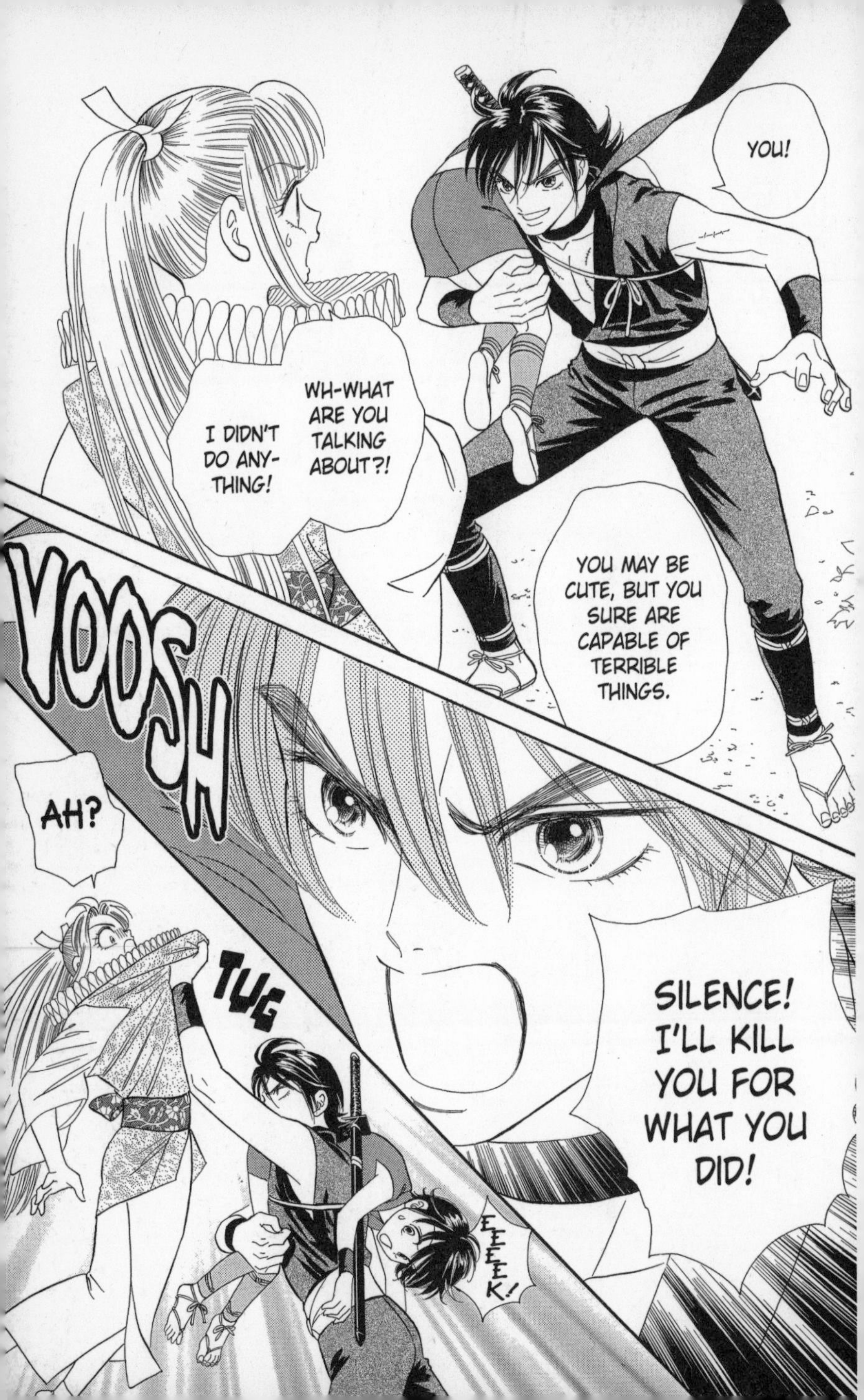
YOU!
YOU MAY BE CUTE, BUT YOU SURE ARE CAPABLE OF TERRIBLE THINGS.
WH-WHAT ARE YOU TALKING ABOUT?!
I DIDN'T DO ANY-THING!
VOOSH
SILENCE! I'LL KILL YOU FOR WHAT YOU DID!
AH?
TUG
EEEEK!

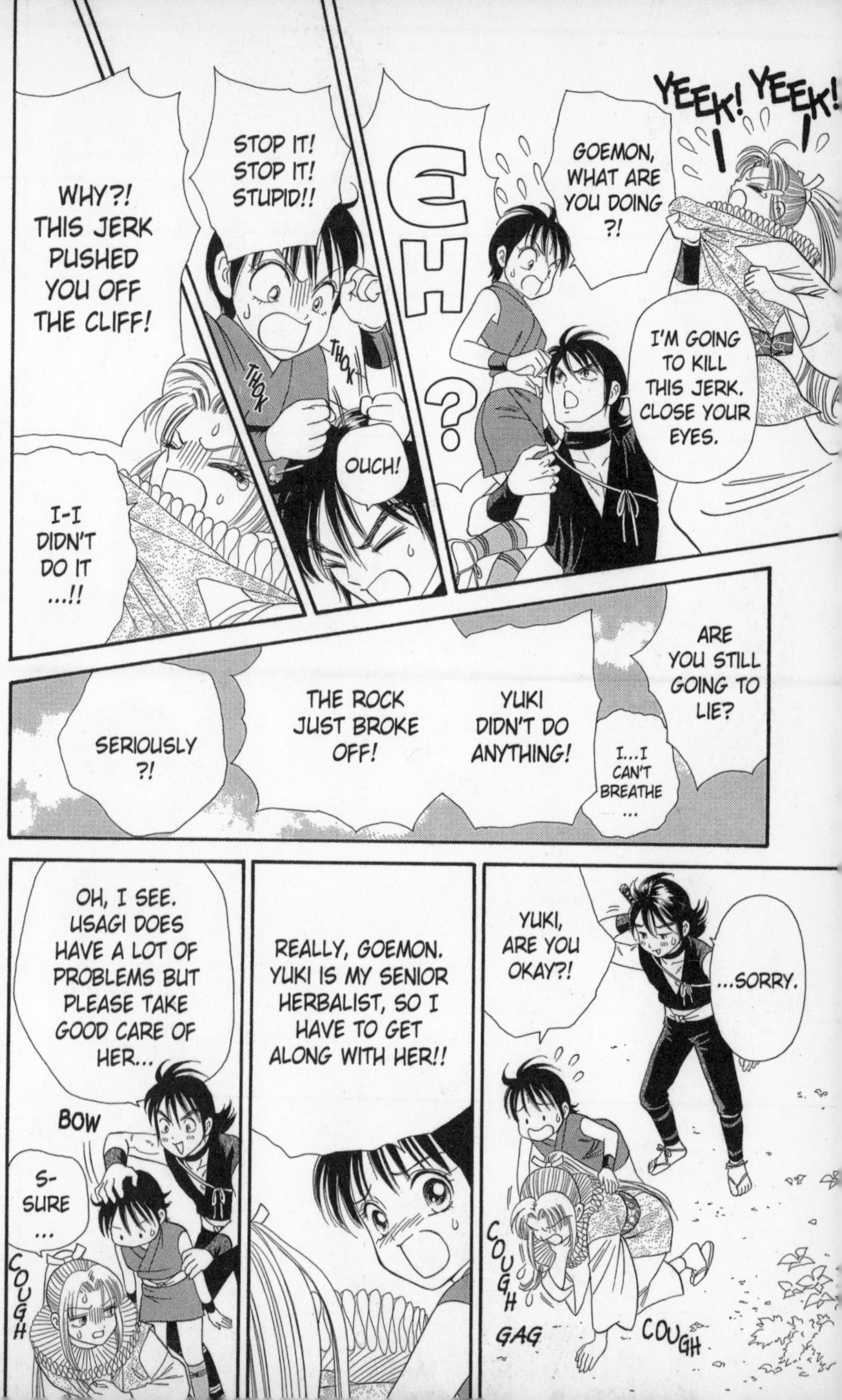
YEEK! YEEK!
GOEMON, WHAT ARE YOU DOING ?!
EH ?
I'M GOING TO KILL THIS JERK. CLOSE YOUR EYES.
STOP IT! STOP IT! STUPID!!
THOK THOK
OUCH!
WHY?! THIS JERK PUSHED YOU OFF THE CLIFF!
I-I DIDN'T DO IT ...!!
ARE YOU STILL GOING TO LIE?
I...I CAN'T BREATHE ...
YUKI DIDN'T DO ANYTHING!
THE ROCK JUST BROKE OFF!
SERIOUSLY ?!
YUKI, ARE YOU OKAY?!
...SORRY.
COUGH
GAG
COUGH
REALLY, GOEMON. YUKI IS MY SENIOR HERBALIST, SO I HAVE TO GET ALONG WITH HER!!
OH, I SEE. USAGI DOES HAVE A LOT OF PROBLEMS BUT PLEASE TAKE GOOD CARE OF HER...
BOW
S- SURE ...
COUGH

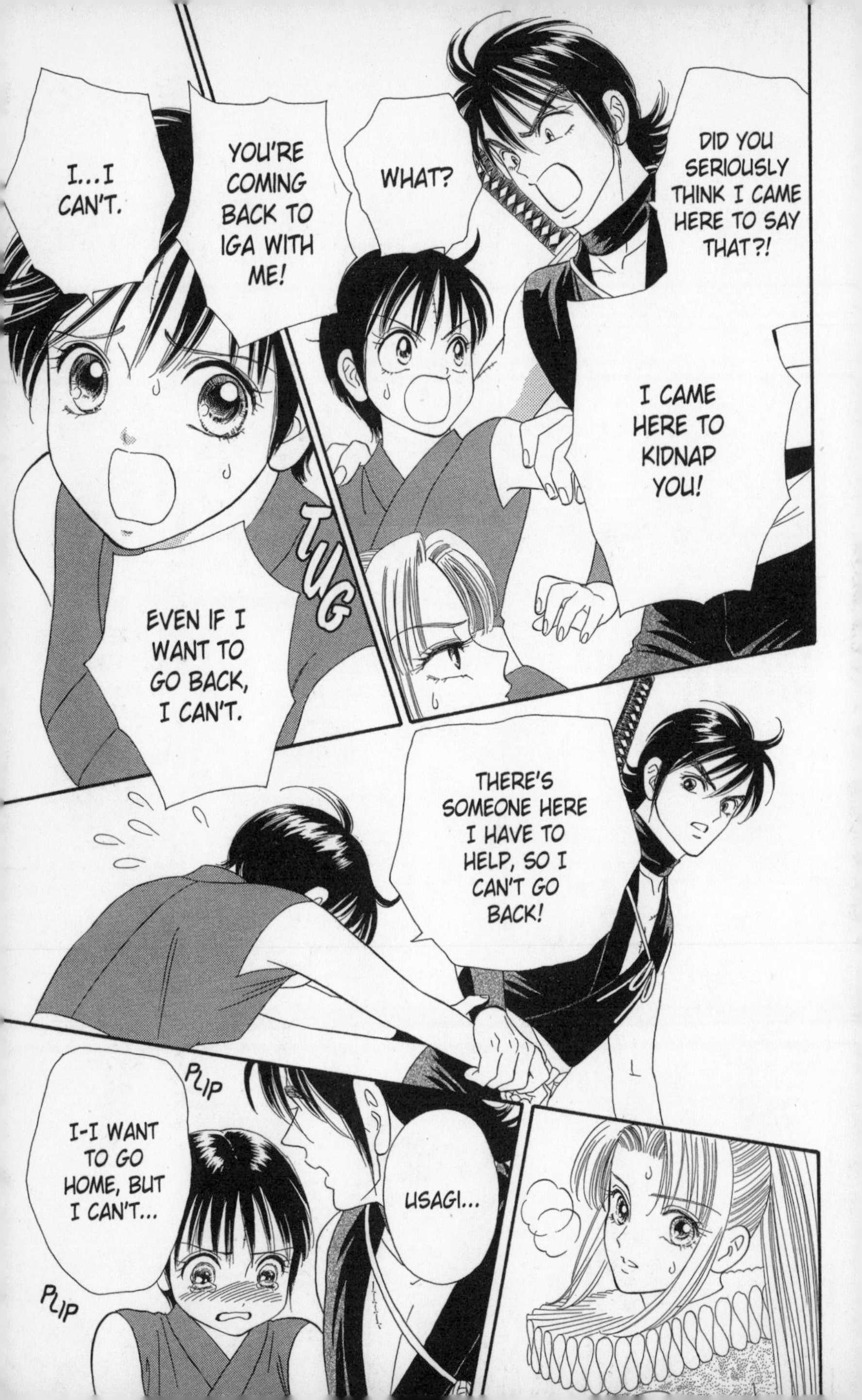
DID YOU SERIOUSLY THINK I CAME HERE TO SAY THAT?!
I CAME HERE TO KIDNAP YOU!
WHAT?
YOU'RE COMING BACK TO IGA WITH ME!
I...I CAN'T.
TUG
EVEN IF I WANT TO GO BACK, I CAN'T.
THERE'S SOMEONE HERE I HAVE TO HELP, SO I CAN'T GO BACK!
USAGI...
PLIP
I-I WANT TO GO HOME, BUT I CAN'T...
PLIP

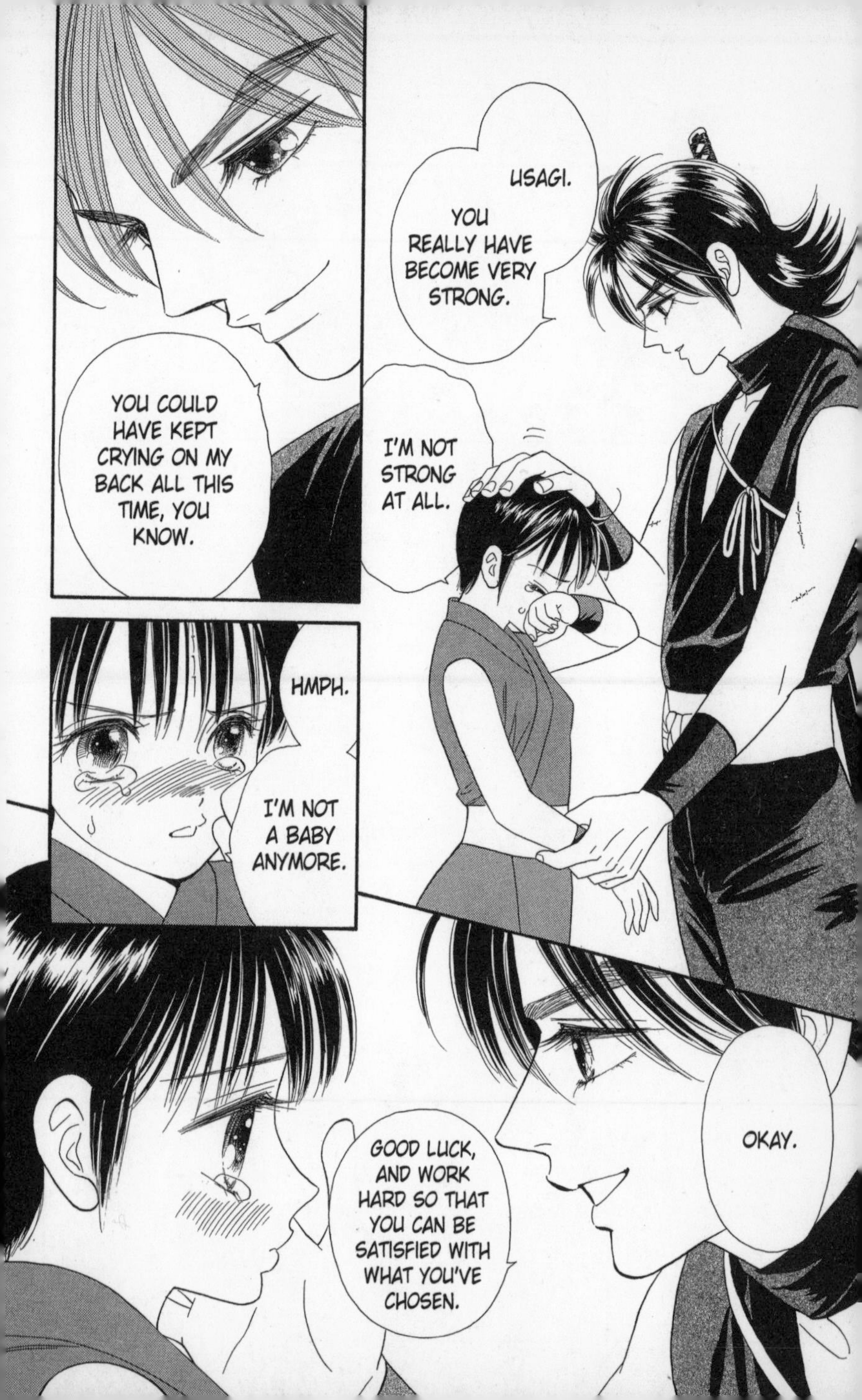
USAGI.
YOU REALLY HAVE BECOME VERY STRONG.
I'M NOT STRONG AT ALL.
YOU COULD HAVE KEPT CRYING ON MY BACK ALL THIS TIME, YOU KNOW.
HMPH.
I'M NOT A BABY ANYMORE.
GOOD LUCK, AND WORK HARD SO THAT YOU CAN BE SATISFIED WITH WHAT YOU'VE CHOSEN.
OKAY.

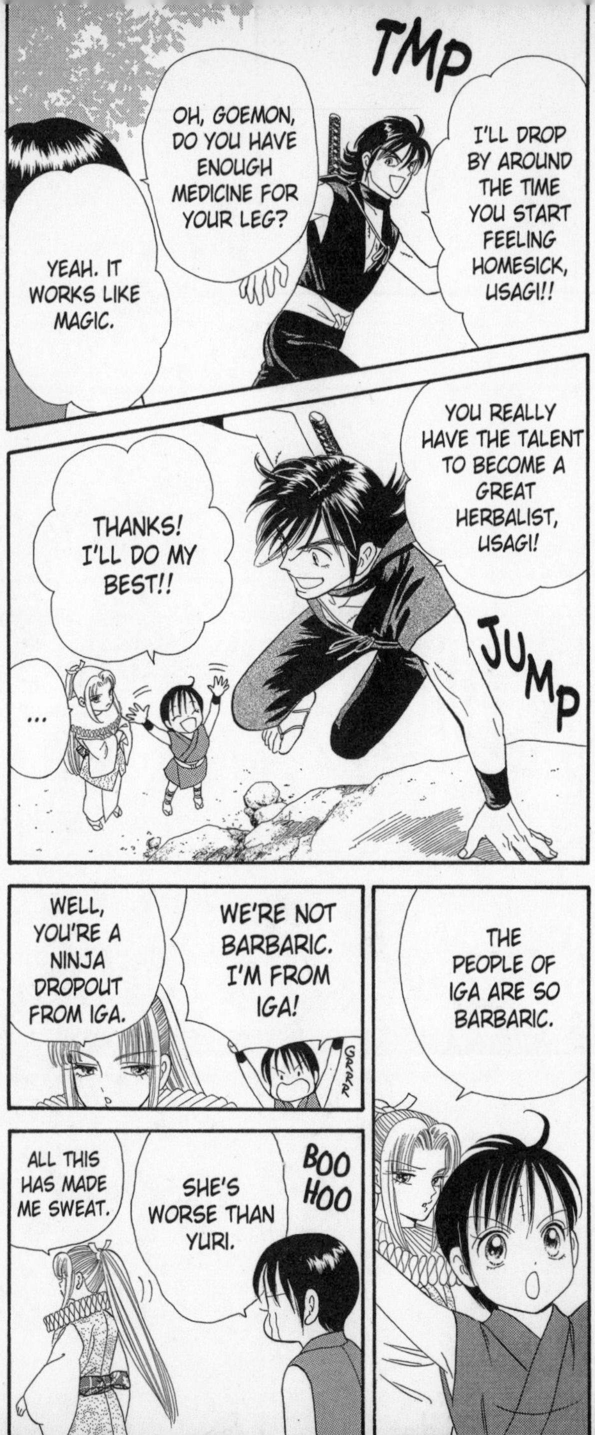
TMP
I'LL DROP BY AROUND THE TIME YOU START FEELING HOMESICK, USAGI!!
OH, GOEMON, DO YOU HAVE ENOUGH MEDICINE FOR YOUR LEG?
YEAH. IT WORKS LIKE MAGIC.
YOU REALLY HAVE THE TALENT TO BECOME A GREAT HERBALIST, USAGI!
JUMP
THANKS! I'LL DO MY BEST!!
...
THE PEOPLE OF IGA ARE SO BARBARIC.
WE'RE NOT BARBARIC. I'M FROM IGA!
WELL, YOU'RE A NINJA DROPOUT FROM IGA.
BOO HOO
SHE'S WORSE THAN YURI.
ALL THIS HAS MADE ME SWEAT.

Thank you everybody for reading this manga.

And thank you to those who sent me messages. They're really encouraging! ♡

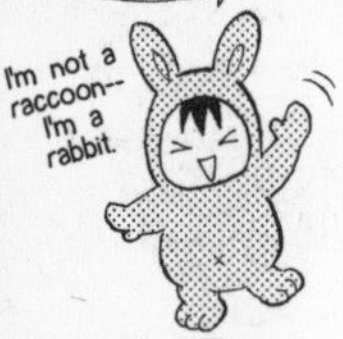
I'm not a raccoon-- I'm a rabbit.

If you have messages, please let me know about them. ♡

Send them to:
Rinko Ueda
C/O Tail of the Moon Editor
P.O. Box 77064
San Francisco, CA
94107

See you all in volume 3!~♪

Rinko Ueda

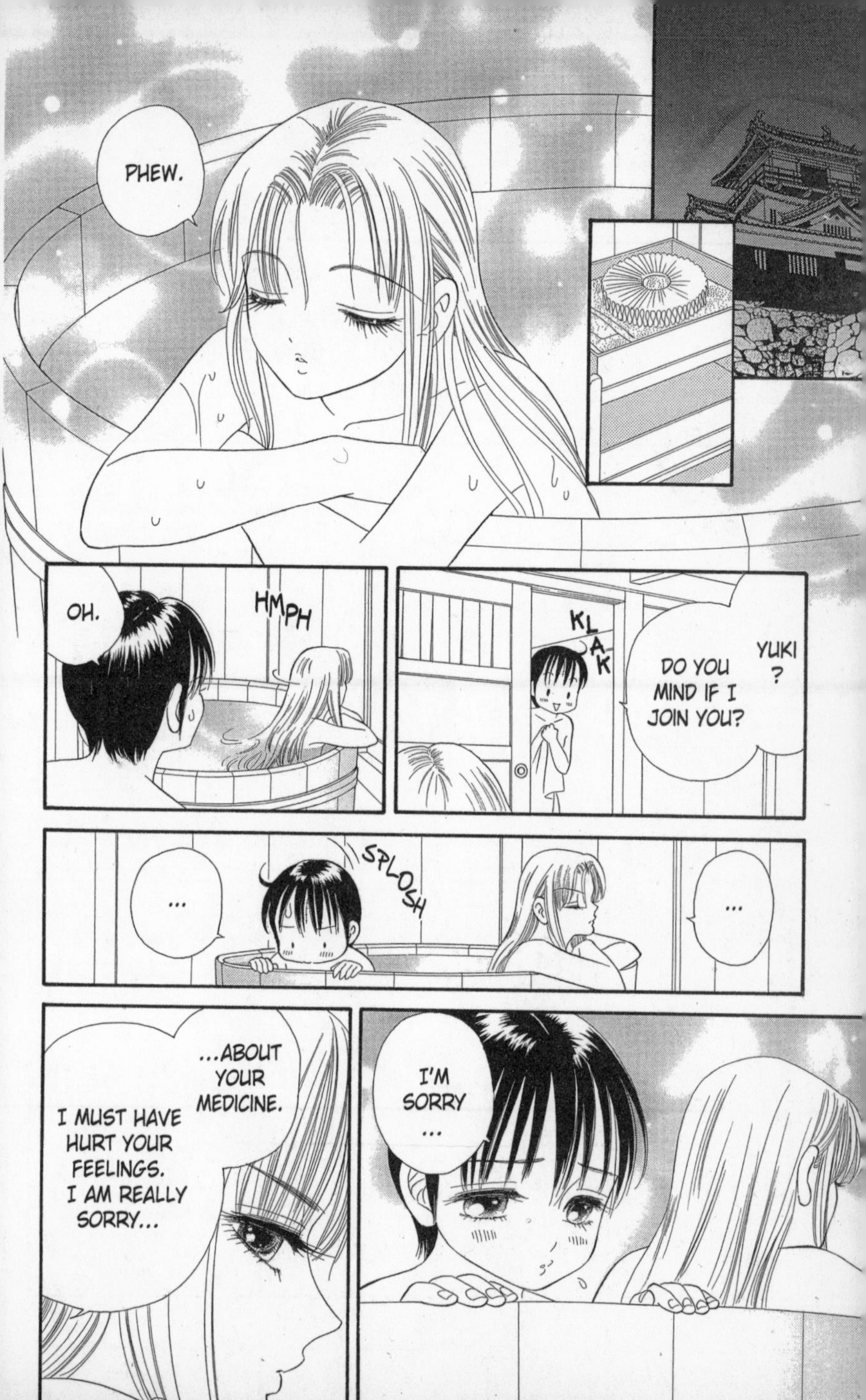
PHEW.
YUKI ?
DO YOU MIND IF I JOIN YOU?
KLAK
HMPH
OH.
...
SPLOSH
...
I'M SORRY ...
...ABOUT YOUR MEDICINE.
I MUST HAVE HURT YOUR FEELINGS. I AM REALLY SORRY...

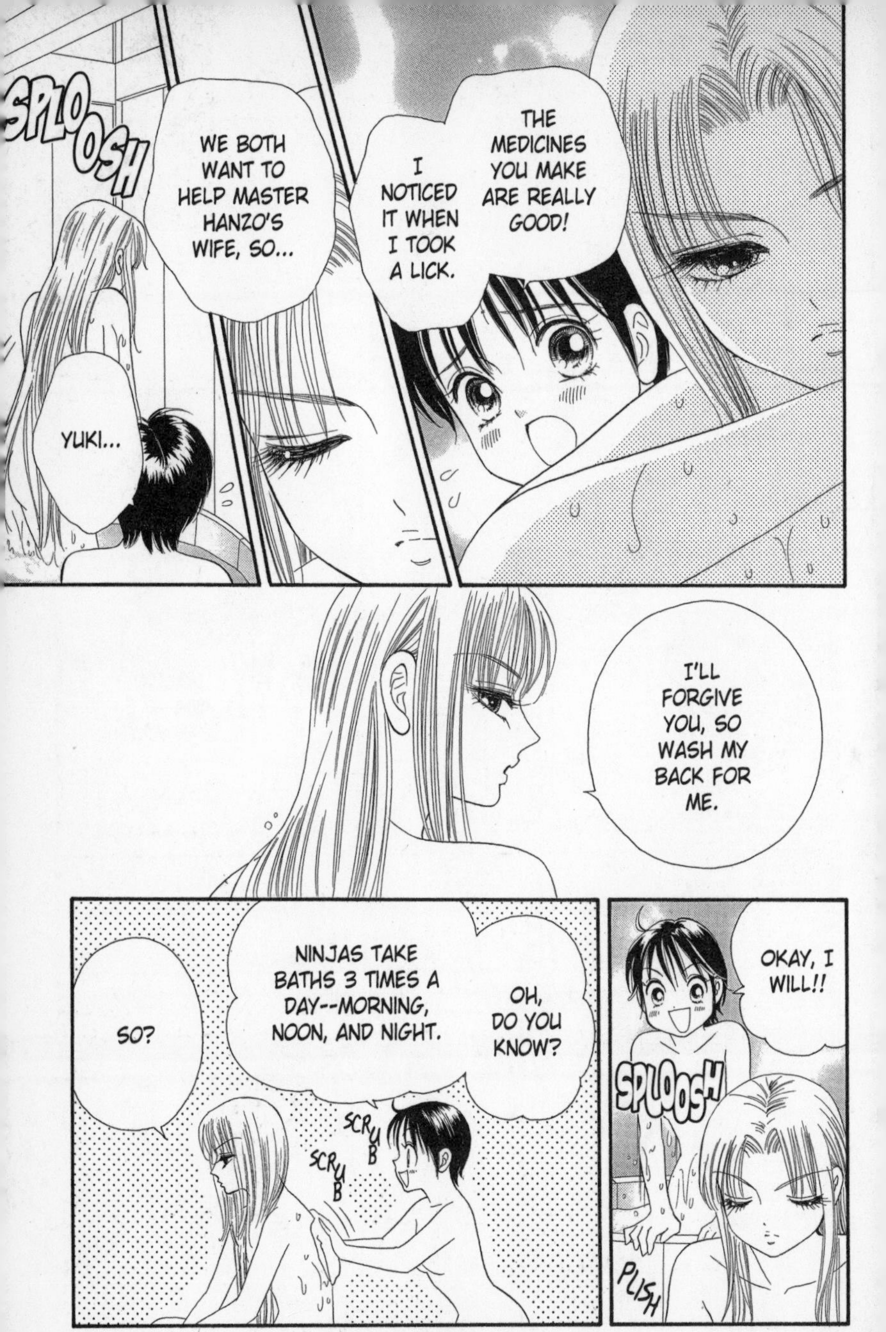
THE MEDICINES YOU MAKE ARE REALLY GOOD!
I NOTICED IT WHEN I TOOK A LICK.
WE BOTH WANT TO HELP MASTER HANZO'S WIFE, SO...
SPLOOSH
YUKI...
I'LL FORGIVE YOU, SO WASH MY BACK FOR ME.
OKAY, I WILL!!
SPLOOSH
PLISH
OH, DO YOU KNOW?
NINJAS TAKE BATHS 3 TIMES A DAY--MORNING, NOON, AND NIGHT.
SO?
SCRUB
SCRUB

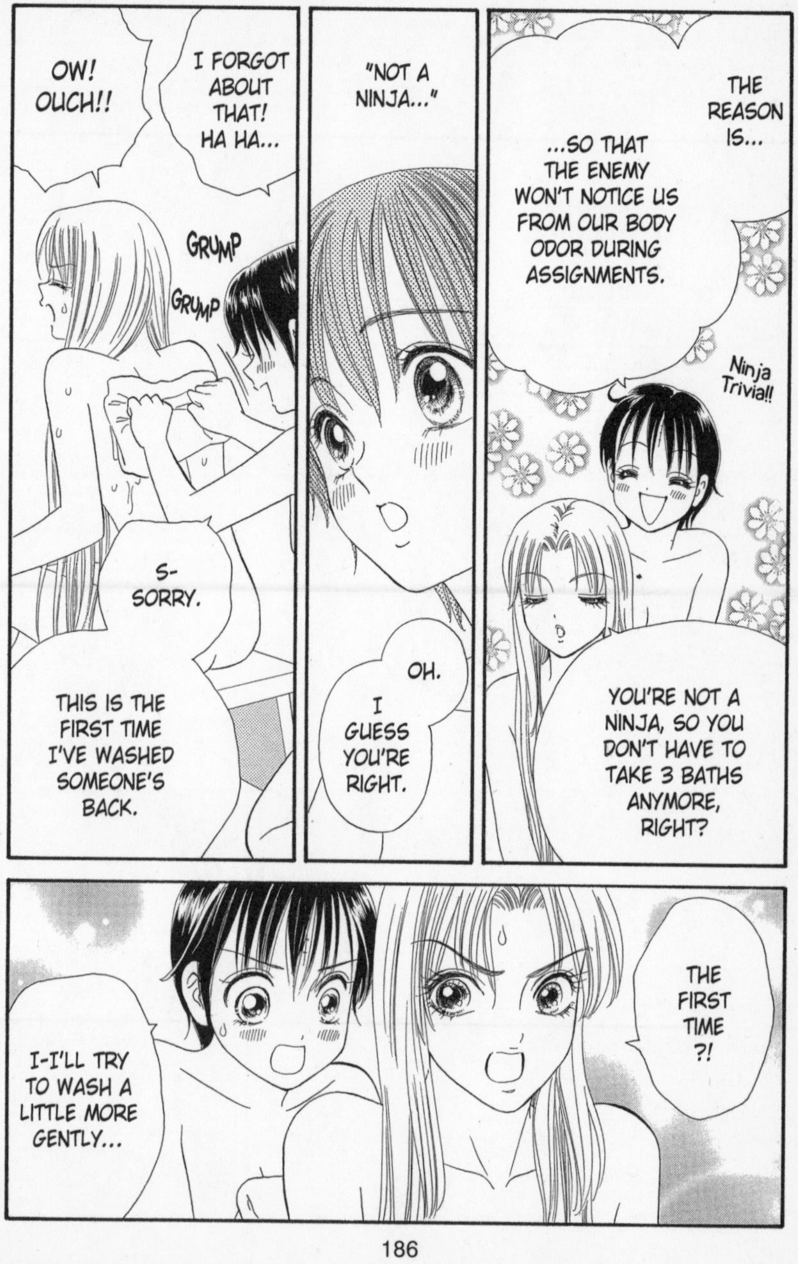
THE REASON IS...
...SO THAT THE ENEMY WON'T NOTICE US FROM OUR BODY ODOR DURING ASSIGNMENTS.
Ninja Trivia!!
YOU'RE NOT A NINJA, SO YOU DON'T HAVE TO TAKE 3 BATHS ANYMORE, RIGHT?
"NOT A NINJA..."
OH.
I GUESS YOU'RE RIGHT.
I FORGOT ABOUT THAT! HA HA...
OW! OUCH!!
GRUMP
GRUMP
S-SORRY.
THIS IS THE FIRST TIME I'VE WASHED SOMEONE'S BACK.
THE FIRST TIME ?!
I-I'LL TRY TO WASH A LITTLE MORE GENTLY...

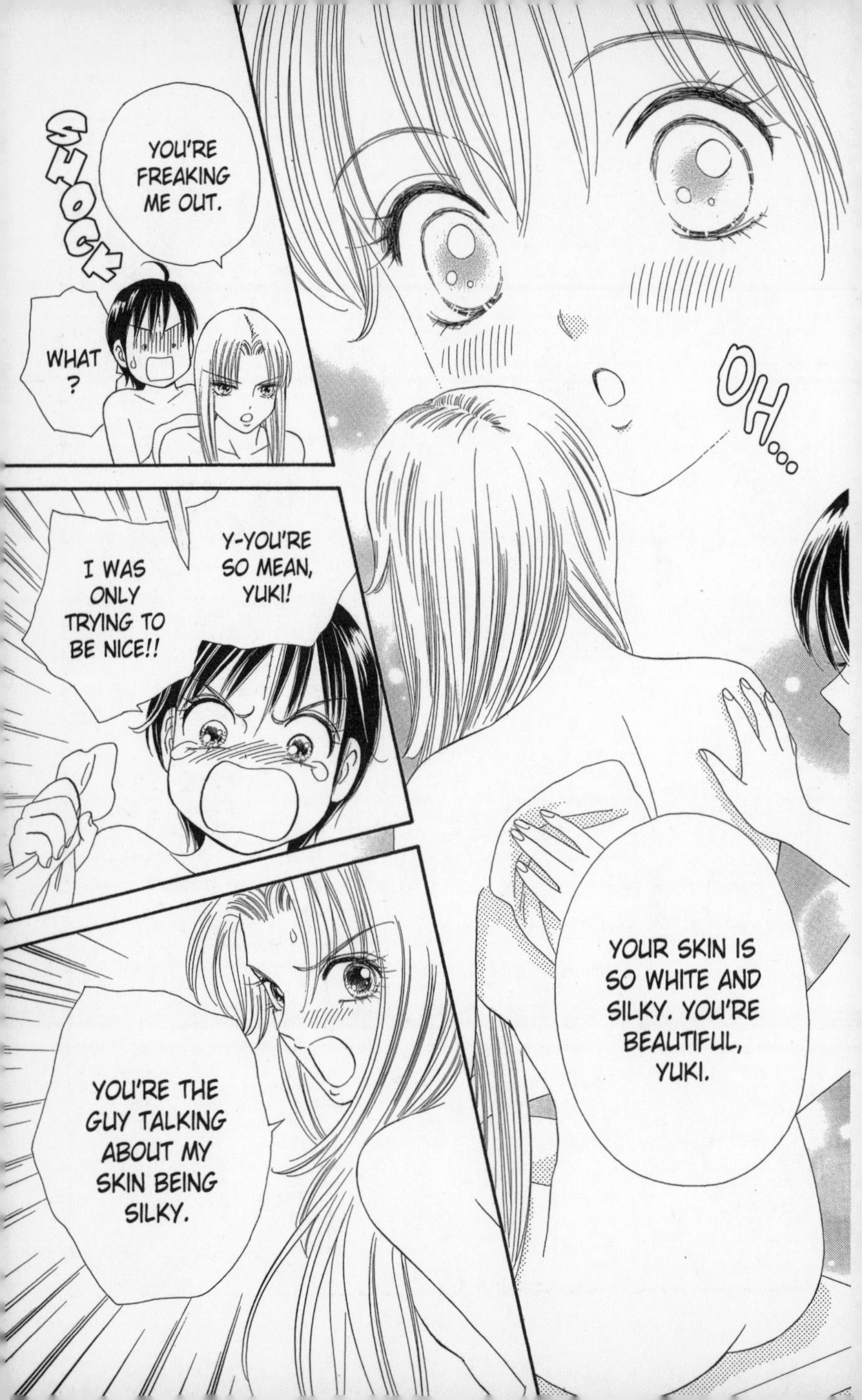
OH...
YOUR SKIN IS SO WHITE AND SILKY. YOU'RE BEAUTIFUL, YUKI.
YOU'RE FREAKING ME OUT.
SHOCK
WHAT?
Y-YOU'RE SO MEAN, YUKI!
I WAS ONLY TRYING TO BE NICE!!
YOU'RE THE GUY TALKING ABOUT MY SKIN BEING SILKY.

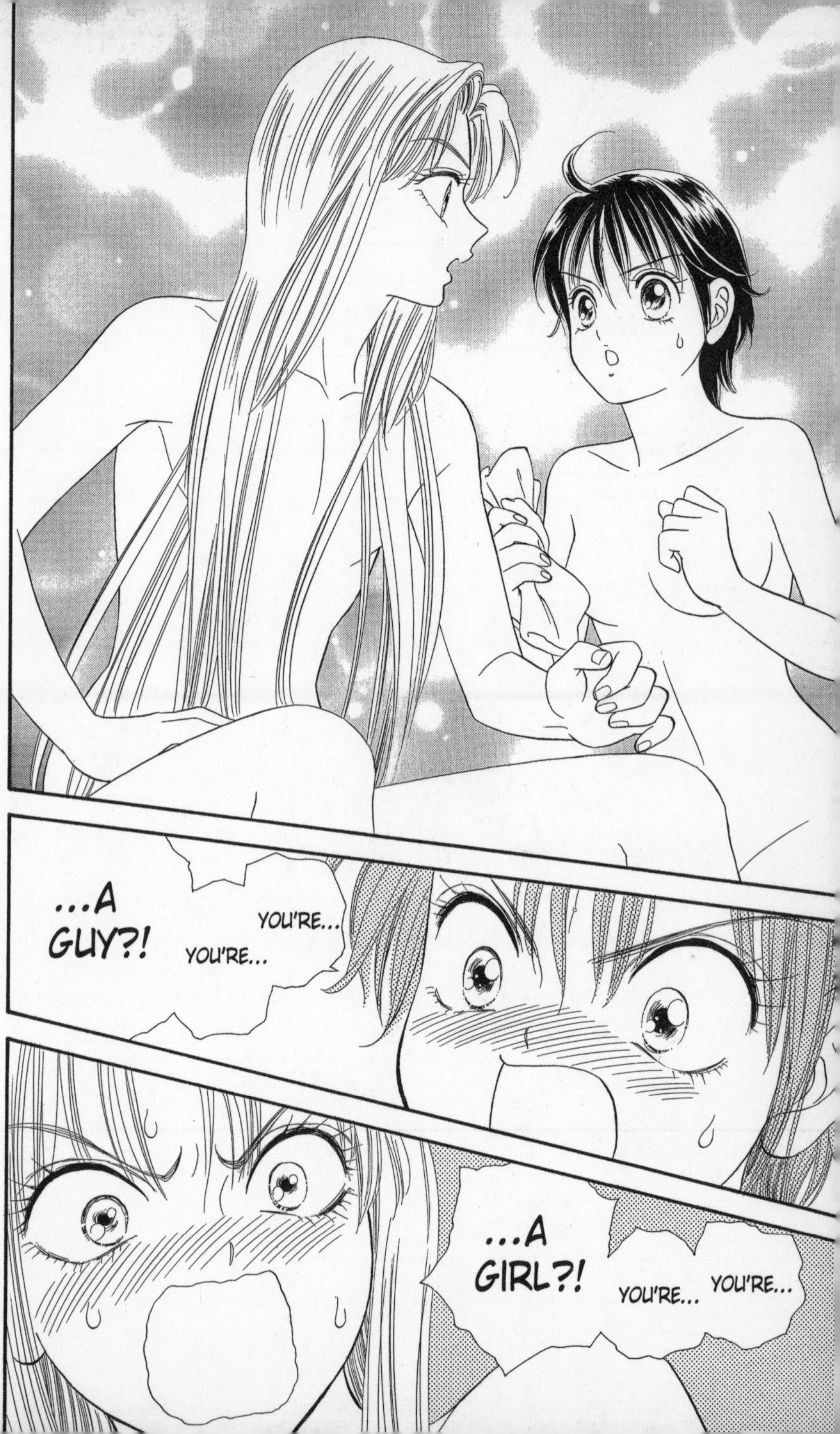
YOU'RE...
YOU'RE...
...A GUY?!
YOU'RE...
YOU'RE...
...A GIRL?!

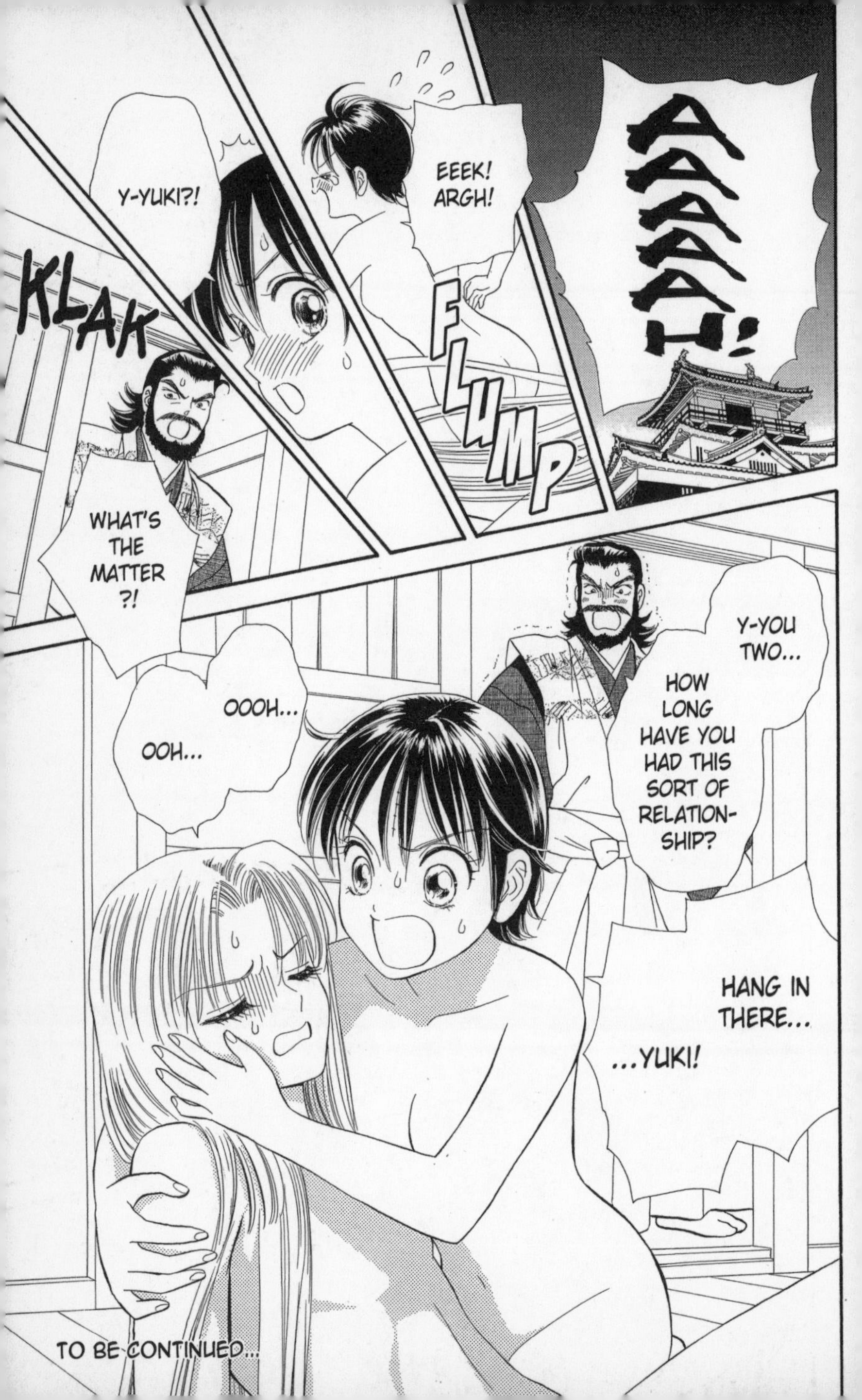
AAAAH!
EEEK! ARGH!
FLUMP
Y-YUKI?!
KLAK
WHAT'S THE MATTER?!
Y-YOU TWO...
HOW LONG HAVE YOU HAD THIS SORT OF RELATIONSHIP?
OOOH...
OOH...
HANG IN THERE...
...YUKI!
TO BE CONTINUED...

The ways of the ninja are mysterious indeed, so here is a glossary of terms to help you navigate the intricacies of their world.

Page 23, panel 2: Iga
Iga is a region on the island of Honshu, and also the name of the famous ninja clan that originated there. Another area famous for its ninja is Koga, in the Shiga prefecture on Honshu. Many books claim that these two ninja clans were mortal enemies, but in reality inter-ninja relations were not as bad as stories paint them.

Page 29: Othello
Although it is called Othello in Japan, it is usually known in the States as Reversi. Reversi actually originated as a German game in the late 1800s, but the modern rule set, which is the universal set being used presently, originated in Japan.

Page 34, panel 4: Hanzo Yasunaga
Hanzo Yasunaga was the founder of the Iga clan. He left Iga along with some of the clan members to work for a warlord. It is said that he was a ninja, but much of his life remains a mystery. His full name was Hattori Hanzo Yasunaga.

Page 50, panel 2: Crossing over
This scene is known as *sanzu no kawa*. In Japanese folklore, people who are dying are first sent to this place. Crossing the river means that you are crossing into the next world. It is the very similar to the "River Styx" in Greek mythology.

Page 116, panel 2: Rice ball
Onigiri, or rice balls, are put in a traditional Japanese packed lunch. Rice is rolled up into a ball-like shape with salty fillings, and is often wrapped in seaweed.

Page 9, panel 3: Tale of Genji
The *Tale of Genji* is a novel that was written in the Heian period (784-1185) about a handsome man and his love affairs at court.

Page 9, panel 4: Lady Murasaki
Lady Murasaki is the narrator of the tale and Genji's true love. She is taken by Genji at a young age and raised by him to be his ideal wife. She becomes his unofficial second wife and remains his favorite until her death.

Page 18, panel 3: Rifle
These rifles are matchlock rifles, which were introduced to Japan by Portuguese and Spanish sailors in 1545. In the original Japanese script, the rifles are called *tanegashima*, which is the place where Japanese gunsmiths adapted the European design to suit their own needs.

Page 20, panel 1: Kami no Hanzou
The term *kami no* means "the Upper," and can refer to social status. However, since Hanzou is a member of a branch family, it is very unlikely that his status is higher than that of the head of the entire clan, Hanzo. The term *kami no* can also refer to a geographic location in relation to an important city center, such as the capital. Hanzou is from Okazaki, which is closer to Edo than Hanzo's home in Segachi.

Page 143, panel 5: Tokugawa Ieyasu
Tokugawa Ieyasu (1543-1616) was the first
Shogun of the Tokugawa Shogunate. He
made a small fishing village named Edo the
center of his activities. Edo thrived and became a huge town, and was later renamed
Tokyo, the present capital.

Page 144, panel 5: Ieyasu's wife and son
It is a historical fact that Ieyasu lost his first
wife and son to Nobunaga, but unlike in this
manga, he was forced to kill his wife and
order his son to commit suicide, in order to
prove his loyalty to Nobunaga.

Page 147, panel 2: Shimo no Hanzo
Shimo no means "the Lower," and in this
case refers to Hanzo's geographic location
rather than social status.

Page 161, panel 1: Tanuki
Goemon is calling Ieyasu a *tanuki*, which is
usually translated into English as "racoon"
or "badger." They look like a cross between
those animals, and are known in Japanese
folklore to trick people.

Page 165: Zhuge Liang Kongming
Zhuge Liang Kongming (181-234), one of
China's most famous hero figures, worked
under military leader Liu Bei of the Shu
Kingdom as a strategist during the Three
Kingdoms Era. His popularity has been so-
lidified by his appearance in the famous epic
novel, *The Romance of Three Kingdoms.*

Page 165: Manjyu
Manjyu is a bun with filling. Manjyu is usually only filled with sweet red-bean paste in
Japan, but in China manjyu is often filled
with meat and other salty fillings.

I visited a Kouga-style Ninja House for reference, which a pharmaceutical company holds in trust. I learned from them that jobs for ninjas became scarce as Japan gradually became peaceful, so many ninja used their pharmaceutical skills to make a living in medicine. I was quite moved to find out that ninja skills changed with the times, and are still among us today.

–Rinko Ueda

Rinko Ueda is from Nara prefecture. She enjoys listening to the radio, drama CDs, and Rakugo comedy performances. Her works include *Ryo*, a series based on the legend of Gojo Bridge, *Home*, a story about love crossing national boundaries, and *Tail of the Moon (Tsuki no Shippo)*, a romantic ninja comedy.

TAIL OF THE MOON
Vol. 2
The Shojo Beat Manga Edition

STORY & ART BY
RINKO UEDA

Translation & Adaptation/Tetsuichiro Miyaki
Touch-up Art & Lettering/Mark McMurray
Design/Izumi Hirayama
Editor/Nancy Thistlethwaite

VP, Production/Alvin Lu
VP, Sales & Product Marketing/Gonzalo Ferreyra
VP, Creative/Linda Espinosa
Publisher/Hyoe Narita

Printed in Canada

Published by VIZ Media, LLC
P.O. Box 77064
San Francisco, CA 94107

Shojo Beat Manga Edition
10 9 8 7 6 5 4 3
First printing, December 2006
Third printing, August 2009

store.viz.com

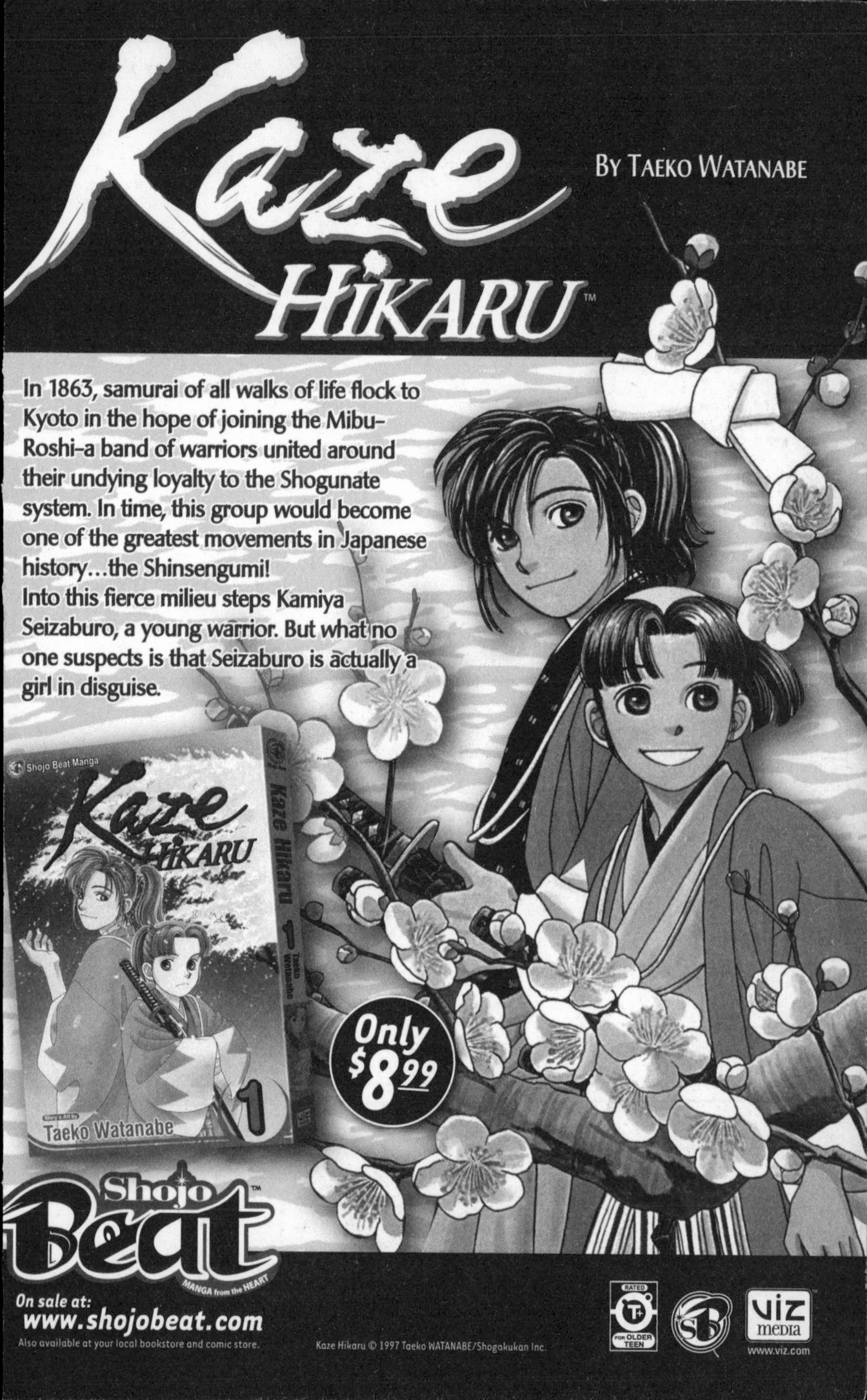

Kaze Hikaru™
By Taeko Watanabe
In 1863, samurai of all walks of life flock to Kyoto in the hope of joining the Mibu-Roshi–a band of warriors united around their undying loyalty to the Shogunate system. In time, this group would become one of the greatest movements in Japanese history…the Shinsengumi!
Into this fierce milieu steps Kamiya Seizaburo, a young warrior. But what no one suspects is that Seizaburo is actually a girl in disguise.
Shojo Beat Manga
Kaze Hikaru
1
Taeko Watanabe
Kaze Hikaru 1 Taeko Watanabe
Only $8.99
Shojo Beat™
MANGA from the HEART
On sale at:
www.shojobeat.com
Also available at your local bookstore and comic store.
Kaze Hikaru © 1997 Taeko WATANABE/Shogakukan Inc.
RATED T+ FOR OLDER TEEN
viz media
www.viz.com

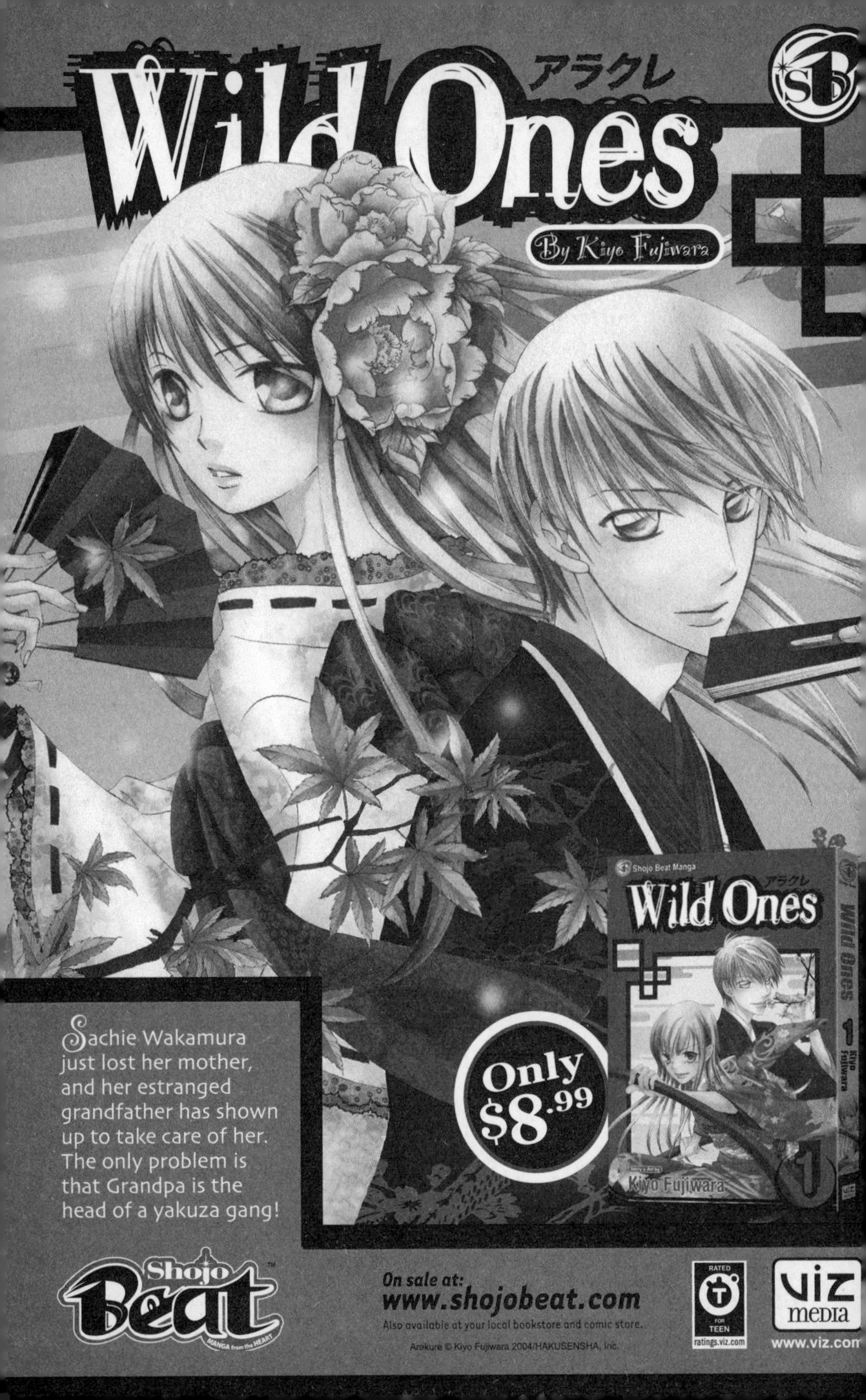
Wild Ones
アラクレ
By Kiyo Fujiwara
Shojo Beat Manga
Wild Ones
アラクレ
Story & Art by
Kiyo Fujiwara
1
Only $8.99
Sachie Wakamura just lost her mother, and her estranged grandfather has shown up to take care of her. The only problem is that Grandpa is the head of a yakuza gang!
Shojo Beat
MANGA from the HEART
On sale at:
www.shojobeat.com
Also available at your local bookstore and comic store.
Arakure © Kiyo Fujiwara 2004/HAKUSENSHA, Inc.
RATED T FOR TEEN
ratings.viz.com
VIZ media
www.viz.com

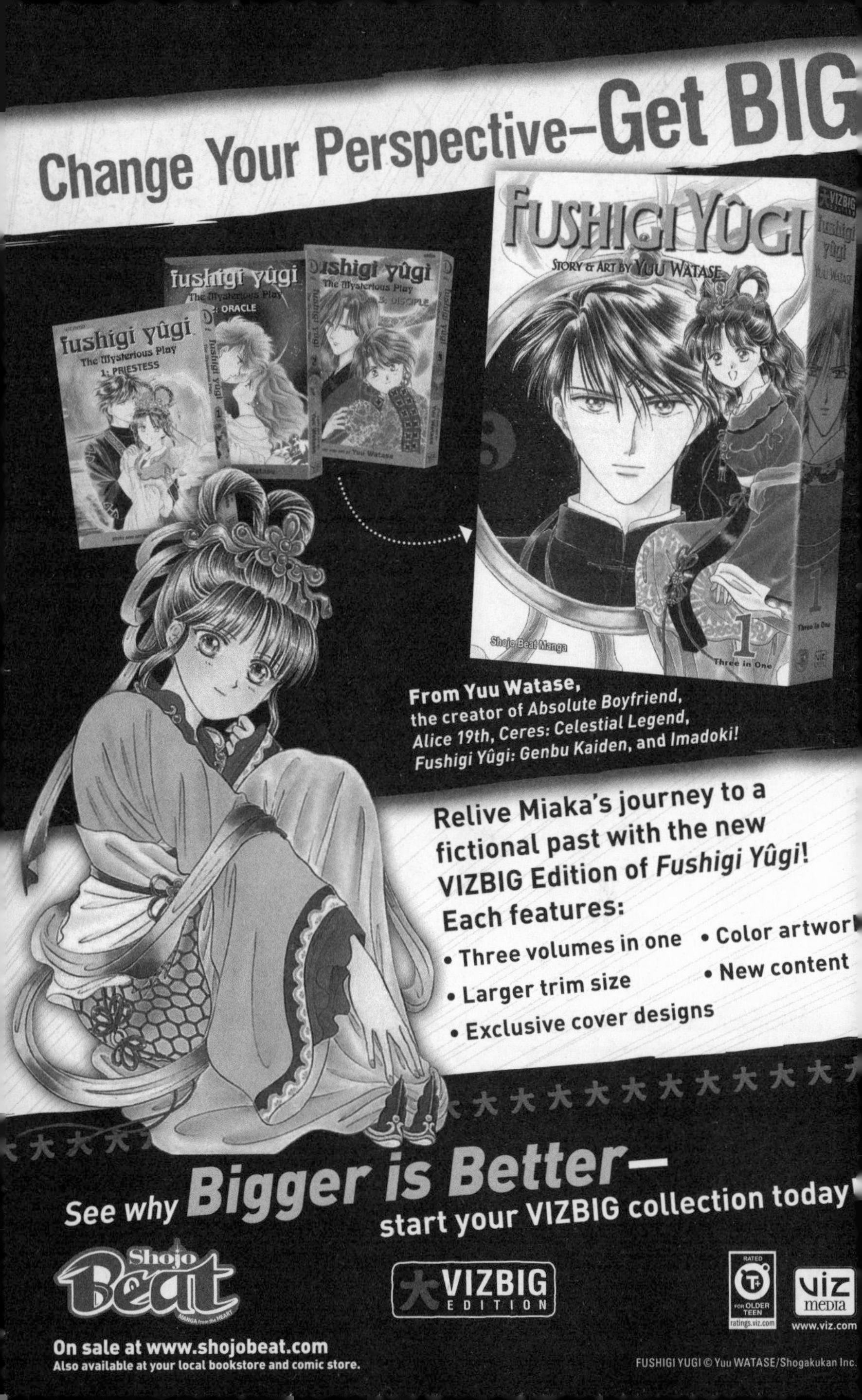

Change Your Perspective—Get BIG
fushigi yûgi
The Mysterious Play
1: PRIESTESS
fushigi yûgi
The Mysterious Play
2: ORACLE
fushigi yûgi
The Mysterious Play
3: DISCIPLE
FUSHIGI YÛGI
STORY & ART BY YUU WATASE
Shojo Beat Manga
1
Three in One
From Yuu Watase,
the creator of Absolute Boyfriend,
Alice 19th, Ceres: Celestial Legend,
Fushigi Yûgi: Genbu Kaiden, and Imadoki!
Relive Miaka's journey to a fictional past with the new VIZBIG Edition of Fushigi Yûgi!
Each features:
• Three volumes in one
• Larger trim size
• Exclusive cover designs
• Color artwork
• New content
See why Bigger is Better—
start your VIZBIG collection today!
Shojo Beat
MANGA from the HEART
VIZBIG EDITION
RATED T+ FOR OLDER TEEN
ratings.viz.com
viz media
www.viz.com
On sale at www.shojobeat.com
Also available at your local bookstore and comic store.
FUSHIGI YUGI © Yuu WATASE/Shogakukan Inc.

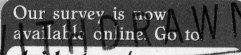